EX LIBRIS:

THE OFFICIAL FULTON FISH MARKET COOKBOOK

ALSO BY BRUCE BECK

Produce: A Fruit and Vegetable Lovers' Guide

THE OFFICIAL FULTON FISH MARKET COOKBOOK

Bruce Beck

Photographs by Richard Lord

E. P. DUTTON  NEW YORK

Published in the United States by E. P. Dutton,
a division of NAL Penguin Inc.,
2 Park Avenue, New York, N.Y. 10016

Published simultaneously in Canada by
Fitzhenry and Whiteside, Limited, Toronto.

Library of Congress Cataloging-in-Publication Data
Beck, Bruce.
The official Fulton Fish Market cookbook / Bruce Beck;
photographs by Richard Lord. — 1st ed.
p. cm.
Includes index.
ISBN 0-525-24773-4
1. Cookery (Seafood) 2. Fulton Fish Market (New York, N.Y.)
I. Title. II. Title: Fulton Fish Market cookbook.
TX747.B36 1989
641.6'92'097471—dc19   88-29976
CIP

Designed by Nancy Etheredge

Grateful acknowledgment is made for permission to reproduce the following:

Recipe for Broiled Fillet of Salmon with Whole-Grain Mustard Breading by Jack Freedman.
Copyright © 1986 by Jack Freedman.

Recipe for Fricassée of Sea Scallops with Corn, Tomatoes, and Leeks by Anne Rosenzweig.
Copyright © 1986 by Anne Rosenzweig.

Recipe for Shrimp, Shanghai-Style by Norman Weinstein.
Copyright © 1985 by Norman Weinstein's Hot Wok.

Recipe for Crabs in Tomato Sauce by Ann Amendolara Nurse.
Copyright © 1980 by Ann Amendolara Nurse.

Recipe for Poached Whole Cod with Tuna Sauce by Joanna Pruess.
Copyright © 1986 by Joanna Pruess.

Recipe for Felipe Rojas-Lombardi's Escabeche of Fresh Sardines.
Copyright © 1985 by Felipe Rojas-Lombardi.

For my parents, Amy and Ed Beck

CONTENTS

Eight pages of color plates follow page 80.

ACKNOWLEDGMENTS

The first thank-you must go to Richard Lord of Fulton Fish Market Information Services, Inc., for generously and enthusiastically sharing his time and his boundless knowledge; also to all the people of the Market for their support, particularly to Robert Smith, Robert Samuels, Terrence Levy, and Mark Rudes, who are, respectively, president and vice-president of Information Services, president of New York Wholesale Fish Dealers Association, Inc., and president of Fulton Market Fishmongers Association, Inc.

Warmest gratitude goes to all the people—too numerous to list here—whose recipes appear in these pages. Chefs, teachers, writers, home cooks, old friends, new friends—the book would have been impossible without their generosity.

Important thanks go to—in alphabetical order—Norman Brouwer of South Street Seaport Museum; Helène Cairo for her help with things clerical and culinary; Mr. and Mrs. Paul Cohen for their kind interest; Joe Enea and the rest of the friendly folks at Pisacane Midtown, one of the best fish stores around; my editor Joyce Engelson for her warmth and wisdom, plus the rest of the staff at E. P. Dutton for making the finalization of this project as painless as possible; William Roy for his patience and palate; and Suzette Surowitz for her kindness. Sincere apologies go to those whose contributions may have been unintentionally overlooked.

Whether aspiring professionals or home cooks in search of new skills and ideas, students are a teacher's best teachers when it comes to the clarity and appeal of a recipe. To all the students and assistants who have cooked and tasted these dishes, many thanks. And for giving me the opportunity to put these recipes to the student test, I thank the New School for Social Research in Manhattan; the Wire Whisk School in Northport, New York; Cookingstudio of Kings Super Markets in New Jersey; and Cooktique in Tenafly, New Jersey.

INTRODUCTION

It seemed impossible that the largest wholesale fish market in the Western Hemisphere—a market whose name is synonymous with seafood all over the country (indeed, the world) and a major tourist attraction to boot—had never told its story in a book all its own. But such was the case. So, a cooking teacher with a strong love for the Market and its wares got together with the heirs to a great New York tradition to assemble just such a record. Without being encyclopedic or unnecessarily technical we wanted to offer an accurate look at Fulton Fish Market past and present, plus a useful guide to what cooks are and/or should be doing with the tons of fine edibles that pass through the Market each year. And we are proud that all of this information comes right from the fish's mouth, if you will.

We are much heartened by the increasing acceptance of seafood as an essential as well as delicious part of the human diet. The word is out that seafood is an excellent source of complete protein, B vitamins, and several minerals, while also being low in calories, sodium, cholesterol, and saturated fats. This good news is, of course, coupled with the excitement about seafood being a rich source of omega-3 fatty acids, and their likely role in reducing the risks of cardiovascular disease and several autoimmune conditions. And, because omega-3s are important to proper nerve function, it even looks like the oldwives were right when they dubbed fish "brain food."

With all the media and medical attention that seafood is generating—with health professionals urging people to eat at least two servings a week, and with shellfish back on low-cholesterol diets—many cooks remain confused and even fearful, still preferring to let professionals tackle fish cookery. This seemed like the perfect time to jump in and demystify the techniques consumers need to derive the maximum enjoyment from their seafood purchases. And with those techniques we have offered a variety of dishes, both old and new, simple and elaborate, delicate and hearty. Many reveal secrets from the kitchens of some of the area's favorite restaurants. All are structured for the home kitchen.

While these recipes reflect seafood cookery in the New York area, with its rich diversity of ingredients and tastes, readers everywhere will be able to locate the necessary foodstuffs, including the occasional local seafood substitute. We sincerely hope that using this book will bring as much joy to the reader as we have experienced in creating it.

PART 1

A HISTORY OF FULTON FISH MARKET

NIEU AMSTERDAM AND OLD NEW YORK

Fish are central to the story of Manhattan—from the earliest permanent settlement that began to thrive as soon as Peter Minuit made his fateful deal with the local Indians in 1626, buying the whole island for goods with a market value of sixty guilders ($24.00 is the oft-quoted equivalent, though $120.00 is closer to modern exchange rates). Proving themselves true sons of a fishing nation, the colonials ceased to buy fish and shellfish from the Indians and began to exploit the seemingly endless abundance in local waters, with no need to venture beyond the safety of the bay. In locally built small craft they took their harvest from seasonal runs of popular species that still migrate through our waters (bluefish, mackerel, shad) as well as those that have been depleted by time or poisoned by industry (striped bass, alewives, and sturgeon). It is said that during the spring shad run one could walk across the Hudson on the backs of the fish that were crowding their way to the spawning grounds upriver.

At least as important as the local fish were the vast oyster beds that ringed the waterlines throughout what is now called New York Bay, as well as those of Long Island, Staten Island, and New Jersey. For about two centuries these resources fed the citizens and provided a steady source of employment. So abundant were these bivalves that legend has it that Pearl Street, which closely follows the original East River waterfront, was paved with oyster shells and named accordingly. Unfortunately, history indicates that this story may be suspect. There is some confusion about the translation of *Perel Straat*— it might be either pearl or peril—so the street may have been named for the guns of Fort Amsterdam above it. But, it may have been paved with shells at a later time, so Pearl Street will do just fine.

As the population of New (*Nieu*) Amsterdam grew, largely hugging the waterfront of the East River, it began to shape lower Manhattan as we know it today. Unfortunately, the old Dutch buildings have been lost to "urban renewal" and devastating fires, but the heritage remains in the layout of the narrow streets of the Financial District and its few broad boulevards, and in certain street names, notably Wall Street (the watergate), and Maiden Lane (*Maagde Paatje*), along which the burghers' daughters trudged on laundry day to the central wash pond and grassy meadow where the laundry was spread to dry. Marketing is, of course, an important part of the social and economic activity of any settlement; by the end of Dutch rule there were three established marketplaces: the fish market at the foot of Broad Street, and general markets at the foot of Maiden Lane and at present-day Peck Slip.

The population of Long Island was also growing rapidly, so that as early as 1638 there was ferry service between Brooklyn, at the site of the present Fulton Street, and Manhattan, in the vicinity of Peck Slip. This is where the two landmasses are closest, and these places served as the neighborhoods for the Brooklyn ferry until it ceased operation in 1924. Market day brought farmers with their produce from Brooklyn and Long Island to the Manhattan side, where they set up shop out of their wagons. Peck Slip was close enough to the population center for the burghers to be able to shop conveniently for fresh farm products, while the islanders on their way to the heart of downtown passed the market at the foot of Maiden Lane, where they could purchase citified goods and imports.

This general market at Maiden Lane and the waterfront established itself in *Smitt's Vallei*, Smith's Valley, so named for the blacksmith who was the first major merchant to take advantage of the traffic between the ferry and downtown. *Vallei* became "fly" in imitation of old Dutch pronunciation. In this quaint way the most important marketplace in colonial Manhattan became the Fly Market when it might have been more pleasantly named Valley Market. Despite its odd name, the Fly Market persisted as a trading center—for fish and meat, primarily—until it was replaced by the new Fulton Market in 1822.

The English takeover of New Amsterdam on September 8, 1664, produced far more than a name change, as the colonial governors sought to exploit the vast natural resources of the new land, particularly fish. The fishing industry got off to a booming start with locally built boats that were large and sturdy enough for deep-sea fishing. Following royal wishes, colonial governor Sir Edmond Andros founded the first stockholder-owned and directed company in the Colonies for the purpose of cod fishing, and also lifted the import duty on salt so that the company could compete favorably on the colonial and European markets. There's an interesting sidelight to this story since the stock offering was made at a price of fifteen beavers or their value per share, reflecting the most important industry prior to English attention to fisheries. In keeping with a commercial atmosphere more capitalistic than England enjoyed at home, the stock company was not granted a monopoly: individuals and partnerships were free to "fish as they might like best." Governor Andros was also responsible for stimulating local trade by encouraging marketplaces with regular weekly or annual market days. To this end he established that "any person coming to or going from these fairs and markets shall be free from arrest for debts on those days."

In 1677 William Beekman purchased a sizable tract of marshland on the northern fringe of civilization—centered around present-day Ferry Street—which became known as Beekman Swamp and was gradually developed as business and population pushed northward. The Swamp is important to our story because the Beekman family prospered, took advantage of water rights to increase the property by landfill, and eventually deeded to the City of New York the land that became the site of Fulton Market.

Whereas New Amsterdam had its town wharf, eighteenth-century New York's East River frontage became rather solidly built up with docks, piers, wharves, and shipyards as far north as Catherine Street by 1755, according to a contemporary map. By then, landfill begun in 1686 had been completed to create a new shoreline, Water Street. Front Street shows up at least partially in place on a map surveyed in 1766. These landfill projects served the dual purpose of creating more commercial space and deepening the harbor by moving beyond the shallows and marshy areas toward greater river depth.

Landfill was seeded by sinking barrels filled with stones and gravel, using these as anchors to support the piling up of other available materials. Recent foundation excavations for the Resnick Tower at 1 Seaport Plaza yielded the skeletons of old wooden boats filled with stones, but it is difficult to say whether they were intentionally scuttled or had "died" naturally in the shallows and been left there. These landfill projects were carried out at a sensible pace with adequate time allowed for the fill to settle and become solid before it was built upon. No one seemed particularly concerned about the damage that all this commerce and construction did to the ubiquitous natural oyster beds, probably because there were so many more nearby.

Even in the eighteenth century New York had begun to develop its "if it's available, it's available here" character. Vast fortunes were made in shipping colonial products to Europe—salted fish, furs, cotton, tobacco, rice, indigo—and importing tea, spices, furniture, fabrics, wine and spirits, and, unfortunately, slaves. New York City was naturally an important plum during the Revolution, one which General George Washington was unable to defend. But after the British occupation ended in 1783, George Washington took office under the new Constitution as the first President of the United States in New York City on April 30, 1789; his new government naturally settled in lower Manhattan. Washington lived on Cherry Street and was a visible part of New York life: of an afternoon, when the weather was fine, he could often be seen strolling along Peck Slip, engaged in an alfresco cabinet meeting. A fun story from the period involves Washington's fondness for shad and his dedication to thrift. According to legend, his cook, Samuel Fraunces of Fraunces Tavern fame, was pleased one spring day to find a particularly fine first-of-the-season shad for the president's breakfast. But Washington was fish-wise enough to inquire about the price of this delicacy. Upon learning that two dollars had been paid, the president declared that he could not countenance such extravagance and would not touch the thing. Mr. Fraunces was not subject to the same compunction, so the shad did not go to waste.

BRAVE NEW CENTURY

In the first twenty-one years of the nineteenth century, the entire character of the Fulton Market area was shaped as some of it exists to this day. The shipping industry was central to this development; as the population continued to live and work in the area, merchants, publicans, boardinghouse operators, and residents were joined by a new kind of tenant. For the first time it became fashionable to rent office space for the keeping of accounts and other business that had previously been conducted at home. Countinghouses were born all over the district. Many of these buildings were in a graceful Georgian-Federal style that looks particularly handsome today in the few remaining examples, especially Schermerhorn Row and the block of fish stalls between Beekman Street and Peck Slip. South Street landfill was begun in 1795 and essentially completed by 1811 when Peter Schermerhorn was busily developing the area. Unlike the care taken with Water and Front streets, this time growth was so rapid that the landfill was *not* properly settled before building was begun, which accounts for the skewed angles that are common in the surviving examples of buildings from the period on or near South Street.

Robert Fulton is the outstanding name in the history of the South Street area, and ironically the steam engine technology he pioneered would both glorify and nearly destroy the neighborhood. Fulton's Folly, the *Clermont,* made its historic maiden voyage from Beekman Slip in 1807. This same site was chosen for the Manhattan dock for regular steam ferry service to Brooklyn in 1814.

In 1816, following Fulton's death the year before, the importance of his contribution was honored by the Common Council of the City of New York with a street naming. The thoroughfare made up of Beekman Slip, Fair Street, and Partition Street was renamed Fulton Street. It became the only cross street in lower Manhattan to have the same name from river to river and remained so until the World Trade Center chopped off the last blocks of its path to the Hudson. Also, the council was so certain that South Street was the permanent waterfront—that landfill was complete—that #1 Fulton Street is on the corner of South, with progressive numbering west to the Hudson, the only street so numbered east to west.

In 1807 the Beekman estate assigned the block bounded by present-day Fulton, South, Beekman, and Front streets to the city for the purposes of a public market. In 1817 the State Legislature ruled that the city might proceed with a plan to take possession of the block by legal actions that would compensate all those who were displaced or inconvenienced. But no final action was taken until after a disaster that proved to be a blessing in disguise.

On the morning of January 24, 1821, at about 3:00, a fire

broke out in the Front Street building occupied by Mrs. Sarah Smith, who was variously described in contemporary newspaper accounts as a resident or keeper of a tavern or sailors' boardinghouse. Severe cold and deep snowdrifts made firefighting efforts extremely difficult; it took three hours to get the blaze under control, at the end of which time only one fireproof building remained salvageable.

In the wake of this disaster came an editorial in *The New York Daily Gazette,* which is generally credited with lighting its own fire under the council. "The late conflagration has exposed to view this beautiful spot of ground which has so universally been considered as the most eligible situation for a market, and which has already been vested in the Corporation for the purpose of a market. Its vicinity to the Ferry, by which the marketing from Long Island will be saved the expense of cartage, a basin for smacks and fish cars, unequalled in its purity, from the depth of its water and rapidity of its current, being decidedly in its favor for keeping and having good fresh fish, which the waters at the Fly market could not furnish, in consequence of the large sewer entering the slip, and, in the summer season, so offensive as to be prejudicial to health."

If the council had been dragging its heels before, it now moved rapidly. The committee's proposed resolutions of February 26, 1821, for action and financing were passed, and Fulton Market was born.

THE BIRTH OF FULTON MARKET

A special meeting of the council on April 23, 1821, passed the following recommendation from the Market Committee: "In making a selection from among the variety of plans which have been presented they have been actuated by the important considerations of combining *Strength* and *Elegance* with Utility and Economy, and have therefore made choice of the plan presented on the drawings made by JAMES O'DONNELL ARCHITECT. . . ." Mr. O'Donnell was a well-respected architect and instructor at Columbia University, but this particular commission was unknown even to his biographers until the above minutes were examined in the 1970s.

The building as planned was indeed elegant, a U-shaped one-story wooden structure (with basement) with rounded classical arches all around and a graceful sloping roof. The grand entrances in the middle of the Fulton, Front, and Beekman wings were two stories, with Greek Revival pitched roofs and three windows in the upper facades. No record exists of the use intended for these entrance towers (they may have been open and purely visual) but they were, curiously, removed sometime after 1869 and roofed over. The building had four other entrances, two each at the corners on South Street and Front Street. The open end of the U, on South Street, was crowned by another Greek Revival pitched-roofed facade with three grand arches wide enough for the passage of carts. The committee altered the design to make the Market open-air, with wooden slats instead of windows filling the arches. This plan was impractical for marketing in all weather and led to hodgepodge wall and stall building in later years. As business increased, canvas awnings gave way to permanent awnings and such commercial sprawl that little of the original structure was visible from the street by the end of the building's life.

Once the new Market was completed in December 1821, stalls were offered at auction (each year's rent to be paid in advance). The central space in the U that opened onto South Street was available to "country people," who could set up shop out of wagons as they had done since 1638. The basement space was also rented, largely by oyster houses and pioneer restaurateurs whose "refreshment saloons" were primitive but bustling in the mornings and afternoons. The official opening was January 22, 1822, which accounts for both "the 1821 Market" and "the 1822 Market" turning up in historical records.

FULTON *FISH* MARKET IS BORN

Though the Market was doing well, many butchers complained that they could not afford the rent and petitioned for a reduction. The council was not impressed and passed a wondrously straightforward resolution: "That the stalls of such persons as were unable to pay should be vacated." The resulting vacancies were heaviest in the Beekman Street wing, so that in October of 1822 there was some rearranging to create an exclusive fish market there. This arrangement worked well and the Market prospered with all the stands occupied: the Beekman Street wing strictly fishmongers; butchers, grocers, greengrocers, and merchandise sellers in the other two wings; "country people" in the middle; and food vendors in the basement. The fish business did so well that by 1830 it was time for expansion. The council was presented a petition in October requesting a new fish market across South Street. As usual, a committee was appointed to study the matter, and its report in favor of the project was passed. Apparently the downstairs neighbors were just as eager for the move as the fishmongers were, because the committee's report included the observation "that water and other nuisances from the fish market descend into the stores below, causing it to be a nuisance."

A bid of $2,847.74 submitted by one John Phillips was accepted, and he built a wooden shed 195 feet long on the waterfront across from Fulton Market. The construction was completed in the spring of 1831 at a cost of $3,223.63, proof that while cost overruns are nothing new, it used to be possible to complete city projects in a sensible period of time.

Business at the Fish Market was so good that seasonal traffic jams in the East River were becoming a problem. The slip was finally ruled exclusive fish territory.

By 1848 a new building to house Fulton Fish Market was clearly needed, and the city appropriated, inexplicably, $2,000 for the construction of a new wooden shed of dimension and design quite similar to the old one (the only explanation for the low cost is that the river bulkhead work was already in place). The dealers who rented the eighteen stalls were able to make do there for twenty-one years and sustain thriving businesses. The importance of this second shed is that it marks the beginning of Fulton Fish Market as a *wholesale* establishment, the factor most responsible for its unique longevity and its relative immunity to the ups and downs of the neighborhood. These fishmongers found a natural market in the provisioning of steamship lines, hotels and boardinghouses, and, later, the retailers and restaurants that would follow an uptown population migration. This is also the point at which Fulton Market and Fulton Fish Market became distinctly separate entities, so the reader will have to note the difference for the rest of our story to avoid confusion.

PROUD TIMES

The early years of steamboating brought bustling activity to South Street as New York continued to be the busiest port in a growing country. But sailing ships were still needed for long hauls and many local runs. Through the century South remained a "street of masts." Graceful clippers and sturdy packets made the international and California runs, smaller sail craft moved Atlantic coast products, while steamboats ferried, tugged, and worked the Erie Canal. This meant an abundance of fresh seafood from nearby, up and down the Atlantic coast, and freshwater fish from the Great Lakes for Fulton Fish Market to handle, plus a sturdy economy and growing population to buy these goods. Contemporary accounts, illustrations, and photographs indicate there will never again be anything to rival the sheer vitality and volume of a business day on nineteenth-century South Street, complete with ships of all sizes, bowsprits jutting into the street, sailors, vendors, businessmen, shoppers, commuters, carts, horses, horse-drawn trollies, traffic jams, mud, and, above all, merchandise of all sorts being carted to its destination or spilling into the streets from overstocked stalls.

This period was something of a golden age for Fulton Market. While the population was certainly moving uptown, Fulton remained a hub because of its Brooklyn connection and its proximity to the Financial District, fashionable shopping on Broadway, fashionable residences around Broadway, and a number of fine hotels, particularly Holt's (later, The United States Hotel) just a block away at Fulton and Water. Eateries were as distinctive a part of the neighborhood's character as any other establishments, and oyster houses were the most popular. Dorlan's, in Fulton Market, was the most famous of all—world famous, according to contemporary accounts—and a must on the tourist itinerary as well as a popular local spot. Charles Dickens is said to have been taken to Dorlan's while on a U.S. tour. Pan roasts, stews, and half-shell oysters, some as big as cheese plates, were served in simple surroundings to people of all classes. Sweet's opened in 1845 across the street at 2 Fulton Street, where it remains today.

The Fish Market badly needed new quarters, and it became apparent that the dealers themselves would have to remedy their situation after they petitioned the city for a new facility in 1868 and were denied. Not only was the 1848 shed inadequate but it looked particularly dismal sitting next to the fine new Fulton Ferry station, a grand cast-iron affair erected in 1863. So in 1869 the dealers organized as the Fulton Market Fish Mongers Association, sold stock, and built a rather splendid new home on the site of the old one. This new building had the same eighteen stalls plus a large second story for office space and a loft for storage. As before, the rear hung over the bulkhead to provide easy access to the floating cars in the river that held live fish. The facade had a proud Victorian look to it, with three large gables on each side plus one at each end and three tall spired cupolas. The new fish market presented the same solid, respectable, ambitious face to the harbor and South Street alike. Though nearly destroyed by fire in 1878, the structure was quickly rebuilt without alteration and remained standing until 1907.

The fine 1869 building was in place when electricity and telephones came to New York. The early phone company gave its customers no overnight service. The fishmongers complained that they could not wait until 8:00 A.M. to begin making business calls, so, thanks to them, the operators began to man their machines at 6:30 for the entire city.

Meanwhile, Fulton Market had grown into an unmanageable mess that came to be called "The Fulton Market Nuisance." Though the health department intervened occasionally and condemned a few add-on stalls, Fulton Market continued to grow higgledy-piggledy. Though the city declared the Market unsafe in 1880 and decided it must be pulled down, the Common Council was saved from the difficulties involved in condemning and razing an entire block, as it had been when the Market was being planned, by a destructive fire that leveled the old wooden building in 1883 (some sources say 1882). The neighborhood as a population center was clearly slipping, with less urgent need for a fine public market than earlier in the century. With the advent of great steamships the shipping industry began to move to the deeper moorings of the Hudson, creating a gradual decline in the general importance of South Street. And with the completion of the Brooklyn Bridge, also in 1883, it was no longer necessary for every last visitor from Brooklyn to pass Fulton Market on his way to any Manhattan destination. The city, however, ignored this trend when it authorized the erection of a new Fulton Market about twice the size of the old one.

The 1883 Fulton Market building was a dark-red brick-and-iron fortress, with whimsical stone animal carvings, no doubt intended to relieve the general air of gloom. In spite of the decline of South Street, the new market enjoyed about two decades of glory.

INTO THE TWENTIETH CENTURY

By 1894 it was time for a new building for the Fish Market and time to widen South Street to ease the traffic problems that plagued the neighborhood. To these ends, the 1869 building was moved one block north along the waterfront so that the city could begin a new bulkhead and necessary pier work. Contemporary photographs show the fine old building sitting in its new location with a shed built in front. Oddly, this shed, intended for business during the transition period, remained, so that the old building which had been moved at considerable expense was never really used again. The city work lagged drastically behind schedule, leaving the fishmongers in their makeshift quarters until a new building could be completed and occupied on March 18, 1907, in time for shad season.

This is the building that stands today between Piers 17 and 18, the prestigious Old Market Building or Tin Building. No one ever accused it of being handsome, even with the bright new paint job it received in time for the summer of 1986 Fourth of July/Lady Liberty festivities. Yet it was considered totally modern when it was designed, and the gradient of the concrete floor plus sinkholes that drained into the river were considered state of the art in sanitation. It had never before been possible to flush out the day's residue with such ease and thoroughness. Each of the eighteen stalls has a ground-floor office for the transaction of sales and a mezzanine countinghouse that looks out over the selling floor much the way the early nineteenth-century countinghouses looked out over the harbor. Two floors above provide locker rooms, offices, and storage space. The steel superstructure is filled in with wooden walls, floors, and ceilings, and the exterior is covered with corrugated metal: the source of the "tin" nickname. With age it has gained character, and a good, utilitarian feel. There is no other atmosphere quite like the upstairs rooms with their smells of old lumber and old machinery, the ghostly quiet relieved only by the occasional squawk of a circling gull or the eerie singing of ancient timbers when temperature changes cause a tiny shift.

Fish dealers who were unable to secure space in the Tin Building convinced the city of the need for another market. In 1909, the newly formed New York Wholesale Fish Dealers Association members moved into new quarters, called the New Market, on the river bulkhead just north of the Tin Building. Few photographs of the original New Market Building remain, but it appears to have been an imposing structure and unlike anything else in the neighborhood, a two-story building with fifteen stalls, built of steel, concrete, and glass. Though it looked quite solid and heavy, all the way up to its domed cupola, these qualities conspired to undermine the strength of the pilings that supported it. The city knew that it was becoming dangerously unsound, but no action was taken.

On the night of August 11, 1936, the north end of the rear of the New Market Building, the part that hung over the bulkhead, gave way and slid into the East River, taking parts of the front with it. Purely by chance it was a Saturday night, so that only a few watchmen were around and there was nothing like the disaster that could have occurred on a busy morning. Market gossip claimed that not long before the accident Captain Tom Kippen of the fish trawler *Whaling City,* a skipper known for his fondness for drink, had miscalculated his departure from Beekman Dock by 180°, dealing a solid blow to already weakened foundation timbers. Whatever the immediate cause of the disaster, the building was hopeless and had to be razed. A new one, the present New Market Building, was dedicated in June of 1939 with Fiorello La Guardia in attendance. Mayor La Guardia was presented with a three-hundred-pound halibut as a token of gratitude for his interest in the project. The 1939 New Market has a clean-lined, functional look that is undistinguished but typical of waterfront building of the period. If it were on the Hudson and said "Department of Docks" instead of "Department of Markets" it would not look out of place.

The 1883 Fulton Market fared less well than the Fish Market. A fire in 1905 did serious damage to one of the towers, and general neglect began to show. In 1914 the City of New York abandoned Fulton as a public market, leaving the structure to the mercy of time and the elements. Then in 1916 the city approved funds for a modest facelift and rented out space. Most of the tenants were fish dealers, made comfortable by their proximity to Fulton Fish Market. Indeed they became a part of the wholesale fish market since Fulton Market had effectively ceased to exist. This arrangement continued until the building was razed in 1950, not to make way for a fine new structure but to avoid the expense of maintaining a white elephant. Twenty fish dealers were forced to find other quarters. In 1953 the old building was replaced by a characterless red brick, one-story, flat-roofed, garagelike building. This was all that remained of Fulton Market when South Street Seaport Museum was entrusted with the care of the neighborhood in 1967. Had the museum accomplished nothing else (which is certainly not the case) it could be commended for the removal of an eyesore more depressing than either previous incarnation of Fulton Market at its worst. The present structure, called Fulton Market, was completed in 1983 as the first part of the Rouse Company's South Street Seaport shopping and dining complex. Though no design satisfies everyone, this one is acceptably respectful of the spirit of the neighborhood. Also, the South Street row of fish stalls in the 1953 garage had become so firmly a part of Fulton Fish Market that it was allowed to remain, embedded in the new building.

One other important part of Fulton's history should at least be mentioned here. In 1899 a few dealers in freshwater fish moved into Peck Slip, soon to be followed by others. By the 1920s there were twenty-five dealers in Peck Slip, and the area was being touted as the greatest freshwater fish market in the world. But even then, in its heyday, there were fatal signs: supplies gradually diminished, prices increased, labor costs increased, and, most important of all, consumer patterns changed. Not only were home cooks less inclined to deal with whole fish than their parents had been, but the advent of supermarket gefilte fish effectively did in Peck Slip. Today there is no freshwater fish market—only two wholesalers, Messing Fish Company and R. J. Cornelius, specialize in freshwater fish, while others carry a few items—and there are only a few dealers of any kind left in Peck Slip.

Changes to the neighborhood since 1953 have had very little effect on Fulton Fish Market because of its special wholesale rhythm of early-morning hours. The gradual encroachment of Wall Street, the beginnings of gentrification, the addition of a major tourist attraction, the loving restoration of vintage buildings, all of these changes have left the Market largely undisturbed. Construction of the elevated FDR Drive in 1953 created nasty traffic problems, but the completed structure effectively removes all express traffic from the neighborhood and also provides a niftily functional, if homely, giant umbrella over South Street.

In the 1960s plans were advanced to move the Market to Hunts Point in the Bronx, where the wholesale produce and meat markets were in the process of locating. A move to the Bronx was first proposed in 1913 as part of a report that led to the City Council's 1914 abandonment of the 1883 Fulton Market as a public marketplace. But not until 1957 was the idea investigated. The city felt the time was right and began planning a modern facility that would centralize wholesaling of perishable goods for the metropolitan area and provide the best possible sanitation, handling, storage, and shipping facilities. But despite the potential benefits, most wholesalers were opposed to the move on financial and convenience grounds. By 1969 the lease for the Bronx site was signed and the press was announcing the inevitability of the relocation project, so it became obvious that heavy artillery would be needed to fight this bureaucratic battle. Leaders from all areas of the seafood industry formed the Committee to Save the Fulton Fish Market and hired consultant Frank Mosco to prepare a persuasive argument. His testimony before the New York State Senate Committee Hearing on Labor in 1975 was a heavy-hitting blend of nostalgia and good business sense that emphasized the potential for many forced closings and the loss of four hundred jobs to prohibitively high rents; the prediction of city revenue lost to New Jersey and Long Island must have been persuasive, too. Eventually the Committee to Save the FFM prevailed, and the relocation project was dropped.

Because the city and the Seaport Museum could realize much greater revenues with retail tenants, there exists the temptation to force FFM elsewhere. In the opinion of some, the neighborhood would smell better if FFM moved somewhere downwind, though this is highly personal. And it is difficult to predict how long it would take for the odor to disappear anyway: the site of London's old Billingsgate market, though admittedly centuries older than Fulton, still bears olfactory reminders of its heritage. Most important, as the only original tenant remaining in the Seaport area, FFM has more right to the space than anyone else. Even for people who never visit the Market during its waking hours it remains an attraction that would be sorely missed, an irreplaceable source of cultural continuity.

THE HUMAN SIDE

Despite the saltiness of South Street, Fulton Fish Market managed to maintain a rather respectable image through the second half of the nineteenth century, while Boss Tweed's Tammany Hall and petty cronyism were the order of the day. The tail end of this period produced one of Fulton's favorite sons and one of New York's best-loved governors, Al Smith. His South Street childhood and early years as a market basket boy held him in good stead in the political arena, adding a little extra to a personality that would doubtless have been colorful anyway. He might refer to a man he did not like as having "an eye as glassy as a dead cod," or another who "shakes hands like a frozen mackerel."

An interesting footnote from the earlier period concerns political chowders, vote-buying events (for men only) that consisted of a boat trip to picnic grounds on Long Island for a day of games and food, lots of food. Big Tim Sullivan staged the largest of these annual summer outings, attended by as many as seven thousand men. Mr. Austin P. Winters of Marco Island, Florida, provided the Seaport Museum with a charming account of his family's involvement in New York's seafood past. Mr. Winters explained that his grandfather, William H. Winters, and *his* brother James were fish dealers who also prepared chowder in quantity for political occasions. According to the family story, the brothers decided one day to avoid the expense of cream by substituting tomatoes, and Manhattan clam chowder was born. We apologize for being unable to offer equal time to all who have the last word on that most incendiary topic, the origin of Manhattan clam chowder.

Partly as a needed source of industry information and partly as a PR scheme, the Fishery Council was formed in 1939, the first industry organization of its kind. The wholesalers' organizations were concerned with internal affairs: the physical plant, working together, working with the city bureaucracy. The neighborhood had never had a press agent and the time was right to get one. The council's press releases from the forties, though timed to coincide with the availability or glut of a particular kind of seafood, are definitely of the "soft news" variety. With the hope that a little wholesomeness or stardust would rub off on the association, the releases invoked names as varied as the Girl Scouts, Boy Scouts, Bette Davis, Wendell Willkie, Dr. Dafoe (who delivered the Dionne quintuplets), George Jessel, Clare Boothe, Gene Tunney (promoting trout, presumably because there was no market for tunny), Lotte Lehmann, Lauritz Melchior, Kay Kyser, the Andrews Sisters, Eleanor Roosevelt, Mayor Fiorello La Guardia, Sophie Tucker, Milton Berle, the St. Louis Cardinals, Winston Churchill, Kitty Carlisle, Dinah Shore, and Tamara Toumanova. With great difficulty we have narrowed these down to two particular favorites that are printed in their entireties on the following pages.

The recipes for the press releases, for radio, and, later, television promos were tested and developed by a young man named John von Glahn, who joined the Fishery Council in 1940. Mr. von Glahn, a passionate and opinionated fish lover, carried out his duties with gusto—cooking, eating, proselytizing, meeting consumer scares head-on, supplying industry information for the media, and image polishing.

In 1951 John von Glahn was named executive secretary (director) of the Fishery Council, a post he held until his retirement in 1983.

BETTE DAVIS' FOOD WISHES
REVOLVE ABOUT SCROD FISH

Celebrities do not necessarily go for the highest-priced foods. Take a simple dish like scrod, which is young cod. Just so Bette Davis, Queen of the cinema, might have the fare she likes best at a dinner in her honor, a large quantity of scrod was shipped to Hollywood from the East Coast, according to the "Food Field Reporter."

When asked what food he would like to have when he was a guest of honor of the Fishery Council, Dr. Allan Roy Dafoe unhesitatingly said "Broiled Scrod."

Housewives can take a tip from these two celebrities--a tip which will save them plenty of money. In fish and shellfish, it is not the highest priced varieties which taste the best, but the variety which is best prepared. Prices of fish are determined by supply and demand at the market. Just because a fish comes to market in heavy volume and thus is low costing, does not mean it is not as palate-pleasing as a fish that is scarce and therefore higher priced.

Another thing the smart Lady of the Kitchen realizes is that a fish in heavy volume is usually a better fish than one which is scarce. It may sound paradoxical, but when a fish is low in price due to heavy volume, it is usually of better quality than the same fish when it is scarce.

The trick is in the preparation. A poor cook can ruin a high priced fish. A good cook can make a gourmet happy with the cheapest fish in the market.

The cooking of fish is an art. To help you develop that art a free "Seafood Cook Book" is sent to all who request it of the Fishery Council, 204 Water St., N.Y.C. Following is a recipe from the book:

COD--GALLICIAN SAUCE

Cut soaked cod in serving pieces; boil. Saute 1 green pepper minced, 1 minced onion and 1 large clove garlic minced in 4 tablespoons oil until beginning to brown. Add 1 cup tomatoes and 1 cup water fish was cooked in. Boil 5 minutes. Add 1 teaspoon paprika. Pour over fish. Shake the dish to be sure fish is coated with sauce. Simmer 1 or 2 minutes. Whole potatoes may be cooked with fish or added to sauce.

GIRL SCOUTS SHOW RARE
SKILL IN COOKING FISH

Recognizing that learning to cook is an important part of every young girl's life, the Girl Scouts recently held a fish cooking contest in conjunction with the Fishery Council. Twelve year old Beatrice Vlach proved that "a child shall lead them" when she demonstrated a culinary skill in winning which won the admiration of 16 top-flight food journalists, Mrs. Wendell Willkie and Louis Diat, chef of the Ritz-Carlton Hotel.

Food experts appreciate that fish is one of the foods from which a well-grounded cook can get a result to please the most exacting gourmet. And they also know that the best fish in the world can be ruined by one who is not versed in the fundamentals of seafood cooking. That is why fish was used as the test for the championship of the Girl Scouts.

Little Beatrice and the five other finalists who had survived troop and district eliminations performed like veterans. The method in which they handled the fish showed they appreciated you can't just throw fish in a pan to get the best results and that the trick in all fish cooking was to retain the natural flavor of the food without drying it out.

Here is the winning Girl Scout fish recipe which won a trip to Washington for Beatrice as guest of the Fishery Council:

BEATRICE'S RECIPE

(Serves Two)

Two fillet of flounder, weighing about one-third pound each.

½ chopped carrot	1 egg yolk
¼ small onion	1/8 cup milk
1½ tablespoons butter	Few drops of lemon juice
½ " flour	Pepper and salt to taste
	4 tablespoons water in which fish is cooked.

Place the chopped carrot and onion in salted water and allow to come slowly to a boil while fish is being prepared. Wash, dry and salt fish, roll and fasten with toothpicks and cook in boiling water over a medium flame. While the fish is cooking, make the sauce in a double boiler by melting--not browning--the butter, stirring in the flour and the egg yolk, which has been mixed with the milk. Add the lemon juice, salt and pepper and four tablespoons of water, in which the fish was cooked. Pour sauce over fish and serve.

To replace himself he hired a young Englishman named Richard Lord, who is carrying on the tradition of information and goodwill solo. And with the changing of the guard the Fishery Council became Fulton Fish Market Information Services, an accurate name for what it has become. The tradition of Market tours for the public that began in the 1950s has been maintained (see p. 34), along with media appearances, lecture/demonstrations, industry information for anyone who wants it, silk-screened posters to promote seafood and warn buyers of holiday schedules, scholarship, articles for trade journals, and international travel to expos and conferences. Already a busy man, Richard Lord would need roller skates if he also had to organize dinner dances at the Waldorf, testimonials, baseball teams, and family outings as his predecessor did. The social conventions that were swept away by the 1960s are only old-timers' memories now, but a sense of community persists; there's no question—people get the Market in their blood!

HOW THE MARKET WORKS

OLD TIMES

When South Street and the Fulton Markets were created in the early nineteenth century, the New York seafood industry did not operate dramatically differently from the way it does now. The important changes are in the transportation of fish to market and in the variety and volume handled. In prerefrigeration days, when all fresh seafood had to be handled live, ingenious boat designs made it possible to keep the catch in the water all the way to market. The most glorious of these was the two-masted schooner, a wholly American invention that was first built in 1713 in Gloucester, Massachusetts. Outfitted with strong bulkheads to protect bouyancy, the holds of the schooners meant for fishing were ventilated to keep seawater circulating continuously through the catch. Ships of this sort were common delivery vehicles in New York Harbor throughout the nineteenth century. Some wholesalers were also fleet owners, so that about seventy-five fishing schooners belonged to the Market until the end of the century when they began to be refitted with engines or replaced by steam trawlers.

Once the live cargo was docked at present-day Pier 17, the fish were transferred to floating wooden holding pens called fish cars, which were tied up in the East River behind the Fish Market. As needed, the fish were removed to woven hampers and carried by "basket boys" to the back of the Market where pulleys were used to hoist the hampers up to the selling floor level. It was common practice for green journeymen to be sent to bail out the cars or initiated into the Fulton Fish Market mysteries at a turtle lassoing, quite an event at a time when green sea turtles weighing as much as two hundred pounds had to be captured and subdued. Iced deliveries began to replace live ones, and gradually, beginning as early as the 1860s, the fish cars began to be less important. But they did not disappear entirely until 1945, long after the swift, clean current of the East River was no longer clean enough to preserve foodstuffs hygienically. With iced seafood shipments, the fish cars were replaced by walk-in coolers, and the old hampers for hauling fish were replaced by hand trucks that could support the weight of large wooden crates filled with fish and ice.

An important influence on the wares at Fulton Fish Market in its infancy was the limited fishing range—from Cape Hatteras to the banks off the coast of New England—which meant that there were fewer available species and a stronger seasonality to the supply. Most dealers carried some poultry and game to tide them over the lean times, a practice that continued well into the twentieth century. When Fulton opened there was no imported seafood and nothing from the Deep South or the Pacific coast. With the opening of the Erie Canal in 1825 it became possible to bring freshwater fish from the Great Lakes to New York City, but it wasn't until the 1850s that the first major exploitation of these resources began. Concurrently, steamboats fast enough to make the Albany run round-trip in twenty-four hours and large enough for safe ocean runs along the Atlantic coast began to compete with an infant rail industry for the business of transporting regional goods to the city. When express companies (Wells Fargo and American Express were the biggies) used stagecoaches there was little chance of hauling fresh fish in good condition, but seafood became an important part of the express business after stagecoaches were replaced by railroads. Then it was possible to transport seafood from distant Atlantic and Gulf ports, adding some species from Southern waters. Now Fulton could receive shipments taken from all major points along the Atlantic coast as the fish swam north in spring and south in the fall or followed other natural migration patterns.

Of course the cargo had to be live in the early days. The first iced shipment of fish arrived from New England in 1858, using natural river ice. The freezing of fish was first accomplished in 1862 with pots of ice and salt set in an insulated room with fish laid out in a single layer. Not until the 1920s was proper rapid deep-freezing perfected. Frozen shrimp and lobster tails are important commodities at Fulton, but frozen fish remains a stopgap—usually stored off-premises—for times when the fresh item is unavailable or prohibitively dear.

Nowadays essentially all seafood deliveries to Fulton arrive in refrigerated trucks after having been hauled overland from the source or from the airport. Whereas boat deliveries were common well into the twentieth century, they dwindled sharply until, by the 1970s, there was only one boat, a scalloper called *Felicia,* that made routine deliveries, the last of which was in 1979. A fishing boat docked at Fulton Fish Market is as rare today as it was common a century ago.

THE MARKET DAY

Fulton Fish Market today is a dinosaur of remarkable vitality. The pace is brisk, the atmosphere is macho, and the ambient odor is unmistakably *eau d'FFM,* at its most exotic in the full heat of summer or mellowed by blending with the smoke of warming fires in cold weather. With all the sales floors open to the elements, the natural atmosphere varies markedly with the seasons. Summer provides some of the most pleasant open-air working conditions in the city: there is enough ice around to temper the effects of the asphalt griddle, and standing in dampness does wonders for the body's summer thermostat. These same conditions produce a cryosphere of marrow-gelling cold in winter, aided by arctic winds that whip through the sales areas. Dawn's early light might bring the first natural warmth of the day or it might bring winds that transform a still night into a more frigid morning. But only visitors are suffering noticeably.

On humid days, particularly in spring, when the temperature is hovering near the dew point, a bizarre set of special effects sets in, an atmosphere of cold steam rising ghostlike from ice and fish. Fluorescent blue is the dominant color and the hustle and bustle, the ordered disorder of business as usual, are wrapped in an eerie muffler of mist.

About seventy-five companies employing about eight hundred people do business here. Many companies are old and stable, while less prudent dealers come and go, reorganize in a new spot with a new name, or, rarely, fly by night. Because the seafood handled at Fulton is largely destined for retail stores and restaurants (processors would be likely to buy direct), the buyers who roam the Market early in the morning consist of owners, chefs, and purchasing agents, plus distributors who do the legwork for businesses that prefer not to send one of their own people. Some distributors are sophisticated wholesalers who rely on their own supply networks as well as Fulton resources. Though restaurants are important customers, they are not necessarily the favorites, owing to the tough financial pressures in the restaurant business in the New York area. This is not to say that restaurants do not pay their bills, but you can be sure they must earn their right to credit. The newest and fastest growing group of buyers is Korean. Current ownership of retail fish markets in the metropolitan area is estimated at seventy percent Korean; their representatives, both individuals and cooperatives, have become the most important single ethnic group of buyers at Fulton, with a corresponding increase in Korean wholesalers. So, buyers at Fulton can be as glamorous as Gilbert Le Coze, chef/owner of Le Bernardin, who ventures down to South Street twice a week (and places phone orders the other market days); or be as uncelebrated as Mr. Kim (the seventy-year-old father-in-law of the owner of Cherry Blossom, a neighborhood fishmarket at First Avenue and East 55 Street) who shops every market day.

At about midnight on market days (Monday through Friday) the loading-in begins. Some of the delivery trucks leave empty, while the ones from distant ports might stay to load a cargo of fish from different locales purchased in advance or after the business day begins, at 3:00 on Monday mornings and at 4:00 Tuesday through Friday. Mondays and Thursdays are the most colorful, the two days each week when southern fish arrive. Canadian dealers time their deliveries to correspond to the southern deliveries, so that they can take home their purchases.

Buyers survey sample goods and strike bargains that are communicated by the floor seller to the cashier in the office, using an ancient microphone and an oblique code (each wholesaler has his own system of letters that stand in for numbers) that keeps the selling price secret from the neighbors. Pricing is a complex system that is based on the wholesaler's cost or what the consignors would like to get for their wares, filtered through the usual laws of supply and demand. Pricing gossip, indeed all gossip, travels with lightning speed through the Market, partly because the customers are mobile and partly because the dealers form a tightly knit community, often with close ties of business or kinship or both.

Volume customers inspect the goods on the top of a case and dicker accordingly, secure in the knowledge that the rest of the case and other cases in the lot will be of the same quality. These cases, whether cardboard, wood, or polystyrene, are normally in the 50- to 100-pound range. Very large fish—swordfish, shark, tuna, Warsaw grouper—might be crated or handled loose. Once a purchase is made and the buyer has paid the bill or secured credit, the cases (or huge fish) are marked with the buyer's parking-space number. These codes instruct the journeymen where to deliver and load the order.

Dealers also have display tables, antique galvanized metal affairs for the most part, from which buyers may hand select their purchases and have them weighed up on equally ancient hanging scales. These loose fish always fetch a premium price. Here, depending on the wholesaler's style, the fish are dumped in gay profusion, glistening silver and rainbow hues or neatly arranged to show off their best sides, carefully iced against damage from the atmosphere. A fairly large purchase might be dumped into a tomato box, or other inexpensive crate that the dealer stocks, and handled as the full-case orders are. Smaller orders are slid into new dog food or fertilizer bags to be carted away by the buyer.

The descriptions above apply to dealers in whole finfish—called headfish—and squid and fresh shrimp. Shellfish dealers receive their stock in a variety of bags, crates, and baskets and rarely split them. The most notable exception is crabmeat in one-pound cans or plastic tubs; the few dealers who handle it normally have open cases for display and might sell as little as one piece. Other shucked shellfish—clams, mussels, small scallops, and oysters—come in plastic containers of various sizes (as well as oysters in the familiar plastic cans that recently replaced the old metal cans with the clear plastic lids). Wholesalers might sell one piece from a case that has been opened. Sea scallops are delivered to the Market in forty-pound muslin bags and sometimes repackaged in plastic tubs.

Fillet houses sell mostly flatfish, cod, pollock, and ocean perch, in round or rectangular twenty-pound plastic tubs. Much of this fish is filleted on the spot and is considered to be of fine quality. "Over-the-road fillet" processed in Gloucester, New Bedford, or some other fishing center is likely to be dipped in various solutions (see p. 73) that make it less desirable from a consumer standpoint, though the price does not always reflect this. Shad is a springtime specialty item that is handled by several dealers. The roe is removed to plastic tubs during business hours and the fish sent to specially trained filleters who normally process it in the evening, then return it to the dealers in the familiar white paper wrappers for sale the next morning. Frozen and preserved seafoods are no more than a sideline for any dealer, with the exception of Meyer & Thompson on Beekman Street, founded in 1912, the last remaining smoker at Fulton. They handle a full line of smoked seafood plus their own finnan haddie (now cod).

Most of the Market merchandise is moved on sturdy hand trucks that are much like their nineteenth-century antecedents. Fork-lifts (generally known as motors or tow-motors in industry) are just beginning to have a presence at Fulton. For many years the United Seafood Workers Union took a labor-protective stand and disallowed their use. In the early 1980s one motor was approved for a loading and unloading operation on the fringe of the Market, and now a few more are in use in the Market proper, and their numbers are growing. The problem with these "labor-saving devices" is that Fulton was not designed for them. The access corridors that define the display/sales/holding/loading space for each wholesaler's stall are too narrow—hand truck width—and South Street is not graded evenly enough for safe operation. Whichever mode of transport happens to be in use, manpower or horsepower, the general din is constantly pierced by the ubiquitous battle cry, "Watch your back!" (the polite version), as crates go zipping by. Even tourists are quick to learn to step lively.

The most common tool at Fulton is the trusty hook. Gaffs a foot long or better are carried by everyone who ever moves a crate or a fish. Because it is an extension of the good right arm, the hook has gained mystical importance. Hooks have been inherited or retired like an athlete's number. Journeymen and salesmen have dangling from their waists hammers that are hatchetlike on one side of the head for opening and closing wooden crates. Other important equipment includes *very* sturdy rubber boots and heavy rubber gloves with a sand-papery finish for gripping slippery fish. Fillet men wear long rubber aprons and white cotton gloves. The fillet knife is unlike any other—a seven- to eight-inch fairly narrow, slightly curving blade with just a hint of flexibility, always carbon steel.

The time of morning that business winds down depends on volume. Lots of fish and brisk sales might keep things bustling until 9:00 A.M. or even 10:00. A truly slow morning might be all over by 8:00. The bulk of the sales are normally completed by 7:30 or so, with the balance of the time devoted to cartage, storage, and cleanup. A central ice station at the north end of the Tin Building dispenses halibut-box loads of ice for re-icing the day's remains before they are stored in the coolers. Cleanup involves hosing down the whole works, leaving the buildings remarkably fresh and South Street an ancient fish soup, actually a running stew. Recent cooperation between the city and wholesalers has greatly improved sanitation on South Street, as befits a major tourist attraction. But no one would mistake the neighborhood for a flower market.

THE WARES

An old boast claimed that Fulton Fish Market could provide a different kind of seafood for every day of the year and now, as then, it happens to be true. But only about half of the seafood varieties that reach the Market can be said to have any real commercial value, perhaps 150 or 200. The best-known and largest sellers read very like the nineteenth-century catch: cod, flounder, fluke, halibut, salmon, mackerel, swordfish, lake whitefish, rainbow trout, red snapper, bluefish, whiting, porgy, smelt, pompano, shad, lobster, shrimp, scallops, oysters, clams, and crab, to name the most familiar. But what are all the other watery fauna and what becomes of them? Many are "normal" species with which the average consumer has at least a nodding acquaintance; others are freak catches on which fishermen hope to make a few bucks rather than having to dump them overboard; still others are exotica that are being flown in from many parts of the world—*bogue* (a sort of sea bream), *rouget* (red mullet), and *rascasse* (red scorpionfish) from the Mediterranean; tilapia (St. Peter's fish, Nile perch) from Israel; New Zealand items as normal as southern bluefin tuna in winter and as exotic as oreo dory or green-lipped mussels; and many others, as many as five new varieties a week.

Even without these flying fish (flyingfish, too) the Market would be chockablock with native species that most Americans never see. Ethnicity is the strongest factor, along with price. To use just one family of fish as an example—the jacks, from Southern waters—pompano makes it to fancy neighborhoods; a shipment of lookdown is likely to find a niche in Chinatown; while amberjack, crevalle jack, scad, permit, or blue runner are most likely to end up gracing the tables of Harlem. Frequenters of sushi parlors may be surprised to learn that yellowtail (not to be confused with yellowtail flounder) is also a jack, a Pacific fish that is imported from Japan or occasionally California, and almost always frozen. The more unusual imports, some of which are handled in startling volume, are likely to end up in a neighborhood with a large population ethnically related to the area where the fish comes from. That is why, for example, you would probably have to go to a Caribbean neighborhood in New York City to ever find parrotfish at retail.

Most of the fish and shellfish handled at Fulton Fish Market, perhaps as much as eighty percent, is consigned to the wholesalers by fishermen or middlemen who acquire it at the source. Wholesalers order what they want, what they think they can sell, but will also accept delivery of unusual fish or unusual volume from consignors who realize the potential for loss but must put their perishable goods somewhere. This no-risk arrangement for wholesalers keeps the markup relatively low.

A natural question here is where does all this stuff come from? The answer is anywhere in the world it can be caught or harvested and shipped to New York in the best condition at the best price, assuming a demand. A few examples follow. The cod family—cod, pollock, hake, whiting, ling—normally come only from New England and Atlantic Canada, not because these resources are always sufficient, but because of the economics of importing relatively inexpensive fish. Flatfish also come mainly from these areas, but a rough winter with a poor catch might result in shipments from Holland of fillets of plaice, a fish no more distinguished than the most ordinary flounder and never worth importing when the domestic flounder catch is normal. Genuine Dover sole, on the other hand, has a steady market and is flown in regularly from Holland, fresh, not just for restaurants but even for neighborhood fish markets with a well-heeled clientele. International commodities such as tuna and swordfish, which inhabit all the world's oceans, are flown in from the closest place where they are biting that has proper air service. While India is the world's major supplier of shrimp, the large ones find a natural market in Japan and only the tiny ones turn up in the United States, in supermarkets in freezer bags and frozen shrimp cocktail. Ecuador and Mexico provide the bulk of frozen shrimp for the American market. If consumers want to buy orange roughy from New Zealand or tilapia from Israel, then these fish are imported. If the Atlantic halibut supply should slacken after the Pacific season opens in April, then some Pacific halibut will be brought in, though the dealers would prefer to handle Atlantic because it really is better.

VOLUME

Fulton remains the largest wholesale seafood market in the Western Hemisphere. Only Paris's amazing Rungis and the three largest markets in Japan—including Tokyo's famous Tsukiji market—can claim larger volume. Poundage figures have been kept for better than a hundred years, though it is difficult to say how accurate they may be. As an indicator of trends, however, a comparison of these figures is instructive: nearly 30 million pounds of seafood handled in 1881, approximately 475 million pounds in 1928 (the period between the world wars was definitely the zenith), and an estimated 88 million pounds for 1987, down from about 140 million at the start of the decade. But with global seafood production at about 195 billion pounds per year, that gives Fulton a .0005 percent share—not bad for one neighborhood. Part of the decline in volume is owed to the growth of frozen and processed seafood industries and other distribution systems. The rest of the decline is on paper, since some Fulton wholesalers have found sophisticated ways to broker product that never reaches the Market. The dollar value of all this seafood is just as difficult to estimate as the poundage; $350 million a year is a figure that pops up often, but $250 million may be more like it.

The reasons for major changes in species volume at Fulton Fish Market, both day to day and over a long period of time, are fivefold and often interrelated: changes in taste, technology, cooking habits, ethnicity, and natural supply.

Among the most dramatic shifts in supply—and price—is the current market for fresh tuna, originally not fished commercially for the fresh market, then seasonally plentiful and offered very inexpensively to the Italian community, now a pricey item sought internationally with a fervor matched only by Japan.

The availability of international swordfish and imported farmed salmon has created supply undreamed of in the nineteenth century, with the longtime perception of these two as highly desirable providing a natural price support. Southern farmed catfish is currently enjoying a vogue, while farmed rainbow trout from Idaho provide a steady, high-quality resource, both fresh and frozen.

Among the great Hudson River fish (which are also native to other rivers that empty into the Atlantic), striped bass is currently making a population comeback from overfishing because its PCB levels make it unfit to eat and illegal to sell in the Northeast; sturgeon—once so plentiful that it was known as Albany beef—is also increasing its depleted numbers because demand is down and the price for the small catch is up. Shad have survived the ravages of industry well enough to become old-fashioned and prized mainly for their roe.

Since Fulton Market was founded, the sea scallop has been discovered, along with dozens of foreign items newly discovered by New Yorkers. Pompano, grouper, and red snapper only graced Northeastern tables after the advent of overnight transport from Florida and the Gulf. Red drum made a sudden appearance on the Fulton scene in the mid-1980s to meet the heavy consumer demand for Paul Prudhomme's blackened redfish. The disappearance of red drum was almost as sudden, as overfishing in the Gulf threatened extinction and forced fishing regulations. Now red drum from the Carolinas turn up occasionally but not with any predictable regularity.

The demand for eel has dropped dramatically, as New Yorkers of English and other European ethnicities have forgotten their fondness for it and the descendants of Italians only clamor for it at Christmastime. Few in the New York area seem to want haddock anymore; even local finnan haddie is smoked cod.

Green turtles have been off-limits for many years following their man-made brush with extinction; lobsters could end up in the same boat despite the hefty price for the dwindling catch (harvest regulations and seeding efforts may help to overcome the danger). While fish can do their own overfishing, the effects of human manipulation of the food chain are more common and usually more dramatic.

Sheepshead Bay in Brooklyn was obviously named for the fish that once teemed in its waters, but a gradual temperature change drove sheepsheads south so that they are rarely seen in local waters and are hardly missed at all. Tilefish were only discovered in 1879; then in 1892 what was feared to be the entire population bellied up, leaving the Atlantic coast from the Carolinas to Long Island littered with bodies. In all likelihood a sudden warm or cold current did the deed. It took better than ten years for the population to recover sufficiently to be fished again.

Waves of destructive algae or parasite growth can sometimes be avoided by fish—they just swim elsewhere—but can be crippling to more stationary bivalves. Scallops tend to be hardest hit, as in the "brown tide" of algae growth that has been suffocating the crop of Long Island bay scallops each summer for the past few years.

Red tides of parasite growth produce the threat of paralytic shellfish poisoning in humans (see p. 71), so the clam, oyster, and mussel populations get a rest from fishing until it's over. Scalloping continues because the muscle meat is not affected by red-tide toxins.

Among other natural changes in the supply, the season of the year is most important. Spring and fall are the boom times, the major migration and spawning seasons. Summer and winter are quieter: summer brings a big rise in lobster, clam, and crab harvests plus an increase in supplies of some fish—particularly weakfish, porgies, and bluefish—but demand is down. Oysters are considered to have a finer texture in cold weather, so that the industry is sluggish for the summer. Winter sunlight lowers the quantity of algae and plankton in the water, creating less food throughout the food chain. Less abundant nutrition and colder temperatures make for slower growth and a tendency for oily fish to become more lean and thus be a little less tasty.

On any Market day, given the seasonal rhythm of supplies, weather is the most important volume factor—weather affects the fishermen's ability to fish. Heavy storms make fishing difficult, dangerous, or impossible. Also, as weather affects water temperature there can be changes in migration patterns as some fish with narrow tolerance seek water temperatures they need and others follow their favorite food.

HOW FRESH IS FRESH?

Fresh seafood is normally shipped the day it is landed, either in the ideal boxed-at-sea containers or after rehandling harborside. Consumers are intrigued by the mystery of how old the fish they consume actually is. No blanket answer will do because of the many variables. Much depends on the retailer. If we realize that temperature control is almost more important than time out of the water, and if we learn to identify quality, there is nothing to fear.

Fish from local waters taken by day boats arrives at Fulton the following morning and should be on sale that day at retail. Farmed fish is handled with similar speed. Trip boats might only fish for two or three days before returning to port, or they might stay out for ten days to two weeks. Ocean scallopers have been known to fish for three weeks at a stretch. Obviously, the longer trips would not be attempted if the entire catch were not salable—and wholesome—but these landings always yield a variety of freshness in the cargo. Here is where your savvy and your retailer's standards are crucial.

SEAFOOD CONSUMPTION

It will come as a surprise to no one to learn that seafood consumption in the United States is on the rise; still the increase is not very dramatic. Figures kept by the National Marine Fisheries Service indicate that the national average for 1927 was 12.2 pounds (boneless, usable weight) per person, that the volume dipped in the mid-thirties to about 8.8 pounds per person, and that the figure has increased rather steadily to a 1986 estimate of 14.7 pounds per person, with perhaps another 4 pounds taken by recreational fishermen. Not surprisingly, 3.3 pounds of the 14.7 was canned tuna. And at least sixty percent of the total is prepared away from home, the largest part of these purchases in the form of fast-food fishburgers. Fulton Fish Market would be hard pressed to survive were it not that the New York metropolitan area is well above the national seafood consumption figures—probably in the 25 to 28 pounds per person per year range.

An unfortunate fact of life for wholesaler and consumer alike is that most of us try only perhaps seven different varieties, ten for the more adventuresome. This places considerable pressure on the supply—and price—of these favorites, many of which are luxury items. Old-timers at Fulton complain that despite all the new items available, people seem to have tastes more fixed than ever; thirty or forty years ago buyers came to the Market to buy *fish,* while now they come for very specific varieties. Consumers have everything to gain from experimenting with unfamiliar species, which are plentiful and relatively inexpensive, with tremendous potential waiting to be tapped.

THE FUTURE

The dumping and seepage of toxic industrial wastes into the water system have rightfully come in for much publicity and attack through the years, with DDT and PCBs the evil stars. Though illegal dumpings and inadequate standards still persist, improvements have been made. But environmentalists are justly concerned that the public may be lulled into a false sense of security. While, alas, new perils will probably develop as years go by, the major threat to the nation's waterways is an old one that grows worse daily. The cause is population density on or near coastlines (marine and freshwater), which has been projected to reach seventy-five percent of the entire national citizenry by the year 2000. The result is the introduction of unnatural levels of nutrients from sewage (both raw and properly treated), garbage, industrial wastes not otherwise toxic, and fertilizer dissolved in rainwater runoff. High levels of nutrients coupled with warm summer weather produce out-of-control algae growth—brown tide or a heavy green sludge—that chokes everything else by robbing the water of oxygen. Though the algae produce oxygen as part of their photosynthetic process during daylight hours, they use it up, and more, during the night, leading in severe cases to a condition known as *hypoxia:* dissolved oxygen less than three parts per million. Hypoxic conditions kill shellfish plus any fish that cannot avoid the area.

The areas hardest hit are the Great Lakes and the estuaries that feed some of our richest seafood beds: North Carolina's Pamlico and Albemarle sounds, the Chesapeake Bay, and Long Island Sound. So it is obvious that even without horrifying "accidents" in our water system, something must be done to prevent the death of our estuaries and the resulting upset of the delicate balance of marine life. Federal and state governments will have to do it, and they must move quickly.

GOING TO FULTON FISH MARKET

TOURS

There are three ways to arrange a tour of Fulton Fish Market. For the general public, the South Street Seaport Museum offers tours on alternate Thursdays beginning at 6:00 A.M. and lasting about one and a half hours. Admission is $15.00; $12.00 for museum members. These tours are guided by pleasant youngsters from the museum staff and begin with a breakfasty snack—a cup of hot coffee can be very welcome on a nippy early morning—and end with a cup of Manhattan clam chowder for those who work up an appetite looking at all the fish. For information and to book, phone 212-669-9416, or write South Street Seaport Museum, 207 Front Street, New York, New York 10038, Attention: Fulton Fish Market Tours.

Those who have a professional or scholarly interest in the Market may contact Richard Lord at Fulton Fish Market Information Services, 212-962-1608, 17 Fulton Fish Market, New York, New York 10038. Mr. Lord is extremely generous with his time and has considerable knowledge of the workings of the seafood industry and will arrange tours, normally on Mondays or Thursdays at 6:00 A.M. or, for the truly committed, at 4:00 A.M. (Mondays and Thursdays are freshwater and southern-fish delivery days, making the Market more colorful). Information Services is a small operation, funded by wholesalers' dues, and welcomes contributions. Tourists are invited to join tours that have already been scheduled, up to a maximum of perhaps ten people.

The New York Aquarium offers an annual tour of the Market, normally in April, from 6:00 to 8:00 A.M. The emphasis is on identification, behavior, biology, and adaptation of familiar and unusual species, plus consumer quality information. The cost is $9.50; $8.50 for members of the New York Zoological Society. For information, contact the New York Aquarium, 718-266-8624, Boardwalk and West 8th Street, Brooklyn, New York 11224. Visitors should simply decide the nature of their interest in the Market, then contact the Seaport Museum, Mr. Lord, or the New York Aquarium accordingly. Wear sturdy footgear, preferably waterproof.

Once the tour is over, somewhere around 8:00 A.M., it seems natural to relax a bit and seek fortification at Carmine's, 140 Beekman Street at Front Street, where a number of locals stop in during the work night and in the morning. There you can have breakfast or simple Italo-American fare with A.M. or P.M. beverages, depending upon your taste and your time clock. Tourists may want to wander a few blocks down to Wall Street to watch the megabillions awake, in plenty of time to be back for the opening of the South Street Seaport shops at 10:00 and 11:00 A.M. In addition to the wide variety of shopping, the Seaport has a host of eateries, anything from international snacks to serious dining. Fixed-up old favorites like Sweet's and Sloppy Louie's coexist with new establishments such as Gianni's, Fulton Street Café, Caroline's, Café Fledermaus, The Ocean Reef Grille, Roebling's, Flutie's, and The Liberty Café, with the pleasant little Bridge Café nearby. Also within easy walking distance are the Battery, the World Trade Center, Chinatown, and Little Italy.

NAVIGATION

The getting there is relatively easy to manage. Those who wish to drive will find city traffic smooth sailing within the early-morning tour hours and parking plentiful in a number of corner lots in the area.

The M-15 bus stops at the intersection of Fulton, Pearl, and Water streets, but it runs infrequently in the early morning and some M-15s terminate on Park Row near City Hall, a pleasant walk in good weather and a taxing experience in bad. Inquire before boarding the bus or avoid the bus altogether in favor of the subway. The Fulton Street Station is serviced by the A, CC, J, M, 2, 3, 4, 5, and even the JFK Express trains. All lines are an easy stroll, under ten minutes, from the Market.

SHOPPING

Visitors to Fulton Fish Market often wish to know if they may purchase seafood in the Market. The answer is both simple and complex. Because it is on city property, Fulton Fish Market is a public market where anyone may visit, but sales are in wholesale quantities, at the discretion of the wholesaler. This could mean ten or twenty pounds of any one item, or it might be considerably less. Tourists who attempt to interfere with the ordered disorder of business as usual— the bread-and-butter deals made with valued clients—will feel distinctly unwelcome. But once the important business of the day has ended (anywhere from 7:00 A.M. to, rarely, 10:00 A.M., with 7:30 as a safe median), many wholesalers are agreeable to unloading a bit of the day's remains. Friday is the best bet, when wholesalers are more likely to part with merchandise that will not store well over the weekend. Before World War II, before coolers became standard, on a Friday one could hold up one finger and get a *box* of fish, maybe a hundred pounds, for a penny a box. Those days are over, but there are still bargains to be found.

Wholesale quantities is the key phrase here. No one will split a bushel of hardshell crabs, a twenty-pound tub of flounder fillets, or a similar unit of commerce, and no one will sell you a piece of a fish, with the exception of the mammoth fish that are routinely split, such as swordfish, tuna, and shark. For instance, a minimum swordfish sale is one "knuckle"—one vertebra—which should weigh in at about ten pounds. If whiting is fetching $.50 per pound there is obviously no good reason for a dealer to bother with a consumer who wishes to purchase a few fish that will weigh in at a few pounds. Yet you should find someone who is willing to part with a salmon, a few pompano, a pound of crabmeat, even a shad roe or a dozen sea urchins. The wisest move is to have an open mind, a wish to entertain grandly, a plan for laying down a home brew of cured, smoked, or pickled seafood, or friends waiting to share the fruits of your wholesale smarts. Look around, ask around, deal with people who are pleasant and seem to have a moment to answer your questions. Be prepared to identify the quality and freshness you want and reject merchandise that is not up to your standards. All sales are "as is" with no cleaning, scaling, or filleting services offered. Only large-volume buyers may arrange to have their purchases dressed to order, for a price.

Wholesale prices vary wildly, while most retailers keep their prices nearly constant to avoid consumer confusion. In times of short supply, the wholesale price of a popular item may approach the retail price, while a glut in the market could send the price of another item plunging to one quarter of the average retail, or even lower.

If the price you are offered is below retail, you should feel that you are getting an acceptable deal, even if it is not the most brilliant deal of the day. Haggling is really only for the big guys, but who knows?

A GUIDE TO FISH
AND SHELLFISH HANDLED
AT FULTON

Included here are all varieties of commercial importance, plus a few others that could or should be. They are grouped, as much as possible, according to families.

FINFISH

BONY FISHES (Class *Osteichthyes*)

Acipenseridae: Sturgeon

The **Atlantic sturgeon,** which also inhabits the major rivers of the Atlantic coast, exists in far fewer numbers than in years past and most often comes to market smoked. Yet there is a fresh market supply, most of which goes to restaurants. Do try it if you can find it at retail. Its distinctive flesh is very meaty and resembles veal as much as other fish. It has the peculiar property of storing its strange-looking yellow fat in a very distinct layer just beneath the skin; some of the fat is always attached to skinned fillets that have not been excessively trimmed. For those who like it, sturgeon is delicious broiled, grilled, panfried, or braised.

Ammodytidae: Sand Lance

The **American sand lance** is rather common at Fulton and is sold as whitebait.

Anarhichadidae: Wolffish

The **Atlantic wolffish,** also known as **ocean catfish,** is in rather steady though small supply, owing to its lack of popularity. Its rather firm, sweet white flesh is excellent for any purpose and is a must try for anyone who can find it at retail.

Anguillidae and *Congridae:* Eels

The freshwater **American eel** and marine **conger eel** are handled year round but are uncommon in mainstream fish stores, except at Christmastime when American eel is handled live. American eel is most often grilled, poached, stewed, or smoked. Congers are considered to have a stronger flavor and are most often included in Mediterranean-style soups or stews.

Ariidae and *Ictaluridae:* Catfish

The marine **gafftopsail** is fairly common at Fulton, but the larger volume is in **freshwater catfish** of various species, most of which are farmed somewhere in the Mississippi valley. The white flesh of both is pleasantly mild and might be used for many preparations; it is most often deep- or panfried for Southern dishes.

Atherinidae: Silversides

Silversides are tasty little fish with a bright silvery stripe along each side. Tiny ones are fried as whitebait, while larger ones are cleaned and panfried like smelts.

Balistidae: Triggerfish

One of the finest eating fish in the sea, **triggerfish** are so highly prized in their native Caribbean that the few that make it north go right to Caribbean neighborhoods. The first dorsal spine is heavy and sharp and once cocked forward can only be released by pulling the second spine like a trigger. If you should find one, either the drab

gray or colorful **queen,** try the sweet white fillets simply broiled and you will be delighted. The next time you happen upon one, see how much more interesting it is than flounder in any of the traditional flatfish preparations.

Bothidae, Pleuronectidae, and *Soleidae:* Flatfish

The first family is the left-eyed flounders, including the **common fluke (summer flounder), Pacific sanddab,** and **southern flounder** (as well as the European **brill** and genuine **turbot,** which are rare in the United States). The next family is the right-eyed flounders: **halibut, blackback flounder (winter flounder), Greenland turbot, gray sole (witch flounder), plaice, sea dab (American plaice), yellowtail flounder,** and a Pacific flounder marketed as **Dover sole,** even though it is neither a sole nor is it from anywhere near Dover. Except for meaty halibut steaks, which are suitable for any cooking technique, and Greenland turbot fillets, which are usually poached and sauced, the flounders are interchangeable and usable in any sort of dish except those that require grilling, braising, and stewing. Gray sole is normally the most expensive of the smaller flounders because it is considered to be the most delicate and because it has the lowest yield. In the United States, **lemon sole** is a marketing term for fillets, usually from the white-skin side, from large flounder—over four pounds whole—most often blackback flounder.

Soleidae is the family of true soles, represented at Fulton by genuine **Dover sole** imported from Holland. Dover sole is usually skinned and broiled or sautéed, or filleted and used in a classic French preparation; it is quite delicate and very special. There are a few other genuine soles imported in small quantites from Senegal, and they are worth trying. There are also a few soles in Western Atlantic waters, but the only one of these you are likely to encounter is a small sole called **hogchoker,** which is caught in small quantities in Southern waters.

Carangidae: Jacks

Florida **pompano** is normally the most expensive whole finfish at Fulton because it is shipped from Gulf or Florida waters and because it has a distinctive buttery goodness, broiled or grilled, or filleted and sautéed. The only other premium jack is Pacific **yellowtail,** one of the finest sushi fish, which is usually handled frozen through the Japanese restaurant network rather than at Fulton. Among the other jacks, **permit** most closely resembles pompano in appearance and taste. The catch is small and there are some people who claim it is actually better than pompano, but unscrupulous dealers (never at Fulton, of course) have been known to trim the long dorsal and anal fins to try to fetch pompano prices for it. **Crevalle** and **amberjack** are cheap and plentiful and tasty, too, though amberjack brings a very low price because it often has a parasite problem, particularly in the tail half. Do try **blue runner, rainbow runner,** or **bigeye scad,** if you can find them, broiled or grilled. **Lookdown** is popular in Chinatown but not an important Fulton item.

Catostomidae: Suckers

Not a pretty name for this family of freshwater fish, but **bigmouth buffalo** is considered by many to be an essential ingredient in gefilte fish. It is also popular in Chinatown, which is the best place to find it at retail.

Centrarchidae: Sunfish

This family includes a number of small freshwater panfish, all of which are tasty and none of which is an important commodity. The members that move through Fulton in any volume are **black crappie, bluegill, pumpkinseed, redear sunfish, warmouth,** and **white crappie.**

Cichlidae: Cichlids

This family includes **tilapia,** which draws some attention under the name **St. Peter's fish.** It is a pleasant, all-purpose sort of white-fleshed fish that is more of a supermarket than Fulton item. Another cichlid is **cherry snapper,** which is also known as **redfish,** not to be confused with ocean perch or red drum.

Clupeidae: Herring

Fresh **Atlantic herring** are delicious panfish, as well as being suitable for the various pickles that are popular in Europe. Small herring are marketed as **sardines,** though that name is more properly applied to genuine **pilchards** imported from Portugal. The other important herring, the giant one, is our wonderful **American shad,** which provides delicious springtime treats, both flesh and roe.

Coryphaenidae: Dolphin

Fish, that is. **Mahi mahi,** the Hawaiian name, is the usual marketing term for this delicious tropical fish that is being brought in from Florida and Central America. It is flavorful and firm enough to be a multipurpose fish, yet delicate enough to suit the more squeamish palate. With luck, it will remain reasonably priced, as premium fish go; it is retailed as low-waste steaks or fillets.

Cyprinidae: Carp

Most often thought of as an ingredient in gefilte fish, the hardy freshwater **carp** may be prepared by any cooking method. Its rich flavor is cleanest in winter. Occasionally **goldfish**—decorative carp hybrids—turn up at Fulton; they have the same culinary uses.

Engraulidae: Anchovies

Fresh **anchovies** imported from Portugal, Greece, Brazil, Argentina, or California are available occasionally. They are usually deep- or panfried.

Esocidae: Pike

The snowy flesh and delicate flavor of **northern pike** have made it a traditional ingredient in gefilte fish as well as the famous French dumplings called *quenelles.* The fresh market supply—from freshwaters in Canada—is small but steady; demand is low because the tiny Y-shaped pinbones make pike difficult to fillet.

Exocoetidae: Flyingfish

The national fish of Barbados, some **flyingfish** move through Fulton for the Bajan community and for restaurants with an Island theme. They are richly flavored and delicious breaded and fried.

Gadidae: Cod

The cod family is the most important commercial group of fish at Fulton, as it always has been. Its members include **Atlantic cod, Atlantic pollock, haddock, cusk, red hake (ling),** and **silver hake (whiting).** All have very lean, sweet white flesh (except for pollock, whose bluish flesh cooks white) that is suitable for any cooking technique.

Haemulidae: Grunts

Grunts—so named for the noise they make when caught—are a large family of small fish taken in tropical and near-tropical Atlantic and Gulf waters. The ones most likely to turn up at Fulton are **pigfish,** porkfish, sailors' choice, tomtate, and white grunt. Though usually fried, they might also be grilled or included in soups or stews; they are considered by many to be more delicate and fine than the costly snappers they slightly resemble.

Istiophoridae: Marlin

Fresh blue marlin and white marlin show up occasionally at Fulton, though most of the small catch is smoked. They are treated like swordfish, which they resemble, though the flesh is not quite so delicious.

Labridae: Wrasses

The only wrasse with any Fulton volume is tautog (blackfish). This underappreciated fish has delicious firm white flesh that is suitable for any cooking technique. Other wrasses—also tasty—that surface occasionally include hogfish and cunner.

Lophidae: Monkfish

Though also known as goosefish, bellyfish, frogfish, sea devil, and poor man's lobster, monkfish is rarely called anglerfish, which is what it is. On restaurant menus it is often called lotte, the French name for its European Atlantic cousin. The Mediterranean version is known as *baudroie* in French and *coda di rospo* (tail of the toad) in Italian. A fearsome beast that looks to be all mouth, the monkfish has very firm white tail meat arranged in two neat, rounded fillets. It is most often used for sautés and for soups or stews.

Lutjanidae: Snappers

Because of the great popularity of American red snapper, there is a flood of other snappers on the market, including Southern red snapper from South America, dusky mangrove snapper, queen snapper, silk snapper, and vermillion snapper (B-liner). All are good but should be less expensive than genuine red. In the high-price category are lane snapper, which looks like a red snapper with yellow stripes, and yellowtail snapper, which some consider the best of all.

Malacanthidae: Tilefish

Though a few other species turn up occasionally, the big seller is Atlantic tilefish, whose fishery is centered off New Jersey. This all-purpose fish is prized for its firmish, very lean white flesh. It is, however, a bit bland for some tastes.

Mugilidae: Mullet

Striped mullet is plentiful and inexpensive at Fulton. Its mild but distinctive, slightly oily flesh is fine for baking, broiling, grilling, and panfrying, but it is underappreciated by upmarket consumers. The roe is considered a great delicacy in Asia and the Mediterranean.

Mullidae: Goatfish

This family includes the famous Mediterranean red mullet called *rouget* in France. These pretty little fish may be panfried, baked, or grilled and are considered essential to an authentic *bouillabaisse.* The Fulton supply is more likely to be a related red goatfish from the Caribbean.

Osmeridae: Smelt

Rainbow smelt are small fish from the North Atlantic or landlocked freshwater in the Northeast and Canada. They have a distinctive, rich flavor and are usually fried.

Percichthyidae: Bass

The star of this family, striped bass, is currently off-limits at Fulton because of PCB levels, so it has been replaced by a hybrid striper called sunshine bass, which is being farmed on the East Coast and in California. Both have a fine flavor and texture that make them all-purpose. Other versatile members of this family include the European sea bass, white perch, and the freshwater white bass.

Percidae: Perch

The two members of this freshwater Canadian family that are popular in the United States are yellow perch, one of the finest panfish, and walleye, also known as walleyed pike and yellow pike. Walleye is mild and delicious and might be used for any purpose, though it is most often used as a substitute for pike and is steamed or fried in Chinese preparations.

Pomatomidae: Bluefish

The single member of this family is our Atlantic bluefish, which is distinctive and tasty baked, broiled, grilled, or cured.

Priacanthidae: Bigeye

Bigeye is a smallish red fish with huge eyes that have earned it the nickname **"jellyeye."** When it does come to the Market, occasionally, it is used as a snapper substitute.

Rachycentridae: Cobia

Cobia is a large sport fish that is all too rarely brought in from the Gulf or Florida. Its firm white flesh is delicious and versatile. Do give it a try if you get the opportunity.

Salmonidae: Salmon and Trout

The salmon family includes a number of important food fish from Atlantic, Pacific, and fresh waters. The two Atlantic versions marketed here are **Atlantic salmon** and a close relation that varies with its habitat—if landlocked, it is **rainbow trout;** if oceangoing it is called **salmon trout** (this is a farmed fish, not to be confused with the wild ocean-run brown trout, not available here, which may be called salmon trout or sea trout). The Pacific variety of rainbow trout may also be oceangoing, in which case it is called **steelhead.** Of the five Pacific salmon in U.S. waters, two are important fresh market fish: **chinook (king),** and **coho (silver).** Coho are also being farmed to produce small troutlike panfish, as well as larger sizes. The other three Pacific salmon, in roughly descending order of quality, are **sockeye, pink,** and **chum.** They rarely show at Fulton, and are more likely to go to canneries or smokehouses. Pacific salmon is less important than Atlantic at Fulton because it is seasonal and the quality varies, while farmed Atlantic salmon has consistent supply and quality. But coho farmers are beginning to catch up. Another salmonid is **lake trout** from the Great Lakes and freshwater Canada; it is a small but steady resource. The surprise members of the family (some taxonomists place them in a family of their own) are **common (lake) whitefish** and **chub (ciscoe).** All members are remarkably versatile and may be prepared by any cooking method, but should not be served raw. (Please see Seafood Safety, pp. 66–68.)

Sciaenidae: Drums

This large family, also called croakers, includes small panfish—**Atlantic croaker, kingfish (Gulf, Southern,** or **Northern),** and **spot**—as well as larger drums. The drums include the famous **red drum** known as **redfish, black drum, spotted seatrout** (the popular

Louisiana **speckled trout**), and our Atlantic **weakfish,** which is marketed as **seatrout.** All drums have tasty white flesh that can be cooked in many ways. But black drum has parasite problems and red drum may not be fished in the Gulf currently because of overfishing, so only a small, sporadic supply from the Carolinas is available.

Scombridae: Tuna and Mackerel

These rich-fleshed beauties share the family trait of possessing lots of colorful swimming muscle. The important mackerels are **Atlantic mackerel,** also called **Boston mackerel,** which is delicious grilled, broiled, baked, cured, and raw; **king mackerel,** also called **kingfish,** which is usually steaked and baked, broiled, or grilled; and **Spanish mackerel,** which is smaller and more delicate, also baked, broiled, or grilled. Of the red-fleshed tunas, larger is better. **Bluefin** is the finest of all, but in short supply; **yellowfin** and **bigeye** are the usual quality tunas at Fulton. The smaller ones, **bonito, blackfin, skipjack,** and **little tunny,** are less fine, but they do respond to soaking in a light brine and will work in cooked preparations. Genuine **albacore,** the only tuna that may be called "white" when canned, has golden flesh that is delicious, but scarce at fresh market.

Scorpaenidae: Rockfish

Ocean perch is the only important rockfish at Fulton. It is used primarily as a less expensive substitute for red snapper. Be sure you trust your retailer on this one. Some **red scorpionfish** are imported from the Mediterranean, where they are used in a variety of ways, including as a component of *bouillabaisse* and other soups and stews.

Scaridae: Parrotfish

Several varieties of **parrotfish** with startling tropical colors arrive at Fulton and are trucked to Caribbean neighborhoods, never to be seen by everyone else. Their beauty is more in the skin than in the flesh, which is undistinguished.

Serranidae: Groupers

Some forty different grouper varieties have turned up at Fulton in the last few years, all interchangeable in the kitchen. These include **black, dusky, misty, nassau, coney, red, snowy, yellowedge, yellowfin, white, rock hind,** and **speckled hind** (also called **Kitty Mitchell** for a prostitute who worked the docks in Florida. Was she fond of polka dots?). Of that group, red grouper has a slightly poorer yield than the others, and yellowfin grouper is considered the most delicate. They all have sweet white flesh that is very versatile. The really distinctive groupers are the two huge ones, **jewfish** and **Warsaw grouper,** which can weigh hundreds of pounds. They are purchased by Chinese restaurants, where the flesh is steamed and the carcass is used for soup stock.

The other important member of this family is the **black sea bass,** among the finest of delicate white-fleshed fish. It may be prepared in a variety of ways, but it is particularly fine steamed.

Sparidae: Porgies

This large family includes a number of **sea breams** on both sides of the Atlantic. The important ones here are our **porgy** (which is also known as **scup**), **sheepshead, red porgy** (called **pink snapper**), and Mediterranean *boque.* With all of them, the sweet white flesh is very tasty. These fish are most often fried, but they might also be broiled or grilled; fillets might be used for many purposes.

Stromateidae: Butterfish

These pretty, silvery little panfish with a buttery texture are most popular with Chinese cooks, but they can be found in neighborhoods beyond Chinatown as well. **North Atlantic butterfish** and **Gulf butterfish** are the most usual varieties, but there is also a long-finned one called **harvestfish** or **star butterfish.**

Tetraodontidae: Puffers

The Atlantic **northern puffer,** also called **blowfish,** is marketed as **"sea squab."** Once the edible tail is removed from the body and skinned, it does not have the toxic dangers of its Pacific cousin, the Japanese fugu. Sea squab tails—which never weigh more than a few ounces—consist of two rounded fillets of firm, deliciously sweet meat joined together by the backbone. Though usually panfried, they might also be used anywhere their firm texture is a plus, including grilling, stir-fries, pasta and rice dishes, and soups or stews.

Trachichthyidae: Roughy

A rather recent discovery, **orange roughy** has become an important export for New Zealand, normally in the form of frozen skinned fillets. Roughy is pleasant, if undistinguished, and may be substituted for snapper or flounder fillets.

Triglidae: Searobin

Northern searobin is plentiful and tasty and could be an important resource if enough people were interested. The incidental catch finds its way mostly to Italian neighborhoods, where cooks are acquainted with a **gurnard** (*cappone* in Italian, *grondin* in French) and appreciate its firm sweetness, as well as the low price.

Xiphiidae: Swordfish

Swordfish is a favorite around the world, partly because it inhabits all the world's oceans, but mostly because it is distinctively meaty and flavorful. This appeal supports the premium price. In addition to the familiar broiled, grilled, and sautéed preparations, consider braising large cuts of swordfish.

Zeidae: Dories

Genuine **John Dory** from the Mediterranean or the European Atlantic is rare at Fulton, but there is a native variety called **buckler dory** (**American John Dory**) that surfaces occasionally in small quantities. Deep-bodied, quite flat, and very long-finned, these strange-looking silvery fish are not likely to become important food fish in the United States, but they are delicately delicious grilled or broiled, or filleted and sautéed. The dark "thumb prints" behind the gills inspired a connection between these fish and various Gospel legends, so that dories are named for St. Peter in many European languages.

Zoarcidae: Eelpout

Though the idea of an edible member of the eelpout family is not likely to inspire confidence, **ocean pout** is very, very good. The firm white flesh has been compared to veal, a reference to the texture rather than the delicately piscine flavor. Here is a plentiful resource waiting for a market.

CARTILAGINOUS FISHES (CLASS *Chondrichthyes*)

Sharks

Of the dozens of shark species, belonging to eleven different families, only four are of commercial importance at Fulton. **Shortfin mako** is the most popular. **Blacktip shark** from Florida is also high quality—the best, according to some people—and is gaining popularity. These large sharks are steaked and cooked like swordfish, which of course they resemble physically. The easiest way to distinguish a crosscut piece of shark from swordfish is to look at the red muscle: in sharks it is a discrete round or oval on either side of the body, while in swordfish the red muscle is almost T-shaped as it follows the clover-leaf pattern of the light muscle. Shark skin is also much thicker than swordfish. When another large shark does reach the Market, chances are that neither the fisherman nor the wholesaler is certain which species it is, unless it has the distinctive *very* long tail fin of the **thresher** or the strange head of a **hammerhead**. Other large sharks do sell, but at a lower price than mako or blacktip.

The other two volume sharks are small ones, **spiny dogfish** and **smooth dogfish**. They can be steaked like their large cousins, but they can also be poached and flaked for certain Central American dishes or for salads. Fillets are delicious panfried.

Skate and Ray

Closely related to sharks, skates and rays have delicate white flesh that is still underappreciated in the United States. The most usual varieties at Fulton are **clearnose skate, little skate, thorny skate,** and **winter skate**. Only the meaty "wings" are marketed. If they are to be poached, there is no need to skin them first. Skate may also be filleted, skinned, and fried or sautéed. It is a popular fish 'n' chips fish in Britain.

SHELLFISH

CRUSTACEANS

Portunidae: Swimming Crab

This is the family of the **Atlantic blue crab,** the "beautiful swimmer" that is big business from the Chesapeake to the Gulf of Mexico. At Fulton it is available live—both hard-shell and soft-shell—in all seasons but the dead of winter, and year round as crabmeat processed where it is harvested. Crabs must be cooked before the meat can be extracted, then the meat is packed into one-pound plastic tubs or pasteurized and sealed in cans (which still require refrigeration and have an extraordinary shelf life but only so long as they are kept chilled). Fresh is better, but canned earns the same or even a slightly higher price because of the extra processing. While all the body meat is of the same sweetness and whiteness, it is graded—and priced— according to the size of the pieces: jumbo lump is the most precious; backfin should be about the same as jumbo, but it may have some broken pieces in it; lump is a mixture of good-sized lumps and broken pieces; special is all smaller pieces. Claw meat is very good, but its brown color makes it less useful. It is usually available as cocktail claws in cans.

Cancridae: Cancer Crabs

These very hard-shelled crabs are represented most famously by the Pacific **dungeness,** which is not a common item at Fulton. As a market for them slowly grows, there is some volume of Atlantic **Jonah crab** and **rock crab,** both of which could be fished in large numbers.

Xanthidae: Stone Crabs

Only the precooked large claws of these sturdy crabs are marketed. They are ready to eat, and are normally served cold with a mayonnaise sauce of some sort (see p. 279), often including mustard. The finest **stone crabs** come from Atlantic Florida, but the Gulf variety is high quality, too. A Chilean stone crab is also being marketed; its quality seems to be fine.

Cambaridae: Crayfish

These freshwater minilobsters are becoming increasingly available in the Northeast, either from the traditional Louisiana resources or from farms in other Southern states. There are some Fulton supplies of live **crayfish,** which of course are known as **crawfish** in the South, and even **soft-shell crayfish.** Both are still a little too unfamiliar and pricey to be big business yet.

Nephropidae and *Palinuridae:* Lobster, Lobsterettes, and Spiny Lobster

The first is the family of our wonderful North Atlantic **American lobster,** which is handled live in large quantity by several Fulton dealers. This family includes the smaller creatures from Europe and the Caribbean called **lobsterettes, Norway lobsters, Dublin Bay prawns, langoustines,** and **scampi,** to mention just a few of their names. At Fulton they are usually handled frozen, and have not yet gained the wide U.S. following they deserve.

Palinuridae are the **spiny (rock) lobsters** from Australia, New

Zealand, South Africa, and, in small quantities, Florida. These are usually handled as frozen tails. Spinies are called crayfish in certain parts of the English-speaking world. Armed with that knowledge, consumers should have no trouble distinguishing between spiny lobster and crawfish in a recipe or other literature.

Penaeidae: Tropical Shrimp
    At least eleven species from this family of warm-water **shrimp** (**prawns** in Britain) are marketed as an important food source around the world. Most of our supply is frozen tails from Ecuador and Mexico, but there is also a large quantity of finer quality fresh tails from Florida. Restaurants seem to get most of those.

Palaemonidae, Pandalidae, Aristeidae, and *Sicyonidae:* Other Shrimp
    These other shrimp are the **freshwater prawn** from Hawaii and Puerto Rico; **northern shrimp** or **Maine shrimp**—the small, red, whole shrimp that are seasonally plentiful; **giant red shrimp** from Spain and Morocco; and **rock shrimp** from Florida, which are plentiful, inexpensive, and usually sold as shelled tail meat.

ECHINODERMS

Strongylocentrotidae: Sea Urchin
    Our **green sea urchins** are harvested by skindivers in Maine waters; they are at their best from fall into spring, but they are fished year round.

MOLLUSCS

Veneridae: Hard-shell Clams
    The most important clam at Fulton is the **hard clam,** which is called—in descending order of size—**quahog** or **chowder, cherrystone,** and **littleneck.** This family also includes delicious **Manila clams** from Washington State.

Myacidae: Soft-shell Clams
    This is the **soft-shell** or **steamer clam,** which is also a big seller.

Arcticidae, Hiatellidae, Mactricidae, and *Solenidae:* Other Clams
    Other clams handled at Fulton, in smaller numbers, include the **ocean quahog** or **mahogany clam;** the giant **Pacific geoduck** from Washington State; **surf clams** from the mid-Atlantic coast; and the

Atlantic razor clam. All are delicious, particularly razor clams, which deserve to be more popular. Surf clams are large and rather tough and are important to the canning industry; the fresh-market supply is likely to be bought by Japanese restaurants, where the foot is thinly sliced and used as a substitute for geoduck in sashimi.

Mytilidae: Mussels

Huge quantities of **blue mussels** move through Fulton because they are cheap and delicious. **Green-lipped mussels** from New Zealand have some presence, and are excellent but a little pricey.

Ostreidae: Oysters

All of the wonderful native **eastern oysters** harvested from New Brunswick to the Gulf of Mexico are the same species; the startling differences in size, shape, and flavor all come from water conditions. The **European flat oyster** is represented by **belons** that are farmed in Maine. Fulton also has some volume of large **Pacific (Japanese) oysters** and some delicious tiny **kumamotos** from the Pacific Northwest.

Pectinidae: Scallops

When **sea scallops** were discovered in the nineteenth century, their size was so impressive that they were dubbed "skate wings" which may account for the persistent rumor that someone is punching out rounds of skate and passing them off as scallops. This is not to say that no one has ever falsified a seafood item, but that one seems unlikely. Fulton also handles what can be harvested from the dwindling populations of the smaller, delicate **bay scallops** from Long Island and New England. The small, lower-quality **calico scallops** from Florida are also handled, the supply supplemented by various small scallops from South America, some of which are as delicate as genuine bays. Essentially all of the scallops at Fulton arrive shucked, because the shelf life is much better than for in-shell, live scallops.

Sepiidae: Cuttlefish

Though not an important commodity, there is some **cuttlefish** at Fulton, usually cleaned and frozen.

Octopodidae: Octopus

Another low-volume item, **octopus** from Florida, usually frozen, is available.

Loliginidae and *Ommastrephidae:* Squid
There is a steady demand for **squid,** though still not as great as it should be. It is available both fresh and frozen.

Strombidae and *Buccinidae:* Conch and Whelk
Live, in-the-shell **conchs** and **whelks** are available at Fulton, as well as shelled, pasteurized meat for those who are not so good with a hammer.

Lacunidae: Periwinkles
The **common periwinkle** is a tasty little sea snail. Once poached or steamed, it is eaten hot or cold by removing the meat with a pin. There are also some land snails at Fulton; they are handled the same way.

MISCELLANEOUS FARE

Manufactured Fish Products
Products made from a Japanese-engineered fish paste called *surimi* are not big business at Fulton, but a few dealers do handle a little. The extensive washing of the Alaskan pollock fillet that forms the base robs it of water-soluble vitamins and some protein, so it is not as nutritious as real fish. But it does have a good shelf life, even when handled fresh rather than frozen. The flavor is bland and sweet, and the texture can be rubbery and/or watery, particularly if it has been handled improperly. The crab-flavored flakes and sticks used for salads and sushi are probably the most successful.

Ranidae: Frogs
Bullfrog legs are not currently available at Fulton, but they may be again. They are most often handled frozen.

Chelydridae and *Emydidae:* Turtles
Live **snapping turtles** and **northern diamondback terrapins** are occasionally available, but they are more often secured through the Chinatown purchasing network.

A CHART TO THE WATERS OF FISH COOKERY

Readers will find this book most useful if they acquaint themselves with the information in this section. It takes the mystery out of choosing and handling fine seafood safely, and gives some general cooking information for the recipes that follow.

CHOOSING FISH AND SHELLFISH

There is really no mystery to choosing fine, fresh seafood in a retail store or at wholesale. Always buy from dealers who keep the premises clean and who carefully ice the wares.

WHOLE FISH

1. Examine the skin. It should have a nice soft sheen and be moist but not covered with mucus (except for blackfish, wolffish, and eels, which normally are). The scales should all be in place, tight against the skin instead of sticking out. Richard Lord of Information Services likes to say that fish should look as if you could put them back

in the water and they would swim away. This is usually wishful thinking because many colors begin to fade rapidly as soon as the fish die. Fish vary in their natural coloring (the cod family and flatfish, for instance, are rather drab), but if you do find fish with a lovely rainbow iridescence or splashes of fresh-looking color, it is a good sign. Silvery skin, as in pompano, behaves rather like aluminum foil in that once crumpled, it cannot be resmoothed. There should be no holes or cuts, which will admit bacteria. Any gaff marks should be on the head.

2. The flesh should feel firm. When pressed gently, it should not leave finger marks. This is a test you will probably not be allowed to perform because no one wants heavy-handed customers bruising his fish. It is not entirely necessary; some fish, bluefish for example, have very soft flesh even when very fresh.

3. Eyes are not the most reliable indicator of freshness, but if they are clear and bright and flush with the skull or bulging, that's great. The interior of the eye begins to whiten with age, but ice-burn can create a cloudy look in good fish. Sunken eyes often indicate moisture loss through age, but it might also be that someone has picked the fish up by the eyes, an excellent way to move it because it does no damage to the flesh.

4. The gills should be neat, not ragged, with a good bright bloodred color and a minimum of mucus. Brownish or blackish color develops with age. If the gills look pale and washed out, you are probably examining a fine-quality fish, like farmed salmon, that has been bled for sweetness and increased shelf life. Consumers want to see gills, but packers want to remove them—a wise move—for increased shelf life. So far consumers are winning that battle, but the situation is subject to change.

5. Fish should smell like the proverbial ocean breeze (or river or lake breeze), but you may not be allowed to get your nose that close, for sanitation reasons. If you can, sniff the gill cavity, the first place off odors develop. Expect something more intense than you would get from smelling the skin, but the odor should be fresh and briny.

FILLETS

Since you will probably be unable to touch or smell fillets at retail, rely on two visual clues:

1. The texture of the flesh. Flesh should look plump and moist with a pearly translucence. The grain should be neat and firm-looking,

with no raggedness, fuzziness, or gaping between the muscle groups. Steak fish should have a flat cut surface with no bulging of muscle groups.

2. The color of the flesh. Though fish vary in flesh color, whatever the color is supposed to be, it should be true: white, not tired beige; pearl gray, not muddy; red, not brown; pearl pink, not yellowish. Shad is a notable exception because it is normally a tired beige color, with gaping muscle groups because of the filleting technique. So pearliness is essential. Swordfish flesh varies from beige to pink to coral to nearly orange, depending on diet and water conditions. All are fine, provided the red muscle is really red.

SHELLFISH

Whole bivalves (oysters, hard-shell clams, and mussels) should be tightly closed, heavy, and moist, with a faint but pleasant odor. Soft-shell clams cannot close their shells, so the meat should look plump and moist with a clean smell. Hard-shell clams come in a variety of shell colors (flesh colors, too), depending on their habitat. Among the finest are those dug from muddy or sandy bottoms on Long Island; the shells are a dark blue-black color—with pale lips—that begins to whiten with exposure to air and light. While natives insist on fresh-dug color, pale is okay too, provided the clams are still alive and tightly closed. And clams from clay bottoms are a pale gray-beige when harvested, while some New England clams from red clay bottoms are red-lipped. To avoid confusion, just be sure the clams are alive and they will be tasty. If you should find whole scallops in the market, the shells will be slightly open, but the muscle should look plump and smell very sweet. The more usual shucked scallops have that same distinctive intense sweet smell with a hint of iodine. Look for scallops that are plump and pearly and almost sticky-looking with no liquid in the container. Color ranges from white to creamy to almost coral. Avoid heat-shucked scallops with their telltale white, fuzzy-looking cut ends.

Shrimp should fill their shells, have little or no black spot, and smell like, well, shrimp. As they go off, the odor becomes intense and ammoniated. Crayfish, blue crabs, and lobsters should be alive and lively. Buy female crabs for soups and stews so you will have the rich flavor of the roe. The large claws of females are tipped with bright orangey scarlet, while the claws of males are tipped in duller red, if they are colorful at all. To be certain, check the modified tail shell, called the apron, which is flat against the underside. Females have very wide aprons (medium width in sexually immature females) and males very narrow. Fresh crabmeat has a characteristic mild, sweet odor; if it is off, you will know it. Because lobsters do not normally feed in captivity (except for the occasional act of cannibalism), they use up stored energy with time, including flesh. When you pick up a lobster, the tail should flap vigorously, then remain tightly clenched against the underbody. This shows that it has lots of tail meat. And for finest flavor and yield, the body shell should be hard, proving that the lobster has inhabited that shell for a long time since molting. You might even look at the underside of the large claws. If they are worn from scraping on the ocean bottom, this is a good sign that it is an old shell, and the lobster will have the most meat. Sexually mature female lobsters (generally over one pound) have wide tail shells, while the males are more rounded. The other sex indicator is the first set of tail swimmeretes, next to the body shell: in females they are soft and feathery; in males they are hard.

Squid are very pale gray when caught. The purplish pigment in the skin develops with time. But if their odor is clean, purple is okay, too.

Sea urchins should be dark green with their spines intact. If you took the trouble really to study one, you would see the spines moving a bit. If there is an open one, look for coral with a rich orangy color and a sweet, briny smell.

Live conch and snails should be tightly locked into their shells by the hard, flat operculum. Precooked conch should smell briny and clean.

STORAGE

Fish must be stored at 32°F. Anything higher than that, even normal refrigerator temperatures, causes rapid deterioration. That's why supermarket seafood displayed in a section of the meat case is bad news. Shaved ice is the best refrigerant, holding goods at a perfect, constant temperature, protecting from freezing as well as warming. If you must store purchases for more than an hour or two—for up to a day or two if necessary—immediately ice them—with shaved ice if you can manage it—and put them in a colander over a bowl or some other setup that allows for melt to run off so the fish does not sit in standing water. Refrigerate. Standing water is not such a problem if items are tightly wrapped, but airtight wrapping is not a good idea for long periods of time because odors can develop, which is another reason why supermarket packaging is bad.

For shellfish that are dead, the same considerations apply as for fish. For live shellfish, ice and standing water can be deadly, particularly for lobsters. Refrigerate, with proper drainage and at least a little ventilation.

While it is safe, home freezing of seafood is not recommended unless the item is just-out-of-the-water fresh. And even then, some damage to the texture—mushiness or graininess—is likely because of the slowness of the freeze. Only professional blast freezing at very low temperatures can guarantee negligible texture change. The professional recommendation for all frozen seafood products (including stock) is that they be stored no longer than two months at 0°F. or lower. It is our experience that up to three months is okay, too. Frozen seafood is best defrosted slowly in the refrigerator. If tightly wrapped, it can be rushed along in a bowl of *cold* water, but that technique is best for shellfish and is not as kind to the texture of finfish.

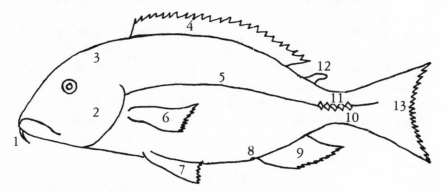

ANATOMICAL TERMS

1 Barbel (*in some species*)
2 Operculum (*gill cover, also called opercle, which is technically the largest of the bones*)
3 Nape
4 Dorsal fin (*there may be one, two, or three*)
5 Lateral line
6 Pectoral fin

7 Pelvic fin
8 Vent
9 Anal fin
10 Caudal peduncle (*tail*)
11 Scutes (*boney plates in some species*)
12 Adipose fin (*in salmon and trout*)
13 Caudal fin (*tail fin*)

CLEANING AND DRESSING FISH

You may have most of these operations performed by your retailer, but they are easy enough to accomplish at home (except for scaling, which is not fun).

SCALING FISH

Scale fish that are to be cooked skin on, but leave scales in place for strength if you are planning to skin the fish. Use a scaling tool, the back of a knife, or a large scallop shell. Start at the tail and scrape forward to pop off all the scales. Be gentle with small or fragile fish. This is a messy job best done in the backyard, but you can minimize flying scales by scaling in the kitchen sink, under water. Or have the fish market do it.

GUTTING AND REMOVING GILLS FROM FISH TO BE COOKED WHOLE

Use a sharp boning or paring knife. Start at the vent and cut all the way to the throat, holding the knife blade up so that it does not pierce the viscera. Remove the gills with good shears or a sharp knife. They are attached together in the front of the mouth and separately in back. When you pull out the gills, part of the guts should come with them. Pull out the rest of the guts through the opening you have cut in the belly. Rinse. Also remove the membrane that lines the cavity, exposing a line of red organ (kidney) that must be rinsed away. Always flush out all blood. Small trout and other panfish can be gutted through the gills without opening up the body cavity.

PAN-DRESSING WHOLE FISH

To pan-dress a fish, scale and gut it but do not bother with the gills. Use a large sharp knife to cut off the head, being careful to make the cut at the base of the skull, not a perpendicular crosscut behind the pectoral fin—that would be wasteful. Cut off the tail. Trim other fins, if you wish, with heavy shears.

CUTTING ROUNDFISH STEAKS

Huge fish are simply cut into pieces of a convenient size. Consumers do not normally deal with a whole swordfish, tuna, shark, or even halibut, which is cut like a roundfish. For salmon, tilefish, king mackerel, and other fish that can be cut into single-serving crosscut steaks, cut off the head as above. Then use your large sharp knife to score the skin to mark steaks 1 to 1½ inches thick. For each steak, turn the fish on its belly and slice through the dorsal flesh until you reach the backbone. If your knife happens to hit a space between vertebrae, go ahead and cut through the backbone. Otherwise use a wooden mallet to tap the knife until it cuts through the backbone. Then turn fish on its side and slice the rest of the way to free the steak. Repeat as needed.

FILLETING ROUNDFISH

To fillet you must have a very sharp boning or paring knife. Also you must remember always to angle the blade slightly toward the bone so that the knife does not wander into the flesh and cause ragged or wasteful cuts. Lay the fish on one side and make a deep cut from the base of the skull down, behind the pectoral fin, to the belly. Also make a crosscut, through the skin and flesh, at the tail. Starting at either end, insert the point of the knife just above the dorsal fin line and, holding the knife parallel to the dorsal fin, begin to slice along the bones from end to end. (If the skin is too tough to cut, make an incision with the point of the knife and insert the knife with the blade turned out, against the skin; you should have no trouble cutting the skin from underneath.) The dorsal fin bones should lead you to the backbone. Hold the emerging fillet with the other hand and try not to tear the muscle groups. When you reach the vertebrae, tease the point of the blade around them and proceed to finish the fillet. You may also cut right through the ribs and remove them later when you trim the fillet. Before you reach the ribs that surround the cavity you may find pinbones, especially in front, that point out from the vertebrae. Cut through them. Tease flesh away from the ribs and complete the fillet. Repeat with the other side of the fish. Some people cut the first fillet only as far as the vertebrae (leaving this side in place), turn the fish over, and fillet the second side completely, and then return to finish the first side. It is a good idea, because starting the second side is much easier if the fish is still in its natural shape. Then complete the removal of the fillet as above. Trim the fillets neatly of all connective tissue and any stray ribs. If the belly flap is very thin or discolored, remove it. Feel with your fingers for pinbones along the central line where the vertebrae were, especially at the head end. Some fish have many, some a few, some none. They always stop at the point where the cavity ends and the fillet becomes symmetrical. Salmon pinbones can be removed with tweezers. There are about thirty on each side. For other fish, make a **V** cut with your knife to remove the bones and the strip of flesh that holds them.

You may also fillet a fish with its belly wall intact and leave the two fillets attached—this is called a kited fillet. If you execute this procedure in reverse, leaving the two fillets attached at the dorsal fin, you will have what is called a butterfly fillet. You may also use a similar technique to remove the backbone and ribs, leaving the head and tail attached. The cut may be made either from the dorsal or ventral side. Use a very sharp knife—or shears if it is a large fish—to sever the ribs as you go. When the flesh is free of the backbone, sever the backbone at head and tail with shears and remove it. Then carefully trim away the ribs from the fillets, doing as little damage as possible to the belly walls. Then remove the pinbones as neatly as possible.

DRESSING FLATFISH

Flounder and sole may be pan-dressed or filleted using a technique similar to that for roundfish, taking into account the difference in anatomy. The white side is filleted first because it is thinner and would be harder to remove second. Flatfish may also be cut into two fillets on each side with the use of a flexible-bladed fillet knife. The first cut is made down the center—the vertebrae—roughly along the lateral line, then the fillets are freed from the backbone from the center one at a time.

SKINNING FILLETS

If you have a large, *very* sharp boning knife—the kind professionals use—you may simply place the fillet in front of you, along the front edge of your board, cut into the flesh at the tail end until you have a little skin to hold on to, then slice the fillet free of the skin, holding the blade flat against the board and using enough pressure to keep the blade flat. Lacking a perfect knife, you may "rip" the skin off using a large dull knife. Hold the blade at about a forty-five-degree angle, using enough pressure to keep it on the board but not so much that you cut through the skin. Again starting at the tail end, free a little flap of skin, then use *tiny* little cutting motions with the knife as you use the other hand to pull on the skin until it is free.

There are a few exceptions worth noting. Eel and catfish both are normally skinned by ripping the skin off the whole fish. With eel, have the fishmonger stun and gut the eels, or take them home and do it yourself: Holding it with a towel, bonk each eel over the head with a sharpening steel or other heavy object, or rap the head on the edge of the kitchen counter. Gut as you would any fish. With a very sharp knife, cut just through the skin all the way around, behind the head. Loosen the skin and begin to pull it back with pliers, holding the head with a towel in the other hand. Once you get it started, the skin will slip right off. With catfish, be sure your towel is heavy so that you avoid the sharp barbels around the mouth. They can give nasty cuts. Dover sole is also skinned whole by making a slit in the skin at the tail and ripping it right off. Only the dark skin is normally removed. Sturgeon and gar are so heavily armored that the flesh must be freed by cutting through chinks in the belly skin and peeling the whole skin away.

CLEANING AND DRESSING SHELLFISH

BIVALVE MOLLUSCS (CLAMS, MUSSELS, OYSTERS, AND SCALLOPS)

Cleaning

Rinse clams or mussels, and then discard any that are open or have broken shells. Scrub them with a brush or a clean scouring pad (not soaped) and rinse thoroughly. Soak in several changes of cold, salted water, leaving them to soak for about thirty minutes between changes if you have the time. For the last soak, you may sprinkle over the water a large handful of flour or cornmeal (cornmeal is not recommended for mussels) to help them cleanse themselves. When sand is minimal, transfer them by hand (leaving any sand behind) to another bowl. For mussels there are two extra steps: Test each one by using thumb and forefinger to push shells in opposite directions to be sure that the hinge is springy. This way you can be sure that each one is alive and not dead and filled with mud that would befoul your whole dish. You must also remove the ropey byssus, or beard, from each one. Use the dull edge of a paring knife to help you pull it off.

Oysters need only to be scrubbed. Shucked scallops need only to have the very pearly-white strip of muscle on the side removed (for most purposes) because it is tough.

Shucking

To shuck a hard-shell clam, plant it in your palm hinge down and insert a clam knife (a special tool that resembles a large dull paring knife) between the shells. Sever the adductor muscles that hold the shells together close to the shells to release the meat. Mussels might also be shucked raw for a broiled half-shell preparation, but they rarely are. To shuck an oyster, place it (large shell down) on your work surface and hold it firmly with a heavy towel to protect your hand. Insert the tip of an oyster knife (shorter than a clam knife and more pointed) between the shells at the hinge. Jimmy from side to side to gain purchase, then give a twist or a downward motion to snap the hinge. Sever the adductor muscles close to the shells to release the flesh.

CRUSTACEANS (SHRIMP, LOBSTER, CRABS)

Shrimp

If shrimp are whole, simply pull off the tails. There are three approaches to shelling and deveining shrimp tails, two of which are recommended:

1. Using small kitchen shears or sewing scissors, make a shallow cut along the back, the length of the shell; lift the flesh out of the shell and remove the vein (intestine) if your scissors have not already done so.

2. Starting at the head end, grasp some of the little swimmers on the underside with thumb and forefinger and pull them around the shrimp tail, taking the shell with them. Repeat until shell is removed. Leave the last shell segment in place (as a convenient handle) or remove it, depending on the recipe. To devein, stretch shelled shrimp out straight on your board and lightly score the back with a sharp knife. If the intestine is visible, remove it. Note that there is never any reason to remove the grayish *nerve* that runs the length of the underside.

There are curved shrimp tools, made of plastic or aluminum, designed to be inserted into the back to pop off the shell and rip out the intestine at the same time. They are effective, but they create such a ragged appearance that they are only suitable for use when the shrimp will be diced or chunked for a salad or puréed for a mousse.

The new stainless steel shrimp knives with a serrated edge do a neater job, but they are still not as neat as the recommended methods above.

Lobster

To split live lobsters for broiling or other purposes, you will first want to kill the lobster by putting it on its back and plunging your knife deep into the mouth and head. The lobster will continue to move, but it is considered dead by humane standards. Lay the lobster on its back and cut in half lengthwise with a large heavy knife. Discard stomach sac behind the mouth, intestine, and feathery gills. Remove coral (if any) and tomalley (liver, green glands) and reserve. Use the back of a heavy knife to crack the claws on both sides. To shell cooked lobster, please see Steamed Lobster *Beurre Blanc* (p. 356).

Blue Crabs

1. To clean hard-shell crabs raw, turn them on their backs and pull apron (the modified tail shell, which is wide in females and very narrow in males) up and off. To remove top shells, place one thumb against the body by the back fin and use the other thumb against the top shell to break the seal and separate it. The stomach and most of the mouth parts should come off with the top shell. If you wish to reserve the top shells for broth, remove and discard mouth parts and the stomach sac behind the mouth. Otherwise, discard top shells, but first inspect them for any greenish tomalley and orangy roe (in females), and scrape it out and reserve. Remove and reserve any more tomalley and roe you find in the body shells. In raw crabs, this should all be in the center of the body shell. Remove and discard the spongy white gills (dead men's fingers) and any mouth parts. Twist off and discard (or save for broth) the swimmerets (the back fins). Snap crab bodies in half and rinse them in cold water to remove any mud or sand.

2. To clean cooked crabs, work over a bowl to catch the juices; break off the apron and save it. Pry off the top shell, working from the back and using your thumbs for leverage. Use a teaspoon to scrape the tomalley and roe from the top shell and from the crab body into the bowl. Remove and discard the stomach sac and save the top shell. From the crab body remove and discard the gills on the sides and the rest of the mouth parts. If the crab bodies are muddy, rinse them. This is the technique for gumbo crabs, when you want cleaned crab bodies for the gumbo and cleaned shells for broth.

3. To clean soft-shell crabs, use shears to cut off the face, then squeeze gently to extract the stomach sac. Carefully lift the points of the top shell, one at a time, and remove the gills, returning the sides of the shell to the original position when you finish. Remove the apron on the underside.

OTHERS

Squid

To clean squid, grasp the head and pull it out, bringing most of the entrails with it (be careful not to damage the silvery ink sac below the head if you intend to retrieve the ink). Cut across the head just to the tentacle side of the eyes and discard eye part and entrails. The tentacles need only have the horny mouth, called the beak, popped out and discarded. Reserve tentacles whole if they are of a manageable size or cut into two or three pieces if very large. Grasp body sac and remove the "pen" (which resembles a clear plastic quill) and flush out all soft matter. Pull off skin and discard. To facilitate skinning, you may place the drawn squid bodies in a bowl with a few handfuls of coarse salt, then manipulate the squid to scour off most of the skin. Rinse and pick off the rest of the skin. To flower-cut squid in the Asian manner, cut the squid body lengthwise, along the thin line where the pen was, to open it up like a shield. Place on a board skin side down. Holding a very sharp knife at a forty-five-degree angle, score the squid with a series of parallel diagonal cuts less than a half inch apart, cutting about halfway through the flesh. Rotate and repeat the cuts on the other diagonal to crosshatch the squid. Slice scored squid into fairly oval chunks roughly the size of a silver dollar. The chunks cannot be uniform, but they should have about the same amount of flesh in them. When blanched for a few seconds, they curl and flower into lovely shapes.

Sea Urchins

Hold a sea urchin in a heavy towel to protect your hand from the spines, insert shears into the mouth, and begin to cut through the shell, turning the shears so that you cut all the way around the base of the shell so that you can remove it like a lid. Inside you will find fingers of orangy roe arranged in a star pattern. To remove them, carefully detach them from their central anchor with a spoon. Gently rinse off any dark viscera, and the roe is ready to eat. If you wish to serve sea urchins in the shell you will have to rinse out the viscera without disturbing the roe. Agitate shells in a bowl of cold salted water, and gently scrape the dark stuff from the shell with a spoon. Rinse, scrape, and rinse until they are clean. Serve the sea urchins just as they are. Diners spoon the roe onto plain toast, adding nothing more than perhaps a drop of lemon juice.

SEAFOOD SAFETY

PARASITES

Some splashy headlines have been created in recent years about possible dangers in eating certain fish or shellfish. Parasites have particular shock value. We believe the facts are actually rather simple and the dangers easily avoidable *provided* a few cooking, handling, buying, and dining concepts are understood. Here are the basic rules:

1. All seafood that has been properly cooked or frozen is free of any parasite danger.
2. Proper cooking is defined as an internal temperature of 140°F. held for five minutes. This temperature produces a full flake (in finfish) with no hint of pearliness remaining, and should produce moist, flavorful results. Many modern cooks prefer a slightly lower temperature, even some fish cooked quite rare, which is common practice for many *saltwater* fish, though obviously this is not as safe.
3. Safe freezing times and temperatures, though still subject to some disagreement, have been set by the National Fisheries Institute at 0°F. for twenty-four hours, with the further recommendation that the freezing time for inefficient home freezers be increased to four or five days. FDA experiments suggest that −4°F. for five days is sometimes necessary, so consumers should freeze fish intended to be eaten raw or eaten cold-cured for a week just to be sure. *Commercially* frozen seafood is usually safe raw because its −40°F. processing temperature kills all parasites within fifteen hours.
4. Never eat freshwater, anadromous (those that spawn in fresh water but mature in salt water), or catadromous (spawn in salt water, mature in fresh water) fish either raw or partially cooked unless they have been adequately frozen. One exception will be noted below.
5. Marination in an acidic liquid (vinegar or lemon or lime

juice) has not been found to kill all parasites all of the time, neither has *cold* smoking or modern light salting. The heavy salting that characterized the "hard cure" of prerefrigeration days killed everything, but it is no longer practiced.

6. In most reputable restaurants or stores, raw fish for sushi and sashimi is either prefrozen or carefully inspected so there is relatively little or no risk in eating these dishes.

With those guidelines in mind, consider what these parasites are. Roundworms called anisakid nematodes are relatively plentiful in certain fish populations—cod, pollock, halibut, flounder, and others— that share coastal ocean waters with seals and sea lions (in the Pacific). *Phocanema decipiens,* the codworm, is the larger of the two common seafood nematodes, and it is more a visual nuisance than a health hazard. Fish handlers and savvy home cooks who find one of these reddish or brownish worms simply cut it out and proceed with cooking. It isn't even necessary to remove them before cooking. They are just another protein source. However, you could become sick from ingesting a whole raw live worm: Roundworms cannot live in the human system, but they can cause severe pain before they die by burrowing through the stomach lining. Codworm problems in humans, even in Japan, are extremely rare because of the ease with which the worms are either identified and removed or rendered harmless by cooking. Fulton wholesalers further reduce the danger by avoiding bottomfish taken from the inshore waters of Canada that are seal territory. Consumers simply do not want fish with worms in it, even if they are harmless.

Anisakis simplex is a smaller ocean roundworm with more potential for human harm. Because it is white and very thin it is less easily spotted during filleting, but easy enough to detect when fillets to be consumed raw are candled (examined over a strong light). However, in living fish simplex is normally found only in the gut cavity, from which it can migrate into the flesh after the fish die. High-quality fish that are gutted immediately after landing should be free of simplex worms. Health officials are justly concerned that the increase in raw fish consumption in the United States might be accompanied by increased incidence of anisakiasis, the gastric disturbance noted above. So far this has not been the case because of the care exercised by restaurateurs and fish handlers.

The only other fish parasites of interest to consumers are the larvae of tapeworms—cestodes—that can infest freshwater species and others that spend any time in fresh water. Obviously, no one wants to gain a tapeworm from eating raw freshwater fish or from raw beef, for that matter. As with roundworms, proper cooking or freezing removes all danger.

Uncooked or undercooked salmon ought to be *verboten,* considering the potential double whammy of nematodes and tapeworms. Indeed, only a fool would consider eating raw Pacific salmon that had not been prefrozen, but *farmed* Atlantic salmon is a different matter. Salmon culture allows for control over the waters so that tapeworms are excluded. Careful handling and rapid gutting at harvest greatly minimize the danger of *A. simplex* infestation.

So far as anyone knows, *all* manufacturers of cold-smoked salmon, be it the humblest deli Nova or the finest Scottish, prefreeze their fish for complete safety. Sushi emporia in the Northeast used to feature only smoked salmon, but fresh salmon is now in use, too. And non-Asian restaurants are offering raw salmon in the kinds of dishes mentioned above. Probably few people have been prefreezing salmon destined to become *gravlax,* but it is a good idea to do so. There is a wonderful hors d'oeuvre popularized by Michel Guérard that consists of thinly sliced raw salmon briefly marinated in lemon juice with a bit of minced shallot and olive oil, served with toast and green peppercorns. Students loved it, and over a period of about five years we never saw a *simplex* in any of the farmed salmon fillets we sliced. Parasites would have been clearly visible. There may be no reports of people eating raw farmed Atlantic salmon with ill effect, but the rule book says don't do it. We have included Jacques Pépin's Salmon Tartare and a suggestion for Salmon Carpaccio (see recipes), because they are delicious and quite mainstream. Please use the above information to make your own informed decision about enjoying such preparations. And know that the incidence of parasite-related health problems, even in the major fish-eating nations, is so low as to be considered rare.

OTHER SUBSTANCES

This is a good place to explain government control and inspection procedures, as they relate to other potential problems in seafood, in the form of natural and man-made additives. The U.S. Food and Drug Administration has not found the need for a uniform, compulsory inspection policy for fresh wild and farmed seafood because of the "naturalness" of the product. The subject is raised from time to time, so the situation is subject to change. Wholesalers are definitely in no rush to see such a program implemented because of the financial hardship it would present. Voluntary inspection is an option for seafood processors, the expense and inconvenience of inspection weighed against the presumed value of an FDA inspection seal in terms of consumer acceptance. So if you examine the frozen seafood products in your grocer's freezer case you will discover that some are inspected and some are not, while all are wholesome or they would not be there. The FDA sets wholesomeness standards for all foodstuffs and monitors their enforcement with the help of state and local health departments. Some examples follow, beginning with chemicals.

The FDA limit for PCBs—polychlorinated biphenyls—is two parts per million. These toxic chemical wastes were spilled into the water system for some years before the dangers became known in 1976. The General Electric plants at Hudson Falls and Fort Edwards on the Hudson River and on other rivers in the Northeast did the worst damage. The chemicals are taken up by microscopic flora and fauna from which they work themselves up the food chain, becoming most concentrated in the oldest and largest of the carnivores at the top of the chain.

PCBs are stored in fat tissues and are not readily broken down or excreted. Though GE claims the Hudson is becoming steadily cleaner as microorganisms digest the residue, Dr. Edward G. Horn of the New York State Department of Health has suggested that it will be at least thirty-three years before local striped bass will again be safe to eat. Therefore all striped bass, even safe ones from the Chesapeake and the Carolinas, are banned from the New York market because of the enforcement difficulties. Chemical levels vary with the location and the season. Though measurable levels of PCBs have been found in American eel, mackerel, drums, and a few others, bluefish is the only species other than striped bass that has created particular concern, and then only very large fish. Though bluefish have been pronounced safe—entirely safe for consumers—the FDA suggested that states warn anglers not to consume large bluefish very often. Authorities have suggested that people not eat fatty fish in general too often. This is in keeping with a commonsensical diet that features variety.

The tomalley (liver), but not the flesh, of some lobsters harvested in bays or harbors has been found to contain unsafe levels of industrial toxins; this is largely a moot point for consumers because lobsters are not normally fished commercially in these areas. But you may avoid eating lobster tomalley if you wish, and you should avoid the tomalley if you or someone you know caught the lobster in a bay or harbor.

The FDA monitors a dozen or so other chemicals as well. DDT is becoming less and less of a threat, as it gradually decomposes with time. Traces of mercury in the form of methyl mercury have been found to be from natural sources as often as industrial ones, and far less toxic than the swordfish scares of past decades led consumers to believe. Spot checks of the domestic catch and of imports occasionally turn up a shipment of Greek swordfish that is slightly above the one-part-per-million limit imposed by the FDA, but that's about it. Imports are inspected at port of entry and promptly returned if they do not meet FDA standards.

Bacterial contamination of seafood in toxic levels is relatively rare and the result of insanitary handling and/or improper chilling. Two kinds of food poisoning are possible: salmonella and scromboid poisoning, a condition that can develop in the dark flesh of the tuna and mackerel family if it is not properly chilled. There is no excuse for toxic levels of these bacteria. It is highly unlikely that any fish so infected could move through Fulton Fish Market. Retail conditions are a different matter, so be sure to patronize reliable dealers.

Viral infections are possible in bivalve shellfish, particularly hepatitis A in shellfish growing in waters that are contaminated by sewage. Elaborate safeguards have been set up by the FDA and health departments to ensure that shellfish are wholesome. The National Shellfish Sanitation Program sets guidelines, aided by the Interstate Shellfish Sanitation Conference. Imports are only allowed from Canada, Mexico, Korea, New Zealand, and Australia. Every container of shellfish must bear an official tag that identifies the waters of harvest. At Fulton every market morning Rudolph Albanese, Inspector for the New York City Department of Health, checks to see that each shellfish container is properly labeled, while he also examines sanitary conditions in general. Further, Mr. Albanese selects random samples which he takes to his laboratory not far from the Market. There he tests for the presence of coliform bacteria, an indicator that fecal matter has been present in the water. Contaminated shellfish are, of course, pulled from sale and the waters are closed to harvesting. Some waters are always safe, some are never safe, others change seasonally. Even with all of these safeguards in place, some people tend to avoid eating shellfish raw in the summer months, when warmer waters promote bacterial and viral growth. Other people avoid raw shellfish entirely. It is impossible to give a blanket recommendation, particularly when conditions are subject to change. But it does seem clear that raw shellfish consumption is unwise for people who are not healthy, particularly if they have liver disease.

Shellfish controls also extend to the prevention of PSP—paralytic shellfish poisoning—which is caused by toxins produced by the parasite infestation called *red tide*. Maine Mariculture explained just how careful the restrictions are. They were prevented in 1987 from shipping whole live scallops because of toxin levels. The muscle meats were totally clean and approved for marketing shucked, the roes were safe, but the scallop bodies contained unsafe levels of toxin. Even though presumably no one in the United States eats scallop viscera, FDA guidelines prohibited the sale of scallops in-the-shell from those Maine waters.

One of the most unpleasant and most easily avoided of the side effects of ingesting the wrong fish is *cigutera* or fish poisoning. First, the good news: In May 1988 doctors discovered by accident that a common diuretic, mannitol, can erase the symptoms of cigutera poisoning almost instantly. And so it is likely that there is now a cheap, effective cure for a condition that had no treatment before. And now, the grim part: A student from New Jersey once told her story about a trip to Florida where she and her friends had feasted on a delicious barracuda that one of them had caught. Later, at home, she (the only one in the group) began to suffer from aching pains deep in the bones and joints and thermostat problems—intermittent chills and hot, burning sensations coupled with vivid skin rash. Others speak of experiencing opposite perceptions of heat and cold. A six-month search finally produced a New Jersey doctor who was alert enough to diagnose her condition. The doctor could offer no treatment, but at least he could assure her that the symptoms would end, and indeed they did, in another six months or so. As you can see from her story, not everyone is susceptible. And the intensity and duration of the symptoms vary considerably among those afflicted.

Cigutoxins are produced by algae or plankton that live around coral reefs in certain well-documented areas of the Caribbean in certain seasons. The toxins are concentrated up the food chain until they can reach harmful levels in many of the common Southern food fish. Locals are cautious about the size (age) of the fish involved, reasoning that small ones are safe to eat. Even so, cigutera poisoning is common in the Caribbean. Barracudas are so peripatetic and voracious that wise diners avoid Atlantic barracuda entirely. For the others, health experts have predicted a sharp increase in cases of cigutera poisoning in the Northeast with the growing interest in grouper and heavy demand for snappers, coupled with increasing imports, but that has not been the case. As stated before, the danger areas and seasons are well known, so shippers and wholesalers alike avoid fish taken from these waters. This self-policing should continue to provide safety.

Fish and shellfish contain natural substances that produce allergic reactions in some people who know who they are and what to avoid. Shellfish allergies are most common, but there are reactions to finfish as well. Some species, a few fish and a few shellfish, produce natural toxins that should always be avoided by everyone. The Pacific puffer (blowfish), fugu, is the most famous of these. Though the flesh is considered a great delicacy in Japan, the viscera contains deadly toxins, while the skin is not safe to eat either. One misswipe of the knife in cleaning fugu, the slightest contact with the liver, and the extensively trained, licensed fugu chef must not only discard that fish but also thoroughly cleanse all utensils before continuing. Even with all the precautions there are about a hundred fugu deaths each year in Japan. Our Atlantic puffer, marketed as sea squab and normally completely cleaned when it reaches Fulton, is safe; even so the skin and viscera must never be eaten.

Giuliano Bugialli recommends wearing rubber gloves when skinning eels; he is the only experienced eel handler we know who is irritated by the secretions from eel skin. Other benign food fish can have toxic livers or roes. Even though these fish are uncommon, it is best not to experiment with viscera unless you know it is safe. For instance, gar innards are off-limits, but first try to find a gar! Edible livers are not terribly popular or exciting, but some of the ones you might want to try are monkfish, skate, and cod. Edible roes, on the other hand, are delicious, particularly shad, salmon, sturgeon (caviar), lumpfish, mackerel, mullet, dolphin (mahi mahi), sea urchin, flatfish, and bluefish. Toxicity of flesh or innards is mainly a concern for anglers, who must either be scholars or learn to trust the folk wisdom of the area where they are fishing when it comes to an unfamiliar catch.

There are very few chemical additives used in the seafood industry. Here are the ones used in fresh market, simple freezing (no processing), and smoking. Fillets cut in New England—called "over-the-road" fillets—are likely to be dipped in a solution containing salt and tripolyphosphate. Phosphates encourage water retention, improving appearance and yield. Tripolyphosphate dips are considered safe and are perfectly legal when used properly. There is also the possibility of potassium sorbate, another FDA-approved substance, added to retard bacteria growth. If you are bothered by the idea or the taste of these additives (some of us swear we can taste them), find a retailer you trust to tell you the truth about his product and buy Fulton fillet or fish filleted there in the store. Fulton fillet houses use only a touch of salt to keep the fish from tasting washed-out by the rinses it goes through as it progresses from whole fish to fillet to skinned fillet.

Sulfites have received a great deal of press in recent years because asthmatics and other sensitive individuals have unpleasant reactions to them. When they are used as antibrowning dips for salad greens and other vegetables—in institutions, downscale restaurants, or packaged foods—sulfites leave a disgusting aftertaste that is offensive even to those who have no medical reaction to them. They are commonly used as preservatives in wines, with flavor and health results that vary with the concentration and the individual who is consuming them. Sodium bisulfate is approved for use in a shrimp dip that has been shown to discourage melanosis, or black spot (no, this is not *Treasure Island*). Only certain shrimp species are prone to developing melanosis after harvest, and the sulfate solution is very weak. Because the dipping is shell-on, residues in the flesh are very low, well under FDA limits. We know of no one who has a palate reaction to sulfate residues in shrimp, but there are some people supersensitive to sulfites who should avoid shrimp just to be safe.

Nitrites are used in some cured and smoked seafoods for some of the same reasons they are used in cured meats—to obtain a pleasant flavor and, most important, to guard against the growth of *Clostridium botulinum* in vacuum-sealed packages. This is the bacterium that produces—only in the absence of oxygen—the toxin that causes deadly botulism. The health concern with nitrites is their conversion to potentially carcinogenic nitrosamines either in the food or in the human system. At this point very little is known about nitrites in cured seafood products, or their tendency to produce nitrosamines. Because they are rarely fried, as bacon is, and because they are sometimes poached (finnan haddie, or kippers) to remove excess salt and in the doing nitrites too, there is the possibility that treated seafoods are less unhealthful than other cured foods. Unfortunately, the facts are unknown. Consumers who wish to avoid treated seafood products may do so by following a visual clue: nitrite-treated salmon is a brash, unnaturally bright orangy color; treated white-fleshed fish will be pinkish.

Now that the perils have been laid out, it should be evident that fresh seafood is perfectly wholesome as an important part of a sensible, varied diet. A little education and a little common sense are needed to avoid the dangers. Most of them are obviated by government programs. We seafood lovers look on fresh fish and shellfish as the cleanest, least adulterated, least tampered with foods around.

ABOUT THE RECIPES

This collection of recipes, most of which have never been published before, reflects seafood cookery in the New York area with all its rich ethnic diversity. Many of these dishes and techniques that transform Fulton Fish Market wares into fine edibles were contributed by area restaurants, from the high-and-mighty with international reputations to simple neighborhood spots that nourish the locals.* Other recipes are from teachers who strongly shape the form of both professional and home cooking in the area. Still others are from people who happen to be fine amateur cooks. And the rest are teaching recipes developed through the years or just for this book because it made a perfect excuse to try some intriguing ideas.

You will find that many of the recipes are quite simple, requiring little effort. Simplicity is certainly a virtue in seafood cookery, because the less doctoring, the more the natural taste and texture shine through. But there are occasions that seem to demand a little more fuss, so there are also plenty of "big" recipes here. We sincerely hope that the style in which they are written will prove properly explicit for cooks at all levels of skill and experience.

Grouping the recipes according to technique seemed the most logical way to present them in the most useful format; further categories were created where pure technique did not quite apply. Where certain techniques receive more attention than others, it is because of their popularity. If one cook or restaurant is represented more often than another, it is simply because the recipes they offered were too interesting to omit. If your favorite restaurant is not represented, it is

---

* Chefs have grown so mobile in recent years that it is difficult to know where they may be cooking tomorrow, and not all restaurants have the longevity their owners wish for. However, the chef/restaurant information in the recipes was accurate when this book was printed.

either through oversight or because the restaurant was ungenerous; that distinction, of course, will remain secret.

COOKING NOTES

INGREDIENTS

All the recipes in this book that use butter are intended to be prepared with good-quality unsalted butter because it has the best flavor. Coarse kosher salt is specified because it is pure and cleaner in flavor than table salt. You might also use sea salt.

CLARIFIED BUTTER

Because butter is only about eighty percent butterfat it is not suitable for high-heat cookery. The moisture and milk solids that give it its creamy texture and wonderful sweet flavor can interfere with sautéing. The milk solids burn and smoke at normal skillet temperatures. This is why some cooks combine butter with vegetable oil; but clarifying is the better way to improve butter's performance in a skillet. Once clarified, butter is fine for sautéing and for adding a little flavor to frying oil, but its smoking point is still lower than that of vegetable oils.

Most cookbooks direct readers to melt the butter, let it settle, skim off the foam, and then pour off the clear liquid. However, this procedure produces a partially clarified result only suitable for sponge cakes, classic egg-yolk-and-butter sauces (these days most cooks use whole butter for the *sauce hollandaise*–family because it is more delicate than clarified butter), and for a lobster dip. For sautéing, a super-clarified butter is required; this is the product Indian cooks call *ghee.* Simmer the butter gently until the moisture has all cooked away. This takes as long as an hour for one pound of butter and considerably longer for larger quantities. Once the foam has dried into a thin crust, push it aside with a spoon and look at the bottom of the pan. When the milk solids have not only dried on the bottom but have just begun to turn a light brown, the butter is totally clarified. Strain it through a high-quality paper towel or a coffee filter and then decant the sparklingly clear golden liquid. (Use a wide-mouthed vessel so that you can get at the butter when it hardens.) It keeps for months at room temperature and many months refrigerated.

OLIVE OILS

Though, technically, olive oils are graded according to their acidity—the lower, the finer—their color and fruitiness are the clues that tell consumers how to use them. Extra-virgin, which is normally from the first cold pressing, usually has the richest color and flavor, followed by virgin, also cold-pressed and distinctive. The virgin oils are most often used as seasonings—for salad dressings and for flavoring cooked foods or other oils—because the heat of a skillet can turn their fruitiness to bitterness. Unfiltered oils (they have a slight cloudiness) must never be overheated or they will certainly taste burned. However, some fine extra-virgins that are pressed from ripe olives have a paler golden color; they can be heated successfully so long as care is used to avoid smoking. Do beware of emerald-green oils, which have had olive leaves added to the pressing. They have a bitter flavor that is unpleasant.

Pure is the lowest grade; heat and even chemical-extraction methods are used to produce it. But pure oils can be delicious (if less olivey), and they are versatile as well. Pure olive oil is a good choice for the sauté pan, to blend (up to fifty percent) with bland vegetable oil for frying, and for mayonnaise. A newcomer in the light-flavor department is the extra-light oil (no doubt someone will market it as "lite") now available. It is an excellent product to use when introducing a good source of monounsaturated fats into the diets of people who claim they do not like olive oil. Extra-light could qualify for extra-virgin status, but that would be too confusing for consumers who expect rich flavor from virgin oils.

NONREACTIVE COOKWARE

Acid ingredients—wine, vinegar, and citrus juice, even tomatoes—should be handled and cooked in materials that will not react chemically with them. These include high-quality stainless steel, glass, glazed ceramic or earthenware, enameled steel, tin, nickle, and nonstick coatings. The reactive materials are aluminum, iron, steel, copper, brass, and plastic (because it absorbs and transfers flavors and fat). When carbon steel woks and cast-iron skillets are properly cured with fat they become essentially nonreactive, yet nothing more than a fast stir-fry is recommended with acid ingredients.

Cream and egg yolks *definitely* require nonreactive materials. Aluminum and iron will only discolor cream slightly, but they turn egg yolks gray-green. Not pretty.

PORTION SIZES

For some years the standard American approach to both restaurant and home cooking has allowed roughly eight ounces of trimmed, usable flesh per dinner serving, a bit less for luncheon main courses, and about half that for first courses. That applies to fish as well as meats and poultry, though shellfish are deemed to be richer and more filling and are often served in smaller portions. Half the norm will provide the needed protein in most diets (three ounces for those who eat three meals a day), even without the careful partnering of complementary incomplete vegetable proteins (rice and beans, peanuts and whole wheat, et cetera); therefore, many modern cooks are serving smaller quantities of animal protein. The recipes in this book tend to require about six ounces of usable flesh per serving for main courses, less when the seafood is "stretched" with other filling ingredients.

YIELD

Obviously different kinds of seafood yield different quantities of skinless, boneless, usable flesh. Shellfish are particularly dissimilar because of their various anatomies; their approximate yields are indicated by the ways they are used in the recipes that follow. The yield for whole fish averages something over 40 percent. There are helpful visual clues:

fish with small heads (lake whitefish, for instance) will yield closer to 50 percent;

fish with very large heads (tilefish, snappers, porgies, pompano) will usually dress out at 40 percent or less;

flatfish other than halibut have an even lower yield, with gray sole at 28 percent the lowest of all.

TEMPERATURE FOR RAW FLESH BEFORE COOKING

Unless a recipe specifies otherwise, fish and shellfish should be at room temperature before cooking to ensure that they cook evenly. This is particularly important with whole fish and with anything to be broiled or grilled. For rare steaks, it becomes essential. A steak started cold turns out raw in the middle and dry on the outside.

MICROWAVES

As people begin to do some serious cooking in their microwave ovens—beyond reheating leftovers, popping popcorn, melting chocolate, and the like—even the most diehard holder-outers must sit up and take notice. It is safe to say that everyone who has experimented agrees that the ovens do a really good job with vegetables and fish. Specifically, microwaves will work well for moist-heat methods: steaming, poaching, braising, and stewing. If the fish needs to be browned—grilling, broiling, frying, sautéing—forget the microwave and use conventional means. There is no appliance they will replace—and they may never appear in the finest restaurant kitchens—but they make good supplemental ovens.

While fish microwave nicely, shellfish are a different matter. Even the slightest overcooking will toughen them and some—particularly scallops, oysters, and whole crayfish or lobster—might explode at high power settings. And users must be mindful of the other safety concerns that are spelled out in owners' manuals. There is also the matter of standing time, an important feature of microwave cooking: The food continues to cook after it is removed from the oven much more than with conventional heating. So perfectly done can turn to overdone on the way to the table. If your oven has a doneness sensor, it may not judge things exactly to your liking. And foods that have been crisped on the outside will become soggy when reheated in the microwave. So nuke away, if it pleases you, but know what you are doing.

Because of the different power levels offered by various ovens and the technical nature of the instructions for using them, no recipes specifically tailored to microwaves are offered here, though a few recipes that are particularly good candidates are so noted.

DONENESS

After freshness, doneness is the most important factor in fine seafood cookery. Overcooked spells dry and/or tough results. Remember that protein is thermosetting or, as Lady Macbeth would have it, "What's done cannot be undone." Too much heat and the texture is irreversibly destroyed along with the natural moisture balance. But undercooking can leave flesh unpleasantly rubbery or mushy in some species, even unsafe in freshwater and anadromous fish (see Seafood Safety, p. 66–68). So the golden mean is what we try to achieve.

Some years ago the Canadian Department of Fisheries and Oceans worked out a doneness system that has come to be known as the Canadian Method. This system recommended that for all direct-heat methods (which for seafood cookery is essentially everything but baking in a slow oven), the proper timing is ten minutes of cooking for each inch of thickness, and twice that if the fish is frozen when you start it. Many modern cooks find this timing a little excessive, preferring to plan on a few minutes less. And this is not even for items that are wanted rare. But no system is perfect because there are too many variables.

The fish themselves vary in the density of their flesh (light textures absorb heat faster); their moisture content (water conducts heat faster than protein); and their fat content (fat heats more slowly than water but holds heat longer). Even the same species will vary seasonally because of spawning and feeding cycles. Whole fish on-the-bone should require a little more cooking time than fillets, but whole fish that are slashed will cook in less time than fillets of the same thickness. And the larger the fish, the less time it requires per inch, as with all types of flesh. And that's just the fish.

The cooking methods are really not equally fast. Obviously oil at 375°F. is hotter than steam at something over 212°F. or water at 170°F., all of which conduct heat faster than a 450°F. oven. So formulas are only just the vaguest of guides. Tests are needed.

If you cooked fish every day you would eventually learn how to judge doneness by feel, just as summer barbecuers get pretty good with a steak by the end of the season. Raw flesh is spongy and cooked is firm. A gentle finger poke to that swordfish steak or even that steamed sea bass and you would know. But fish is tricky, even for experts, because of all the variables mentioned above.

Yes, you may stick a fork in to see if the protein fibers will flake, but that doesn't do much for the appearance. A chopstick inserted into a slash in a whole fish will tell you when the flesh will just pull away from the bone, leaving the bone still slightly pink and pearly, which is the ideal. And, again with whole fish, if the eye has turned white and bulged, the fish is probably done; if the eye has popped out, the fish is probably overdone. But the very best test for doneness is the skewer test for temperature. It isn't that no one ever thought of such a thing before, but we owe the careful refinement of this technique to Gilbert Le Coze of Le Bernardin. It is a foolproof test for any kind of seafood, and it does no damage to the texture or appearance of the food: Insert a thin metal skewer—a turkey lacer or such—well into the flesh. Leave it about two seconds, then immediately apply it to your lower lip: cool means raw, warm means rare, *very* warm means perfectly done, and uncomfortably hot means overdone. It is that simple.

SERVING A WHOLE FISH

Because whole fish are tastier than fillets, home cooks should become comfortable with the notion of *presenting* a whole fish as well as cooking one. There is only a bit of anatomy and method to be learned, and no matter what cooking technique is used and at what temperature the fish is served (hot or cold or something in between), this always applies.

Most of the large fish that are routinely cooked whole cannot be neatly portioned with a knife. Salmon is the major exception: a cold poached salmon can indeed be carved. Other fish are broken into portions with two large serving spoons. As the fish lies on its side, examine the up side and visualize the central line that divides the dorsal (upper) half from the ventral (lower) half of the fillet. Starting just behind the head, use your spoons to gently dislodge portions from the dorsal half. When you reach the tail, start on the ventral half. When you get to the rib cage, be as careful as possible to leave the ribs and pinbones on the skeleton. (No matter how careful you are, you will probably end up serving a few bones from this section; savvy diners will not mind.) There may not even be enough flesh to bother with on the ventral fillet where it covers the ribs. When you have served the top fillet, use your spoons to break through the vertebrae at the base of the skull and at the base of the tail. Gently lift the backbone—it should come away in one piece—and place it aside on your platter. Proceed to portion the remaining fillet just as you served the top one.

Eating a whole fish—a trout, small flounder, or other panfish— is really the same proposition in miniature. This is why fish knives are dull and more spoonlike than other table knives.

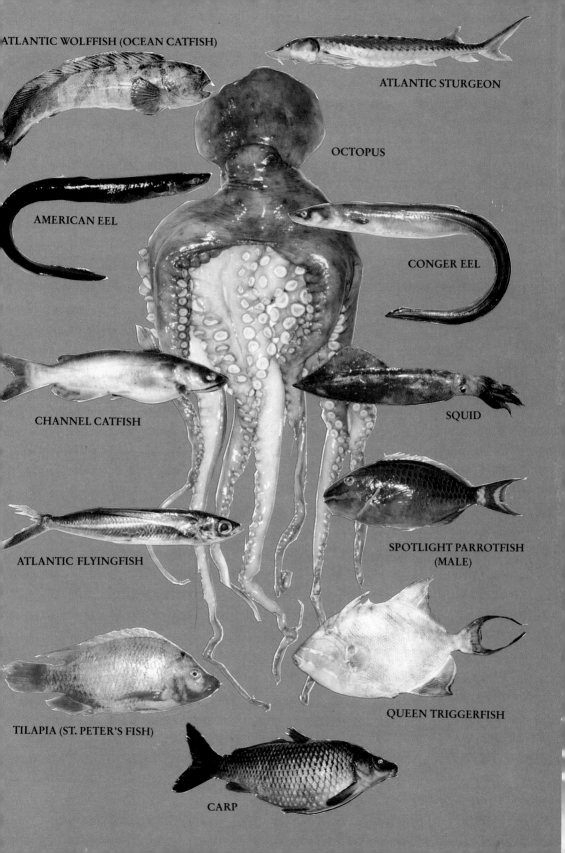

ATLANTIC WOLFFISH (OCEAN CATFISH)

ATLANTIC STURGEON

OCTOPUS

AMERICAN EEL

CONGER EEL

CHANNEL CATFISH

SQUID

ATLANTIC FLYINGFISH

SPOTLIGHT PARROTFISH
(MALE)

TILAPIA (ST. PETER'S FISH)

QUEEN TRIGGERFISH

CARP

ATLANTIC HALIBUT

GRAY SOLE (WITCH FLOUNDER)

SWORDFISH

DOVER SOLE (EUROPEAN)

FLORIDA POMPANO

PERMIT

CREVALLE JACK

WALLEYE (WALLEYED PIKE,
YELLOW PIKE)

YELLOW PERCH

LOOKDOWN

FLUKE (SUMMER FLOUNDER)

OCEAN PERCH

RED SCORPIONFISH

ATLANTIC HERRING

YELLOWTAIL SNAPPER

AMERICAN SHAD

MAHI MAHI (DOLPHIN)

ATLANTIC COD

ATLANTIC POLLOCK

SILVER HAKE (WHITING)

MONKFISH

AMERICAN RED SNAPPER

VERMILLION SNAPPER (B-LINER)

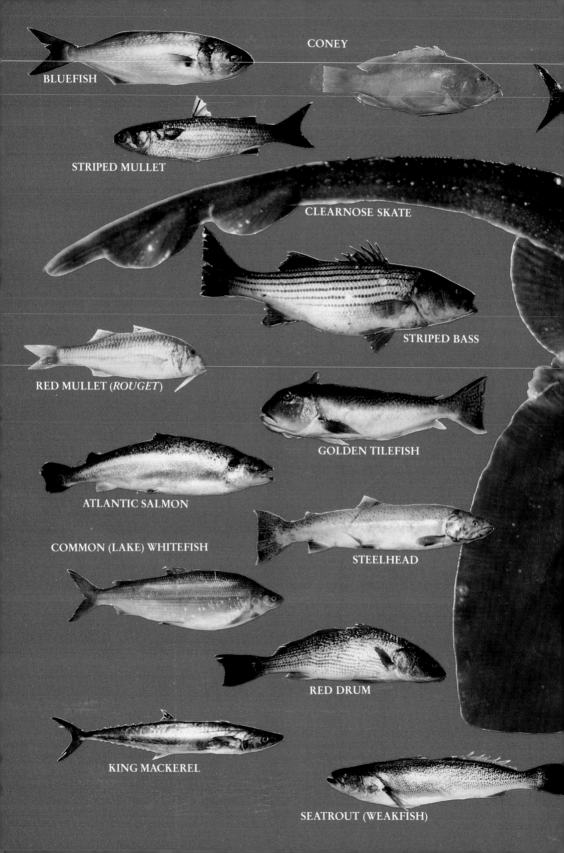

CONEY

BLUEFISH

STRIPED MULLET

CLEARNOSE SKATE

STRIPED BASS

RED MULLET (*ROUGET*)

GOLDEN TILEFISH

ATLANTIC SALMON

COMMON (LAKE) WHITEFISH

STEELHEAD

RED DRUM

KING MACKEREL

SEATROUT (WEAKFISH)

BLUEFIN TUNA

YELLOWFIN GROUPER

SPECKLED HIND
(KITTY MITCHELL)

SHEEPSHEAD

NORTH ATLANTIC BUTTERFISH

PORGY (SCUP)

BLACK SEA BASS

ATLANTIC MACKEREL
(BOSTON MACKEREL)

HYBRID STRIPED BASS (SUNSHINE BASS)

NORTHERN
SEAROBIN

SHORTFIN MAKO SHARK

BUCKLER DORY
(AMERICAN
JOHN DORY)

OCEAN POUT

NORTHERN PUFFER
(BLOWFISH, SEA SQUAB)

TAUTOG (BLACKFISH)

MOLTING
ATLANTIC
BLUE CRAB
(FEMALE)

ROCK CRAB

ROCK SHRIMP

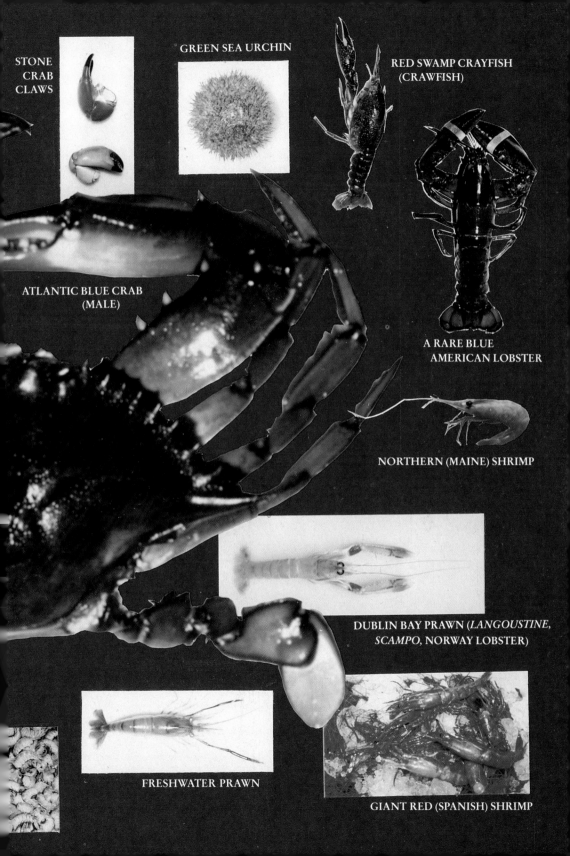

STONE
CRAB
CLAWS

GREEN SEA URCHIN

RED SWAMP CRAYFISH
(CRAWFISH)

ATLANTIC BLUE CRAB
(MALE)

A RARE BLUE
AMERICAN LOBSTER

NORTHERN (MAINE) SHRIMP

DUBLIN BAY PRAWN (*LANGOUSTINE*,
SCAMPO, NORWAY LOBSTER)

FRESHWATER PRAWN

GIANT RED (SPANISH) SHRIMP

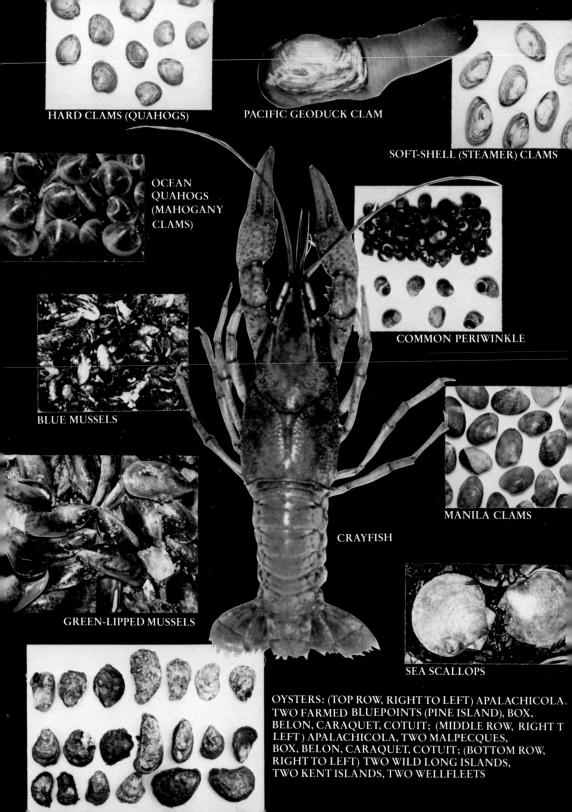

HARD CLAMS (QUAHOGS)

PACIFIC GEODUCK CLAM

SOFT-SHELL (STEAMER) CLAMS

OCEAN QUAHOGS (MAHOGANY CLAMS)

COMMON PERIWINKLE

BLUE MUSSELS

MANILA CLAMS

CRAYFISH

GREEN-LIPPED MUSSELS

SEA SCALLOPS

OYSTERS: (TOP ROW, RIGHT TO LEFT) APALACHICOLA, TWO FARMED BLUEPOINTS (PINE ISLAND), BOX, BELON, CARAQUET, COTUIT; (MIDDLE ROW, RIGHT T LEFT) APALACHICOLA, TWO MALPECQUES, BOX, BELON, CARAQUET, COTUIT; (BOTTOM ROW, RIGHT TO LEFT) TWO WILD LONG ISLANDS, TWO KENT ISLANDS, TWO WELLFLEETS

PART 2

BAKING

See p. 78 for ways to determine proper cooking time.

Now that thermostatically controlled ovens are standard equipment in all kitchens, cooks may take some seafood, season it, and bake it until it is done. That is the best definition for baking: oven roasting (as opposed to spit roasting). It is no longer necessary to use protective coverings of clay, salt, or leaves to minimize the effect of intense or uneven heat on delicate flesh. Covering and wrapping techniques are still in use because they can produce delicious results, but they are not the same as roasting. Whenever you seal the fish—even with a lid or foil or parchment—you are doing something else to it: braising it in its own juice, or steaming it, as in Pierre Baran's Red Snapper *aux Ecailles de Concombre.* The recipes in this section are, as much as possible, for oven roasting. There are also three shellfish gratins included, because the shellfish start out in their market state, get mixed with other things, and are then popped into the oven and baked until done.

VARIETIES BEST SUITED

Any kind of seafood may be baked. As with all techniques, whole fish will emerge from the oven tastier than fillets, also more attractive because they will have had time to develop a nice crust.

EQUIPMENT

No special equipment is required for baking, just ordinary ovenproof vessels of the right size.

TECHNIQUE

Fish and shellfish to be oven roasted are seasoned (sometimes marinated) and always filmed with a little fat for protection. Whole fish are often slashed to let the flavorings in and to equalize the cooking time of the head and tail halves. Stuffings are fairly common, but present the same danger as stuffed poultry—you may have to overcook the beast to cook the stuffing. Fresh herbs and aromatic vegetables are safer. So roasting technique is really very simple. Only when it comes to oven temperature do we start to run into some confusion.

High heat, moderate heat, low heat, and combination heat— each has its logic and devotees. High-heat roasting is most like broiling and gives a nice appearance, but some people feel that it is likely to dry out fish and toughen shellfish. Moderate heat, therefore, ought to be safer. The low-heat people, however, reason that they can work the least texture damage and achieve moist, tender results that are most like the natural raw creature. We're talking *real* low here: 225°F. to 250°F. It produces fine results. The combination-heat people, who start the fish on high and then reduce heat to moderate or low, want to get the best of two worlds. All four approaches are used here for different reasons. It should be mentioned that a few people bake whole live lobsters, to serve as is or to precook the meat for another purpose. It works, but steaming (p. 356) seems to be kinder to the flesh and maybe to the animal, too.

THE PREFERRED BAKED FISH, FULTON FISH MARKET-STYLE

For those who want to know what fishmongers eat (if they eat fish), here it is. It is fitting that the first recipe in this book should also be the most typical.

Preheat oven to moderate: 325°F. to 375°F. Take some nice fish and season it to taste with salt, pepper, lemon juice, and softened butter. Bake until done. Serve hot.

VARIATION 1

Sprinkle with Italian bread crumbs before baking.

VARIATION 2

Wrap fish with foil before baking. When it is almost done, unwrap it and brown it a little by raising the oven heat or by running it under a broiler.

ROAST GROUPER WITH FRESH HERB SAUCE

About 4 servings

Here is a satisfying, basic wintry dish for homey occasions. It can be varied ad infinitum by changing the fresh herbs. Any mild, white-fleshed fish will do admirably, as will salmon and large trout. Boiled potatoes are the perfect accompaniment; string beans might be nice too.

4 pounds whole grouper (1 or 2 fish), scaled, gutted, gills removed,
  pectoral fins removed, rinsed well
Coarse salt and freshly ground white pepper to taste
1/3 cup minced shallots
10 tablespoons softened butter
2 small bay leaves
2 pinches dried leaf thyme
1 cup crème fraîche *or heavy cream*
1/2 cup dry white wine
1 cup Fish Stock (see recipe)
1/3 cup finely chopped parsley, preferably flat leaf
1 to 2 teaspoons finely chopped fresh herbs, such as tarragon, savory,
  dill, chervil, or chives
Parsley sprigs
Lemon wedges

Slash fish crosswise on both sides at 2-inch intervals just to the bone, holding knife at a 45-degree angle inclined toward the head. Season lightly with salt and pepper. Combine the shallots and 6 tablespoons of the softened butter. Smear mixture evenly over the fish, including the cavity. Place bay leaves and dried thyme in cavity. Place fish in a roasting pan just large enough to hold it. Hold it in the refrigerator if prepared in advance. Fish needs at least 30 minutes at room temperature before cooking.

Preheat oven to 350°F.

Pour cream into a medium-size heavy, nonreactive saucepan, and reduce by half. Bake fish until it is just done. Because of the oven temperature you can plan on about 12 minutes per inch of thickness. Do not overcook. When fish is done, remove it to a platter and keep warm. Place the roasting pan on a stove burner and add white wine. Over fairly high heat reduce by half, being careful not to scorch the pan. Add stock and reduce by half. Strain mixture through a sieve into the saucepan with the reduced cream. Bring sauce to a boil. At this point the texture should be about right—very light but still slightly creamy—but you may reduce it slightly if you feel the need. Add chopped parsley and other fresh herb(s), and heat through. Swirl in remaining 4 tablespoons butter. Correct seasoning. If you arrange vegetables around the fish you are all set to serve. If not, pour ac-

cumulated platter juices into the sauce and neaten the platter. Pour a
little sauce over the fish and serve it immediately, garnished with
parsley sprigs and lemon wedges, passing the remaining sauce in a
sauceboat.

ROAST LOTTE CHEZ LOUIS

6 servings

New York–based cookie magnate David Liederman's restaurant Chez Louis is part of a return to hearty, generous bistro
fare. Many of the menu items are roasted, as in this monkfish
recipe contributed by Chef Arthur Borkan. It is served with an
appropriate green vegetable—broccoli, string beans, or snow
peas—and an interesting potato preparation, perhaps grati-
néed or a croquette. If you cannot locate the fresh herbs for
the marinade use one teaspoon each of dried.

THE MARINADE

> *1 1/2 cups corn or vegetable oil*
> *1/2 cup extra-virgin olive oil*
> *3 sprigs fresh thyme*
> *3 sprigs fresh rosemary*
> *3 sprigs fresh tarragon*
> *4 cloves garlic, peeled and bruised*
> *1 lemon, thickly sliced*

> *4 pounds whole monkfish tail, filleted, trimmed of all dark flesh, and*
>   *cut into 6 serving pieces (about 3 pounds fillets)*
> *18 cloves garlic, unpeeled (about 1 head)*
> *A little vegetable oil*
> *1 1/2 cups* **Beurre Blanc** *(see recipe), strained or not, as desired*
> *Coarse salt and freshly ground pepper to taste*
> *Flour for dredging (optional)*
> *Clarified butter (p. 75) (optional)*
> *6 sprigs fresh thyme*
> *Vegetables of choice*

In a medium to large nonreactive bowl, combine the oils for the marinade. Bruise the three kinds of herbs with the flat side of a heavy knife. Add to the oil along with the peeled garlic cloves and lemon slices. Add fish and marinate, refrigerated, turning from time to time, for 12 to 24 hours.

About 1 hour before fish is to be baked, preheat oven to 300°F.

Film 18 garlic cloves lightly with a little oil, and place in a baking pan. Roast garlic 45 minutes or more, until very tender. Set aside.

Begin the wine/shallot reduction for the preparation of *Beurre Blanc.*

While garlic cloves are roasting, allow fish to come to room temperature—at least 30 minutes—then remove from marinade. Dry well with paper towels. Season lightly with salt and pepper. If you are nervous about skillet-browning the fish naked, you may dredge it very lightly in flour, dusting off excess. Heat a large skillet to very hot. Film with a little oil or clarified butter and brown each piece of fish on all sides, removing pieces as they are browned to a baking dish. When all pieces have been browned, roast until done, 10 to 15 minutes, adding the roasted garlic cloves for the last few minutes to warm.

While fish is roasting, complete *Beurre Blanc.* Ladle a little pool onto each of 6 warmed dinner plates. Top with a piece of fish. Garnish each plate with 3 garlic cloves, a sprig of thyme, and vegetables of choice, and serve immediately. The buttery garlic pulp from the skins can be spread on the fish, if desired.

TANDOORI FISH STEAKS

6 servings

This recipe is based on the richly spiced and brightly colored meats that are meant to be cooked in the traditional clay oven called a *tandoor.* Chicken and kebabs are the usual fare, and are served in Indian restaurants around the world. A neighborhood place called India Pavillion does a fish version, which inspired the one below. King mackerel is the best choice, but you might try tilefish steaks or bluefish fillets. If you find the indicated spice mixture daunting, you may substitute 2 tablespoons good curry powder plus 1 ½ tablespoons *garam masala,* which is available in Indian shops. The results will be less exciting, but acceptable. Prepare all the accompaniments if you can—none is time-consuming—although you may simplify if you wish. If you decide on a fresh coriander chutney, you might add a little chopped mint to the *Raita*.

6 king mackerel steaks, 1 inch thick (about 3 pounds)

THE MARINADE

1 1/2 cups plain yogurt
1 medium onion, finely chopped
3 cloves garlic, peeled and finely minced
2 tablespoons finely minced fresh gingerroot
2 tablespoons lime juice
1 teaspoon grated orange zest
2 teaspoons coarse salt
1 teaspoon freshly ground black pepper
1 teaspoon freshly ground white pepper
1 1/2 teaspoons cayenne
1 teaspoon ground coriander
1 teaspoon ground cumin
1/2 teaspoon ground fenugreek
1 teaspoon ground cardamom
1 teaspoon ground fennel seed
1 teaspoon ground cinnamon
2 teaspoons ground turmeric
Orange or red Indian food-coloring powder (optional)

Approximately 6 ounces clarified butter (p. 75) (or ghee*)*
1 large Spanish onion, peeled and sliced into rings
Lime wedges

ACCOMPANIMENTS

Plain White Rice (Basic Western or Boiled) or Saffron Rice, preferably basmati (see recipes)
Yogurt and Cucumber Raita *(recipe follows)*
Fresh Onion Chutney (recipe follows)
Fresh Coriander or Mint Chutney (recipe follows)
Mango chutney (store-bought), sweet or hot (optional)

Arrange fish steaks in a single layer in a nonreactive dish just large enough to hold them. In a bowl, combine yogurt, onion, garlic, ginger, lime juice, orange zest, and salt. Combine the remaining marinade spices, except the food-coloring powder. Heat a small skillet and add the spice mixture. Toss over moderate heat just until mixture is fragrant. Add to the yogurt mixture. You may also add coloring powder, starting with about ¼ teaspoon, until you are satisfied with the color. It may be made quite bright without overcoloring the finished dish. Pour the mixture over the fish and marinate, turning occasionally, for 12 to 24 hours, refrigerated. An hour or two at room temperature will yield some limited results, but a long marination is much better. Bring fish to room temperature before baking.

Preheat oven to 450°F. Also preheat an ovenproof baking-serving dish of the right size to hold fish in a single layer.

Remove fish from the marinade, leaving just a thin film on each steak. Warm the clarified butter and brush or rub a thin film of fat all over the steaks. Open oven door and place steaks in the preheated dish. Bake until done, about 10 minutes.

While the fish is baking, rinse onion rings in cold water and pat dry. Heat a large skillet, add a little clarified butter, add onions, and toss over high heat briefly, until they start to lose their raw look and threaten to wilt. Do not cook to tenderness.

When fish is done, remove it from the oven, strew with the onion rings, and bring to the table immediately, still sizzling. Spritz with the juice of 1 or 2 lime wedges, and serve immediately, with additional lime wedges and any or all of the dishes that follow.

YOGURT AND CUCUMBER *RAITA*

Combine 1 cup plain yogurt with about ¾ cup shredded cucumber, preferably seedless, and a little salt.

FRESH ONION CHUTNEY

Combine about 1 cup chopped onion, rinsed with cold water and dried, with tomato ketchup to moisten and Tabasco to taste. Make this one quite hot.

FRESH CORIANDER OR MINT CHUTNEY

1/3 cup chopped fresh coriander or mint
1/4 cup minced onion
2 teaspoons minced fresh gingerroot
1 teaspoon sugar
2 teaspoons lime or lemon juice
1 tablespoon minced fresh green chile (jalapeño or serrano), or to taste
  (optional)

Combine ingredients. Use chiles only if you want a hot chutney. For other purposes it could be made very hot indeed. It could also be puréed.

SLOW-BAKED SHAD, ITALO-AMERICAN

4 to 6 servings

There are several Market men in their sixties whose Italian mothers still cook every day and have a much-appreciated way with seafood. Come shad season, the ladies work a similar preparation on this jumbo herring. And just so we don't offend anyone by leaving her out, the recipe below is a composite version. In the days before professionally filleted shad became available, most shad were cooked whole and given a long, slow baking in an effort to render the myriad tiny pinbones harmless. Unfortunately, the flesh was likely to be destroyed along with the bones. But as long as the timing is sensible, the low oven temperature is still a good idea; the results are moist and meaty. The light spinach purée was added for piquancy. Sorrel is another possibility, but it is still too expensive and too difficult to find, and it seems a shame to add a Loire Valley touch to a very New York dish.

2 shad fillets, 2 to 2 1/2 pounds
1/4 cup light olive oil
2 large cloves garlic, peeled and well mashed
1 teaspoon chopped fresh rosemary, or scant 1/2 teaspoon dried
1 teaspoon fresh thyme leaves, or 1/4 teaspoon dried
1/4 cup white wine
1/4 cup lemon juice
Coarse salt and freshly ground black pepper to taste
3/4 cup fine fresh bread crumbs
1/4 cup melted butter
1/4 cup extra-virgin olive oil
Spinach Purée (recipe follows) (optional)

Rinse shad fillets, pat dry, and place them in a nonreactive dish, skin side down. Combine light olive oil, garlic, herbs, wine, lemon juice, and salt and pepper to taste. Pour over fish and baste. Let marinate for at least 1 hour; refrigerate if you let it sit longer than that. Turn and baste once or twice.

Preheat oven to 225°F.

Choose a baking dish just large enough to hold the shad in a single layer. Remove shad from marinade and scrape off any large pieces of garlic. Place fillets in the baking dish, skin side down, and sprinkle on a light, even coat of bread crumbs. Combine melted butter and extra-virgin olive oil, and drizzle over all, as evenly as possible. Also drizzle on a few spoons of marinade. Place in oven and bake until heated through and very lightly browned, anywhere from 1 to 1 1/2 hours, depending on your oven and the size of the fillets. Reserve the pan juices for the Spinach Purée. Serve as is, or remove to a platter filmed with the Spinach Purée.

SPINACH PURÉE

1 pound fresh spinach, thoroughly washed, coarse stems removed
About 1/2 cup Fish Stock (see recipe)
Large pinch sugar
1/2 teaspoon coarse salt
2 tablespoons lemon juice, approximately
Pan juices from the baked shad

Combine spinach, 1/2 cup stock, sugar, and salt in a heavy nonreactive saucepan, cover, and bring to a simmer. When spinach is wilted—30 seconds or so—purée mixture in a food processor as finely as possible, adding a little more stock if it seems thick. Return to saucepan. At serving time, reheat to a simmer and stir in 2 tablespoons lemon juice and strained pan juices. Correct seasoning and serve immediately.

BAKED WHOLE FISH AU POIVRE

4 to 6 servings

Veteran teacher Miriam Brickman has been planning for years to drop this recipe from her seafood classes because of its simplicity. But just in time a former student will say, "Love that peppered fish; it's the only thing from the class that I make," or some such comment that both pleases and vexes, and back into the curriculum it goes. It *is* simple, and therein lies its charm. The pepper forms a nice crust, just as surely as salt would but with a zestier flavor. This will only work with whole fish, and large ones are best. You might choose any of the usual roundfish—red snapper, black sea bass, grouper, seatrout, tilefish—but Miriam's favorite is bluefish. She recommends that you use the larger amount of pepper; diners may choose how much of the skin they wish to eat.

1 whole roundfish, 5 pounds or more, scaled, gutted, gills removed, pectoral fins removed, rinsed well, and brought to room temperature
Juice of 1 lemon
Olive oil, as needed
1 or 2 large cloves garlic, peeled and bruised
Coarse salt to taste
Parsley sprigs
1/2 to 1 ounce (up to 2 1/2 tablespoons) black peppercorns, rather coarsely ground in a pepper mill or spice grinder

GARNISHES

Lemon slices
Parsley sprigs
1 black olive

Preheat oven to 450°F.

Score the fish on both sides, 2 slashes per side. Hold a sharp knife at a 45-degree angle inclined toward the head, and make crosscuts just to the bone, about 2 inches apart. Sprinkle the lemon juice over the fish and rub it evenly around. Oil fish generously all over. Rub with garlic and a little salt, and place the garlic in the cavity along with a few parsley sprigs. Coat the skin with pepper.

Place fish in a well-oiled pan. Measure the width of the fish at the thickest point to give you some idea of timing, which should be 8 or 9 minutes per inch.

Bake until done. Remove to a platter and garnish with lemon slices and parsley sprigs. Remove the visible eye and replace it with the olive. Serve immediately, offering the pan juices in a sauceboat for those who wish to spoon a little over to moisten. This dish is also delicious at room temperature.

HELEN VON GLAHN'S MUSTARD-BAKED FILLETS

4 to 6 servings

This book would be incomplete without the delightful little quickie below, which was developed by the wife of John von Glahn, who for many years ran what is now called Fulton Fish Market Information Services. The recipe has appeared in several publications through the years and was a highlight of Mr. von Glahn's cooking manual (which is now, sadly, out of print) called *Fish 'n' Tips*. Despite its simplicity it seems to have magical powers, particularly for people who claim they are iffy about fish. Any fish fillet or steak will do, but use flounder and you will be *really* safe. This preparation may also be broiled.

4 to 6 fillets of desired size, skinned or not
Salt and freshly ground pepper to taste
6 tablespoons melted butter or margarine
2 teaspoons lemon juice
1 1/2 teaspoons Dijon mustard
1 clove garlic, crushed

Preheat oven to 350°F.

Let fish reach room temperature, at least 30 minutes. Trim fillets of all bones and season lightly with salt and pepper. Combine remaining ingredients. Dip fish into the mixture to coat lightly and place in a baking pan just large enough to hold fillets in a single layer, skin side down. Plump up fillets and even out the thickness by folding tail ends under, if that applies. At this oven temperature you can expect about 12 minutes of cooking time per inch (thickness) of fish. Bake until done. Serve hot.

TROPICAL FISH

4 to 6 servings

One of the better palates in New York belongs to a Wall Street type named June Sabah. Some ten years ago she served a memorable summer luncheon shortly after she returned from a few years in San Juan, Puerto Rico, where her food mentor was Marta Casals Istomin. It was a perfect combination of good food, good company, good wine, and good weather, as we lazed the afternoon away in the garden of her family's extraordinary old house in Brooklyn. For the wonderful fish dish she prepared, June used a handsome striped bass because it was the freshest local choice at the time. Red snapper, black sea bass, grouper, and seatrout are good choices these days. We like bluefish best of all. June insists this fish must be served at room temperature and she is right, but if you should decide to serve it hot I don't suppose she will find out. The chayote salad is also a must if you want to get it right.

4- to 6-pound whole fish (1 large or 2 medium), scaled, gutted, gills removed, pectoral fins removed, rinsed well
Juice of 1 lime or lemon
Light olive oil, as needed
1 or 2 large cloves garlic, peeled and bruised
10 to 12 thin slices fresh gingerroot
3 scallions, split lengthwise
Coarse salt to taste
1 teaspoon freshly ground black pepper, or to taste
1 to 2 tablespoons thinly sliced hot chile (jalapeño or serrano) (optional)
1 bunch fresh coriander sprigs, with most of the stems removed
1 1/2 cups unpeeled, seeded, juiced, and diced tomatoes
1 thinly sliced lime or lemon

ACCOMPANIMENTS

> *Chayote Salad (recipe follows) (optional)*
> *Lettuce and Coriander Salad (recipe follows) (optional)*

Slash prepared fish crosswise on both sides at 2-inch intervals just to the bone, holding knife at a 45-degree angle inclined toward the head. Pour the juice of 1 lime or lemon over the fish and rub it in. Oil fish generously all over and place it in an oiled roasting pan just large enough to hold it. Rub the garlic all over the fish and then place in the cavity. Season with salt and pepper to taste, inside and out. Place half the ginger, half the scallions, half the chile, one-third of the coriander, and one-third of the tomatoes in the cavity. Place the remaining ginger slices and scallions on the fish, followed by the remaining chile, coriander sprigs, and a row of overlapping lime or lemon slices. Be sure to cover the eye so you will not have to worry about it later. Sprinkle the remaining diced tomatoes over all and drizzle on another tablespoon or so of oil. Put fish aside for about 1 hour to marinate and to come to room temperature.

Preheat oven to 425°F.

Place fish in oven, and roast for 10 minutes. Reduce temperature to 250°F. and continue roasting until done. This could take 1 hour. Do not open oven door until fish has cooked for at least 30 minutes. Let cool to room temperature, 1 or 2 hours at least. Carefully transfer the fish to a platter and spoon the pan juices over it. Serve, offering the optional salads on the side. The fish is best served the day it is made, but leftovers are also good, and are best if allowed to come to room temperature before serving.

VINAIGRETTE FOR SALAD ACCOMPANIMENTS

> *½ cup fruity olive oil*
> *¼ cup red wine vinegar or lemon or lime juice*
> *Coarse salt and freshly ground pepper to taste*

Combine vinaigrette ingredients in a covered jar and shake to blend. Set aside.

CHAYOTE SALAD

> 3 to 4 medium chayotes (mirliton, vegetable pear)
> 1 cup unpeeled, seeded, juiced, and diced tomatoes
> 1/2 cup chopped red or white onion, rinsed with cold water and dried,
>   or thinly sliced scallions
> 2 tablespoons chopped parsley

Simmer chayote in salted water until just fork tender, about 45 minutes, maybe longer. Drain and cool. Peel. Dice flesh—seed, too, if it is tender—and combine with tomatoes, onion or scallions, and parsley. Moisten with half of the vinaigrette. Correct seasoning.

LETTUCE AND CORIANDER SALAD

> 1 large head green leaf lettuce, washed, dried, and torn into bite-size
>   pieces
> 1 bunch fresh coriander, leaves only

Toss lettuce and coriander with just enough vinaigrette to film the leaves. Do this at serving time, not in advance.

MULLET ROAST, HOME-STYLE

Though striped mullet are seasonally plentiful in the Atlantic and estuarine inland waterways and at Fulton, they generally go only to neighborhoods where their low price makes them attractive. Do give them a try if you locate some, and be sure to use any roe you find, for breakfast with scrambled eggs perhaps. In Tidewater Virginia and the Carolinas when mullet are running, sport fishermen stretch gill nets across the appropriate waters and haul the catch onto the beach, where preparations have been made for a traditional mullet roast. A large hardwood or driftwood fire is built and allowed to burn down to glowing coals. The mullet are cleaned, slashed, seasoned with salt and pepper, and skewered lengthwise on sticks. The sticks are thrust into the sand at an angle just right for fat to drip down the sticks rather than into the fire, as the fish slowly roast to a crispy brown. Bourbon also seems to be an important

ingredient in this ritual. A bibulous gent known only as Mr.
Fisher, who by the 1960s was perhaps the last of what you
could call landed gentry in the countryside near Coinjock,
North Carolina, used to say, "Well, you don't hardly ever see
a preacher at a mullet roast." With or without the bourbon,
you can prepare a decent mullet roast at home that will lack
only the smell of wood smoke and the appetite stimulation
of riverine air. Offer baked potatoes, melted butter, and corn
and peas or whatever is fresh. Mackerel is also tasty prepared
this way.

*1 striped mullet per person (or 1 for 2 people, if large), scaled, gutted,
     gills and pectoral fins removed, and rinsed well
2 to 3 strips bacon per fish
Coarse salt and freshly ground black pepper to taste*

Preheat oven to 250°F.

Slash prepared fish three times on each side. Rub each from
head to tail with a piece of bacon to film it with fat, then season with
salt and pepper, inside and out. Place fish in a baking dish, belly down,
and drape with strips of bacon. Bake until done. Serve hot with
vegetables of choice and melted butter.

BAKED CLAMS WITH HAZELNUT AND HERB PESTO

12 clams; 4 or more servings

Chef Steven Mellina of The Manhattan Ocean Club has
worked a sea change on the traditional Mediterranean basil
and pine nut pesto and teamed it with clams for an interesting
flavor combination. He specifies filberts for the pesto. Strictly
speaking, the filbert is a nut of English origin that is related to
European hazelnuts, though the two terms are commonly used
interchangeably for hazelnuts, the ones that are most available.
So the more common term is used here to avoid confusion.
Sorry, Steve. Do not be daunted if you cannot locate verbena
(also called lemon verbena). You may substitute about a half
teaspoon grated lemon zest. If chervil is also missing from your
greengrocer's inventory, substitute a little more parsley and
you will not notice a dramatic difference because of all the

other herbal flavors. If you have the time and are willing to flirt with preciosity, you might create a garnish for each plate of a tiny bouquet of one sprig of each of the herbs tied with a chive.

5 ounces hazelnuts
5 ounces (1 ¼ sticks) softened butter
1 teaspoon chopped garlic
2 teaspoons chopped shallots
1 ounce (2 tablespoons) dry white wine
2 teaspoons chopped fresh oregano
2 teaspoons chopped parsley
1 teaspoon chopped fresh basil
1 teaspoon chopped fresh verbena
1 teaspoon chopped fresh chervil
1 teaspoon chopped fresh chives
Freshly ground white pepper to taste
12 medium-small clams (large littlenecks or small cherrystones)
Lemon wedges

To prepare hazelnuts: Preheat oven to 375°F. Place hazelnuts in the oven for about 10 minutes. They should begin to color slightly and become fragrant. A handful at a time, wrap them in a coarse kitchen towel and rub vigorously to scour off the skins. The residue will have to be picked off by hand. Make sure nuts are very hot while you are working them in the towel. Cool and reserve.

Melt half the butter in a small skillet and gently sauté the garlic and shallots until translucent. Add the wine and simmer for about 1 minute to mellow the flavor of the wine. Add all the herbs and stir until they are well combined. Pour mixture into a bowl and cool.

Combine the nuts, remaining butter, and herb mixture in the bowl of a food processor and process to a smooth paste, stopping to scrape down the sides of the bowl often. Season lightly with the pepper. Note that salt has been omitted because the clams are naturally salty enough.

Shuck the clams as described on p. 63, reserving the juice for another purpose. Place the clams on the half shell and discard remaining shells. Place clams on a baking tray lined with coarse salt (for stability) and divide the herb pesto evenly over them, masking each one neatly. You may do this in advance—the same day—and refrigerate.

Preheat oven to 450°F.

Bake clams in preheated oven just until topping is browned and crunchy. Do not overcook. Transfer clams to platter or plates, and garnish with lemon wedges. Serve immediately.

GRATIN OF OYSTERS, SAUSAGES, AND APPLES

4 to 6 servings

Oysters have a curious affinity for sausages, even good old American breakfast sausages. This recipe combines the two with apples for a homey cold-weather side dish that is fine for brunch, a buffet, and especially as a kind of savory "dressing" to accompany roasted poultry. Most of it can be prepared well in advance and then reheated with the oysters.

8 ounces (8 count) small breakfast link sausages
2 firm red apples (Cortland, Empire, McIntosh, or any of the fine local varieties)
2 tart green apples (Granny Smith, Rhode Island Greening)
2 tablespoons butter
1/3 cup minced shallots
1/4 teaspoon dried sage (crumbled leaf sage, if available, or rubbed)
1/4 teaspoon dried leaf thyme
Salt and freshly ground white pepper to taste
18 large oysters, shucked, or two 8-ounce containers raw oysters
1/4 cup fine fresh bread crumbs
3 tablespoons very cold butter

Cook sausages in a skillet according to maker's instructions, under-cooking them slightly. Drain on paper towels. Use a pastry brush to paint a thin film of the sausage fat in an oval or round 2-quart baking dish. Discard remaining fat, but reserve skillet without washing it.

Preheat oven to 375°F.

Slice the apples in half lengthwise and core with a melon baller. Use a paring knife to trim stem and blossom ends. Slice apples *crosswise* into 1/8-inch slices. Toss to mix the two kinds of apples. Place the apples in the prepared dish and shake to compact and distribute them evenly. Smooth the surface, and set aside.

Reheat the skillet, melt the 2 tablespoons butter, and add the shallots. Stew gently until tender. Add sage and thyme. Pour mixture over apples, using the pastry brush to be sure there is a thin film of butter over all. Season to taste with salt and pepper. Cover well with foil. Bake in preheated oven until apples are tender and juicy, about 30 minutes. If prepared in advance and refrigerated, bring to room temperature before proceeding.

About 30 minutes before serving, preheat oven to 450°F. and return dish to the oven, uncovered. Bake until heated through and very slightly browned, about 10 to 15 minutes. Remove from oven. Arrange sausages on top like the spokes of a wheel and add oysters to the open spaces. Sprinkle on bread crumbs. Use a coarse grater to grate the 3 tablespoons cold butter evenly over the top. Return dish to oven and bake until hot and lightly glazed, about 10 minutes. Serve as soon as possible.

OYSTERS SUZETTE

4 to 8 servings

Oysters are delicious teamed with bacon as well as sausages, as in this Creole favorite, which is also called Oysters *Vieux Carré.* Students have consistently preferred it to oysters Rockefeller, and it is easier to make. You will notice that the ingredients are similar to those for clams casino (though spicier and more fun), so the mixture will also work well with clams. Creole baked-on-the-half-shell oyster dishes are traditionally prepared with the shells nestled in a bed of hot rock salt, which not only keeps them from tipping but also retains heat. Since not many home kitchens are equipped with individual ovenproof dishes for this purpose, use a large metal platter. Kosher salt is fine if you cannot locate ice cream salt. You might also, inauthentically, skip the salt and the shells and assemble servings in individual ramekins. For dishes of this sort, many people lightly poach or bake oysters in advance to plump them up and eliminate excess moisture that dilutes the sauce, but it does not seem necessary for this particular dish. Allow three to six oysters per serving, depending on your menu.

8 ounces sliced bacon, chopped or thinly sliced crosswise
2 ounces (1/2 stick) butter
2 cups diced green peppers
1 cup sliced scallions, green and white or just green if you have extra
1 teaspoon Tabasco
3/4 cup diced bottled pimiento or roasted red pepper
Salt and pepper to taste
24 large bluepoint oysters, shucked, large (bottom) shells reserved
Rock or kosher salt
French bread

In a large skillet, sauté bacon very gently until you have rendered most of its fat; do not crisp or brown. Pour out most of the fat and add the butter. Add green peppers and scallions, and sauté just until tender. Stir in Tabasco. Pour mixture into a bowl and stir in pimiento. Cool. Taste for seasoning, and add a little salt and pepper if you feel the need.

Preheat oven to 550°F.

Scrub reserved oyster shells well and dry. Drain oysters well and make sure there are no bits of shell. Place an oyster in each shell and mask with some of the cooled sauce.

Line baking dish(es) with a layer of rock or kosher salt about 3/8 inch deep. Preheat dish on the top rack of the preheated oven. Just before serving time, remove dish from oven and quickly nest oyster shells in the salt, close together, keeping them as level as possible. Return dish to oven and bake until hot and bubbly, up to 15 minutes. Serve as soon as possible, with French bread to sop up the juices.

SCALLOPED OYSTERS

6 to 8 small servings

There are plenty of fellow nonnatives in New York to jog the memories of those of us who have forgotten some of the best regional fare from back home. This Southern favorite got remembered through one of those friend-of-a-friend chance meetings, and we've all been preparing it ever since as a side dish for winter holiday meals. It takes no more than five minutes to assemble, and can be baked at whatever oven tempera-

ture you are using for the rest of the menu. Use more oysters
if you are feeling flush. Freshly shucked oysters are best, naturally, but you can have the fish market shuck them a day ahead
of time; and the canned raw ones from the Chesapeake and
thereabouts are just fine. The canned raw oysters from the
Pacific Northwest that have been turning up in supermarkets
lately are second best—they do not have tasty liquor and
should be drained and rinsed. If using them, increase the cream
or half-and-half.

*24 medium oysters, shucked, liquor reserved, or two 8-ounce tins raw
    oysters*
One row of saltines (4 ounces), coarsely crushed by hand
1/3 cup heavy cream or half-and-half
Freshly ground pepper to taste
Large pinch ground mace (optional)
2 to 3 ounces (4 to 6 tablespoons) cold butter

Pick over the oysters to remove any bits of shell. Lightly butter a 9-
or 10-inch round baking dish and line it with half of the crushed
saltines. Arrange the oysters evenly over the saltines. Combine cream
with enough oyster liquor to make about 3/4 cup. Drizzle evenly over
oysters. Season with pepper and optional mace. Top with remaining
saltines in an even layer. Grate the butter evenly over all (or go
through the tedious process of dotting with butter, if it is not cold
enough to grate). Bake in a moderate or hot oven, whichever you
need for the other dishes on your holiday menu, until heated through
and lightly browned, 20 to 30 minutes.

DEVILED CRAB

Serves 6 to 8 as a first course, 4 as a main course

Another Southern goodie, this is one of those comfort foods
from childhood inextricably linked to summers at the shore,
beachcombers who knew how to find intact sand dollars at first
light, hurricanes, and glorified diners with wonderful drafty air
conditioning. For just plain good eats or for satisfying a nostalgia fit, this one can be made anytime of the year with the

high-quality crabmeat from Florida and other points along the Atlantic coast. It need not be super-deluxe jumbo lump or backfin, but the less expensive smaller grades require a little more time for sorting out bits of shell. Pasteurized crabmeat in the sealed cans that require refrigeration is not as good as fresh, but it will do in a pinch. The two standard approaches to deviled crab use either a white sauce or a mayonnaise binder. The mayo version is best, and it must not be just any mayo, but Hellmann's bottled mayo (called Best Foods in some parts of the country). This is a necessary ingredient, not a shortcut. The unforgivable shortcut is serving this dish in aluminum facsimiles of crab shells rather than the real thing. However, ceramic crab or scallop shells or ramekins, or natural scallop shells are fine.

3/4 cup Hellmann's mayonnaise
2 tablespoons minced onion
2 tablespoons minced green pepper
2 teaspoons minced parsley
1 1/2 teaspoons dry mustard
2 teaspoons Worcestershire sauce
Dash Tabasco
1/4 teaspoon cayenne
2 teaspoons lemon juice
Coarse salt and freshly ground black pepper to taste
1 pound fresh or pasteurized crabmeat, either select or one of the lump grades, carefully picked over to remove all bits of shell
3 to 4 tablespoons butter
1 cup fine fresh bread crumbs
Parsley sprigs
Lemon wedges

Put the mayonnaise in a bowl and whisk in the vegetables and seasonings. Go very easy on the salt and pepper. Cover bowl and put aside for 15 minutes or so for the flavors to marry. Correct seasoning. Gently fold in the crabmeat. Reserve, refrigerated, if you are doing this in advance.

Melt 3 tablespoons butter in a small skillet and add the bread crumbs. Cook over low heat until just golden, adding a little more butter if it seems too dry. Scrape into a bowl and cool.

Preheat oven to 425°F.

Arrange natural or ceramic crab or scallop shells or ramekins on a baking sheet. Divide crab mixture among containers, mounding it a bit in the center so that it looks generous. Sprinkle the crumbs over the crab mixture. Bake on the top rack of the oven until bubbly and lightly browned, 10 to 15 minutes. Serve hot with parsley sprigs and lemon wedges.

BRAISING

See p. 78 for ways to determine proper cooking time.

Braising is practiced far more frequently than most cooks realize. Though classically it is a technique reserved for large whole fish, for our purposes this is the most useful definition: When a whole fish, steaks, fillets, or even occasionally shellfish, browned or not, are placed in a covered pan with some liquid (not enough to cover), and cooked on top of the stove or in the oven until the fish is done, it is braising. Braising seafood is a simpler affair than the care required with meats and poultry; there is less worry about desiccating the beast because the stock was too thin or the heating too rapid. Braises have the advantage of advance preparation for everything but the final heating, and can often be served from the container in which they were cooked.

VARIETIES BEST SUITED

Any fish may be braised, though large fish and large cuts will be the most interesting. The texture and flavor of the fish should suit the other ingredients, or vice versa. Among shellfish, squid and cuttlefish are likely candidates, as in the stuffed squid recipe that follows. Lobster might be braised—cut in half lengthwise—but it is more usually prepared in other ways.

EQUIPMENT

No special equipment is required for braising, though it would be nice to have round or oval brasiers about three inches deep, of various sizes to hold the fish in a single layer. Heatproof gratins, casseroles, baking dishes, roasting pans, skillets, even a fish poacher might do. An electric skillet will work if it is the right shape for what you are preparing. These vessels need not have proper lids of their own; an imperfect seal is often desirable and the dish can always be covered with foil lined with parchment. Flameproof cookware is fastest and best, and often eliminates the need for washing an extra pan. But ovenware is fine too—though it will require extra time to heat up—and often can be brought to the table, eliminating the need to wash a platter.

TECHNIQUE

Whole fish for braising are traditionally topped with sheets or strips of salt pork or bacon, unless a meatless dish is desired. The usual

stock vegetables and herbs (p. 266) are sprinkled around or underneath, and the braising liquid—half wine (red or white) and half fish
stock—is poured in to cover the fish by three-fourths. The liquid is
brought almost to the simmer on top of the stove if the vessel is
flameproof, loosely covered, then braised in a moderately slow oven,
325°F. to 350°F., and basted often until the fish is done. The vessel
is uncovered for the last ten minutes or so in hopes of getting a nice
glaze as fish is basted. Though it is technically incorrect, braises may
also be completed on top of the stove, keeping the liquid at a proper
poaching temperature of 170°F. to 180°F. At this temperature the
surface of the liquid will quiver slightly, so it is called "the shiver."
The cooked fish is removed to a serving platter and the pan juices are
strained and degreased, maybe reduced, and either served as a sauce
or folded into the sauce that has been made separately.

Variations can be worked to accommodate steaks, big chunks of
large fish, fillets, and shellfish. As with meat and poultry, there are
brown braises and white braises, so there will be times that you want to
brown the fish in hot fat before you proceed. Sometimes the braising
liquid, instead of being a wine-and-stock combination that is later used
as a sauce component, *is* a sauce that has been assembled in advance.
The Braised Tuna, Milanese-Style, Stuffed Squid, and Redfish Courtbouillon are in that style. If that sounds like a stew or a fricassée, there is
a relationship, but semantic lines must be drawn somewhere. And
Andrée calls her Mediterranean dish a casserole and, because of the
rice, it *is* a casserole, but the cooking technique for the fish—by our
definition anyway—is braising. Mediterranean flavors leap to mind for
this technique; it just so happens that all of the following recipe choices
include them. But you could just as easily braise a fish, then add to the
strained pan juices dill or mustard or horseradish to your heart's
content. You could also get lovely results with a soy-based Asian-
flavored liquid. The possibilities are international.

One other note is in order. Richard Lord of Fulton Fish
Market Information Services has a new favorite fish cookery technique: He browns the fish in a little fat, then covers the pan and very
gently cooks the fish through. That makes Richard one of the few
people who practice *poêlage,* for poêling is the only accurate name
for what he does. It is mentioned here because it is a sort of braising-
in-its-own-juice that is useful for fish or cuts that are too large to
pan-fry to doneness without burning them. The results are similar
to those achieved when fish is wrapped in foil and cooked in the
oven.

BRAISED SALMON WITH ROSEMARY

4 servings

This technique is based on the pan roasts (not to be confused with those good rich oyster stews of Oyster Bar fame) that were commonplace in Europe and the United States in the days before thermostatically controlled ovens were standard home equipment. Joints, cuts, and whole animals that were not spit roasted before the hearth fire were often pot roasted on the stove or *in* the hearth fire (think of Dutch ovens, which were heaped with coals to provide an even heat source). The flavors here are standard for Northern Italian roasts, and the specific technique is traditional for tender young poultry. With some slight adjustment—in the timing and the precooking of the pan sauce—it is delicious applied to fish as well. Whole trout and other freshwater fish are good candidates, as are fat steaks or chunks of swordfish or tuna. Salmon steaks make good sense because they are tasty and very popular. The preliminary browning and the braising liquid may be completed in advance with nothing more to do at serving time than heat things through. Four salmon steaks fit perfectly into an electric skillet, so if you have one, use it. Blanched broccoli with some pan juices spooned over is a good vegetable choice. Rice or boiled potatoes would complete the course.

4 salmon steaks, 1 to 1 1/4 inches thick
Light olive oil
Freshly ground black pepper to taste
Coarse salt
2 tablespoons butter
4 medium cloves garlic, peeled
4 small sprigs fresh rosemary, or 4 large pinches dried
8 narrow strips of lemon peel ("twists"), 2 inches long, cut with a
    v-knife or a paring knife
4 sprigs thyme, fresh or dried, 1 inch long (optional)
1/2 cup dry white wine
1/2 cup Fish Stock (see recipe)

Bring steaks to room temperature. Pat dry with paper towels. Film lightly but evenly with a little olive oil. Pepper rather generously to taste. Heat a heavy skillet until very hot. Add steaks in a single layer and sear them until nicely browned on each side, turning once. Remove steaks to a platter, salt very lightly on each side, and reserve.

If the skillet seems burned, wipe it out with a paper towel. Let skillet cool a bit so it won't scorch the butter. Add 2 tablespoons olive oil, the butter, then the garlic and rosemary. Cook over medium heat, turning the garlic until it is fragrant and just threatening to color a bit. Add lemon peel, optional thyme, wine, and stock and cover. Lower heat and let mixture simmer for about 10 minutes. Put skillet aside, still covered, and let it cool as long as time permits, up to 1 hour. Uncover and add salmon steaks in a single layer (plus any juices that have accumulated on their platter), basting them with pan juices and placing a garlic clove, rosemary sprig, 2 lemon twists, and a piece of optional thyme on top of each steak. Replace the lid. Put aside to let the flavors marry for 15 minutes or so.

Just before serving, set skillet over medium heat until the liquid reaches a simmer. Lower heat and cook mixture very slowly, basting once or twice, just until steaks are heated through. Remove them to a platter or plates. Reduce pan juices briefly over high heat only if they seem very thin. Spoon over steaks, and serve immediately.

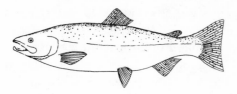

BRAISED TROUT WITH SPINACH AND PINE NUTS

4 servings

This delightful dish is equally good made with baby coho salmon or even whiting. Most of the work can be done in advance. Though this is not essential, it is especially good if you cook a few ounces of chopped pancetta or bacon in the olive oil, decreasing the amount of oil a bit to compensate for the pork fat. Notice that you should be careful to avoid contact between the spinach and the wine (except at the edges) to avoid discoloration.

4 rainbow trout or baby coho salmon
Salt and freshly ground black pepper to taste
Flour for dredging
1/2 cup vegetable oil
1 pound spinach, leaves as large as possible, washed
3 to 4 ounces pancetta or bacon, chopped (optional)
2 to 4 tablespoons olive oil, light or golden extra-virgin or a blend
1/4 cup pine nuts
3 large cloves garlic, minced
1/2 cup white wine
1/2 cup Fish Stock (see recipe)
2 tablespoons butter, at room temperature (optional)

Rinse and dry the fish, scaling them if you feel the need. Trim off pectoral fins. You could bone the fish if you felt you had to, but they will be tastier if left whole. Season lightly all over with salt and pepper. Dust very lightly with flour. Heat vegetable oil in a heavy skillet large enough to hold the fish in a single layer, if possible. Brown fish lightly on each side and remove. Pour out and discard oil but reserve skillet.

Drop spinach into a pot of boiling water and blanch a few seconds, just until wilted. Drain immediately and shock with cold water. Working in a large bowl of cold water so that you can easily spread out the leaves, select enough large ones to wrap the fish. Remove tough stems and drain leaves on paper towels. Reserve remaining spinach for another use. (It could be chopped and stuffed into the cavities of the fish, for instance.) Wrap each fish neatly with spinach leaves, leaving the tails and part of the heads exposed so they do not look like mummies. Set aside.

Reheat the reserved skillet with the optional pancetta or bacon and 2 tablespoons olive oil, and cook until fat is rendered but pork is not browned. If pancetta or bacon is omitted, use 4 tablespoons olive oil. Add pine nuts and cook until golden. Add garlic and heat briefly. Pour out mixture and reserve. Deglaze skillet with the white wine and stock and reduce by one-third. Pour into a shallow casserole or gratin dish, preferably flameproof, that is just large enough to hold the fish in a single layer.

Arrange the fish in the casserole and pour the pine nut mixture evenly over them. Cover with a lid or foil lined with parchment. Bring to a simmer on top of the stove—if container is flameproof—and cook fish gently until just done, 10 to 15 minutes, either on top of the stove or in a preheated 350°F. oven. Allow an extra 15 minutes of oven time for a nonflameproof dish that has not been preheated on top of the stove. When done, remove fish to a platter or plates, and strain pan juices into a saucepan, spooning any solids back over the fish. Bring pan juices to a boil. Reduce slightly if they seem very thin. Swirl in optional butter until melted and creamy, spoon sauce around fish, and serve immediately.

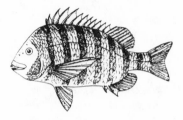

REDFISH COURTBOUILLON

4 to 6 servings as a main course, 8 servings as a first course

A legendary fish dish from New Orleans, Redfish Courtbouillon has been very popular with my students. It is a fine example of French tradition reworked for New World ingredients and tastes. Without being either a soup or what you could properly call a stew, it bears some small resemblance to *bouillabaisse* and partakes of the "Creole holy trinity"—onions, celery, and green peppers—plus the usual tomatoes and aromatics that are typical of Louisiana cookery. The results are both hearty and elegant, and representative of this food tradition influenced by Mediterranean classics and defined by skilled black cooks who brought to it their own African and Caribbean heritage. It is easily reproduced here in the Northeast, except that red drum—which used to be so plentiful and inexpensive in the Gulf states—is now very difficult to find anywhere. Substitute any white-fleshed, mild-flavored fish that you like, including red snapper, black sea bass, seatrout, grouper, large porgies, or sheepshead. I like seatrout best. If you wish to buy fillets, you will need to bring some bones home from the market or use fish stock in place of water and decrease the lemon juice to one tablespoon. The sauce can be prepared a day or two in advance and refrigerated.

4 to 5 pounds whole redfish or other fish, 1 or 2 fish
4 to 8 uniformly thin center slices of lemon, seeds removed
1 quart water
1/2 cup light olive or corn oil
2 ounces (1/2 stick) butter
1/2 cup flour
2 cups chopped onions
1 cup thinly sliced scallions, white and green parts
1 1/2 cups diced green peppers
3/4 cup chopped celery
1 tablespoon minced garlic
2 teaspoons coarse salt, or to taste
1/2 teaspoon freshly ground black pepper
1/2 teaspoon freshly ground white pepper
1/2 teaspoon cayenne
2 bay leaves
1/2 teaspoon dried leaf thyme
1/4 teaspoon ground allspice
One 28-ounce can imported tomatoes, crushed by hand
2 tablespoons minced parsley
1 cup dry red wine
2 tablespoons lemon juice
4 to 6 cups freshly cooked Plain White Rice (Basic Western or Boiled)
     (see recipes)

Fillet fish, skin the fillets, and remove pinbones. Rinse and pat dry. Cut fillets into 4 to 8 portions of equal weight (1 large fish will yield either 4, 6, or 8 portions; 2 fish can yield 4 or 8 portions). Fold tail portions skin side in so that they are of uniform dimension and thickness. Top each with a lemon slice, cover, and refrigerate.

Remove and discard gills from fish head(s) and rinse bones well to remove all blood. Place skeleton(s) in a pot with the water and bring to a boil. Lower heat and simmer gently, skimming from time to time, for 30 minutes while you prepare the remaining ingredients. Strain and reserve broth, discarding bones.

In a heavy nonreactive flameproof casserole or other vessel just wide enough to hold the fish in a single layer, heat the oil and butter and whisk in the flour. Cook the roux over a fairly high flame until it turns medium brown, stirring constantly and lowering the heat once roux begins to color. Add onions, scallions, peppers, and celery, and cook, stirring often, until vegetables are thoroughly wilted, about 10 minutes. Stir in garlic and seasonings and heat briefly. Add tomatoes, parsley, wine, lemon juice, and about 3 cups of the reserved broth. Bring mixture to a boil, then reduce heat and simmer 30 to 45 minutes, partially covered, until vegetables are tender and flavors are well married. Sauce should be fairly thick but not pasty. Uncover and reduce if it seems thin or add a little more broth if it is too thick. Correct seasoning. Set aside, covered.

Just before serving, bring sauce to a simmer and add the lemon-topped fish pieces in a single layer. Depending on the dimensions of your vessel, the sauce may cover the fish or not. No matter. Cover and cook gently just below a simmer, until fish is heated through, probably less than 10 minutes. Serve immediately with white rice.

STUFFED SQUID BRAISED IN TOMATO SAUCE, SPANISH-STYLE

10 to 12 tapas portions

Here is a delicious *tapa* from Felipe Rojas-Lombardi at The Ballroom. It keeps well for as long as a week in the refrigerator and is actually best when prepared a day ahead and reheated at serving time. That way the acidity of the tomatoes and wine in the sauce will gradually tenderize the squid without the need to cook it until it is characterless and the filling overcooked.

THE SAUCE

> *3 tablespoons light olive oil*
> *1 medium onion, peeled and finely chopped*
> *1 tablespoon minced garlic*
> *2 ounces* chorizo *(Spanish sausage), skinned and finely diced*
> *1/2 cup finely chopped carrot*
> *1/2 cup finely chopped celery*
> *1 1/2 tablespoons fresh thyme leaves, or 1 teaspoon dried*
> *1/2 teaspoon cayenne*
> *Two 35-ounce cans (8 cups) imported canned plum tomatoes with some*
> *of their juice, crushed by hand*
> *1 tablespoon coarse salt*
> *2 cups white wine*

THE SQUID AND STUFFING

> 2 1/2 pounds medium squid (or 2 pounds cleaned): at least 12 pieces
> in good condition
> 1/2 pound fresh pork, finely ground
> 3 tablespoons raisins soaked in 1/4 cup dry sherry
> 1 large clove garlic, peeled and minced
> 2 teaspoons coarse salt
> 1/4 cup green peas (defrosted frozen peas are usually best)
> 1/2 teaspoon ground mace
> 2/3 cup fresh bread crumbs
> 1/3 cup pine nuts, toasted
> 1 egg
>
> Vegetable oil for frying
> 1/2 cup flour
> 1 quart water, Fish Stock (see recipe), or chicken stock
> 1 cup chopped flat-leaf parsley

To prepare the sauce: In a large skillet, heat the olive oil and add the onion. Sauté a few minutes until wilted. Add garlic and sauté briefly. Add *chorizo* and cook an additional 5 minutes, stirring occasionally. Add carrot, celery, and thyme, and cook another 5 minutes, stirring occasionally. Add cayenne, tomatoes, coarse salt, and white wine. Bring to a boil, stirring frequently, reduce heat, and simmer, uncovered, for about 30 minutes, stirring now and then. Set aside.

Meanwhile, clean the squid as described on p. 65 if they are whole. After you have sliced off the tentacles and popped out the beak, chop tentacles rather finely—you should have about 1 cup—and place them in a large bowl. Make sure squid bodies are very clean, inside and out, and free of any holes. Leave them whole. Set aside. Add the stuffing ingredients to the bowl with the chopped tentacles and mix thoroughly.

Fit a large pastry bag with a plain tip with an opening about 1/2 inch in diameter or a little more: number 7 or 8. Fill the bag with the stuffing mixture and pipe it into the squid bodies so that they are about two-thirds full. (If you have no pastry bag you may spoon the mixture into the squid bodies, but it is messy and slow.) Leave about 1/2 inch of the open end unfilled. Secure the openings with toothpicks. Set aside.

Heat vegetable oil for shallow frying or deep-frying in a deep skillet, large saucepan, or wok to 375°F. Dredge squid lightly in flour, shaking off excess. Fry squid until lightly golden, 3 to 5 minutes. Drain and reserve.

Add half the liquid (water or stock) to the reserved sauce and bring sauce to a boil. Add browned squid to the sauce, and simmer 20 to 30 minutes, partially covered, stirring carefully from time to time to prevent sticking, and adding more liquid, up to the full quart if sauce seems too thick. Remove from heat and gently stir in the parsley. Correct seasoning. Rest briefly, then reheat and serve, or cool, refrigerate, and reheat at serving time.

MEDITERRANEAN FISHERMAN'S CASSEROLE

4 to 6 servings

Andrée's Mediterranean Cuisine (now reopened as Café Crocodile) is the source of this hearty and delightful braise. It reflects Andrée's own sunny sensibilities, which are keen on the Middle-Eastern style of her native Egypt but sensitive to the cooking of the other countries that border the Mediterranean. This can be prepared largely in advance. Cod is a good choice these days, now that striped bass is off-limits in the New York area, but you might consider seatrout, mako, grouper, or steaks cut from a fairly large red snapper. Something more flavorful such as king mackerel is also a good choice.

4 to 6 fish steaks at least 1 inch thick, about 2 pounds
Flour for dredging
Olive oil
2 onions, sliced
1/4 cup pine nuts
1 teaspoon ground cumin
1/4 teaspoon powdered saffron, or an equivalent amount of crumbled
    thread saffron, about two-thirds of a .2-gram vial
2 or 3 cloves garlic, minced
Coarse salt and freshly ground white pepper to taste
1/2 cup white wine
2 tablespoons vegetable oil or light olive oil
2 cups long-grain white rice
1/2 cup lemon juice
3 cups Fish Stock (see recipe)
Lemon wedges
Parsley sprigs

Dredge fish very lightly in flour, shaking off excess. Heat 3 table-spoons olive oil in a heavy skillet until very hot and lightly brown the fish, no more than 2 or 3 minutes per side. Set fish aside on a platter. Add onions to skillet and sauté gently until golden, adding a little more oil if necessary. Add pine nuts, cumin, and half of the saffron, and continue to cook. When pine nuts threaten to color, add garlic and cook briefly until fragrant; stir in a little salt and pepper to taste. Pour mixture over the fish. Deglaze pan with the wine and reserve the liquid.

Heat the vegetable oil or olive oil in a heavy medium-size nonreactive pot and stir in the rice. Cook and stir until rice grains whiten. Rice should not brown but no harm will be done if it starts to color just a bit. Add the reserved wine, lemon juice, 2 cups of fish stock, remaining saffron, and a little salt and pepper, being careful to protect yourself from any spatters when the first liquid goes in. Bring to a simmer, cover, reduce flame to low, and let simmer for 10 minutes. Remove from heat and let rest—do not lift lid!—for another 10 minutes, or until about 30 minutes before serving time.

Preheat oven to 350°F.

Place cooked rice in the bottom of a baking dish large enough to hold the fish steaks in a single layer. If pan is slightly too large, mound rice so it is a little thicker around the border of the dish. Arrange fish and onion mixture evenly over the rice and pour the remaining cup of fish stock over all. Seal dish with a lid or foil lined with parchment, and bake for 20 minutes. Uncover, and return to oven for 10 more minutes. Garnish with lemon wedges and parsley sprigs and serve immediately.

BRAISED TUNA, MILANESE-STYLE

6 servings

Here is an idea based on the balance of flavors in a traditional Milanese ossobuco. Though intended for veal shanks, the flavors are also delicious with a meaty fish. Swordfish and sturgeon are other fine choices. This is a variation on Italian tuna braises, many of which feature capers, which do not seem right with this particular dish. Here is also an excuse to indulge a passion for Risotto alla Milanese (recipe follows), presenting it with the main course and getting away with it.

Six 6- to 8-ounce squarish chunks of tuna (2 1/2 to 3 1/4 pounds tuna loin)

THE MARINADE

1 cup dry white wine
1 teaspoon minced garlic
1 tablespoon extra-virgin olive oil
1 bay leaf
3/8 teaspoon dried leaf thyme
1 teaspoon freshly ground black pepper
2 teaspoons coarse salt

THE SAUCE MIXTURE

1 1/2 cups finely chopped onions
1/2 cup finely diced carrots
1/2 cup finely diced celery
2 cups canned imported tomatoes with their juice, coarsely crushed or chopped
1 cup Fish Stock (see recipe) or white veal or chicken stock
1/4 cup chopped fresh basil (optional)

THE GREMOLATA (OR GREMOLADA)

1 teaspoon finely minced garlic
2 teaspoons grated or finely minced lemon zest or a combination of lemon and orange zest
2 tablespoons finely chopped parsley

1/2 cup light olive or vegetable oil
Flour for dredging
2 ounces (1/2 stick) butter

Risotto alla Milanese *(recipe follows)*

Trim tuna of skin and most of the blackish flesh. Cut into 6 uniform chunks, as thick as possible. Combine the marinade ingredients in a nonreactive bowl, and add the tuna. Let marinate, turning and basting occasionally, for 4 to 6 hours in the refrigerator or 1 or 2 hours at room temperature.

While the tuna is marinating, prepare the sauce mixture: In one bowl combine the onions, carrots, and celery; in another combine the tomatoes, stock, and optional basil. Set aside. Combine the *gremolata* ingredients and set aside.

Remove tuna from marinade, reserving marinade, and dry it well with paper towels. Heat ½ cup light olive or vegetable oil in a heavy nonreactive skillet or flameproof casserole large enough to hold the tuna in a single layer. Dredge dried tuna pieces lightly in flour, shaking off the excess. Brown them lightly on all sides in the hot oil. Remove to a platter and blot off the cooking oil with paper towels. When cool, refrigerate.

Pour out and discard the cooking oil, and wipe the skillet out with paper towels only if it seems burned. Melt the butter, add the onion mixture, and sauté over low heat until tender, up to 10 minutes. Add half the *gremolata* and cook briefly. Add the tomato mixture and the reserved marinade. Bring to a boil, lower heat, and simmer mixture very gently, covered, for about 1 hour, stirring occasionally. Correct seasoning.

Add tuna pieces to the sauce in a single layer and baste. Remove from heat, cover, and put aside to rest for a while, 30 minutes to 1 hour. Just before serving time, return to low heat or preheat oven to 350°F., and heat through, basting several times. Sprinkle on the remaining *gremolata* for the last 5 minutes of cooking. Remove tuna to a serving platter or individual plates. Sauce should be thick but not pasty. If necessary, reduce sauce over high heat or thin with stock or water. Correct seasoning, pour sauce over the tuna, and serve right away with Risotto alla Milanese.

RISOTTO ALLA MILANESE

6 servings

You might use fish stock just for this one partnering, but white veal or chicken stock is more successful. The stock should be fairly light, like a soup stock. Thin with water if it is too robust. The traditional cheese is retained, even though cheese is almost never used with seafood dishes in Italy.

3 tablespoons butter
3 tablespoons light olive oil
1 cup finely chopped onions

2 cups Arborio or other short-grain rice
1/2 cup dry white wine
About 5 1/2 cups hot white veal or chicken stock
*1/4 teaspoon powdered saffron, or an equivalent amount of crumbled
    thread saffron (about two-thirds of a .2-gram vial), mixed with
    1/2 cup white veal or chicken stock*
Coarse salt and freshly ground pepper to taste
*1 1/2 cups freshly grated Parmesan (*parmigiano reggiano*) (op-
    tional)*

In a heavy medium-large saucepan, heat the butter and oil. Add the
onions and sauté gently until translucent. Add rice and sauté, stirring,
for a few minutes, or until rice starts to whiten. Do not brown. Add
wine and stir over medium heat until liquid is absorbed. Proceed to
add a little of the hot stock, about 1/4 cup at a time, stirring constantly,
then adding more stock only after the previous addition is absorbed.
When about half the stock has been used, add the saffron-infused stock
in two additions. Season lightly.

Continue cooking and stirring and adding stock until rice is
done. The outside of the rice grains will be tender and creamy but the
center must retain a decided firmness, even a slight crunch. Correct
seasoning. Stir in about 1/2 cup Parmesan. Serve immediately, passing
the remaining cheese in a bowl.

BROILING AND GRILLING

See p. 78 for ways to determine proper cooking time.

123

Grilling is enjoying a healthy vogue, and broiled seafood is a steady favorite. We will follow current American usage and define *broiling* as the placing of food under a flame or electric element, and *grilling* as the positioning of the food over an element or charcoal or stone or ceramic coals. *Barbecue* is a nebulous term that, in the case of seafood, is normally only applied to grilled, marinated shrimp. But the term *barbecue* is useful to identify the outdoor barbecue grill. Included here is so-called *pan broiling* or *pan grilling,* because the results are similar to grilling and nothing like a sauté.

VARIETIES BEST SUITED

Among the most likely candidates for broiling and grilling are oily fish, fish with a sturdy, steaklike texture, and crustaceans (shrimp, lobster, et cetera). Oily fish do especially well because they are self-basting and will form a fine natural crust; they often have a rich flavor that will be complemented, rather than overwhelmed, by the assertiveness of a lightly charred finish. Steaks and meaty textures handle well for the same obvious reasons that meat steaks are the preferred cuts for broiling and grilling. Bivalves (clams, oysters, mussels, scallops) are sometimes broiled, but rarely grilled unless they are skewered. Small fillets of flatfish are the worst grilling choices, but even they can be successfully broiled.

EQUIPMENT

The broiling elements in home ovens vary in their ability to produce the intense heat necessary for successful broiling. Electric ovens generally do best, while gas is better suited to poultry and other items that need relatively long cooking times. Most gas ovens are not great for fillets or steaks, but will do an acceptable job of broiling whole fish, oysters, clams, or mussels in half-shell preparations, even lobsters and large shrimp. Electric toaster ovens that are designed for broiling are fine if they are powerful enough to broil quickly.

There are two types of professional gas broilers, large and small, both of which are called *salamanders* (not to be confused with the amphibian or the iron disks for glazing desserts). The large ones perform a variety of restaurant tasks and produce such intense heat—from the flame above and from retained heat in the adjustable grill below—that they almost simulate grilling. The smaller ones, which are often installed in well-designed (for the well-heeled) home kitchens, are really meant for top browning, and are tedious to clean after use in "almost grilling" where food is placed directly on the grill, but they work very well. These small salamanders are best suited to broiling foods on a pan, and to finishing or glazing a dish that has been assembled and then warmed by some other means.

Pans used for broiling in home ovens can be of a variety of materials and need only be heavy enough to resist warping and be of an appropriate size to hold the food in a single layer. The slotted broiler pans that are standard equipment with most stoves are generally not appropriate for broiling seafood because they drain away liquids that are essential for the juiciness and flavor of the dish. The most successful broiling pans are the professional oval "sizzle pans," or "sizzle plates" of heavy aluminum that come in several sizes from about ten inches to twelve inches. These should be easy enough to find in a good cookware shop because of their vogue some years ago as serving plates, complete with wooden liners, for steaks. Forget the liners. The only limitation for sizzle pans is that even the largest ones will accommodate, at most, about two servings.

Pan broiling requires a heavy skillet, and American cast iron is the only excellent material. A useful hybrid appliance is the cast-iron grill pan. It consists of raised parallel ridges added to the design of a traditional round skillet or squared-off griddle. The only drawback is that it can produce copious smoke even if only a light layer of fat clings to the fish, so adequate ventilation is essential.

Outdoor barbecue grills come in a wide range of sizes, shapes, designs, and prices. Whether fired by charcoal or gas, all can work well, provided they are used properly. Indoor grills are wonderful luxuries that only require good ventilation to make them very useful appliances. The countertop electric grills, which have the advantage of being essentially smokeless, do not generally get hot enough to brown seafood nicely, and are best for poultry and larger cuts of meat.

Many cooks feel safest when seafood to be grilled is enclosed in a hinged, handled wire cage, either in the shape of a whole fish or a rectangular shape for multiple fish, steaks, or fillets. Cages are recommended for small and fragile items. Buy sturdy ones.

TECHNIQUE

Fish to be broiled or grilled may be whole, pan-dressed, steaked, filleted, or cubed and skewered. Whole and pan-dressed roundfish will do best if they are slashed in the thickest part to help equalize the cooking time of the flesh. Small and fragile fish—mackerel, sardines, herring—are best left untreated. Whole fish for broiling or grilling should be between 1 and 2½ inches thick at the widest part behind the head; 2 inches is ideal. Cookbooks often speak of broiling at a distance of 4 or 5 inches from the element, but experience proves that most equipment designed for home use is simply not that powerful and requires a closer proximity. Skewered cubes of fish should be about 1½ inches square (if thin, folded and threaded so that the completed skewer is 1½ inches square) and are turned three times: a half turn, a quarter turn, then a half turn.

Fillets should be about 1 inch thick, steaks slightly thicker, and as uniform as possible. The exception here is the case of fish that are often cooked rare—tuna, swordfish, even salmon—where an oversize piece might be exactly what you want, as in the Grilled Marinated Filet Mignon of Tuna. Very lean fish should receive a dusting of flour or fine crumbs to help the appearance and the surface sear. There is no other way to achieve an attractive, crisp finish. A dusting of paprika is purely cosmetic and not very, at that. And it burns.

Broiled fillets are usually cooked skin side down and are not turned. Grilled fish and broiled steaks are turned once. For a professional look when grilling, you may easily achieve *quadrillage* (cross-hatched grill marks) by gently picking up the steak when it is half done on the first side and rotating it about 90 degrees so that it will be marked by crossing lines. It is not necessary to crossmark the second side, which will be against the plate when it is served.

In broiling and grilling, the most important preparatory step is to preheat the appliance to very hot. An underheated grill all but guarantees that food will stick, tear, and break. Once heated, the grill should be rubbed with a little oil. When broiling in a home oven, gas or electric, be sure to put the door ajar for several minutes before you start (after a preheating time of at least fifteen minutes) and leave it that way for the duration. This way you create just enough draft on the thermostat to trick it into signaling a steady heat source. A trick for achieving handsome results in a less than perfect home oven or with fillets that are too thin is to remove fish from the broiler when it is perhaps half done, let it cool for five minutes or so, and then return it to the heat, repeating the cooldown if necessary, until the fillets are just done with a fine, golden finish.

A light layer of fat is usual before fish is broiled or grilled.

Skipping this ingredient results in tired-looking and slightly dry results without an appreciable saving of calories. Keep in mind that most of the oil or butter melts away as its protective work is done. Many restaurant chefs refuse actually to broil dry because of the inferior results, preferring instead to blot the fish after cooking to remove the surface fat. Grilling totally naked fish is definitely not recommended, but the amount of fat should always be just adequate to coat the fish with a light film, to avoid flareups.

Pan broiling, either in a skillet or grill pan, resembles grilling in that intense heat is required and the pan is dry while the fish is lightly filmed with fat. Carried to the extreme, there is Paul Prudhomme's blackened fish, which bears little resemblance to other skillet work. As with all grilling, it is essential that the fish be dried of all surface moisture before it is lightly filmed with fat.

The basic technique for broiled fish fillets served plain or with a sauce prepared separately is standard restaurant procedure and perfect for fast meals at home: Take the pan and splash in a little white wine, enough to just film the pan. Dust the flesh side of fillets very lightly with flour if they are very lean, add them to the pan skin side down (even if they are skinned), and shape them to uniform thickness. Brush on a light layer of melted butter or oil of choice and season lightly with salt and freshly ground white pepper. Broil until done, blot, and serve immediately. The pan juices may be spooned over the fish or added to a sauce.

The choice between broiling and grilling is often determined by the available equipment or the weather, but there is the following consideration in favor of grilling when either technique is an option: Only grilling will produce a rich "barbecue" flavor, and it has the advantage of allowing for the wonderful smoke flavors imparted by dried wood chips, herbs, roots, bark, or twigs. If you decide to use one of these (no pine or other resinous wood), be sure to soak it in warm water (and drain, of course) to promote smoking. Scatter the damp vegetation over the coals just the moment before you begin grilling so that no flavor is lost. Repeat applications if you feel the need.

Oversize fish should be grilled or broiled only until they are nicely browned, then heated through in a slow to moderate oven. This is a useful technique for any grilled or broiled seafood item when you want to get most of the work done in advance.

GRILLED MARINATED FILLET MIGNON OF TUNA

2 servings

Here is a signature dish at Union Square Café. It is a wonderfully conceived notion in that fresh tuna has a dense, steaklike texture that is best enjoyed raw or extremely rare, as devotees of Japanese food know; in this preparation Japanese flavors and Western rare-steak tradition meet beautifully. The near cubes of "fillet mignon" are nicely charred like a fine steak with a center similar to warm sashimi. Be sure to buy the finest tuna of rich, clear red color that you can find. Yellowfin (for which bigeye is often substituted with negligible quality difference) is the usual quality tuna on the market in the Northeast. Do try bluefin in the event that your fishmonger has been able to get some away from the Tokyo tuna brokers who buy the bulk of the global catch for export to a discerning Japanese clientele who will pay astronomical prices for the very best. In order for this preparation to work properly you must use very thick steaks cut from a *loin* of tuna rather than a crosscut. If this loin is from the center of a large fish, divide it in half lengthwise so that you can keep the thickness you need in a steak of about eight ounces. Union Square Café recommends serving the steaks with grilled vegetables—zucchini or baby eggplant rubbed with a little oil—and the optional wasabi sauce was added for zip. Be certain to caution your guests about its heat. If you feel the marinade is too salty you may reduce the soy sauce or use sodium-reduced "lite" soy. Use less soy sauce the longer you intend to marinate. In the absence of a grill, pan grilling will do nicely but broiling will not.

Two 8-ounce yellowfin tuna steaks, 2 to 2 1/2 inches thick
1 cup light soy sauce
3 tablespoons lemon juice or rice vinegar
1/4 cup dry sherry
2 tablespoons finely chopped fresh gingerroot
1 large clove garlic, finely chopped
1/4 cup thinly sliced white of scallion
Dash cayenne
2 tablespoons freshly ground black pepper
1 teaspoon sugar
2 tablespoons soy or peanut oil

GARNISHES

> *Pickled ginger*
> *2 or 3 scallion greens, thinly sliced on the diagonal*
> *Wasabi, mixed with cold water to form a paste and thinned to the*
> *texture of heavy cream (optional)*

Place tuna steaks in a nonreactive bowl with soy sauce, lemon juice or vinegar, sherry, ginger, garlic, scallion, cayenne, pepper, and sugar, and marinate, turning occasionally, for 5 to 8 hours. Tuna should be refrigerated for the marinating period, but it must be brought to room temperature before grilling; allow at least 1 hour.

Just before serving time, preheat grill to very hot. Remove tuna from marinade and blot dry. Film with the oil. Grill for 1 or 2 minutes on each side, including the edges, until nicely seared all over. Serve immediately with a bit of the marinade spooned over and the garnishes you have chosen. You may simply strew a few slices of pickled ginger over the steaks or roll it into rosettes. A sprinkling of scallion green on top of the steaks is a good idea. Pass optional wasabi sauce separately.

GRILLED RED SNAPPER MARGARITA

4 to 6 servings

This was inspired by the rather new interest in the New York area in fine dishes from the Southern states of Mexico, where simply prepared seafood touched with sparkling tropical flavors is important fare. Dishes of this sort are not limited to Mexican restaurants, however. Melissa Lord is turning out a similar one at John Clancy's. Using a few mesquite, hickory, or fruitwood chips is an excellent idea. A 1-pound fish per person is ideal, but you may also use fish of any manageable size and share from a platter. Remember to finish large fish in the oven, p. 127. Black sea bass, grouper, and seatrout are other good choices. Add some black beans and rice and you are all set. If the name seems a little silly, the marinade *is* almost a margarita cocktail.

4 to 6 pounds whole red snapper or other fish, divided into 1 to 6 pieces

THE MARINADE

3 ounces white or gold tequila
4 ounces triple sec
3/4 cup lime juice
2 teaspoons coarse salt
2 large cloves garlic
1/4 cup corn oil

THE *SALSA CRUDA*

2 pounds ripe tomatoes, diced
1 medium to large white onion, chopped
Minced chiles to taste (a combination of sweet and hot is best)
3 tablespoons chopped fresh coriander
Salt to taste
Pinch sugar, as needed

Corn oil
Freshly ground black pepper to taste
Coriander sprigs for garnish

Scale, gut, remove gills and pectoral fins, and rinse the fish well. Use a very sharp knife to slash the fish crosswise at 2-inch intervals, cutting toward the head with the knife held at a 45-degree angle, just to the bone. Repeat on the other side. Place fish in a nonreactive dish just large enough to hold it in a single layer, if possible. Combine marinade ingredients and pour over fish, rubbing it all over, inside and out. Leave to marinate for at least 1 hour, preferably 3 hours, turning and basting occasionally. Refrigerate if fish will stand for more than 1 hour, but bring to room temperature before grilling.

At least 1 hour before serving time, combine the tomatoes, onion, chiles, chopped coriander, salt, and sugar. After the flavors have had time to marry, you will want to correct the seasonings. This *salsa cruda* will keep for 1 or 2 days refrigerated. Bring it to room temperature before serving.

Heat grill to very hot. Remove fish from marinade, pat dry, film with a little corn oil, and pepper lightly. Grill until just heated through and nicely colored. Meanwhile, heat marinade in a saucepan and let it boil vigorously while you swirl it over high heat for about

2 minutes. When fish is done, remove it to serving platter or plates, and strain a little of the hot marinade over it to moisten. Spoon *salsa* around, garnish with coriander sprigs, and serve immediately.

LESLIE REVSIN'S BROILED MACKEREL WITH MINT AND VINEGAR

4 to 6 first course servings

> The peripatetic Ms. Revsin has cooked at some of New York's most interesting restaurants, including Café Leslie, 24 Fifth Avenue, Bridge Café, Metropolis, and Argenteuil. The appetizer below is a delicious example of her fresh, clean approach to food.

> *Four 6-ounce fillets of very fresh Atlantic mackerel, about 3/4 inch thick*
> *3 tablespoons light olive oil*
> *Coarse salt and freshly ground black pepper to taste*
>
> *2 tablespoons red wine vinegar*
> *Scant 1/4 cup extra-virgin olive oil for dressing*
> *1/2 cup thinly sliced onion*
> *12 lemon slices, 1/16 inch thick*
> *Generous tablespoon coarsely chopped fresh mint leaves*
> *Boston lettuce leaves, washed and dried*

Preheat broiler to very hot. Place the mackerel fillets on a sheet pan with low sides and dribble on the 3 tablespoons olive oil. Lightly rub an even coat of oil onto the fish and be sure that the pan is oiled as well. Lightly season fish all over with salt and pepper. Place fillets skin side up.

Broil fish close to the source of heat just until barely heated through. The skin should begin to char and blister—a flavor bonus—and the flesh should be barely opaque, but still glistening and juicy. This mackerel is a likely candidate for the repeated partial broilings described on p. 126. Carefully transfer the fillets to a nonreactive platter. Pour any pan juices over the fish.

To make the dressing, pour the vinegar into a nonreactive

bowl and slowly whisk in the olive oil to create an emulsion. Season to taste with salt and pepper. Set aside.

While the fish is still warm, scatter the onion and lemon slices over it and pour on the dressing. Sprinkle on the mint. Incline the platter slightly and use a large spoon to baste the fish several times. Cover with plastic wrap and set in a cool place (refrigerate in hot weather) for about 2 hours. Baste several more times during this mellowing period.

Arrange attractive lettuce leaves on 4 to 6 individual plates. Break—*do not cut!*—the fish fillets into 2-inch sections. They will break into natural, jagged shapes, each different from the other. Place these pieces next to and on top of one another to create mounds of interesting angles. Take half of the marinated onion and scatter it over the portions. Also place 2 to 3 marinated lemon slices on each plate. Divide the juices over the fish. Serve at room temperature.

GRILLED SWORDFISH WITH ORANGE, OLIVE, AND ROAST CUMIN

4 servings

Orange, olives, roasted cumin seed—these are among the Mediterranean flavors in this slick presentation from Andrew Ziobro. It is from his time as executive chef at the Upper West Side grand café Metropolis (R.I.P.). Though the combination may seem rather exotic, the result is suavely balanced.

THE GARNISH

> *12 calamata olives*
> *2 to 3 large California navel oranges*

THE SAUCE

> *1 1/2 teaspoons whole cumin seed*
> *1/2 cup chopped shallots*
> *3 ounces white wine*
> *3 ounces orange juice (from above)*
> *4 ounces (1/2 cup) red wine vinegar*
> *1/2 pound butter, cool but not cold, cut into pieces*

*

Four 8-ounce swordfish steaks, 1 to 1 1/4 inches thick
Olive oil
Coarse salt and freshly ground pepper to taste

Cut in half and pit the olives. Slice the oranges into *suprême* by slicing
off the ends, then peeling neatly to remove all of the skin, including
the white pith, and making vertical cuts to remove 20 neat, mem-
brane-free segments. Reserve these for the garnish, and squeeze the
carcasses for juice for the sauce. Discard peels and set juice aside.

Toss the cumin seed in a small skillet over medium heat until
fragrant and toasty—2 or 3 minutes—then remove from heat, wrap
in the corner of a towel, and crack with a meat pounder or mallet or
the bottom of a saucepan. Set aside.

In a smallish heavy nonreactive saucepan, combine shallots,
wine, orange juice, and wine vinegar. Simmer mixture over medium
heat until reduced to just a few tablespoons of liquid. Remove from
heat and whisk in the butter, a piece at a time, until it is emulsified
into a creamy butter sauce. Warm the pan as needed to keep the butter
melting, but do not overheat. Strain the sauce into a small warmed
bowl and whisk in half of the toasted cumin seed. Hold sauce in a
warm place or over very warm water. Reserved orange segments
should also be *very* gently warmed in a saucepan or double boiler.

Preheat grill to very hot. Film swordfish steaks with olive oil
and season them with salt and pepper to taste. Grill until medium rare,
turning once. Remove steaks to warmed dinner plates and pour equal
amounts of the sauce over each steak. Garnish each plate with 5
warmed orange segments and 6 olive halves. Sprinkle remaining
cumin seed over all, and serve immediately.

BROILED TILEFISH STEAKS PAVED WITH
TOMATOES AND ONIONS

1 serving

Here is a fine, fast, summery dish to throw together when
really good tomatoes are available. It is best done for one or
two, unless your broiler is large enough to accommodate two
sizzle pans, in which case it is perfectly easily prepared for four.
Any fresh fish steak will be fine, particularly cod, pollock, mahi

mahi, or king mackerel. Tilefish was chosen because it is bland on its own and responds well to Mediterranean flavors.

Light olive oil, or a mixture of oil and melted butter, as needed
2 tablespoons dry white wine
1 tilefish steak, about 1 inch thick
½ teaspoon mashed garlic
½ teaspoon chopped fresh herbs: basil, thyme, oregano, marjoram, or
    parsley, or a combination
Coarse salt and freshly ground pepper to taste
7 thin slices ripe plum tomato
6 thin half slices medium onion

With a pastry brush, film a sizzle pan with oil. Add the white wine and swirl it around. Place the steak in the pan and film it lightly with oil. Pat garlic into the surface of the steak. Sprinkle on herb(s) of choice. Season lightly with salt and pepper. Cover steak with a horseshoe of overlapping alternate slices of tomato and onion, beginning and ending with tomato. Brush on a film of oil. Season lightly with salt and pepper. Put aside to come to room temperature.

Preheat broiler to very hot.

Broil steak about 4 inches from heating element until done. Serve on a warmed dinner plate with the pan juices spooned over. This will also be tasty served at room temperature.

BROILED FILLET OF SALMON WITH WHOLE-GRAIN MUSTARD BREADING

1 serving

This simple and appealing preparation is from Jack Freedman, former chef at the New York Restaurant School restaurant. Nearly any fish could be prepared this way, but salmon is particularly good with mustard and is wildly popular as well. The mustard breading will keep for a long time in a covered container.

2 tablespoons vegetable oil
6 to 8 ounces fillet of salmon or other fish, skin on

2 tablespoons lemon juice
1 tablespoon whole-grain mustard
2 tablespoons Whole-Grain Mustard Breading (recipe follows)

Preheat the broiler.

Use a few drops of the oil to film lightly a sizzle pan or other broilerproof vessel. Place the salmon in it, pour the lemon juice over, and rub in evenly. Brush mustard over salmon. Sprinkle the mustard breading evenly over the salmon. Drizzle remaining oil over the breading and pat it in evenly. Broil about 4 inches from the heating element until done. Transfer fish to a plate, and serve immediately.

WHOLE-GRAIN MUSTARD BREADING

Makes enough for 8 servings

1/2 cup mustard seeds
1/2 cup fine dry bread crumbs
1 teaspoon coarse salt
1/2 teaspoon freshly ground white pepper

Put mustard seeds in the corner of a kitchen towel and crack them with a mallet or the bottom of a saucepan. You may also crack seeds in a blender or processor, but a processor will only do a good job if the mustard seeds are first toasted in a moderate oven and then cooled. Combine with crumbs, salt, and pepper, and blend well.

ALAMBRES DE CORVINA ROSA MEXICANO

4 to 6 servings

Corvina is a Pacific fish highly prized in Central and South America for its fine texture and flavor. Here in the Northeast we are lucky to have a plentiful and relatively inexpensive substitute, a close relation in the drum family, weakfish or seatrout. Josefina Howard makes excellent use of it in her East Side haven for those beguiled by fine and authentic regional Mexican cooking, the acclaimed Rosa Mexicano. *Alambres* (literally wires) are skewers. The texture of the lightly cooked bacon is very appealing to those who like it. Otherwise, the bacon could be blanched in advance, but the results will be neither as authentic nor as tasty as the version given here.

5 pounds whole (about 2 pounds fillets) seatrout
1/2 cup light olive oil
*1 1/2 cups tomato purée (*not *tomato sauce)*
1/2 cup water
1 tablespoon dried oregano, toasted in a skillet until fragrant and
    crumbled
1 tablespoon finely minced parsley
2 cloves garlic, minced
2 tablespoons white vinegar, wine or distilled
1/3 to 1/2 pound bacon, cut into 1 1/4-inch lengths
Dash cayenne
Coarse salt and freshly ground black pepper to taste
4 medium ripe tomatoes
16 medium slices of medium-small onion, preferably white
4 to 6 whole serrano chiles (optional)
4 cups cooked Plain White Rice (Basic Western or Boiled) (see recipes)

Skin the seatrout and cut into 1 1/4-inch squares; the thin tail end should be cut long and later folded square to obtain pieces consistent in size.

In a nonreactive bowl, combine olive oil, tomato purée, water, herbs, garlic, vinegar, bacon, cayenne, and salt and pepper to taste. Add fish, stir gently with the hands to coat, and marinate, stirring occasionally, for at least 1 hour at room temperature, or as long as overnight if refrigerated.

Use a very sharp or serrated knife to slice sixteen 1 1/2-inch discs from the walls of the tomatoes (reserve remaining tomato hearts for another purpose). Arrange fish on 4 to 6 heavy stainless steel skewers, alternating the fish pieces with bacon, onion, and tomato slices, ending with an optional chile on each skewer. Simply calculate the number of fish pieces you have per skewer and alternate the elements as you wish. Be careful to recover as much of the marinade as possible to make the sauce.

At serving time, heat a grill to very hot. Place the marinade in a heavy nonreactive saucepan and bring to a boil. Simmer for about 5 minutes, adding a little water if it gets too thick. Grill fish until nicely browned and just cooked through, about 2 minutes on each of the four sides. Do not overcook.

Arrange a line of hot cooked rice along the center of each serving plate and present the skewers on top of the rice, with some sauce on either side.

GRILLED HALIBUT ALLA CUCINA NUOVA

4 servings

Though balsamic vinegar has an ancient history in and around Modena, it is not normally used in fish cookery. Hence the rather pretentious name for this simple and delicious "new" dish. It really needs the rich smoky flavor of grilling—you may certainly use wood chips for extra smokiness—but broiling is also okay. You might try these flavors with any fish steak, particularly swordfish, king mackerel, and mahi mahi. Grilled fennel is a possible vegetable accompaniment; if you decide to use it, parsley is the best herb choice.

1/2 cup balsamic vinegar
1/2 cup white wine
2 teaspoons honey, or to taste
2 large cloves garlic, peeled and slightly mashed
Coarse salt and freshly ground black pepper to taste
1/2 cup olive oil
1 1/2 to 2 pounds halibut steak, 1 to 1 1/4 inches thick
2 ounces (1/2 stick) butter
1 generous tablespoon chopped fresh herb(s): parsley, basil, or marjo-
*   ram, or a combination*

In a nonreactive dish large enough to hold the fish in one layer, combine vinegar, wine, honey, garlic, salt and pepper, and 1/4 cup olive oil. Cut fish into 4 serving pieces. Place them in the dish and marinate, turning occasionally, for at least 2 hours, or refrigerate overnight.

Just before serving, preheat grill or broiler to very hot. Remove fish from marinade—reserve marinade—and pick off any pieces of garlic. If you are grilling you will want to dry fish well and film it

lightly with a little olive oil. Cook until just done, planning on about
8 minutes per inch, turning once. Remove to warmed serving plates
or a platter.

As fish is nearing doneness, combine the remaining ¼ cup
olive oil, butter, and about 2 tablespoons reserved marinade in a small
saucepan. Swirl over high heat until it reaches a simmer and cook
about 1 minute. Pour over the fish, sprinkle on herb(s), and serve
immediately.

GRILLED TROUT ROSEMARY

4 servings

Here is another simple Italian-style grill, a more traditional
one, based on a haunting memory of a luncheon in Verona that
included a perfect trout perfectly prepared. Grilling is best, but
broiling will do. The trout are best grilled in a cage; if you lack
one, you will probably find the fish easier to handle if it is not
slashed. Baby coho salmon also work well.

4 rainbow trout, gutted, gills removed, rinsed well
2 cloves garlic, peeled
4 large sprigs fresh rosemary
Coarse salt and freshly ground black pepper to taste
¾ cup dry vermouth
½ cup olive oil

If using the farmed trout from Idaho, they are normally neatly pre-
cleaned and ready to go. Dry trout with paper towels, then slash them
(unless you are grilling without a cage) at 1½-inch intervals on both
sides. Place in a nonreactive dish.

With the side of a heavy knife, bruise garlic and rosemary and
rub all over fish. Add salt and pepper, vermouth, and olive oil. Let
marinate, turning occasionally, for at least 1 hour, or for as long as 12
hours, refrigerated.

Just before serving, preheat grill or broiler to very hot. Remove fish from marinade—reserve marinade—and place a rosemary
sprig in each cavity. If you are grilling you will want to dry fish well
and film lightly with a little olive oil. Cook fish close to heat, turning

once (if your timing is right) until done. Serve immediately. If you wish, while fish is cooking you may bring the marinade to a boil in a small saucepan, simmer a few minutes, and spoon a little over each fish at serving time. Fish prepared this way are also lovely served at room temperature.

GRILLED MAKO WITH FRESH HORSERADISH SAUCE

4 servings

> Though horseradish may seem a more likely flavoring for cold, maybe smoked fish, there are also possibilities for hot dishes. Sailing, a pleasant spot downtown on Hudson Street, does a quickie combination of prepared horseradish, mustard, and mayonnaise to be smeared on a tuna or swordfish steak for the last minute of broiling. Below is a fancier version that is also very easy to make. The horseradish is best in long shreds from the julienne or shredding disk of a food processor. Be sure to fold it immediately into the cream so that it will not be exposed to air for long. Swordfish is another good choice. Grilling and pan grilling are best, but broiling will do.

> *4 mako steaks (about 8 ounces each), 1 1/4 inches thick*
> *1/2 cup white wine*
> *1 large clove garlic, peeled and smashed*
> *Coarse salt and freshly ground white pepper to taste*
> *2 firm red apples*
> *1 cup heavy cream or* crème fraîche
> *Large pinch sugar*
> *3/4 cup freshly shredded horseradish*
> *About 1 teaspoon lemon juice*
> *8 scallions*
> *4 ounces (1 stick) softened butter*

Trim steaks and put them on a nonreactive dish with the wine, garlic, and salt and pepper. Core apples and cut 12 even center slices, crosswise, 1/4 inch thick. Add to the fish, turning to expose all surfaces of the fish and apple slices to the wine and seasonings. Let marinate for 30 minutes or so, turning occasionally. If prepared in advance it must be refrigerated, then returned to room temperature before cooking.

Whip cream with sugar and a little salt until it is lightly thickened. Do not beat until stiff. Peel and grate horseradish and immediately fold it into the cream, along with lemon juice to taste. Slice off the roots of the scallions, then trim the greens to leave scallions about 7 inches long.

Preheat grill, broiler, or heavy cast-iron skillet to very hot. Drain fish and apples, discarding marinade, and pat dry. Smear with a very light film of butter, melting it if necessary. Film scallions too. At serving time, grill steaks and apples until lightly browned and fish is just heated through. Grill scallions until lightly charred. If cooking space is limited, do apples and scallions first. Arrange apple slices on platter or plates and place steaks half covering apples. Spoon on a little horseradish sauce, strew scallions over steaks, and serve immediately, passing the remaining sauce.

SWORDFISH SCALLOPS AL PIATTO

4 servings

Here is a popular dish from Chef Alessandro Prosperi of Barocco, a Tuscan restaurant in TriBeCa. It is also very easy and versatile; it can be served at room temperature for warm-weather luncheons and suppers. Mako and tuna are two other fine fish choices; if you use tuna, slice it a little thicker so that it can be broiled rare. In fact, any fish would be delicious prepared with these ingredients, cut into scallops, steaked, filleted, or whole. In a restaurant kitchen a dish like this is prepared one serving at a time on a sizzle plate, hence the name.

½ cup extra-virgin olive oil
2 tablespoons lemon juice
2 tablespoons chopped flat-leaf parsley
2 tablespoons chopped fresh oregano leaves
Coarse salt and freshly ground black pepper to taste
2 pounds swordfish
Lemon wedges

Preheat broiler to very hot.

In a small bowl, blend olive oil, lemon juice, parsley, oregano, and a touch of salt and pepper. Divide mixture in half and reserve half to use as the sauce. To trim the swordfish, remove and discard the skin and most of the red muscle. Slice into 12 scallops approximately ¼ inch thick. Do not be too concerned about waste as you shape scallops into neat rectangles. Dip fish into the other half of the mixture to coat and arrange scallops in a single layer on a broilerproof pan or platter, and broil close to the element, until just warmed, 3 to 4 minutes. Chef Prosperi suggests lifting the edge of a scallop to see that the bottom has whitened. Do not overcook.

Transfer fish to warmed dinner plates, 3 scallops per serving. Whisk up the reserved sauce and divide it among the servings. Serve immediately with lemon wedges, or cool and serve at room temperature.

BRACIOLE DI PESCESPADA

GRILLED STUFFED SWORDFISH ROLLS, SICILIAN-STYLE

4 to 6 servings

And now for something completely different. . . . Here is one version of a traditional Sicilian dish. With its typical combination of anchovy and raisins in the filling, it reflects the influence of Spain and North Africa on the foods of Sicily. This recipe was developed by chef/teacher Richard Glavin for his students at The New School for Social Research. Grilling yields the finest flavor, but broiling is easier to handle.

2 pounds swordfish

THE FILLING

> 1 medium onion, peeled and finely chopped
> 2 tablespoons olive oil
> 1 ½ cups fresh bread crumbs
> 2 anchovy fillets
> 1 large clove garlic
> 2 tablespoons pine nuts
> 1 tablespoon golden raisins, rinsed and drained
> 2 tablespoons grated Romano cheese
> 1 tablespoon lemon juice
> 1 tablespoon orange juice
> 1 egg, beaten
> Coarse salt and freshly ground black pepper to taste

THE COATING

> 1 egg, beaten
> 1 tablespoon olive oil
> 1 cup dry bread crumbs
> 2 tablespoons grated Romano cheese
> ½ teaspoon dried oregano
> 1 tablespoon chopped parsley
> 1 clove garlic, peeled and minced
> Coarse salt and freshly ground black pepper to taste

> Olive oil, for basting

THE GARNISHES

> Lemon wedges or slices
> Thin slices red onion
> Parsley sprigs

To trim the swordfish, remove and discard skin and most of the red muscle. Slice into 6 scallops approximately 5 by 3 by ¼ inches. Do not be too concerned about waste as you shape scallops into neat rectangles. Dice trimmings and reserve for the filling. Put scallops between sheets of wax paper and *very* gently pound them with a meat hammer or the bottom of a small skillet until they are about 20 percent larger. Do not tear holes. Set aside.

Sauté onion in 2 tablespoons oil until translucent, adding the diced swordfish trimmings when the onion is nearly tender. Transfer mixture to a bowl, cool slightly, and mix in remaining filling ingredients until thoroughly combined. Divide mixture among the scallops and spread it thinly and evenly over them. Starting at the narrow end, roll up scallops tightly and secure with toothpicks.

Preheat grill or broiler.

Stir the beaten egg and oil together with a fork. In a separate bowl, combine remaining coating ingredients. Dip swordfish rolls into the egg mixture, then the crumb mixture, pressing to help the crumbs adhere. This can be done up to 30 minutes before cooking. Grill or broil rolls, turning as needed, until nicely browned all over and heated through, 12 minutes or less. Baste twice with olive oil during cooking. Transfer rolls to individual plates, garnish, and serve immediately.

ANNA TERESA CALLEN'S CHRISTMAS EEL

8 small servings, or 4 large

Teacher and food writer Anna Teresa has fond memories of the fat, delicious eels of her native Italy. These are not congers (ocean eel), but *capitoni:* freshwater eels that live in river mouths and bays (the ones from near Rome and the Comacchio Valley south of Venice are the most famous) where the meeting of salt and fresh water brings them more food than their upstream cousins can manage to find. Here is a traditional Christmas Eve treatment, meant to be served as part of a seafood feast that might feature seven different dishes. But feel free to serve it anytime during the fall-into-winter eel season. Our American eel does nicely. Be sure to caution the uninitiated not to eat the bay leaves. The eel skin crisps nicely and is a treat for some; others will want to avoid it.

About 2 pounds live eel (3 to 4 eels)
4 large cloves garlic, peeled and bruised
1/2 cup lemon juice
1 cup light olive oil
Coarse salt and freshly ground black pepper to taste
Small bay leaves or pieces of large ones, fresh if possible, almost as many
    as you have pieces of eel

The easiest way to handle live eels is to have the fishmonger bonk them over the head with something heavy, such as a sharpening steel, and quickly gut them. Then you are all set to take them home. Or if it appeals to you, take them home live and kill them yourself. Clean eels well to remove all blood. Scrub skin to remove slime, and dry. Slice eels crosswise into lengths of 2 to 3 inches, discarding head and tail ends. Combine remaining ingredients in a nonreactive dish, then add eel pieces and baste. Marinate, refrigerated, for up to 12 hours, even longer is okay. Turn and baste occasionally.

Preheat grill or broiler to very hot.

Thread eel pieces onto skewers—either metal skewers or bamboo skewers that have been soaked in water to minimize burning—threading a piece of bay leaf between each piece of eel. Anna Teresa threads them crosswise, but you may thread the eel pieces the long way—with the backbone—if you wish. Grill until nicely browned and heated through, turning as needed. For broiling, line up skewers on a baking sheet with low sides and cover skewer ends with a strip of foil to reduce burning. Serve hot or tepid.

SEAFOOD FAJITAS

6 to 8 servings

One of the more fun approaches to informal summer entertaining is the Tex-Mex event called fajitas, where diners choose from among a savory array of fixings to create their own rolled flour tortillas. Skirt steak is the usual meat, though breast of chicken is very popular, as is seafood. Use shrimp for sure, and add fillet of monkfish, ocean pout, blackfish, even tuna, if you wish. Though there are a number of components, none is difficult and all can be prepared well in advance of the final grilling. Canned refried beans are fine. Use some mesquite or other wood if you have it. When pan grilling, you might sneak a little *pure* liquid smoke, about ¼ teaspoon, into the marinade. If you have a large griddle, heat it at serving time, strew with peppers and onions, and add the grilled seafood and bring it to the table, sizzling.

*3 pounds large shrimp, shelled and deveined, or a combination of
    shrimp and trimmed fillet of monkfish, tuna, or other fish*

THE MARINADE

> 6 large cloves garlic, peeled and mashed
> 1/2 cup lime or lemon juice
> 1/4 cup white wine
> 1 teaspoon sugar
> 2 tablespoons Worcestershire sauce
> Salt and freshly ground black pepper to taste
> Tabasco to taste, about 1/2 teaspoon
> 1/4 cup corn oil or light olive oil

THE PAN-FRIED ONIONS AND PEPPERS

> 1/4 cup corn oil or light olive oil
> 2 large white onions, peeled and sliced
> 2 or 3 large bell peppers, green or a mixture of colors, trimmed and
>   cut into strips

THE TORTILLAS

> 24 flour tortillas
> Corn oil or light olive oil

ACCOMPANIMENTS

> Refritos (recipe follows)
> Guacamole (recipe follows)
> Pico de Gallo (a chunky salsa cruda) (recipe follows)

Place seafood in a nonreactive dish and add marinade ingredients. Let marinate for at least 1 hour at room temperature, or overnight, refrigerated, turning several times.

To prepare the onions and peppers, heat a large skillet until very hot. Swirl in oil and heat until barely smoking. Add onions and peppers, and sauté, stirring often, until nearly tender. Set aside.

Purchased flour tortillas need to be warmed. Remove them from their plastic wrapper, rewrap in foil, and place in a moderate 350°F. oven for 15 minutes or so. The package could also be warmed on the side of the barbecue grill; turn often so that it does not scorch.

At serving time, remove seafood from marinade, pat dry with

paper towels, film with a little oil, and place on a preheated grill close
to a hot fire. Cook, turning once or twice, until heated through. If you
use tuna, cook it rare. Shrimp are left whole. Fish is sliced on the
diagonal. Remove to a warmed platter lined with peppers and onions
that you have reheated. Serve immediately with all accompaniments.

REFRITOS

> 1 pound black, pinto, or red kidney beans, picked over, rinsed, and
>   soaked overnight in cold water to cover by several inches
> 1 bay leaf
> 1/2 cup lard or light olive oil
> 2 medium onions, finely chopped
> 3 large cloves garlic, peeled and minced
> Coarse salt and freshly ground black pepper to taste

Drain soaked beans and place in a heavy pot with water to cover by
1 inch and add the bay leaf. Bring slowly to a boil, reduce heat, and
simmer very gently until tender, adding water as needed to prevent
scorching. In a large skillet, heat half of the lard or oil, and sauté
onions until tender, adding garlic for the last 30 seconds or so. Add
to beans and simmer until everything is very tender and fairly dry.
Season with salt and pepper to taste.

Remove and discard bay leaf. Purée half the mixture in a food
processor. In the large skillet, heat the remaining lard or oil and slowly
work in the whole beans, mashing them coarsely. Add the purée and
mix well; heat to a creamy, fairly dry paste. Correct seasoning. Reheat
as needed, adding a little water if mixture becomes too dry.

GUACAMOLE

> 1 small clove garlic, peeled
> 1/2 teaspoon coarse salt
> 2 ripe Hass avocados, cut in half, flesh scored
> 2 teaspoons lime or lemon juice
> 1 tablespoon chopped fresh coriander
> 1/4 cup minced white onion

In a nonreactive bowl, combine garlic and salt and mash with a fork
until you have a paste (or nearly). Scoop avocado flesh out of skins
with a spoon and add to the bowl. Mash slightly with the fork. Add

remaining ingredients and combine well. Correct seasoning. Even if you are not superstitious you may bury an avocado pit in the mixture before you cover it closely—on the surface of the mixture—with plastic wrap and refrigerate until needed.

PICO DE GALLO

> 3 large ripe tomatoes, juice and seeds removed, coarsely chopped
> 1 medium white onion, peeled and chopped
> Finely chopped sweet and hot chiles (a combination is best) to taste
> 3 tablespoons chopped fresh coriander
> Coarse salt and freshly ground black pepper to taste
> Large pinch sugar

Combine ingredients for *pico de gallo* in a nonreactive bowl and correct seasoning. It should be quite hot. Cover and refrigerate until needed.

BROILED MACKEREL WITH PEPPERS

4 to 6 servings

Just a rustic luncheon or supper idea, this recipe features one of the least expensive and most flavorful fish. You might also try king mackerel steaks or even tuna, if you are feeling flush.

> 2 pounds fillet of Atlantic mackerel (from about 4 pounds whole fish)
> 2 ounces (½ stick) softened butter
> Coarse salt and freshly ground pepper to taste
> ¼ cup dry white wine or vermouth
> ½ cup light olive oil
> 1 green bell pepper, cleaned and sliced into strips
> 1 red bell pepper, cleaned and sliced into strips
> 1 yellow bell pepper, cleaned and sliced into strips
> 1 large Spanish onion, peeled, cut in half lengthwise, and sliced
> 2 to 3 cloves garlic, peeled and minced
> Dash cayenne to taste
> ½ teaspoon sugar
> 1 tablespoon red wine vinegar (optional)
> 3 tablespoons finely minced fresh herb(s): parsley, basil, oregano, or
>   marjoram, or a combination

Using a very sharp knife or razor blade, lightly score the skin of the fillets, about 5 cuts per fillet. Brush a broilerproof pan or 2 sizzle plates with a little of the butter and add the fillets. Brush with butter to film and season to taste with salt and pepper. Arrange fillets skin side up, and plump them to make the flesh as uniform as possible. Pour the wine around the fillets and set aside.

Heat the oil in a large skillet. Add the pepper strips and onion, and toss or stir over high heat just until the vegetables begin to wilt. Add the garlic for the last 30 seconds or so. Pour mixture into a large sieve set in a bowl and reserve (save for another use the flavored oil that drains from the mixture). Reserve skillet too.

Preheat broiler.

Broil fish, close to the source of heat, until it is heated through. As fish nears doneness, return drained pepper-and-onion mixture to skillet and heat. Transfer fish to platter or plates, and add the pan juices to the skillet, along with the remaining ingredients. Heat the mixture through, correct seasoning, spoon over fish, and serve immediately.

FRYING AND SAUTÉ

See p. 78 for ways to determine proper cooking time.

Every developed cuisine features some sort of cooking in fat as a fundamental technique, producing both elegant and rustic foods. Chemically, hot fat sears foodstuffs faster and more thoroughly than water-based liquids, guaranteeing plump, tender, and juicy results if handled properly. And if the fat is properly hot and the food is drained or blotted after cooking, it should gain very little in the way of added calories.

Deep-frying is the most obvious of the techniques, where pieces of seafood and sometimes whole fish of various sizes—usually with some starchy coating—are wholly immersed in hot fat until done. Shallow frying is nearly the same, but the food must be turned so that it is nicely crusted on both sides. Panfrying is for skillet-sized whole fish, steaks, or large fillets, using at most 1/4 inch fat. Stir-frying speaks for itself—the food is cooked by just enough hot fat to lightly film it as it is energetically stirred and tossed so that all sides are rapidly exposed to the heat of the wok.

Sautéing is a little trickier. Technically, the food should be of a uniform thickness of 1/4 to 1/2 inch and normally lightly dusted with flour. A hot skillet is filmed with fat and the seafood is quickly cooked, with one turn, until lightly colored and heated through. Then it is removed to a platter or plates, and a sauce is made in the skillet. However, the term *sauté* is also applied to preliminary searing for fish that is to be finished another way, as in braising. And some cooks use a nonstick skillet to achieve a sautéed effect using little or no fat. A true sauté is completely cooked in the skillet with a little fat; if the sauce ingredients are added to the skillet and the seafood is heated through in the sauce, then you have a *fricassée,* a term that in seafood cookery is normally only applied to shellfish. However, some fricassées are called sautés and vice versa. So long as the technique is understood, there is no reason to be confused by semantics.

VARIETIES BEST SUITED

Any seafood is appropriate for any of the techniques, except that stir-frying requires a sturdy texture such as that of shellfish and firm fish like monkfish, ocean pout, blackfish, wolffish, searobin, and sea squab.

EQUIPMENT

Deep-frying is best done in a thermostatically controlled fryer, just as electric skillets are good for shallow frying. Standard spun carbon steel woks are also very good, but the temperature must be monitored. Large saucepans will also do, provided they are deep enough to be safe. A good deep-fry thermometer is needed for all top-of-stove vessels.

Skillets of various sizes for sauté and fricassée need only be sturdy to work well. After the modern resin coatings, cast iron and black steel have the best nonstick properties, followed by aluminum and enamel. Stainless is the most likely to cause sticking, but any metal will work if it is properly preheated *before* the fat is added. Oval fish pans just the right size and shape to hold a couple of trout are not only handsome but highly functional for panfish and fillets too. The traditional French tin-lined copper pans are very expensive but built to last forever (except for periodic retinning). Wear-ever made an excellent, affordable aluminum fish pan that is difficult to find these days; grab one if you come across it.

TECHNIQUE

Soy oil (the most common vegetable oil) is the most common fat used for these techniques. Any of the other light oils will do if the flavor is right. Olive oil is delicious, used straight for sautéing or blended with bland oil for frying, but it is distinctive and best used precisely when its flavor is desired. French peanut oil is light and clean—and very expensive—while American peanut oil is so flavorful that it is best reserved for Asian foods. Of the saturated fats, pure lard and rendered beef fat, while tasty, are steadily losing ground for health reasons. Palm and coconut oils are unacceptable (except for a touch of *dendé* oil in certain Brazilian dishes). Hydrogenated vegetable fat (Crisco, et cetera) produces superior fried foods, but it is used less and less because it seems foolish to introduce saturated fat where none is needed. Though not suited to any kind of frying, butter is often used in sautéing for its fine flavor. Of course its milk solids will burn at high temperatures, so it is often clarified or blended with oil or both.

Oil temperature is the most crucial factor in achieving light, greaseless frying. Within the range of 360°F. to 400°F., with 375°F.

as the norm, results will be good. Cooler temperatures produce soggy food and higher temperatures will burn the oil, making it smoky and unpleasant. If you lack a thermometer, there are a few tests you can perform that will indicate a proper temperature. The oil is hot enough if: You flick in a little flour and it turns golden immediately; you drop in a slice of fresh ginger and it rises to the surface immediately; you insert the tip of a new, dry bamboo chopstick or wooden spoon and it begins to bubble immediately; you add a chunk of bread and it browns nicely in 30 seconds. To keep the oil at a proper temperature, fry small batches and give the heat a chance to recover in between. Provided the oil is strained thoroughly after frying—through a paper towel or a coffee filter—it can be reused a time or two. The addition of some fresh oil with each reuse will improve its flavor and frying properties. Old oil browns foods much faster than fresh, so it is possible to get a "false positive" reading from the appearance of foods cooked in old oil.

Coatings are usual for both frying and sautéing, usually just a dusting of white flour for sauté, but often more substantial breadings for frying. Cornmeal, cornstarch, rice flour, bread crumbs, cracker or matzo meal, oatmeal (rolled oats—old-fashioned, quick, or instant— not steel-cut, it is too tough), ground nuts, and grated cheese are possibilities. The standard one-two-three for breading is flour, egg or egg and milk, then crumbs or other granular substances. Breadings will form a better seal if they are completed in advance of frying. Simple dustings must be executed immediately before cooking or they will turn to library paste, and fried library paste is just what you would expect. Batters are sometimes used in place of breadings, with variable results. Properly made tempura is ethereal, while an overdense batter is stodgy and awful.

Safety is a paramount consideration in frying. Make certain cords and handles are out of the way and the wok is stable. Avoid splashes from introducing food into the fat by easing it in with an away-from-you motion rather than dropping it from a distance. Avoid splattering and bubbling over by being sure the food is dry and the vessel is never more than half full of fat; one-third is safer.

Fried foods are drained on paper towels and served immediately or kept in a *warm* oven while the rest of the recipe is completed. Never cover or overlap, or you will cause the food to steam itself into limpness. Sautéed food is blotted to remove cooking fat; if left to drain on paper towels, the food will lose flavorful juices.

PICCATA OF MAKO SHARK

2 servings

This perfectly simple dish is from the Grand Central Oyster Bar. It is delicious made with other meaty fish—swordfish, of course, but also monkfish, ocean pout, blackfish, and wolffish. Fillets of flounder or other white-fleshed fish are also tasty prepared this way, if less interesting texturally. In fact, this could be called *à la grenobloise,* a traditional preparation that is also applied to panfish, particularly trout. It is easiest prepared for two, but four servings can be managed in two skillets by sautéing in both skillets and finishing the sauce in just one of them.

Four 3-ounce slices of mako shark, ¼ inch thick
Coarse salt and freshly ground white pepper to taste
Flour for dredging
4 ounces (1 stick) butter
1 teaspoon chopped parsley
1 lemon, peeled and cut into segments (see technique for suprême of
*   orange, p. 133)*
2 teaspoons drained tiny (nonpareil) capers, or more to taste

Season fish with salt and pepper and dredge lightly in flour, shaking off excess. Heat half the butter in a large heavy skillet until the foaming subsides and the butter threatens to start browning. Add fish in a single layer and allow it to color lightly, about 1 minute on each side. Remove to warmed platter or plates, blot, and sprinkle with parsley.

Wipe out skillet and add remaining butter. When foaming subsides and butter just begins to brown, add lemon sections and capers and toss briefly to heat through. Spoon over fish and serve immediately.

PANFRIED FILLET OF POMPANO WITH RUM RAISINS

2 servings

Marvelous fish, marvelous spirit, marvelous restaurant—what's not to like? This elegant dish is also from the Grand Central Oyster Bar. It is a perfect main course for a romantic dinner for two, but, again, you may double it if you use two skillets to sauté and just one of them to prepare the sauce. Despite the title, this is a classic sauté. The Oyster Bar serves it with boiled potatoes.

1/4 cup dark raisins
6 ounces dark rum
2 fillets, 6 to 8 ounces each, from 1 large pompano
Coarse salt and freshly ground white pepper to taste
Flour for dredging
1/4 cup clarified butter (p. 75)
2 ounces (1/2 stick) butter, firm but not cold, cut into pieces

Soak raisins in rum in a covered container for at least 1 hour, or better still, for 1 or 2 days if you have the time.

Trim pompano fillets neatly. If you wish, you may cut the fillets in half lengthwise as you might with flatfish fillets; they will be easier to handle. Season lightly with salt and pepper and put aside to come to room temperature. Heat a skillet to very hot. Dust fillets lightly with flour, shaking off excess. Add clarified butter to the hot skillet, swirl it around, and immediately add fillets, skin side down. Sauté until golden, turn, and finish cooking. Remove to warmed serving plates and blot with a paper towel.

Pour off and discard cooking fat. Wipe out skillet, and return it to the burner. Add rum-raisin mixture, and bring to a boil. Do not be alarmed if it flambés. Reduce liquid slightly, then add the butter pieces and swirl until sauce is just creamy. Spoon over pompano and serve immediately.

POMPANO WITH PARSLEY SAUCE

2 servings

Despite the tradition for richly seasoned pompano dishes in Louisiana, where Gulf waters produce a plentiful crop, the distinctive buttery flavor and texture of pompano are best enjoyed simply broiled or sautéed, with just enough sauce to add interest. The most expensive whole finfish at Fulton deserves respectful treatment. This second pompano sauté is inspired by one served at Le Bernardin. Once again, it may be doubled using two skillets for sautéing and one for finishing the sauce.

2 fillets, 6 to 8 ounces each, from 1 large pompano
Coarse salt and freshly ground white pepper to taste
Flour for dredging
4 tablespoons clarified butter (p. 75)
2 ounces (1/2 stick) butter
2 tablespoons minced shallots
1/4 cup white wine
1/2 cup Fish Stock (see recipe)
2 tablespoons heavy cream (optional)
2 teaspoons lemon juice
2 tablespoons minced parsley

Trim fillets neatly and cut them in half lengthwise along the lateral line. Season lightly with salt and pepper. Heat a large skillet to very hot. Dust fillets *very* lightly with flour. Add clarified butter to the hot skillet, swirl it around, and immediately add fillets, skin side down. Sauté until golden, turn, and finish cooking. Remove to a platter and keep warm.

Pour off and discard cooking fat. Wipe out skillet if it is burned. Return to heat and add 2 tablespoons of the butter and the shallots. Cook briefly until fragrant. Add the white wine and reduce by half. Add the stock and reduce by half. Add the optional cream, return to a boil, and reduce slightly. Add the remaining 2 tablespoons butter and swirl it in. Add the lemon juice and parsley and swirl them in. Correct seasoning. Divide sauce between 2 warmed dinner plates, top with pompano, and serve immediately.

FRICASSÉE OF SEA SCALLOPS WITH CORN, TOMATOES, AND LEEKS

6 servings

This lovely dish is the creation of Anne Rosenzweig of Arcadia and the new "21" Club. Notice that it elevates some good old American ingredients to *haute cuisine* status by the use of sophisticated (but by no means difficult) technique. The result is fresh, modern, and elegant.

2 pounds large sea scallops
Coarse salt and freshly ground pepper to taste
Flour for dredging
1/2 cup soy or other light vegetable oil
1/2 cup (1 stick) butter
3 tablespoons minced garlic
1 1/2 cups thinly sliced leeks
3/4 cup dry white wine
1/2 cup Fish Stock (see recipe)
3/4 cup corn kernels
1 1/2 cups peeled, seeded, juiced, and chopped tomatoes, fresh or canned
*3/4 cup lightly packed, thin shreds (*chiffonade*) of fresh basil leaves*

Clean scallops, removing the tough whitish strip on one side. If the scallops vary greatly in size, you will want to slice the larger ones in half crosswise to make them as uniform as possible. Season scallops lightly with salt and pepper, and dust lightly with the flour.

Heat 2 large sauté pans over moderately high heat, and divide the oil between them. When the oil is very hot, add the scallops in a single layer, dividing them between the pans. Add 1 tablespoon butter to each pan and cook until scallops are lightly browned on one side, 3 to 5 minutes. Turn scallops and sauté for about 2 minutes more until lightly browned. Scallops should be medium-rare. Remove from pan and drain briefly on paper towels. Hold in a warm place while you proceed with the sauce. You have now finished with one of the pans.

Discard oil in remaining pan and add 2 tablespoons butter. Return to the heat and, when the butter is melted and sizzling, add the garlic and leeks. Sauté 1 minute, stirring often. Add the wine, increase heat to high, and cook, stirring often to deglaze and reduce by half, 3 to 5 minutes. Stir in the stock and cook 1 minute longer. Add corn, tomatoes, and remaining 4 tablespoons butter. Cook 2 minutes, stirring constantly, until juices are no longer watery but slightly creamy. Stir in basil and adjust seasoning to taste. Divide sauce among 6 warmed plates. Arrange scallops on the sauce and serve immediately.

PANFRIED CATFISH WITH SALPICON OF SOUTHWESTERN VEGETABLES AND ANCHO SAUCE

6 servings

Fresh, modern approaches to Southwestern cooking are important fare in some New York restaurants, spearheaded by Brendan Walsh during his tenure at Arizona 206. Actually, this recipe is only partly influenced by that style of cooking, having also had the unlikely inspiration of a dish with Mediterranean flavors from Chef Gérard Pangaud of the elegant Aurora. The distinctive ingredients should be easy enough to find in a specialty store with a well-stocked Mexican or Southwestern foods section. Any white-fleshed fish that can be cut into neat fillets will do. Yellow perch is particularly delicious.

THE ANCHO SAUCE

2 large dried ancho chiles, about 1 ounce
Coarse salt to taste
10 to 12 ounces crème fraîche

THE *SALPICON*

1 cup diced red bell pepper
1 cup thinly sliced scallions
1 cup diced peeled jicama or sunchoke
1 cup yellow corn kernels, fresh or frozen
1/4 cup light olive oil
1 tablespoon minced fresh hot green chile (jalapeño or serrano), or to taste
1 teaspoon minced garlic

¹/₄ cup canned tomatillos *(Mexican green husk tomatoes), puréed, or*
  ¹/₄ cup tomato purée combined with 1 tablespoon lime or lemon
  juice
Coarse salt to taste

2¹/₂ to 3 pounds catfish fillets, trimmed
Coarse salt and freshly ground pepper to taste
¹/₂ cup flour
¹/₄ cup yellow cornmeal
Corn oil

1 large bunch fresh coriander, trimmed into sprigs
Lime wedges

Soak anchos in hot water to cover until softened and plumped, at least
30 minutes. Drain, reserving the liquid. Remove and discard caps,
seeds, and membranes. Purée in a food processor with the salt and
about ¹/₄ cup of the soaking liquid, scraping down the bowl often,
until mixture is as smooth as possible. Add the *crème fraîche* and pulse
to blend. Strain mixture through a fine sieve and discard solids. Correct seasoning. Reserve, refrigerated, if prepared well in advance.
Bring to room temperature before serving.

 To prepare the salpicon: combine red pepper, scallions, jicama,
and corn, and set aside. Reserve other *salpicon* ingredients separately.

 Just before serving time, season catfish fillets lightly with salt
and pepper. Combine flour and cornmeal and put it on a platter or a
sheet of wax paper. Heat 2 large skillets to hot and add ¹/₃ inch oil
to each. When oil is very hot, dredge fillets in flour mixture, shaking
off excess. Fry until golden and heated through, 1 to 3 minutes per
side, depending on thickness. When fish is done, remove to a platter
lined with paper towels and put in a warm place. Remove the oil from
1 skillet and wipe it out if it is burned. Add the ¹/₄ cup olive oil and
heat. Add the chile and garlic and heat briefly, just until fragrant. Add
the *salpicon* mixture and the *tomatillo* purée and toss over high heat to
warm through, about 1 minute. Add salt to taste. Arrange fish and
vegetables on warmed plates. It looks particularly nice if the *salpicon*
rings the fish. Garnish generously with coriander sprigs and lime
wedges and serve immediately, passing the ancho sauce separately.

SHAD ROE WITH DANDELION AND BASIL

4 servings

This delightful partnering of springtime favorites is another winner from Leslie Revsin. The ingredients are perfectly balanced, so you will want to measure with care and avoid substitutions. Only bacon fat lends the right flavor to the greens; do not be tempted to try olive oil, but a little warm butter mixed with corn oil might do in a pinch. The smallest, tenderest first-of-spring leaves of genuine dandelion are best. Catelonian chickory, with its long rather pale green leaves, is marketed as dandelion many times of the year, and it is acceptable. Should you be unable to locate either genuine or *faux* dandelion the same day fine, fat shad roe is in the market, try spinach with the chickory. While sorrel might seem like a logical choice, it is really the wrong flavor to pair with a basil *beurre blanc.*

THE GREENS

1/2 to 3/4 cup smallest, tenderest dandelion leaves
1/2 to 3/4 cup pale inner leaves of chickory (curly endive) or escarole
3 to 4 tablespoons rendered bacon fat, warm
1 teaspoon red wine vinegar
Coarse salt and freshly ground black pepper to taste

BASIL *BEURRE BLANC*

3/4 cup dry white wine
1 1/2 tablespoons minced shallots
Generous 1/4 teaspoon coarsely crushed white peppercorns
Generous 2 teaspoons thin strips (chiffonade*) of purple or green basil*
*   leaves*
1/2 cup (1 stick) cool butter, cut into pieces
1/4 teaspoon coarse salt
Few drops of lemon juice
1/4 teaspoon chopped purple or green basil leaf

THE SHAD ROE

2 pair (8 to 12 ounces each pair) shad roe
1 tablespoon butter
Coarse salt and freshly ground white pepper to taste

Flour for dredging
1 teaspoon chopped purple or green basil leaves for garnish

Tear the dandelion leaves in half or, if large, into 1½-inch lengths. Tear the chicory into 1½-inch pieces. Wash greens and dry thoroughly. Wrap in paper towels and refrigerate. Whisk together bacon fat and vinegar with salt and pepper to taste and set aside in a warm place.

To prepare the beurre blanc: Combine wine, shallots, crushed peppercorns, and 2 teaspoons basil strips in a small nonreactive saucepan. Simmer until liquid is reduced to about 1 teaspoon, being careful not to scorch the mixture. Remove from heat and whisk in the cool butter, a piece at a time, returning the pan to low heat from time to time, if necessary, to keep mixture just warm enough to melt the butter. Do not overheat. (Ms. Revsin works over very low heat all the while, which is sound technique but perhaps a little risky for amateurs.) Strain the sauce into a warmed nonreactive container. Whisk in the salt, a few drops of lemon juice, and the ¼ teaspoon chopped basil. Set sauce aside in a warm place. It may stand up to 1 hour, if necessary.

Separate the roe sacs by trimming the membrane that connects them, being careful not to cut the "skin" that encloses the eggs. Bring roe to room temperature. Just before serving time, heat the tablespoon butter in a heavy skillet. Season roe with salt and white pepper and dredge in flour, removing the excess. Handle gently. When the butter has ceased to foam and just begun to color, add the roe and cook over medium heat until it is a rich golden color on both sides, about 6 minutes altogether. The roe is done when it just begins to feel springy to the touch or "medium-rare." Do not overcook.

Remove roe to warmed plates. Whisk up the warm vinegar and bacon fat, and toss it with the greens, and divide greens among the plates, putting the mixture next to the roe. Spoon a little butter sauce over each roe and sprinkle a little of the basil for garnish on each. Serve immediately.

SEARED TUNA WITH SEA URCHIN ROE

6 servings

Now ensconced in its spiffy new quarters in the AT&T Building, the Quilted Giraffe continues to produce some of the most remarkably good food in New York, which is as it should be since it is generally considered the most expensive restaurant in New York. Notice how few ingredients there are in this lovely dish; all must be of finest quality. The sea urchin roe must have a rich coral color or it is likely to be pallid of flavor too. If you are nervous about getting a perfect golden sear on the tuna without any sticking, you might consider a *very* light dusting of flour just before you sauté.

3 pounds finest tuna (yellowfin, bigeye, or bluefin, if you can find any)
3 cups dry white wine
¾ cup peeled and thinly sliced shallots
1 pound cool butter cut into pieces
Coarse salt and freshly ground white pepper to taste
Juice of 1 lime (about 2 tablespoons)
3 large sea urchins
Flour for dredging (optional)
Clarified butter (p. 75)

Remove and discard skin (if any) and the blackish dark muscle from the tuna. (Save trimmings for another use.) Slice flesh into neat 1½-inch cubes. Let tuna come to room temperature.

Combine wine and shallots in a medium-small nonreactive saucepan and reduce over medium heat until nearly dry, reducing heat toward the end and taking care that shallots do not scorch. Whisk in butter, a piece at a time, warming saucepan over low heat from time to time as needed to keep it warm enough to melt the butter. Do not overheat. Strain sauce into a warmed nonreactive vessel, discarding solids, and season it with a little salt and pepper and lime juice to taste. Hold the sauce in a warm place or over warm water.

Clean sea urchins (p. 65) and gently remove pieces of roe in whole fingers. You will need 12 perfect pieces. If you can manage 18 pieces, that is even better. Just before serving time, add sea urchin roe to the sauce to warm it through slightly, being careful to keep the roe pieces intact.

Heat a large heavy skillet until very hot. Season tuna cubes lightly with salt and pepper, and dust very lightly with flour if you are timid. Film hot skillet with clarified butter and add the tuna pieces in a single layer. Let tuna achieve a rich golden crust before you do any turning. Then rotate tuna cubes so that they sear for about 30 seconds on each side (cubes have 6 sides). Remove from pan as they are done.

Slice tuna on the diagonal and arrange overlapping slices on warmed plates so that the richly seared side and the rare center are clearly visible. Spoon on sea urchin roe pieces and a line of sauce across the middle of each serving, then a little more sauce around. Serve immediately.

SHRIMP WITH CIDER SAUCE

6 servings

The sweetness of spiced cider is balanced by aromatics and the pungency of wilted arugula in this elegant Quilted Giraffe creation. The ease of preparation is nearly as impressive as the beautiful combination of flavors, colors, and textures. Here is that rare bird: exquisite restaurant fare that can be tossed off at home by any careful cook with basic skills.

2 quarts best-quality apple cider
2 sticks cinnamon, broken up
1 bay leaf
2 tablespoons whole black peppercorns
4 unpeeled cloves garlic, bruised
4 unpeeled shallots, bruised
1/2 cup (1 stick) cool butter, cut into pieces
Coarse salt, as needed
Juice of 1/2 lime
Butter for sautéing
2 pounds medium-large shrimp, shelled and deveined
2 large bunches arugula, carefully washed, tough stems removed*

Pour cider into a heavy nonreactive saucepan and add cinnamon, bay leaf, peppercorns, garlic, and shallots. Bring to a boil and reduce to 1 cup liquid, skimming from time to time to remove any scum. Strain through a fine strainer. Wipe out saucepan and return the reduction to it. Set aside.

Just before serving time, bring reduction to a boil, remove from heat, and whisk in the stick of butter. Season with salt and a few drops lime juice to taste. Put sauce in a warm place or over warm water but do not let it overheat.

---

* Be particularly careful to rid arugula of all sand by gently agitating it in basins of cold water until it is thoroughly clean. Dry gently with paper towels without bruising.

In a large skillet, heat a few tablespoons butter and add shrimp in a single layer. Sauté until lightly colored on each side and just heated through, in batches if necessary. Do not overcook (1 tablespoon butter per 10 shrimp should be about right). As they are done, remove shrimp from skillet and put them aside in a warm place.

In the same skillet, toss arugula quickly and lightly over heat just until it is slightly wilted. Timing is crucial. Immediately remove arugula and drain it for a few seconds, if necessary. Divide arugula among warmed plates, forming nests. Place some shrimp in the center of each plate, spoon over some sauce, and serve immediately.

ANDY JOHNSTON'S SWORDFISH SCALLOPS WITH CORIANDER SEED AND LIME

4 servings

Here is a fresh, modern dish from Andy Johnston, former chef at the New York Restaurant School restaurant. It was on the menu at Seventy-One Seventh, the Brooklyn restaurant that he ran with his wife, Kathleen. If you do not have a spice grinder, you may combine the coriander seed and flour in a processor bowl and process until it is as smooth as possible, but grinding is better.

1 1/2 pounds boned, skinned swordfish, sliced into pieces 1/3 inch thick
Coarse salt and freshly ground white pepper to taste
2 tablespoons coriander seed, coarsely ground
1 cup flour
Clarified butter (p. 75)
2 tablespoons minced shallots
1/4 cup dry white wine
Juice of 1 lime
Zest of 2 limes, cut into fine julienne
1/2 cup heavy cream
6 ounces (1 1/2 sticks) butter at room temperature
Snipped chives, about 1/2 inch long

Season prepared fish lightly with salt and pepper. Combine coriander seed and flour on a large plate.

Heat a large skillet until hot and film with clarified butter. Dredge swordfish. Sauté until nicely browned on each side, turning once. Fish should be on the rare side. Remove to a platter, blot cooking fat, and set aside in a warm place.

Degrease skillet. Add shallots and toss. Deglaze with white wine. Add lime juice and zest and reduce by half. Add cream and reduce again by half. Add butter and whisk constantly until it is incorporated. Spoon sauce over fish, garnish with chives, and serve immediately.

GULF GROUPER SAUTÉED WITH ESCAROLE, ROMAINE, PINE NUTS, AND GARLIC

4 servings

Here is another winner from chef Andrew Ziobro. It is both hearty and suave in its combination of flavorful Mediterranean ingredients and *haute cuisine* technique.

1/2 cup white wine
1/4 cup water
1 tablespoon lemon juice
1/2 cup pine nuts
Four 6- to 8-ounce fillets of grouper, skinned or not as desired, and lightly pounded to a uniform 1/2-inch thickness
Coarse salt and freshly ground white pepper to taste
Flour for dredging
1/4 cup clarified butter (p. 75)
4 loosely packed cups escarole, cut crosswise into 1/2-inch slices
4 loosely packed cups romaine, cut crosswise into 1/2-inch slices
1 teaspoon minced garlic
6 tablespoons butter
Boiled new potatoes, or another potato choice

Combine the wine, water, and lemon juice, and set aside. Toast the pine nuts in a 350°F. oven for about 10 minutes, then set aside. Just before serving time, heat a large heavy skillet. Season the fillets lightly with salt and pepper and dredge in flour. Film pan with clarified butter, shake off excess flour from fish, and add fillets to the skillet, presentation (bone) side down. Sauté for 2 to 3 minutes, or until golden. Turn and sauté for 2 to 4 minutes, or until slightly underdone. Remove to warmed platter or plates, blotting off the excess cooking fat. *Do not overcook;* the retained heat will continue the cooking process. Set aside in a warm place.

Pour the fat out of the skillet. Return to medium heat and add wine, water, and lemon juice mixture. When it boils, add the escarole and stir as mixture returns to the boil (escarole needs a bit more cooking time than the remaining ingredients), then add romaine, pine nuts, garlic, and butter. Continue cooking, stirring, to wilt greens, reduce liquid, melt butter, and emulsify the liquids into a light butter sauce. Correct seasoning. Spoon greens and sauce over the fish, add potatoes, and serve immediately.

STEVEN MELLINA'S SCALLOPS OF SALMON AND FROGS' LEGS WITH SUN-DRIED TOMATO BUTTER

4 servings

The chef of The Manhattan Ocean Club serves a number of interesting and ambitious dishes that reflect modern tastes and his own sensibilities. As with most sautés finished with a pan sauce, this one should not be attempted for more than four, and is obviously well suited to a special occasion. You may omit the frogs' legs entirely or replace them with a half pound of picked crawfish tail meat.

4 ounces (1 stick) butter
8 sun-dried tomatoes in oil, drained
Coarse salt and freshly ground white pepper to taste
1 teaspoon chopped parsley
1 teaspoon chopped fresh chives
1 teaspoon chopped fresh basil
1/2 teaspoon lemon juice
Four 6- to 8-ounce skinless fillets of salmon
8 pair frogs' legs
Clarified butter, as needed (p. 75)
Flour for dredging, lightly seasoned with salt and white pepper

2 tablespoons white wine
1 tablespoon cognac

Prepare the tomato butter by processing the 4 ounces of butter and the sun-dried tomatoes in a food processor until smooth. Season with a pinch of salt and pepper to taste. Place in a bowl and fold in herbs and lemon juice. Set aside.

Make sure salmon is neatly trimmed and entirely free of bones. Trim frogs' legs by chopping off the ends of the feet and excess hip bone. Make a tiny incision in the "calf muscle" in one leg of each pair and insert the other leg to cross the legs so they will remain flat when they are cooked.

Just before serving, heat a heavy skillet just large enough to hold the salmon in one layer and film generously with clarified butter. Dredge salmon lightly in the flour and sauté until nicely browned on both sides and cooked medium-rare. Remove to a platter, blot with paper towels, and keep in a warm place. Dredge frogs' legs and sauté until golden. Remove to the platter. Pour the fat out of the skillet and add the wine. Boil until it is reduced slightly, then add the cognac and return to a boil. Finish sauce by swirling in half of the tomato butter until mixture is warm and creamy. Return frogs' legs to the skillet to warm them and coat them with sauce.

Place a piece of salmon in the center of each serving plate and arrange the frogs' legs in sauce around. Place a dollop of the remaining tomato butter in the center of each piece of salmon, and serve immediately.

SCALLOPS IN CHIPOTLE SAUCE

4 to 6 servings

This lovely creation is from Josefina Howard. Unlike the strict authenticity of most of her dishes, this one is her own interpretation of Mexican ingredients and techniques applied to a new idea. You may simply serve it with white rice, or you may follow the striking plating, described below, that Mrs. Howard developed for her restaurant, Rosa Mexicano. In case you should be unable to locate canned *chipotles en adobo* but you happen upon dried ones, there is a homemade *adobo* method (see following recipe). It is not as good but it is better than missing out on this dish entirely. There is a generous amount of sauce here, so you might even serve eight with the addition of some extra scallops; two skillets would be needed for the sauté.

2 ounces (½ stick) butter
¾ cup finely chopped white onion
2 teaspoons minced garlic
3 cups cored, seeded, juiced, and diced ripe, red tomatoes, the outer walls only
3 large chipotles en adobo, drained; stems, seeds, and veins removed; finely minced
Coarse salt to taste
1½ cups heavy cream
Clarified butter (p. 75)
2 pounds large sea scallops, trimmed and sliced in half crosswise
4 to 6 cups Plain White Rice (Basic Western or Boiled) (see recipes)
1 to 2 cups broth from Squid Stewed in Its Own Ink (see recipe) (optional)
1 large red pepper, roasted, peeled, cleaned, and cut into thin strips

Melt the butter in a skillet and sauté onion very gently until tender. Add garlic and sauté briefly. Add tomatoes and *chipotles* and a little salt. Cover and simmer gently, stirring occasionally, until all is tender. Cool mixture to lukewarm and process to a fine paste, scraping down the sides of the processor bowl as needed. Pour mixture into a non-reactive saucepan and add the cream. Heat mixture over a very low heat or in a double boiler until the flavors are married and the cream no longer has a raw taste. Do not simmer. Correct seasoning. Keep the sauce warm but do not overheat.

Heat a large skillet and film it with clarified butter. Sauté scallops gently without browning just until they are heated through. This will probably have to be done in 2 batches. Blot scallops to remove cooking fat and place them in single layers on opposite sides of warmed serving plates, leaving a center line vacant for the rice. Fold squid broth (if you are using it) into the rice, and spoon a line of rice down the center of each plate. Decorate rice with some criss-crossed strips of red pepper. Mask scallops with warm sauce, and serve immediately.

HOME-PICKLED DRIED *CHIPOTLES*

> *2 tablespoons corn oil*
> *¼ cup sliced white onion*
> *1 clove garlic, sliced*
> *½ teaspoon dried oregano, toasted in a skillet until fragrant*
> *¼ cup wine vinegar*
> *¼ cup water*
> *12 dried* chipotles, *rinsed in cold water*

Heat oil in a small saucepan and add onion. Sauté gently until almost tender. Add garlic and sauté briefly. Add oregano, vinegar, and water, and bring to a boil. Add chiles, cover pan, and simmer for about 5 minutes or so. When chiles begin to plump and tenderize, pour mixture into a bowl, cover closely, and cool. Refrigerate mixture and let it cure for a few days before using, if possible.

MACADAMIA-BREADED MAHI MAHI WITH PASSION FRUIT SAUCE

4 servings

As the word gets out and the supply increases, mahi mahi is becoming a more mainstream fish, no longer a Hawaiian exotic. Though the fish live in all tropical oceans and our supply is mostly Atlantic, mahi mahi is the best marketing name to use, for now at least; *dolphin* still scares some people who ought to know better than to think that someone is putting marine mammal on the table. This dish exploits the tropical theme. You might use a cup of fresh mango purée in place of the passion fruit.

4 mahi mahi fillets, 6 to 8 ounces each, with skin on
Coarse salt and freshly ground white pepper to taste
1 egg, beaten
¼ cup milk or buttermilk
One 3½-ounce bottle shelled macadamia nuts
Flour, as needed
3 passion fruit
¼ cup lime juice
1 teaspoon sugar, or to taste
¼ cup vegetable oil
¾ cup white wine
Zest of 1 lime, cut into fine julienne
4 tablespoons butter cut into pieces, at room temperature

Season fillets lightly with salt and pepper and set them aside to come
to room temperature. Combine egg and milk or buttermilk in a shallow bowl and set aside. Pulse nuts in a food processor or blender just
until they are rather finely ground. Do not overprocess. They may also
be chopped by hand. Combine ground nuts with ¼ cup flour and set
aside. Cut passion fruit in half, spoon out the pulp, and put it in a small
sieve over a small bowl. Mash pulp with the back of a spoon to extract
as much juice as possible, and pour through the lime juice to "wash"
the seeds. Discard seeds. Dissolve sugar in the passion fruit–lime juice
mixture and set aside.

Heat a large skillet to very hot. Put a large handful of flour on
a sheet of wax paper and the chopped nuts–flour mixture on a separate
piece of wax paper. Dust the fillets with flour, shaking off the excess,
then dip them into the egg and buttermilk bath, moistening the flesh
but not the skin as much as possible. Then press the flesh into the
chopped nuts to coat, leaving the skin plain. Add the oil to the hot
skillet and heat it until almost smoking. Add the fillets to the pan, skin
side down, and sauté until golden, about 2 minutes. Turn and sauté
until the nut crust is golden, another 2 minutes or so. Turn again,
set heat on low, and cook until heated through. Remove to a platter
and keep warm. If the fillets are very thick, remove them from the
skillet when they are nicely browned and then heat them through in
a 300°F. oven.

Wipe out the skillet and return it to the heat. Add the white
wine and reduce by half. Add the fruit juice mixture and reduce
slightly. Add the lime zest. Add the butter and swirl it in off the heat.

Correct seasoning. Blot cooking fat from the platter, pour the sauce around the fillets, and serve immediately.

SEA SQUAB PROVENÇALE

4 servings

One of the sweetest and easiest to handle of all seafoods is the meaty tail of our Atlantic puffer (blowfish), which is marketed as sea squab. The flesh is arranged rather like monkfish in two rounded fillets divided by a central backbone, so there is very little waste. Some sort of panfrying is usual, though there is no reason why they could not be included in stews and other preparations as well. This recipe is particularly well suited to the Northeast, where cherry tomatoes are often the most flavorful ones available, unless it happens to be August or September. This same preparation works nicely for many other seafoods, including fillets of searobin and frogs' legs. It is also tasty prepared in advance and served at room temperature.

About 2 pounds sea squab tails, 8 to 12 pieces
½ cup buttermilk

THE COATING

1 cup all-purpose flour
1 tablespoon coarse salt
½ teaspoon freshly ground black pepper
½ teaspoon freshly ground white pepper
¼ teaspoon cayenne

Light olive oil, as needed
2 tablespoons minced shallots
1 tablespoon minced garlic
¼ cup dry white wine
½ teaspoon grated or finely minced lemon or orange zest
1 pint very red, small cherry tomatoes, stems removed, rinsed, and dried
1 tablespoon tiny (nonpareil) capers, drained
2 tablespoons chopped parsley or fresh basil or a combination
Coarse salt and freshly ground black pepper to taste

Rinse and dry fish, and put it in a dish with the buttermilk. Bring it to room temperature. Prepare coating and set aside.

Just before serving time, spread the seasoned flour on a plate or sheet of wax paper. Heat a large skillet until very hot and add oil to a depth of ¼ inch. Heat oil until it threatens to smoke. Dredge fish in flour and shake off excess. Cook in hot oil until nicely browned and heated through, a few minutes on each side. Remove to a platter lined with paper towels to drain, and put in a warm place. Plate fish or remove and discard paper towels from the platter.

Discard oil and wipe out the skillet if it is burned. Add ¼ cup fresh oil to skillet and heat. Add shallots and garlic and sizzle briefly, just until fragrant. Add white wine and zest and reduce by half. Add tomatoes and heat them through, shaking the pan often to roll them around. Cook tomatoes just until they are warmed but still retain their shape. Add capers, herb(s), and salt and pepper to taste, and toss to distribute. Be careful with salt because of the capers. If the skin of the softest tomato splits, you know they have all had enough. Spoon mixture over or next to the fish, and serve immediately.

OLD-FASHIONED CRAB CAKES

4 to 8 servings

Crab cakes are important fare these days, but if you intend to get them by the critics they should consist of only jumbo lump crabmeat and just enough other stuff—mostly a little egg—to hold it together. While there is nothing wrong with such extravagance, a more traditional approach, such as the one below, is enjoyable too. Make sure the mixture is well seasoned. You may form eight cakes, dust with flour, and sauté in butter for an elegant starter or main course served with Lemon Butter (see recipe) or another sheer sauce, or you may crumb and deep-fry smaller cakes; they will work as finger food if they are not too large. Tartar sauce is a possible accompaniment for the little fried guys, but it is not essential that you offer any sauce at all.

4 tablespoons butter
¾ cup minced onion
1 teaspoon dry mustard

Large pinch cayenne
1/2 teaspoon coarse salt
1/2 teaspoon freshly ground pepper
1 teaspoon Worcestershire sauce
1 teaspoon lemon or lime juice
3/4 cup fresh bread crumbs
2 tablespoons minced parsley
2 eggs, beaten
1 pound crabmeat, jumbo lump or a smaller grade, carefully picked
over
Flour for dredging (optional)
1 1/2 cups bread crumbs for dredging (optional)
Clarified butter (p. 75) or vegetable oil
Parsley sprigs and lemon wedges for garnish (optional)

In a medium skillet, melt butter and sauté onion gently until tender and translucent. Pour mixture into a bowl and stir in mustard, cayenne, salt, pepper, Worcestershire, and lemon or lime juice. Stir in 3/4 cup bread crumbs and minced parsley, then eggs. Gently fold in crabmeat. Correct seasoning. Chill well.

At serving time, form mixture into cakes of desired size, and then either dredge lightly in flour and sauté in clarified butter until golden, or roll in bread crumbs and deep-fry in 375°F. oil until lightly browned. Drain and serve immediately garnished with parsley sprigs and lemon wedges.

FRIED PORGY WITH SPICY THAI SAUCE

About 4 servings

A number of Thai restaurants in the New York area serve delicious crispy spicy whole fried fish with a sauce that is very like the tomatoey Hunan Chinese version. The principal difference is in the use of lime juice instead of rice vinegar and fish sauce instead of soy. Both styles are wonderful. This version is based on a composite of dishes sampled in Thai restaurants plus techniques learned from Norman Weinstein. Many restaurants use black sea bass because of its popularity, but such an elegant fish should be reserved for steaming. Porgies have a perfect flavor and texture for frying. Ocean perch is another good choice.

4 pounds whole porgies (2 to 4 fish), gutted, scaled, gills removed, rinsed well
Coarse salt to taste

THE AROMATICS

1 generous tablespoon minced garlic
¹⁄₄ cup minced fresh gingerroot
3 to 4 tablespoons minced fresh hot green or red chiles (jalapeño or serrano), or to taste
Thinly sliced green tops from 4 scallions

THE SAUCE

¹⁄₄ cup lime or lemon juice
¹⁄₂ cup brown sugar (light or dark)
³⁄₄ cup tomato purée
¹⁄₃ cup Asian fish sauce
¹⁄₄ cup water

Peanut or soy oil for deep-frying, about 2 quarts
Cornstarch for dredging

THE GARNISHES

Julienned whites from 4 scallions
1 bunch fresh coriander, in sprigs

Cut 3 deep slashes—to the bone—on each side of the fish, holding the knife at a 45-degree angle to the head. Salt lightly, inside and out. Combine aromatics. Combine sauce ingredients and correct seasoning.

Heat the oil in a wok to 375°F. Dredge fish in cornstarch, being sure to coat the insides of the slashes. Holding it by the tail, slide fish, one at a time, into the hot oil and fry until golden and cooked through. If the fish is not totally immersed in oil, baste the exposed head and/or tail to ensure even cooking. When done, remove to a platter lined with paper towels to drain, and then fry the remaining fish. Let oil return to temperature between fryings, and keep it hot.

Remove ¼ cup oil to another wok or a heavy skillet that has been heated. When the oil threatens to smoke, add the aromatics and stir-fry briefly until fragrant. Stir in the sauce mixture and bring to a boil.

Return fish to the hot oil for a few seconds to crisp. Drain again. Place fish on a platter. Pour the hot sauce over the fish, strew scallion whites over the fish and coriander around it, and serve immediately.

FRIED WHITEBAIT

6 to 8 servings

Though never quite so popular in the United States as in Europe, fried whitebait is relished here by folks in-the-know. Particularly in late spring and in the fall there are generous supplies of small fry at Fulton. While baby herring and related fish are usual in Europe, our whitebait are likely to be young silversides or sand lances. They are delicious when prepared and presented simply. Fried parsley makes a lovely garnish, and presents no particular extra work since the oil is already heated to frying temperature.

2 pounds fresh whitebait
½ cup lemon juice
2 cups flour
1 tablespoon coarse salt
1 teaspoon white pepper
1 teaspoon black pepper
¾ teaspoon cayenne
Vegetable oil for frying
Lemon wedges
1 large bunch fried curly parsley (optional) *

---

* To prepare parsley for frying, trim the stems to a length of 2 to 3 inches, wash parsley well and dry it *extremely* well. Set aside on a paper towel. At serving time, fry the prepared parsley in oil heated to 375°F., a handful at a time, for 30 seconds or less, or just until crisp. Drain well.

Rinse and drain fish well. Place in a bowl with the lemon juice and let sit for a few minutes or longer. Combine the flour and seasonings. Heat oil to 375°F. At serving time, drain fish and dredge a handful at a time in seasoned flour, dusting off excess flour in a strainer. Deep-fry until lightly browned, about 1 minute, then drain well. Repeat the procedure for the remaining fish, holding the finished fish in a warm oven. Do not cover. Let oil return to frying temperature between batches. (Fry parsley at this point, if you are using it.) Garnish the whitebait and serve it hot.

CREOLE SPECKLED TROUT MEUNIÈRE (OR AMANDINE)

6 servings

The most plentiful and popular fish in the Gulf, speckled trout (spotted seatrout) is not a trout at all but a member of the drum family along with red drum, black drum, and our Atlantic seatrout or weakfish. Seatrout is quite similar to speckled trout and makes a fine substitute in all Louisiana trout dishes. If you add sliced almonds to the basic meunière preparation, then it becomes amandine.

6 skinless speckled trout or seatrout fillets, 6 to 8 ounces each
2 cups flour
2 tablespoons coarse salt
1 teaspoon freshly ground black pepper
1 teaspoon freshly ground white pepper
1/2 teaspoon cayenne
2 eggs
1/2 cup milk
Vegetable oil for frying
8 ounces (2 sticks) butter
1/4 cup lemon juice
1/2 cup sliced blanched almonds (optional)
2 tablespoons finely chopped parsley
1 teaspoon Worcestershire sauce

Trim fillets neatly and bring them to room temperature. Combine flour with seasonings and have it ready on a platter or a sheet of wax paper. Beat eggs with milk until smooth, and set aside. Pour 1 inch of oil into a large skillet or, preferably, a wide heavy pan with sides 3 or more inches high.

Heat oil to 375°F.

While oil is heating, swirl butter in a medium skillet over heat until it is lightly browned. Arrest cooking by adding half the lemon juice. Set aside. Toast the almonds in a 375°F. oven if you are using them.

Just before serving, dredge fillets in seasoned flour, dust off excess, dip into egg mixture, and dredge again. Fry until golden and heated through, turning once. Do not crowd pan or add fillets so quickly that oil temperature drops below 360°F. As pieces are done, remove them to a platter lined with paper towels and hold them in a warm oven.

Transfer fish to a platter or plates, and sprinkle with parsley, optional almonds, and remaining lemon juice. Heat up the melted butter and add the Worcestershire. Swirl to combine, pour over fish, and serve immediately.

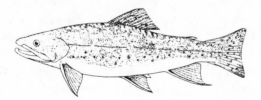

SKATE WITH VINEGAR SAUCE

4 to 6 servings

Here is a variation on a recipe from Andrée's Mediterranean Cuisine, which has been remodeled and reopened as Café Crocodile. We all think of skate with black butter and may forget that there are many other possibilities as well as that classic. Yet a touch of vinegar is lovely with skate no matter what else happens to it; that is why this treatment seemed so appropriate. Andrée herself uses fillets of seatrout—an excellent choice—which, of course, do not require preliminary poaching. Skate may also be skinned and trimmed or filleted raw, but poaching makes it easier to handle.

4 pounds skate wing (this could be 2, 3, or 4 pieces)
Coarse salt, as needed
Red or white wine vinegar, as needed
Freshly ground black pepper to taste
Flour for dredging
Vegetable oil for shallow frying
1 tablespoon olive oil
1 tablespoon flour
1 clove garlic, minced
2 teaspoons chopped fresh rosemary leaves, or 1 scant teaspoon dried
1/2 cup white wine
About 1 teaspoon honey
Rosemary sprigs for garnish

Rinse skate well, scrubbing it if it feels slimy. With a very sharp knife or kitchen shears, trim off and discard the thin outer fins; the point where the usable meat begins will be clearly visible. Also trim off any "shoulder" bones on the inside. Cut crosswise into fairly large serving pieces. Put skate, dark skin down (it seems to curl more) in a heavy pan large enough to hold it in a single layer. Add cold water to cover well, measuring the amount of water. For each quart, add 2 tablespoons coarse salt and 1/4 cup vinegar. Bring water almost to a boil, lower heat, and poach until heated through. Do not overcook. Remove skate from poaching bath and, when it is cool enough to handle, remove and discard skin. You will find a thin gelatinous film and a thin layer of beige flesh that you also want to remove, working your knife lightly with the grain to avoid tearing the neat white flesh. When skate wings are huge you can fillet them, but the more normal sizes should be left with the central horizontal bones intact. They present no problems for the diner. Season skate lightly with salt and pepper and have flour for dredging ready.

Heat 1 inch of vegetable oil in a large skillet until very hot. Handling carefully, dredge skate pieces lightly, shaking off excess flour. Fry them in a single layer until golden on both sides and warmed through. Drain on paper towels and place on a serving platter. Keep warm.

Heat the olive oil in a medium skillet and add 1 tablespoon flour. Cook and stir until flour just begins to color. Add garlic and chopped rosemary, and stir for a second or two, until fragrant. Whisk in white wine and 1/2 cup vinegar, being careful to avoid spatters. Add the honey. Whisk and cook for about 1 minute. Correct seasoning. Pour sauce over skate and serve immediately, garnished with rosemary sprigs.

OYSTERS KATSU-RETSU

4 to 8 servings

New York City has a charming abundance of neighborhood restaurants of nearly every ethnic persuasion, with Japanese restaurants high on the list of favorites. The one called Seto on East 51 Street near First Avenue is one of those good little places. Along with their selection of sparklingly fresh raw fish and shellfish offerings, Seto serves a few very pleasant cooked seafood dishes. At home you may use this method to produce either a first or a main course, as simple or as elaborately garnished as you wish. Here is how they do it. Allow four to eight oysters per serving.

32 oysters, freshly shucked, or four 8-ounce cans raw oysters
1 cup flour, lightly seasoned with salt and white pepper
3 eggs, beaten
2 cups fresh bread crumbs, not too finely ground, partially dried in a
    warm oven
Soy or peanut oil for deep-frying
1 bunch broccoli
2 cups bean sprouts
Lemon wedges
Tonkatsu *sauce,* * *diluted with water to the texture of a thick sauce,*
    or Spicy Dipping Sauce, Japanese-Style (recipe follows)
Yellow mustard (Dijon is fine)
White rice, Basic Chinese (see recipe)

Drain the oysters. Bread them by rolling them first in the flour, then in egg, then in the crumbs. Place them as they are breaded on a rack to dry a bit while you prepare the garnishes and the rice, if desired, and while you preheat the soy or peanut oil to 375°F.

---

* *Tonkatsu* is a dark, fairly thick Japanese condiment purchased in Asian food shops that specialize in Japanese products. The best-known source in Manhattan is Katagiri, 224 East 59 Street, New York, N.Y. 10022.

Cut the broccoli into florets. Steam or blanch bean sprouts and broccoli for either 1 minute for steaming or a few seconds for blanching.

Deep-fry the oysters, a few at a time, in the preheated oil until they are "red fox color." Drain on paper towels and serve as quickly as possible with the hot vegetables, the lemon wedges, the sauces in little individual bowls, if possible (tiny for the mustard and smallish for the *tonkatsu*), and rice on the side in Asian rice bowls. Chopsticks are appropriate.

SPICY DIPPING SAUCE, JAPANESE-STYLE

> *¼ cup Japanese soy sauce (Kikkoman is fine)*
> *¼ cup orange juice*
> *2 tablespoons molasses*
> *1-inch piece fresh gingerroot, peeled and finely chopped*
> *1 large clove garlic, mashed*
> *1 tablespoon rice vinegar*
> *2 tablespoons Worcestershire sauce*
> *½ to ¾ cup tomato ketchup*

Combine ingredients and let flavors marry at room temperature for about 30 minutes. Strain. Correct seasoning.

SHRIMP, SHANGHAI-STYLE

4 to 6 main course servings, 10 first course servings

This simple charmer is from Norman Weinstein, whose classes at various area schools and classes and catering at his Hot Wok in Brooklyn are perennial pleasers. This recipe takes advantage of the fine flavor of shrimp cooked in their shells, even to the point of making the shells an edible part of the dish. Therefore, you will want to be sure not to use shrimp much larger than the 36/40s (count per pound) that Norman specifies; in general, the larger the shrimp the harder the shell. Instructions are given below for preparing the dish to be served either hot or at room temperature. Room temp gets many votes. Ginger wine is the rice wine or dry sherry used to store odds and ends of fresh ginger. If you have none around, use plain rice wine or sherry and increase the ginger a hint. Norman uses Yeo's Sweet Chili Sauce, which he buys at Wing Woh Lung, 50 Mott Street, in Chinatown. You may substitute any of the more available chili sauces from Asian shops or even the Chinese section of some supermarkets, but watch the quantity. Because this sauce mixture is completely combined before it is cooked, you can start with only 1 teaspoon of chili sauce, tasting and adding more until the flavors are balanced. A little more sugar will probably be needed.

1 pound medium shrimp, preferably 36/40s (count per pound)

THE SAUCE

3 tablespoons tomato purée
3 tablespoons ginger wine, or rice wine or dry sherry
1 tablespoon red wine vinegar
1 tablespoon thin (light-color Chinese) soy sauce
1 tablespoon sugar
1 tablespoon Yeo's Sweet Chili Sauce (or other)
1 tablespoon minced fresh gingerroot
¼ teaspoon five-spice powder

5 to 6 cups peanut or corn oil
¼ cup very thinly sliced scallions, green and white parts

ACCOMPANIMENTS

Freshly cooked Basic Chinese Rice (see recipe), if served hot
1 or 2 bunches watercress, tough stems trimmed, if served cool
Thinly sliced scallions for garnish (optional)

Snip off the legs of the shrimp with small kitchen shears or other available tool, even sewing scissors. Rinse shrimp and pat them thoroughly dry with paper towels. Put aside. Combine all the sauce ingredients and set aside.

Heat a wok and add the oil. Heat to 375°F. Add one-third of the shrimp and cook for about 45 seconds, or until shrimp flesh has whitened. Remove to a platter and fry the remaining shrimp in two more batches, making sure that the oil temperature is correct before the shrimp are added. For extra crispiness, you may redip the shrimp in the hot oil, in three batches, but only for a few seconds. Be very careful not to overcook them.

Drain all but 1 tablespoon of the oil from the wok. Heat over high flame for 5 seconds, then add the sauce mixture. Stir to mix well and bring to a boil. Add the shrimp and the thinly sliced scallions, stir once just to combine, and serve immediately with rice. If serving cool, let mixture come to room temperature and serve in a nest of watercress, sprinkled with extra scallions, if you wish. If cooked more than 1 or 2 hours before service, cool and refrigerate but return to room temperature before serving.

CAMARÃOS PAULISTA

FRIED SHRIMP, SÃO PAULO-STYLE

4 servings

Here is another shell-on shrimp fry, but Brazilian this time. The recipe is based on a dish served at the Brazilian Coffee Restaurant and Brazilian Pavillion (same ownership). Diners are free to eat the shells if they wish, or to remove the shells and eat only the flesh if they prefer. The optional sauce was added for moistness, but it is not essential.

1 pound medium shrimp
Coarse salt and freshly ground black pepper to taste
5 to 6 cups vegetable oil for frying
1 tablespoon minced garlic
1 small bunch curly parsley, washed, stems trimmed, thoroughly *dried*

THE SAUCE (OPTIONAL)

2 tablespoons butter
2 tablespoons flour
2 tablespoons garlic-scented oil (reserved from above)
1 cup dry white wine
1 cup Fish Stock (see recipe)
Coarse salt and freshly ground pepper to taste

Lemon or lime wedges

Use very sharp kitchen shears to cut through the *underside* of the shrimp shells almost to the tail end, cutting through about half of the flesh as you go. Season shrimp with salt and pepper and set aside for about 30 minutes to come to room temperature.

Just before serving, heat the oil in a wok or deep saucepan. When it is hot, add the garlic, which will begin to color instantly, and immediately skim it out while it is still golden. Do not let it brown. Set it aside. If you are making the sauce, reserve 2 tablespoons of this garlic-scented oil in a medium skillet. Bring the oil temperature to 375°F.

Carefully dry the shrimp with paper towels. Fry them, a handful at a time, until lightly browned and heated through, up to 1 minute. As they are done, remove them to paper towels to drain, and keep them warm in a slow oven while you fry the rest. Then fry the *very* dry parsley, a handful at a time, for a few seconds, or until almost crisp. Drain and keep warm.

If you wish to make the sauce, add butter and flour to the reserved 2 tablespoons of garlic-scented oil in the medium skillet. Melt butter and cook the roux 1 minute. Whisk in the wine and stock and bring to a boil. Reduce heat, simmer 2 minutes, and then add the reserved garlic. Place the shrimp on a platter or plates, and top with the optional sauce or sprinkle on the reserved garlic. Add the fried parsley, garnish with lemon or lime wedges, and serve immediately.

FRIED SOFT-SHELL CRABS

4 servings

Though still largely a cottage industry, the soft-shell crab business is now so well organized that the product is available up to nine months of the year, with frozen stock available in the three winter months for those who can't wait for the finer live crabs to resurface in April or May. Sautéing is considered the elegant preparation for these gems, but many of us prefer frying, for two reasons. First, a crisp golden coating seems to be the perfect foil for the tender flesh inside. Second, soft-shells vary in their softness because of the rapidity with which crabs begin to strengthen their new armor. Faced with a shell that has gone even a little bit "buckram," the cook will find it impossible to sauté this critter into a wholly edible treat. Only deep-frying will produce the crackling crispness that renders shells palatable, as it does with shrimp, too (see Shrimp, Shanghai-Style). As soft-shell crawfish become more available, you might try them in this same preparation. Properly fried soft-shells need only a spritz of lemon juice to make them perfect, but you may offer a sauce if you wish.

4 large, 8 medium, or 12 small soft-shell crabs
1 tablespoon coarse salt
1/2 teaspoon ground black pepper
1/2 teaspoon ground white pepper
1/4 teaspoon cayenne
1 cup all-purpose flour
Vegetable oil, preferably soy, for frying
Lemon wedges

SUGGESTED SAUCES

Red Sauce with Basil, or Tartar Sauce with Chile and Coriander, or Southwestern Tartar Sauce (see recipes) (optional)

Clean crabs as described on p. 65, rinse, drain, and set aside. Add seasonings to flour and whisk with a dry whisk to combine. Set aside.

If using a large skillet or electric frying pan, add oil to a depth of about 1 inch. For a wok, fryer, or large saucepan, make it deeper. Heat oil to 375°F. Dust crabs with seasoned flour, shaking off excess. Fry crabs in batches, without crowding the vessel, until nicely golden, turning as needed. By all means use a spatter screen if you have one. Small crabs in deep oil should be done in 2 to 3 minutes. Large crabs in shallow oil might need as much as 3 minutes on each side. As crabs are done, remove them to a platter lined with paper towels to drain. Hold them in a warm oven while you fry the rest. When all are done, serve them immediately with lemon wedges and a sauce, if you wish.

FRIED SQUID

About 4 servings

There are not many more wonderful foods than fried squid, but technique is important. Perhaps you assumed that everybody just tossed the cleaned and cut squid with seasoned flour, fried it until golden, drained it, and served it forth. Not so. At Sloppy Louie's on South Street, Chef Antonio Pascual uses *fine* cracker meal. It's good. Chef Louis Leichter claims to have found, through extensive experimentation, the very best way to fry squid in order to achieve a nice crisp crust and tender, moist innards. He determined that blanching the squid for a few seconds before breading it is the secret. He also uses a three-step breading: flour, egg bath, flour. The version below was inspired by his, but it omits the first flouring for delicacy. No sauce is needed with fried squid, but you could provide Red Sauce with Basil (see recipe) for those who want it.

2 pounds squid
1 egg
1 cup buttermilk
2 cups all-purpose flour
2 tablespoons coarse salt
1 teaspoon black pepper
1 teaspoon white pepper
¼ teaspoon cayenne
Vegetable oil, preferably soy, for frying
Lemon wedges

Clean the squid as described on p. 65, and slice bodies into rings ⅜ inch wide. Cut tentacles in half if they are large. Bring a saucepan of water to a boil. Add squid, stir just until pieces separate, and immediately drain and shock with cold water. Drain well and reserve. Beat egg lightly, add buttermilk and squid pieces, and set aside.

Heat oil to 375°F. Combine flour and seasonings. A handful at a time, drain squid pieces and toss them in seasoned flour. Shake off excess flour in a strainer. Deep-fry until golden, less than a minute if oil is properly heated. Remove to a platter lined with paper towels to drain. Keep warm in a slow oven while you fry the remaining squid. Do not cover. Serve as soon as possible with lemon wedges.

STIR-FRIED MONKFISH AND ASPARAGUS

4 to 6 servings

New York's neighborhood Chinese restaurants of the Szechuan/Hunan ilk celebrate the changing of the seasons with a special asparagus menu for spring. Here is a version of one of those seasonal specialties. Of course, the increased availability of asparagus makes this one possible at many times of the year. You might want to substitute about a pound of other seafood—shrimp, scallops, squid, or ocean pout—alone or in combinations.

> *1 1/2 pounds monkfish, trimmed of dark flesh, boned, and cut into*
>   *1-inch cubes*
> *1/2 teaspoon coarse salt*
> *1/4 teaspoon sugar*

THE VEGETABLES

> *1 1/4 pounds medium asparagus*
> *Coarse salt*
> *1 red bell pepper*
> *3 larged dried shiitake mushrooms*

THE AROMATICS

> *1 tablespoon minced garlic*
> *1 tablespoon minced fresh gingerroot*

THE SAUCE

> *2 tablespoons light soy sauce*
> *3 tablespoons rice wine or dry sherry*
> *About 1 teaspoon sugar*
> *1 to 2 tablespoons Chinese chili sauce or paste (depending on the brand*
>   *and your taste)*
> *2 tablespoons hoisin*
> *1 tablespoon ketchup*
> *1/2 teaspoon dark sesame oil*

*

3 scallions, thinly sliced
1 tablespoon cornstarch mixed with ¼ cup water
2 cups soy or peanut oil
1 tablespoon cornstarch
Basic Chinese Rice (see recipe)

Toss fish in a bowl with salt and sugar and let marinate.

To prepare the vegetables: Remove and discard tough ends of asparagus and cut on a steep diagonal into slices about ½ inch thick. Keep tips separate. Blanch stems in salted boiling water for about 30 seconds, depending on size. Add tips and drain almost immediately. Shock with cold water and set aside. Wash the red pepper, clean out membranes and seeds, and slice into thin strips. Soak mushrooms in hot water until plump, then drain and slice them. Combine vegetables and set aside.

Combine garlic and ginger and set aside. Combine sauce ingredients and taste for seasoning. If your chili sauce is vinegary, you may need to add more sugar to balance it. You now have, in separate bowls, fish, vegetables, aromatics, sauce, scallions, and cornstarch mixture.

In a wok, heat the oil to 375°F. Stir 1 tablespoon cornstarch into the fish, by hand, gently but thoroughly. Fry the fish chunks, a few at a time, until crisp and heated through. They will color very lightly. Drain and reserve.

Pour out all but about 1 tablespoon of the oil and heat the wok until it just starts to smoke. Add aromatics and stir-fry briefly. Add vegetables and stir-fry about 30 seconds. Add sauce and toss. Add fish and toss. Add scallions and toss. Dribble a little of the cornstarch mixture in from one side and toss until it is cooked. You will need only just enough of the mixture to set the sauce so it clings lightly to the solids. Pour onto a platter and serve immediately, with rice on the side.

LEFTOVERS

Imaginative recycling makes good sense, particularly when there is a surfeit of expensive ingredients. Rather than let leftovers sit in the fridge until they grow green-and-gray fur, why not put them to good use? Seafood dishes are usually pleasant to eat simply reheated or at room temperature, but most people prefer a little novelty. So the recipes for this section were chosen with the thought that they are fun to make and to eat, but that you might not dash out to the fish market to provision them. There are only a few basic considerations to keep in mind when planning creative reuse.

If the seafood has been heavily flavored by a marinade or assertive herbs or spices, those flavors should be welcome in the new dish. Mild-flavored, white-fleshed fish are the most versatile, but shellfish and assertive or colorful fish have their uses too, particularly shrimp and salmon. If the fish was cooked in butter, it will probably only be useful for hot makeovers. Oil-based and fat-free preparations will do for either hot or cold.

The recipes assume that the leftover is cooked. But sometimes you will have been working with a fish that needs to be cut to very specific dimensions, leaving a good quantity of usable flesh that is not usable for the recipe at hand. In the case of raw trimmings, simply poach them in salted water or bake them in a slow oven. When cool enough to handle, remove skin and bones and flake or chop or whatever is needed, just as you would with cooked leftovers.

SEAFOOD FRITTATA

4 to 8 servings, or 24 or more hors d'oeuvre squares

People in the United States are discovering the considerable charms of a well-made frittata, the traditional Italian open-faced omelet flavored with nearly anything savory that a cook might have on hand. Just be sure there are no raw ingredients that could make the mixture watery as it cooks. Unlike French omelets, frittatas are cooked slowly until firm but not dry and served in wedges, either warm or cool, as a starter or a luncheon or supper main course. Most any leftover fish or shellfish will do. This is one of the few Italian preparations where it is safe to go ahead and include cheese with the seafood.

2 tablespoons light olive oil
1 tablespoon butter
1 cup thinly sliced onions
1 medium zucchini, thinly sliced
1 large clove garlic, minced
6 eggs
1 cup flaked or diced leftover seafood
1 1/2 cups cooked spaghetti or other thin pasta
2 tablespoons chopped fresh herbs, parsley or basil or a combination
1/2 cup grated Parmesan, preferably genuine parmigiano reggiano
Coarse salt and freshly ground black pepper to taste

Heat the oil and butter in a 10-inch skillet or omelet pan. T-fal or another quality nonstick is easiest to handle, but any heavy material will do. Add onions and cook gently until wilted. Add zucchini slices and cook gently until tender and the moisture has reduced, adding the garlic for the last 30 seconds or so. Pour mixture into a large sieve set in a bowl to drain and cool. Reserve drippings.

In a bowl, beat the eggs until they are nearly homogenous, then stir in the cooled onion mixture and the remaining ingredients. Heat the skillet and put about 1 tablespoon of the reserved drippings in it. When the drippings are hot, add the egg mixture and distribute the solids evenly. Cook over moderate to low heat until lightly browned and softly set. Use a fork to pierce the bottom in several places, and lift it slightly to allow fluid egg to flow in. This will help the frittata to set up evenly. When almost set, use a plate to flip the frittata and slide it back into the pan to cook the other side. The second side should only need 1 or 2 minutes to lightly color it. Do not overcook. You may also cook the second side briefly under a broiler instead of flipping it. Slide onto a plate and serve either warm or cool, cut into wedges. You could also cut small squares for hors d'oeuvres.

SALMON CROQUETTES

6 to 12 servings

Here is the first of two recipes from Robert Posch, former executive chef of the New York Restaurant School restaurant, now the head of an executive dining room and a teacher at The

New School for Social Research. Both recipes grew out of his experience in restaurant kitchens, where extravagant quantities of trimmings accumulate. This is one to make when you have leftovers from a poached salmon or when you get a good deal on a whole salmon and need a use for the good parts that remain after you have cut your uniform steaks or fillets. Bob recommends beer and a creamy cole slaw as accompaniments. An honorable man, he credits the spine of the recipe to a crab cake recipe by his mother, Ruth Posch.

1 1/2 pounds (usable weight) salmon meat, trimmed of skin, bones, fat, and any darkened areas
2 tablespoons butter
1 cup minced onions
1 cup minced celery
1 small clove garlic, finely minced
1/4 cup chopped parsley
1/4 cup all-purpose flour
2 cups half-and-half
1/2 teaspoon coarse salt, or to taste
1/2 teaspoon freshly ground white pepper, or to taste
2 tablespoons chopped fresh dill
Vegetable oil for frying
About 2 cups fine fresh bread crumbs

If salmon is raw, poach it in salted water just until heated through. Drain, cool, and flake. Set aside.

Melt butter in a skillet. Add onions and celery and cook over low heat until onions are tender and translucent. Add garlic and parsley and cook 1 minute. Sprinkle the flour over the mixture and stir it in. Cook briefly, stirring. Stir in the half-and-half. Bring to a boil, still stirring, then reduce heat and let simmer, stirring occasionally, for 5 minutes. Scrape into a bowl, season with salt and pepper, and let cool to room temperature.

Combine cooled mixture with salmon and dill and blend well. Correct seasoning. Cover and refrigerate for at least 1 hour. The better chilled it is, the easier it will be to form and the less likely it will be to fall apart during frying.

Form chilled mixture into 12 balls about 4 ounces each. Flatten to form patties approximately 3/4 inch thick. Pour oil into a large skillet to a depth of 1/2 inch. Heat to very hot—375°F., if you are able to measure it at that depth, and coat patties with bread crumbs, gently shaking off excess. Brown cakes on one side, then turn and brown the other. As cakes are done, drain them briefly on paper towels, and serve immediately.

FRESH TUNA AND RED BEAN VINAIGRETTE

4 to 6 servings

Just as satisfying as the suave richness of Salmon Croquettes is this combination of earthy flavors, also from Robert Posch. Again the amount of leftover fish is rather unusual for the average home kitchen. Buy a little extra when preparing Grilled Marinated Fillet Mignon of Tuna or another dish that requires that the fish be cut to very specific dimensions. That way you can look forward to this dividend. Bob recommends it as a starter or a luncheon main course with a green salad and a crusty loaf. If you are in a rush you might substitute drained canned beans, even though they are rather mushy and not as clean-tasting as home-cooked; we just won't tell Bob.

1/4 pound (generous 1/2 cup) dried red, red kidney, or pinto beans, picked over and rinsed
Coarse salt (about 2 teaspoons)
1 1/2 pounds (usable weight) tuna meat, trimmed of any skin and dark flesh
1 small red onion, halved lengthwise, and sliced crosswise into thin slivers
1/2 small clove garlic, minced
2 tablespoons chopped fresh oregano leaves
2 tablespoons chopped parsley
2 tablespoons white wine vinegar
2 to 3 tablespoons lemon juice
1 cup extra-virgin olive oil
1/2 teaspoon coarse salt, or to taste
1/2 teaspoon freshly ground black pepper

Soak beans overnight, or follow the package instructions for quick soaking. Drain. Simmer very gently in fresh water to cover until tender, adding some salt toward the end. Drain and cool.

   If tuna is raw, poach it in salted water just until heated through.

Drain and cool. Dice the tuna or break it into chunks, whichever seems more practical for the shapes you have.

Combine tuna with beans, onion slices, garlic, and herbs. Whisk or shake vinegar, lemon juice, olive oil, and salt and pepper into a vinaigrette. Add to tuna mixture and combine well. Cover and refrigerate for at least 1 hour so the flavors have time to marry. Correct seasoning. Serve cold or at room temperature.

9TH AVENUE FRITTERS

About 12 snack portions

Among the ethnic treats one can expect to find at the annual 9th Avenue International Food Festival are thin, shallow-fried Asian fritters something like the ones below. It is difficult to know what to call them. They are not really fu yung; in fact they are nothing like the snowy egg-white-and-minced-chicken concoctions of Northern China. Anyway, they are delicious and a perfect use for leftover seafood and leftover pasta, too. Dust off the old electric frying pan if you have one. It will give you temperature control and just the right squarish shape for frying 4 fritters at a time.

1 tablespoon cornstarch
1/4 teaspoon baking powder
4 eggs
2 teaspoons soy sauce
1/2 teaspoon sugar
1/2 teaspoon dark Asian sesame oil
Dash Tabasco or hot chili oil, or to taste
1/2 teaspoon minced garlic
1 teaspoon minced fresh gingerroot
1/4 teaspoon coarse salt, or to taste
1 cup flaked or diced leftover cooked seafood
3/4 cup mung bean sprouts, rinsed and drained well
*3/4 cup cooked spaghetti or other thin pasta, cut into lengths not more
    than 6 inches*
1/3 cup thinly sliced scallions
Soy or peanut oil for frying

In a medium bowl, whisk together cornstarch and baking powder to combine and eliminate lumps. In another bowl, whisk eggs until just blended and gradually whisk into cornstarch mixture. Whisk in soy sauce, sugar, sesame oil, Tabasco, garlic, and ginger. Fold in remaining fritter ingredients.

Pour ¼ inch oil into an electric frying pan, or large skillet, and heat to 375°F. The easiest way to form the fritters is to scoop up about ¼ cup of batter with a ladle, using tongs to ensure a good balance of liquid and solids. Ladle into the hot oil with a circular motion and quickly spread batter with the tongs so that it is thin and about 4 or 5 inches in diameter. Repeat to fill the pan. When fritters are golden, turn and brown on the other side. When done, remove fritters to drain on paper towels and hold in a warm place while you fry the rest. Serve hot.

SEAFOOD FRITTERS

About 24 small fritters

Here is quite another fritter, something more akin to the conch fritters that are enjoying a healthy vogue in Caribbean and Key West–type restaurants. By all means use conch if you can find it; its rich flavor is ideal for this preparation. But any other seafood will do nicely. There are several Bahamian bottled sauces on the market, in various shades of red and green, all devilishly hot. Try these, if you can find them, but also offer the more readily available Jamaican Pickapeppa Sauce. Failing that, you might try Tartar Sauce with Chile and Coriander (see recipe).

1 cup flaked or chopped leftover seafood
1 cup fine fresh bread crumbs
1 egg, lightly beaten
½ cup finely chopped onion
1 small clove garlic, minced
¼ teaspoon Tabasco, or to taste
1 teaspoon lime or lemon juice
2 teaspoons chopped parsley
Milk, if needed
Salt and freshly ground pepper, if needed
Vegetable oil for frying
Lemon wedges

In a bowl, combine seafood, bread crumbs, egg, onion, garlic, Tabasco, lime or lemon juice, and parsley. Moisten with a little milk if mixture seems too dry to hold together. Season to taste with salt and pepper. Chill mixture for at least 1 hour.

Pour oil into some sort of fryer, either shallow or deep, and heat to 375°F. Meanwhile, form mixture into balls using a generous tablespoon for each. Fry, a few at a time, until nicely browned. As they are done, drain fritters on paper towels and hold them in a warm place while you fry the rest. Serve hot with lemon wedges and sauce(s) of choice.

STUFFED JALAPEÑOS

24 to 30 pieces

Years ago a coworker who had spent some time in Mexico used to stuff pickled jalapeños with canned tuna for a zesty hors d'oeuvre that everyone who liked the heat loved. If you wish to try the *authentic* item, order chiles stuffed with sardines at Rosa Mexicano. Tasty as that is, the corrupt version below is more fun, and ideal for leftover tuna, herring, sardines (small herring), or mackerel. Try it for casual occasions when spicy food is to follow, suggesting to diners, as the inventor did, that they pop the whole thing into their mouths—nibbling can cause lip discomfort, even blisters for the uninitiated. Now that bottled *jalapeños en escabeche* are readily available, even in supermarkets, assembling the ingredients for this one is a snap.

1 cup flaked cooked leftover fish: tuna, herring, sardines, or mackerel
Few tablespoons bottled mayonnaise or homemade mayonnaise with a
    pinch of sugar added
1 teaspoon lime or lemon juice
Coarse salt, if needed
12 to 15 bottled pickled jalapeños, depending on size
Chili powder (the supermarket kind with cumin in it, not pure ground
    chiles)

Pick over the fish to remove any bones. Moisten with mayonnaise and season with lime or lemon juice, plus a little salt if the original preparation of the fish was bland. Set aside.

Slice jalapeños in half lengthwise and remove caps. Use a teaspoon to scrape out seeds and membranes, then discard them. Stuff jalapeño halves with fish mixture, mounding it slightly. You will probably need 1½ to 2 teaspoons mixture per piece, depending on the size of the chiles. Refrigerate if prepared in advance. Sprinkle very lightly with chili powder and serve cool.

PASTA WITH TUNA AND TOMATO SAUCE

2 to 4 servings

If you keep a pint of homemade red sauce in the freezer for emergencies (as everyone should), then you can put this one together in minutes and be proud to serve it to anyone. Even from scratch it is quick and easy. Leftover mackerel, herring, or sardines are other good candidates. Remember, purists say no cheese with seafood pasta, even with red sauce, but suit yourself.

2 cups homemade Red Sauce with Basil (see recipe)
4 to 6 ounces cooked leftover tuna, broken into chunks
2 to 4 anchovy fillets, chopped
½ to 1 tablespoon tiny (nonpareil) capers, drained
8 ounces spaghetti or other pasta
Coarse salt
1 tablespoon softened butter
*1 tablespoon thin strips (*chiffonade*) fresh basil or mint*
Freshly grated Parmesan, preferably genuine parmigiano reggiano
  (optional)

Prepare the red sauce, if you have not already done so, and warm it in a nonreactive saucepan. Add tuna, anchovies, and capers, and heat through. Correct seasoning, and keep warm.

Cook pasta in well-salted water until it is *al dente,* drain, and toss with the butter. Put pasta on platter or plates, and top with the sauce. Sprinkle on the basil or mint. Serve immediately, offering cheese if you wish for those who may want it.

RICE OR NOODLE SOUP WITH SEAFOOD, JAPANESE-STYLE

About 4 servings

This is based on the *zosui* served around town that is so very satisfying in cold weather. Precooked Japanese short-grain rice is the normal ingredient, but long-grain rice will do. If you have some noodles around and want to use them, then you will have to call this dish noodle soup; there seems to be no authentic Japanese preparation quite like it. The Japanese ingredients (except for sake from the liquor store) are available at specialty shops, at neighborhood greengrocers, and, increasingly, even in supermarkets.

THE SOUP

> *1/4 cup soy sauce (Kikkoman is fine)*
> *1/4 cup sake or mirin*
> *1 envelope (.35 ounce) powdered instant dashi*
> *One 2-inch piece dried kombu (kelp) (optional)*
> *2 or 3 thick slices of fresh gingerroot*
> *1/2 teaspoon sugar*
> *5 1/2 cups water*
> *Coarse salt, if needed*

> *4 cups cooked short- or long-grain rice (from 1 1/3 cups raw rice), slightly undercooked if possible, and rinsed, or 4 cups cooked noodles (from 10 ounces dry), udon or soba, or spaghetti or a finer gauge of Western pasta, slightly undercooked if possible, and rinsed*

THE GARNISHES

> *1 cup leftover cooked seafood, flaked or shredded*
> *3 dried shiitake mushrooms, soaked in hot water until tender, drained, stems removed, and sliced*
> *1/4 cup very thinly sliced carrot*
> *1/3 cup thinly sliced scallions*
> *One of the following: 1 sheet dried nori for sushi, toasted and shredded; 1 tablespoon dried instant wakame (seaweed), reconstituted in*

*hot water and drained; 1 cup fresh spinach leaves, washed,
trimmed, and torn or shredded; or ½ bunch watercress, coarse
stems removed*

Choose a lidded pot of at least 4 quarts capacity that can come to the
table: a Japanese *donabe,* a Chinese sandy pot or other flameproof
earthenware, Western enameled cast iron, or whatever is presentable.
Combine the soup ingredients and bring to a boil. Lower heat and
simmer 2 or 3 minutes. Correct seasoning. Remove and discard
kombu and ginger. Add the rice or noodles, and return to a boil. Turn
off heat and quickly add the garnishes, each type grouped together.
I'd put the seafood in the middle and the four others in clumps around
it. Immediately put on the lid and take the pot to the table. Remove
lid and let diners admire the beauty of your work. Stir just to distribute
ingredients and serve in deep soup bowls if you have them; otherwise,
flat Western soup plates will do.

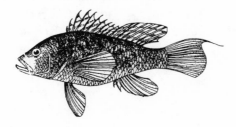

A SIMPLE SOUP

About 4 servings

Here is an outline for a very satisfying soup that is particularly
appropriate for a cold-weather supper with a crusty loaf and a
salad. Feel free to add any vegetables you have around, including carrots, zucchini, corn, and cooked dried beans. Fresh
herbs are also welcome. Mild white fish and shellfish are the
best leftover choices.

2 tablespoons butter
2 tablespoons light olive oil
1 cup chopped onions
1/2 cup chopped celery
One 28-ounce can tomatoes
1 large clove garlic, minced
1/2 cup dry white wine
2 cups Fish Stock (see recipe)
2 1/2 cups water
2 cups peeled potatoes cut into 1/2-inch dice
1 bay leaf
1/4 teaspoon dried leaf thyme
2 tablespoons chopped parsley
Coarse salt and freshly ground black pepper to taste
1 cup leftover cooked seafood, flaked or diced

Heat butter and oil in a medium soup pot, and add onions and celery. Cook gently, without browning, until tender. Slice canned tomatoes and set aside; strain juice from can and reserve. Stir in garlic and cook for a few seconds. Add tomatoes, juice, and remaining ingredients, except for the seafood, and bring to a boil. Reduce heat and simmer gently, uncovered, until potatoes are tender, about 20 to 30 minutes. Add seafood, correct seasoning, discard bay leaf, and serve hot.

PASTA AND GRAIN DISHES

See p. 78 for ways to determine proper cooking time.

It is no secret that vast quantities of Fulton wares are turned into pasta and rice dishes, reflecting an American passion in general, and the area's strong Italian influence in particular. Add the influence of other Mediterranean kitchens and all the Asian styles that are represented in the New York area, plus the most visible stronghold of traditional American rice cookery, Louisiana, and the total of farinaceous dishes is substantial. If you want to make your own pasta, you will find exhaustive treatments elsewhere. We have included a polenta recipe because polenta is delicious with stews and braises.

VARIETIES BEST SUITED

Shellfish turn up more often than not in seafood pasta and rice dishes because of their firm texture as well as fine flavor. Firm-textured fish—monkfish, ocean pout, blackfish, wolffish, searobin, and sea squab (puffer)—are also good candidates. The exceptions that come immediately to mind are the use of smoked salmon in creamy pasta preparations and the myriad fish used in sushi.

EQUIPMENT

Of course a large pasta pot—8 to 16 quarts—is needed for cooking many pastas. That is standard kitchen equipment, as is everything else needed for these recipes.

TECHNIQUE

Everyone has heard by now that dried pasta is normally cooked just until it retains some bite—*al dente*—but area teachers who cook pasta have a rough time convincing people to use enough salt in the water. Pasta takes up little salt as it cooks, and can be so bland that it throws off the balance of a carefully made sauce. For a pound of pasta, start with 4 or 5 quarts of cold water, bring it to a boil, covered (fresh water boils faster than salt), and then add ¼ cup coarse salt. Return water to a boil, add pasta, stir with a wooden spoon, and cook until done: a matter of seconds for fresh pasta and perhaps 8 to even 15 minutes for dried, depending on its gauge. Do not oil the water or rinse the pasta unless you are planning to make a salad. People on a salt-free diet should of course ignore the salt instructions and continue to do what they need to do.

PÂTES AUX MOULES

4 to 6 servings

This dish is from A. J. Battifarano, who has developed a thriving business styling food for photography. When we can get her back into the classroom, her students delight in her fine pasta dishes, as well as other fare. This one is particularly well suited to the delicate texture of homemade narrow taglierini or wider tagliatelle (similar to the gauge of fettuccine), but commercial pasta will do. You will have better results with good-quality store-bought "fresh pasta" than with the packaged dried varieties. The flavors are so perfectly balanced that you should not be tempted to alter any of the proportions. Notice that the natural brininess of the mussels coupled with the white wine in which they steam makes the addition of salt unnecessary, provided the pasta water is properly salted.

3 pounds mussels, soaked, scrubbed, and debearded (p. 62)
1/2 cup dry white wine
1 bay leaf
1/4 cup minced shallots
4 tablespoons butter
4 cloves garlic, minced
4 tablespoons minced parsley
1 cup heavy cream
1 pound homemade or purchased fresh egg pasta, narrow- to medium-width noodles
Coarse salt
Freshly ground black pepper

Place mussels in a large saucepan with the white wine and bay leaf. Cover tightly and cook for 3 to 5 minutes, or until shells have opened. Shake the pan once or twice to redistribute the mussels for even cooking. Remove mussels with slotted spoons or a skimmer to a large platter to cool. Strain liquid through a sieve lined with cheesecloth or high-quality paper towel, and reserve. When mussels have cooled, remove them from their shells. Discard the shells and the bay leaf, and transfer the mussels to a bowl and cover to keep them from drying out.

In a medium saucepan, gently sauté the shallots in butter until tender. Add garlic and parsley, and cook 1 minute. Add reserved mussel broth, and cook for 5 minutes, or until reduced by half. Stir in heavy cream and simmer another few minutes, until thickened slightly.

Bring 4 to 5 quarts of water to a boil and add ¼ cup of the coarse salt. In the meantime, reheat sauce, add mussels, and heat them through. Cook pasta just until it is tender. Drain, transfer to a serving platter, and add the mussel sauce. Toss to combine. Serve immediately, offering pepper at the table.

PASTA WITH MONKFISH, BROCCOLI, AND SUN-DRIED TOMATOES

4 to 6 servings

A chunky pasta is in order for this lovely combination of sunny flavors. Penne seem right, particularly if you can find the ridged ones, penne rigati. Imported Italian pasta is a must. Remember that only firm-textured fish will stand up to tossing with the pasta; other than monkfish, you might use ocean pout, blackfish, wolffish, or searobin. Shrimp and scallops are also good choices. If you buy monkfish with bone in, buy the larger amount given below.

1 bunch broccoli
¼ cup pine nuts
¾ cup light olive oil
1 ¼ to 1 ¾ pounds monkfish tail, trimmed of dark flesh, boned, and sliced into chunks 1 by 1 by ½ inch
Flour for dredging
4 to 6 large cloves garlic, peeled and thinly sliced
½ cup dry white wine
½ cup Fish Stock (see recipe)
8 to 10 sun-dried tomatoes in oil, thinly sliced
1 pound penne, or other pasta of choice
2 tablespoons tiny (nonpareil) capers, drained
3 tablespoons chopped fresh herbs: basil or parsley or a combination
Coarse salt and freshly ground black pepper to taste

Peel the broccoli stems with a swivel-blade peeler. Slice off and discard woody stem ends. Slice off and reserve florets, then thinly slice stems on the diagonal. Blanch sliced stems and florets in salted water for about 15 seconds. Drain and shock with cold water. Set aside. Lightly toast the pine nuts in a skillet or a 375°F. oven. Set aside.

Heat the oil in a large skillet or wok until very hot, almost smoking. Dredge fish *very* lightly in flour. Add to hot oil in batches, and cook until slightly golden, about 1 minute on each side. Drain on paper towels. The oil and the skillet should be fairly clean. If there is a lot of browned residue on the bottom of the skillet, pour oil through a strainer, wipe out skillet, and put oil back in.

Add garlic to the hot oil, and cook and stir briefly, just until fragrant. Do not brown. Add wine and stock, and boil for about 1 minute. Add sun-dried tomatoes and heat through. Turn off heat and cook pasta.

Bring a large pot of well-salted water to a boil, add pasta, and stir well. Cook just until *al dente*, stirring occasionally. Drain and place in a serving bowl. As pasta nears doneness, reheat reserved skillet, toss in broccoli, monkfish, capers, pine nuts, and herbs and heat, stirring gently, just until everything is heated through. Pour mixture over cooked and drained pasta, season well with pepper, and toss to combine. Correct seasoning and serve immediately.

LA CÔTE BASQUE'S SEAFOOD RAVIOLI

6 or more servings

Chef/proprietor Jean-Jacques Rachou is famous for elegant presentations with precious foodstuffs, elaborate garnishes, sauce painting, and the like. This creation is within the realm of possibility for home cooks because so much of the work can be achieved in advance (indeed, must be), and the ingredients and garnishes may be varied to suit the occasion and the budget. Any sensible combination of fish and shellfish could be interesting, and the pasta dough can be purchased as fresh pasta or egg roll skins. Most wonton skins are too thick, but if you wish to buy the thin ones in Chinatown, they are ideal. Fashion the ravioli in the desired size and shape and serve them as a first course or luncheon or supper main course.

THE FILLING

2 ounces (½ stick) butter
Finely chopped white of 1 leek
Few sprigs fennel leaves, finely chopped
1 small shallot, minced
6 ounces salmon fillet, cut into ¼-inch dice
¼ pound sea scallops, cut into ¼-inch dice
¼ pound cooked lobster meat (or substitute raw shrimp, in addition
    to the quantity below), cut into ¼-inch dice
1 ounce Pernod or Ricard
½ cup thin slices (chiffonade) of basil, loosely packed
¼ pound shrimp, peeled and deveined
2 teaspoons coarse salt
1 teaspoon freshly ground white pepper
Pinch freshly grated nutmeg
1 cup heavy cream, very cold

1 pound fresh egg pasta, homemade or purchased, rolled thin and
    wrapped to keep it moist
1 egg beaten with 1 tablespoon heavy cream

THE SAUCE (SAFFRON *BEURRE BLANC*)

2 cups white wine
2 tablespoons white wine vinegar
3 medium shallots, minced
Scant ¼ teaspoon powdered saffron, or an equivalent amount of
    crumbled thread saffron—about half a .2-gram vial—or to taste
12 ounces (3 sticks) cool butter, cut into pieces

THE GARNISHES

12 whole Caribbean freshwater prawns, heads left on, tails peeled
    except for the very end, and deveined (optional)
Butter
Salt and freshly ground white pepper, to taste
1 medium leek, cut into 2-inch julienne, blanched and shocked
1 small carrot, cut into 2-inch julienne, blanched and shocked

For the filling: Melt the butter in a skillet and add chopped leek and fennel sprigs, and shallot. Sauté over low heat until soft. Add diced salmon, scallops, and lobster meat (or shrimp substitute). Turn heat fairly high and toss until seafood is warmed through and juices are reduced. Add Pernod or Ricard and basil, and mix well. Spread mixture on a sheet pan, cover, and chill.

Purée the 1/4 pound shrimp with the seasonings in a chilled food processor bowl until very smooth. Process in the cream, one-third at a time, scraping down the sides of the bowl between additions. Process just until smooth. Chill mixture for a bit if you have the time. Combine with the chilled seafood mixture and correct seasoning. Chill until needed.

To assemble the ravioli: Lay out the pasta on a cloth or lightly floured surface. Mr. Rachou cuts the pasta into eighteen 4-inch squares. Spoon the filling mixture onto the pasta—1 tablespoon for the large squares and less for smaller ravioli—and lightly brush the edges with egg wash. Fold diagonally into triangles and press edges to seal. Bring a pot of water to a boil and salt generously. Add ravioli and cook for 2 to 3 minutes, depending upon size, until ravioli are plump. Remove with a skimmer to a bowl of cold water and reserve. Reserve the hot water and keep it hot.

To prepare the saffron beurre blanc: Bring wine, vinegar, shallots, and saffron to a boil in a heavy nonreactive saucepan. Reduce to 3 tablespoons. Whisk in the butter, a tablespoon at a time, rewarming the pan over heat if necessary. Do not overheat. Strain and reserve sauce in a warm place.

To prepare garnishes: Sauté the optional prawns in a little butter until golden. Season lightly with salt and pepper. Remove to a platter and reserve. Wipe out skillet, add a little more butter, and sauté julienned leek and carrot, adding a little salt and pepper, until almost tender. Reserve.

Reheat ravioli in the salted water for about 1 minute, or until heated through. Drain and pat dry on paper towels.

Now, place 2 prawns, back to back, on the top of each warmed plate, if they are being used. Divide the julienned vegetables among the plates and spread them on the bottom third of each. Lay 3 ravioli on top of the vegetables. Spoon sauce over ravioli and the rest of the plate. Serve immediately.

CRABS IN TOMATO SAUCE

4 to 6 servings

This rustic charmer was supplied by teacher Ann Amendolara Nurse, who specializes in down-home Italian cooking, mostly southern. If you can find a fishmonger who will remove the top shells from the crabs for you (within only a few hours of cooking time), that's great; you can also do it yourself without much fuss as long as you are careful to avoid the claws while the crabs are alive. Handle them with tongs and cover claws with a towel while you work. You might want to simmer the top shells and swimmerets in water to make a broth that you can use in soup or add to a fish stock. Be sure to provide plenty of napkins and a big bowl for shells. Bibs are not a bad idea; finger bowls, too. You might offer picks and lobster crackers, but diners will really do better with hands and teeth.

12 hard-shell blue crabs, preferably female, alive when purchased
3/4 cup light or blended light and extra-virgin olive oil
4 large cloves garlic, peeled
Two 28-ounce cans tomatoes with purée
1 teaspoon dried oregano
3 tablespoons chopped flat-leaf parsley
Coarse salt, as needed
2 dried hot red peppers
1 pound linguine or spaghetti, best-quality imported
Butter

If crabs are whole, rinse them well and soak them in two changes of well-salted cold water. Clean the crabs (p. 64), reserving the crab body halves and the tomalley and roe. Mash innards with a whisk until pasty.

Heat olive oil in a heavy casserole large enough to contain the crabs, and cook the garlic cloves until just barely golden. Do not brown. Add crabs and toss them in the oil until they start to change color—the exposed flesh will whiten and the shells begin to redden. Add tomatoes, oregano, parsley, a little salt, and the peppers. Stir to combine. Whisk mashed innards into the juices at the edge of the casserole, then stir to combine. Bring mixture to a boil, then lower heat. Partially cover and simmer mixture about 30 minutes. Correct seasoning.

Just before serving, cook pasta in well-salted boiling water until just done. Drain, and toss with a little butter. Pour onto serving platter or casserole, and top with hot crab tomato sauce. Serve immediately.

SCALLOPS, BROCCOLI, AND MUSHROOMS WITH LINGUINE

4 to 6 servings

This is from Sailing, a pleasant downtown fish house that offers fine, fresh seafood, simply prepared, in an informal atmosphere. Best of all, the price is affordable. Notice that Asian flavors are combined with Italian pasta without any fuss or pretense. Sailing uses sea scallops, though you may want to try shrimp, monkfish, ocean pout, or a combination. Use medium shrimp, shelled and deveined and left whole; cut fish into one-inch cubes.

3/4 pound sea scallops, trimmed of tough muscle and sliced in half crosswise, if large
4 tablespoons peanut or soy oil
1 bunch broccoli, cut into florets, the stems peeled and sliced thinly on the diagonal
1/4 cup white wine
Coarse salt, as needed
1 teaspoon sugar
1 pound imported linguine (regular or fine)
1 tablespoon finely minced fresh gingerroot
1 teaspoon minced garlic
8 to 10 mushrooms, sliced
Dash hot chili oil, or to taste
Light-color or low-sodium soy sauce

Toss scallops with 1 tablespoon of the oil until they are evenly filmed. Set aside. Blanch broccoli in boiling salted water for about 30 seconds. Drain and shock with cold water; set aside. Combine white wine, 1 teaspoon coarse salt, and sugar, and set aside.

Put pasta into a large pot of well-salted boiling water, stirring a few times. Sauce will cook in about the same amount of time.

Heat a wok or large skillet until very hot. Add 2 tablespoons oil and swirl around. Add ginger and garlic, and stir-fry a few seconds, just until fragrant. Add mushrooms and stir-fry about 1 minute. Add scallops and stir-fry about 1 minute more. Add broccoli and wine mixture, and stir-fry about 2 minutes more, or until broccoli and seafood are heated through. Do not overcook.

When pasta is just done, drain and pour into a serving bowl or onto a platter. Toss with the remaining tablespoon of oil and chili oil to taste. Pour sauce over pasta, toss lightly (either in the kitchen or at the table), and serve immediately, offering a cruet of soy sauce for those who wish it.

SAUTÉED SQUID WITH CLAMS AND PASTA

4 to 6 servings

This shellfish combination is particularly tasty with homemade spinach noodles or black pasta colored and flavored with squid ink. If you choose to buy your pasta, consider tagliatelle (similar to the gauge of fettuccine) or whatever noodle shape pleases you. There is now a high-quality black pasta made by Raffetto's that is available at the 144 West Houston Street store and, among other places, at Fairway Fruits and Vegetables, 2122 Broadway. The clams are not absolutely essential, but they add drama to the presentation and their broth makes an important flavor contribution. You could substitute about a half cup fish stock, boiled with the wine until the raw taste of the wine is gone.

12 littleneck clams
3/4 cup dry white wine
Coarse salt, as needed
2 pounds whole squid
1 pound pasta of choice
6 tablespoons plus 2 teaspoons butter
6 tablespoons light olive oil
2 tablespoons minced garlic

1 tablespoon minced fresh oregano leaves, or ¹/₂ teaspoon dried
2 tablespoons chopped parsley
Freshly ground black pepper to taste
Dash cayenne

Scrub clams and soak them in several changes of salted cold water to remove sand. In a heavy saucepan, bring wine to a boil and add the clams. Cover and steam until they open, 5 minutes or so. Remove clams and set them aside in a warm place. Strain liquid to remove sand. Reserve.

Clean squid and reserve ink sacs as described on p. 65. Reserve tentacles and slice body sacs into ¹/₂-inch rings.

Have the pasta pot boiling and salt the water well. Organize the finishing of the dish according to whether you are using dried pasta that will take 10 to 12 minutes to cook, or fresh pasta that will take 1 minute or less. Just before serving time, heat 6 tablespoons butter and the oil in a large skillet or wok. Add garlic and sauté for a few seconds. Do not color. Raise heat to high, add squid, and cook, stirring constantly, for about 15 seconds. Add reserved clam broth, herbs, and seasonings, and stir over high heat just until heated through. Do not overcook or squid will toughen.

Drain cooked pasta and toss it with the remaining butter in a large pasta bowl or on a platter. Pour squid mixture over the pasta, add whole clams for garnish, and serve immediately.

RISOTTO WITH MUSSELS

4 to 6 servings

Of all seafood risotti, traditional and modern, ones that feature mussels will probably remain the most popular because of the special, rich flavor of the broth. The lemon zest and hint of saffron are delicious touches that make this recipe a wee bit different from the classic version. A fine risotto requires about twenty minutes of undivided attention and is never at its best reheated. However, you may stop in the middle of the cooking process and finish at serving time with negligible texture damage. In Italy rice and pasta dishes that include seafood are rarely if ever served with cheese, but you might offer freshly grated Parmesan for those who crave it.

This recipe assumes that you have on hand the required quantities of broth and shucked mussels left from a full batch of *Moules à la Marinière* (see recipe). If not, prepare one-half of that recipe and you will have plenty of broth and mussels for this use.

Large pinch saffron
2 cups hot mussel broth (see above)
3 tablespoons butter
3 tablespoons olive oil
1 cup finely chopped onions
2 cups Arborio or other short-grain rice
1 teaspoon minced garlic
½ teaspoon grated or minced lemon zest
¼ to ½ cup dry white wine
About 4 cups hot Fish Stock (see recipe) or water
Coarse salt and freshly ground pepper to taste
2 tablespoons chopped parsley
1 to 1½ cups shucked steamed mussels (see above)

Add the saffron to the mussel broth and keep warm. In a heavy medium-large saucepan, heat butter and oil, and add onions. Sauté gently until translucent. Add rice and sauté, stirring, for a few minutes. Add garlic and lemon zest, and stir until fragrant. Add ¼ cup wine (or ½ cup if you will be using water instead of fish stock later) and stir over medium heat until liquid is absorbed. Proceed to add ¼ cup of the hot saffron-infused mussel broth at a time, stirring constantly, adding more only after the previous addition is absorbed. When you have used all of the mussel broth, begin to use the stock or water.

When about half of the liquid has been used, season risotto lightly with salt and pepper and add parsley. Be very cautious with salt because of the saltiness of the mussel broth. Continue cooking and stirring and adding liquid until the rice is done. The outsides of the rice grains will be tender and creamy but the centers must retain a decided firmness, even a slight crunch. Correct seasoning. Gently stir in mussels. Stir briefly, just to warm the mussels through, and serve immediately.

RISOTTO OF SEAFOOD AND WATERCRESS

4 to 6 servings

Here is quite a different risotto, one that reflects the myriad possibilities for combinations of seafood and fresh herbs. Chefs devise their own—as home cooks should feel free to do— keeping good technique and common sense in mind.

1/2 pound medium shrimp
1/2 pound fillet of white-fleshed fish, such as black sea bass, snapper,
*   grouper, tilefish, or cod*
About 6 cups hot Fish Stock (see recipe)
3 tablespoons butter
3 tablespoons olive oil
1 1/2 cups finely chopped onions
1 teaspoon minced garlic
2 cups Arborio or other short-grain rice
1/2 cup dry white wine
1 1/2 bunches watercress, stems removed, then coarsely chopped
Coarse salt and freshly ground pepper to taste
6 sprigs watercress for garnish

Shell, devein, and slice shrimp into 1/2-inch chunks. Reserve shells. Skin, trim, and cut fish into 1/2-inch cubes. Add shrimp shells and any bones and trimmings from the fish to the stock. Let stock simmer in a saucepan for 15 to 20 minutes, strain it through a sieve, and discard solids. Wipe out the saucepan, return the hot stock to it, and bring it to a simmer. Add the seafood and stir gently to separate the pieces. Poach seafood for about 15 seconds, then skim it out and reserve. Keep stock hot.

In a heavy medium-large saucepan, heat butter and oil and add onions. Sauté gently until translucent. Add garlic and rice, and sauté, stirring, for a few minutes. Add wine to rice mixture, and stir over medium heat until reduced. Add 1/4 cup hot stock at a time to the rice, stirring constantly, adding more when the previous addition is absorbed.

When about half of the stock has been used, add the chopped watercress. Season lightly. Continue cooking and stirring and adding stock until rice is done—the outsides of the rice grains will be tender and creamy but the centers must retain a little crunch. If you run out of stock, use hot water. Stir in seafood, and correct seasoning. Stir gently over heat briefly, just until seafood is heated through.

Portion the risotto, garnish each serving with a watercress sprig, and serve immediately.

SHRIMP AND OYSTER JAMBALAYA

6 servings as a main course, or 10 as a first course

Though based on the famous *paellas* of Spain, jambalaya has a long Louisiana history of its own. Jambalayas may contain nearly any shellfish or land animal that happens to be available. Here is an unorthodox approach that produces authentic results. A properly made jambalaya should be fairly dry, so it is nice to spoon a little sauce Creole (which may be derived from Cajun sauce piquante) around it to moisten it. Rather than handle many of the same ingredients twice, you may prepare the sauce and the flavor base at the same time. There is no need to resort to converted rice in order to get a good texture—the film of fat that coats the rice should allow for long cooking without mushiness—but you may use it if you wish. The texture and flavor are inferior, but converted rice is safer for timid cooks and slightly more nutritious than long-grain white.

1 pound medium shrimp
24 oysters, shucked, liquor reserved
3 cups water
2 bay leaves
1/2 teaspoon dried leaf thyme
2 teaspoons coarse salt
1 teaspoon pepper (a mixture of black and white is good)
1/2 teaspoon cayenne
1/4 teaspoon ground allspice
4 tablespoons butter
3 cups chopped onions
3/4 cup chopped celery
1 1/2 cups diced green peppers
Corn oil, as needed
1 cup thinly sliced scallions

1 tablespoon minced garlic
¼ cup chopped parsley
One 28-ounce can imported tomatoes, coarsely crushed by hand
2 cups tomato purée
½ pound smoked ham, cut into small dice
*¾ pound smoked garlic sausage (*andouille *or* kielbasa*), cut into*
    ¼-inch slices
2 cups long-grain white rice, rinsed well, drained, and left to dry

Shell and devein shrimp. Put shells into a medium saucepan. Strain oyster liquor into the saucepan. Refrigerate shellfish. Add the water and all the seasonings to the saucepan. Cover and bring to a boil. Reduce heat and simmer for about 30 minutes.

In a large, wide saucepan, heat 3 tablespoons of the butter and add the onions, celery, and green peppers. Sauté until tender but not browned, 10 to 15 minutes, adding a little corn oil if it seems dry. Add scallions, garlic, and parsley, and sauté until they are tender. Add tomatoes and tomato purée. Strain the liquid from the shrimp shells and seasonings into this mixture, and discard the solids. You now have the makings of a sauce Creole flavored with shellfish. Let it simmer for 20 minutes or so, covered, stirring occasionally.

Preheat oven to 375°F.

Heat the remaining tablespoon of butter in a flameproof casserole of about 4 quarts capacity. Add the ham and sauté over low heat until it has rendered its fat. Add the sausage and cook another 10 minutes or so without browning. Add the rice and cook about 5 minutes over fairly high heat, stirring almost constantly. The rice is not really supposed to brown, but if it becomes a little golden here and there, that's all right. Reserve 2 cups of the sauce and measure the rest. You should have 5 cups. Add water if necessary. Add the 5 cups of hot sauce to the rice mixture. Stir once. Bring to a boil and stir again. Cover, lower heat, and simmer gently for 15 minutes. Let rest for 10 minutes without opening the lid. If you wish to prepare this in advance, cook the rice mixture for only about 10 minutes and put it aside for 1 or 2 hours, then warm it before you proceed.

Remove lid and gently fluff rice with a fork. Correct seasoning. Gently fold in the reserved seafood and replace the lid. Place casserole in the preheated oven and bake 10 minutes, then remove cover and bake 10 minutes more. Reheat the remaining 2 cups of sauce. Spoon the jambalaya onto plates and spoon a little sauce around it. Serve hot.

PLAIN WHITE RICE, THREE WAYS

Because rice is such an important accompaniment to many seafood dishes, here are three approaches to cooking it. They are all for long-grain (or extra long-grain) white rice, the basic Chinese rice, which is also known generically in the United States as Carolina. These methods will also work with white basmati, the special Indian rice now grown here as well. Basmati has a rich, nutty aroma and flavor, and, as it cooks, has the curious habit of swelling lengthwise into very long grains rather than the usual fat ones. Brown rice normally requires half again as much water and twice the cooking time. Rice is usually washed to remove surface starch that would make it gummy. Enriched rices carry a proscription against rinsing or draining, but the small amount of added B-vitamins lost in washing will only be missed by those with poorly balanced diets. Cooked rice yields 3 times its raw volume: 1 cup raw yields 3 cups cooked, which is 3 to 6 normal servings. All recipes may be prepared in desired quantities.

BASIC WESTERN RICE

The usual approach to rice cookery in the Western world, this one is usually salted and also slightly buttered to help the grains stay separate. When cooking more than 2 cups of raw rice, begin to decrease slightly the proportion of water, salt, and butter. This rice may also be cooked with no salt when you want a very bland foil for spicy food, and cooked with no fat at all.

1 cup long-grain white rice
1 1/2 cups water
1/2 teaspoon coarse salt
1 teaspoon butter

Wash rice thoroughly in a sieve until the rinse water runs clear. Leave it to drain, shaking a few times, until it is dry or nearly so. Allow at least a generous 30 minutes for drying. If you are in a rush and the rice is still wet, decrease the water by about 2 tablespoons.

Add the water, salt, and butter to a small saucepan, cover, and bring to a boil. Add the rice and bring rapidly back to boiling. Stir once with a fork to be sure grains are separate. Cover closely. Reduce heat to very low and simmer gently exactly 15 minutes. Remove from heat. Let rice rest undisturbed for at least 5 minutes. Do not open lid! If rice is to rest more than 15 minutes, reheat it slightly over low heat. Uncover, fluff with a fork, and serve.

BASIC CHINESE RICE

> Long-grain white rice
> Water

Put rice in a saucepan and rinse it well in several changes of water until water is clear. Add cold water to cover rice by 1 inch. This is customarily measured with the tip of the forefinger or thumb. Bring to a boil. Some cover the pan and others leave it open. If covered, boil rice until a little starchy liquid starts to boil over the side of the pan. Then reduce heat to low and simmer gently 15 minutes. If open, boil 2 minutes, or until the surface looks dry and pocked with steam holes. Cover, reduce heat to low, and simmer gently 15 minutes. Whichever way you have started the rice, now remove from heat and let rice rest for 5 minutes before opening. Instead of observing the 15 minutes of simmer and 5 minutes of rest, you may continue to simmer the rice very gently until you hear a faint crackle and smell a slight nuttiness. This will not only flavor the rice a bit but will also yield the dividend of a thin, lightly browned crust on the pan, which is considered a tasty munch as well as an ingredient in a few Chinese recipes.

BOILED RICE

> This one produces results similar to Basic Western Rice with less fuss but a slight loss of flavor. It is particularly well suited to preparation in advance, in quantity, or for salads. The touch of vinegar is very effective in helping to keep the grains separate.
>
> Long-grain white rice
> Water
> White vinegar: wine, rice, or distilled
> Salt (optional)
> Butter (optional)

In a saucepan, bring to a boil about 3 cups of water for each cup of rice you are using. Add ¼ teaspoon vinegar per cup of rice. Add rice and return to a boil. Stir once with a fork. Lower heat and simmer gently, uncovered, for 15 minutes. Drain. For serving right away, rinse rice with hot water and drain well. Return rice to saucepan, tossing it with a little salt and butter, if you wish. Cover, and warm over low heat for about 5 minutes, or until heated through. Fluff with a fork and serve. If preparing in advance, wash rice with cold water and drain well. Toss with a little salt and bits of butter, if you wish, and return to the saucepan or put it in a casserole. Cover. Before serving time, reheat over low heat or in a moderate oven.

SAFFRON RICE

6 to 8 servings

This is prepared exactly as Basic Western Rice with the addition of flavorings that make it appropriate as a complement to Indian dishes such as Tandoori Fish Steaks (see recipe). It is also delicious with Middle Eastern and North African dishes, with or without the currants and almonds.

2 cups basmati or long-grain white rice
3 cups water
2 teaspoons lime or lemon juice
1 teaspoon coarse salt
¼ teaspoon powdered saffron or an equivalent amount of crumbled thread saffron (about two-thirds of a .2-gram vial)
1 tablespoon butter
1 cup dried currants, soaked in hot water and drained (optional)
1 cup toasted sliced almonds (optional)

Wash, drain, and dry rice, and proceed as for Basic Western Rice (see recipe), cooking rice in a mixture of water, lime juice, salt, saffron, and butter. At serving time as you fluff the rice, gently combine the optional currants and almonds.

POLENTA

About 8 servings

Finally catching on in the United States is this cornmeal mush that has been an important staple in northern Italy for several centuries. There it is served on its own with butter and cheese and with a number of stewed and sauced dishes, particularly game, veal, poultry, sausages, and earthy mushrooms. It is also served, hot or cold, with hot or cold stews of squid or cuttlefish (see Squid Stewed in Its Own Ink). Like mush and grits, polenta can also be prepared in advance and chilled, then sliced and fried, or stuffed with cheese, covered, and reheated in the oven. It can also be reheated plain. Polenta meal can be yellow or white, and it may be a special fine grind or standard stone-ground cornmeal.

8 cups water
1 tablespoon coarse salt
2 cups cornmeal or fine polenta meal

Bring water to a boil in a heavy medium pot, and add salt. Pour in meal gradually in a fine stream, stirring constantly with a wooden spoon. When all of meal has been added, continue to stir, slowly, over moderate heat, until polenta is very thick and begins to pull away from the sides of the pot. This should not take more than 30 minutes. If the mixture gets too thick before the cornmeal grains are tender, add a little more boiling water. Let mixture sit over low heat for 1 or 2 minutes to set slightly. Stir just around the edges to free it from the pot, and pour it onto a platter. Quickly smooth it into an even, thick disk. Serve immediately, cut into wedges, or allow to cool for another use.

POACHING

See p. 78 for ways to determine proper cooking time.

Excellent results can be achieved in poaching seafood if the timing and temperature are accurate. It is a technique second only to steaming in its respect for the natural flavor and texture of the flesh. Properly poached seafood tastes like itself, so the success of the dish depends on the skill and taste involved in the saucing or finishing. A mini-poach, called *blanching,* is valuable as a preliminary step in many dishes, particularly with shellfish.

VARIETIES BEST SUITED

Any fish or shellfish could be poached, but assertively flavored fish and fish with colorful flesh are rarely poached, except for salmon and trout.

EQUIPMENT

Any vessel that will hold the seafood and enough liquid to cover it well can be used. Long narrow fish poachers—which come in several sizes, all of them long enough to fit on 2 burners—are ideal for poaching whole fish. Otherwise, a deep roasting pan or even an oval wash tub can be used.

TECHNIQUE

In classic French cookery, fish are normally poached in a fla-vorful court bouillon (p. 267). However, this does tend to alter or dull the flavor of a fine fish, so it is used much less often in modern cooking. Well-flavored poaching liquids are only required when they are to become a soup, a sauce, or a jelly for decorating cold dishes. Seawater is the original and still the best poaching medium. Consider that both fresh- and saltwater fish have a natural salinity similar to land animals—near the mean of .9 percent of body fluids—which is consid-ered low sodium for dietary purposes. Even shellfish that can have up to twice the salinity are still low in sodium. For most palates, a hint of added salt makes things perfect. Seawater, at about 3.5 percent salt, can add that subtle touch without masking the natural flavor or making the fish unhealthfully saline. *Very* little salt is absorbed.

The best substitute for seawater is fresh water with 2 table-spoons coarse salt per quart added. Undersalted water will leech out natural sodium, leaving the flavor palid indeed. A teaspoon of white vinegar (wine, rice, or distilled) per quart helps to give fish a clean flavor, particularly if they are a day older than we would like. There are only three major exceptions to this formula: oysters are usually poached in their own liquor (p. 231); skate and shark, because of their chemistry, are normally poached in a liquid with considerably more vinegar (p. 178); and finnan haddie is often poached in milk (p. 230).

The temperature of the poaching bath is of critical importance. If the liquid is held at 170°F. to 180°F.—the shiver—results will be good. Use a thermometer if you are in doubt. At higher temperatures fish are likely to explode and shellfish to toughen. Whole fish are normally started in cool or warm liquid so the least amount of damage will be done to their appearance. The exception is the famous blue trout of Germany and Switzerland, where sudden heat causes the just-killed fish to contract into a desired C shape. Fillets, steaks, and shellfish are usually introduced into liquid that is already up to temperature. This plumps and firms them and actually creates a slight surface seal that holds in juices.

When shellfish are briefly poached to plump them up and stabilize their moisture content, you may call this *blanching* or *parboiling*. As with vegetables, they are sometimes drained and shocked with cold water to arrest the cooking, as in Fried Squid (see recipe). If they are fully cooked, this becomes poaching. Poaching is the most popular cooking method for whole lobster, even though it is usually called boiling. Many professionals find steaming, p. 346, a superior technique for lobster.

POACHED WHOLE FISH

1 to 2 servings per pound of whole fish

Now that striped bass is off-limits in the Northeast, salmon is the only large glamour fish that is regularly poached whole for a dramatic presentation either hot or cold. However, other attractive fish do nicely, including black sea bass, snappers, grouper, pike, walleye, whitefish, salmon trout, and seatrout. Rainbow trout and baby coho salmon make popular single-serving poached fish, usually served cold. Among the sauces you might choose to serve with a hot poached fish are *Beurre*

Blanc, Beurre Rouge, Lemon Butter, Red Pepper Purée, any of the Compound Butters (see recipes), and Hollandaise sauce or any of its variants. For cold, consider Green Sauce, *Skarpås, Taratoor,* Vinaigrette, and Tartar Sauce with Chile and Coriander (see recipes). For instructions for decorating a cold poached fish, see p. 244. For simple presentations, hot or cold, lemon wedges or slices are usually appropriate garnishes, as are sprigs of fresh herbs that echo or complement the flavors in the sauce.

Whole fish of desired size
Water to cover by 1 inch
Coarse salt
White vinegar: wine, rice, or distilled

To prepare a fish for poaching, scale it and gut it carefully so as to keep its shape. There is no hard and fast rule, but in the West a whole fish is normally presented on its side with the head on the left: make your vent-to-head cut on what will become the underside—the right side of the fish—so the cut will be invisible. Remove gills with shears or a sharp knife and discard. Wash fish thoroughly to remove all traces of blood. Be sure to remove the membrane that lines the cavity so that you can flush out any blood along the backbone. Trim off the pectoral fins (on the sides, behind the gills), but leave others intact. If the fish is too long to fit in any available vessel, cut off the tail, even the head, if necessary. Poach the head and tail, too, and reassemble the fish at serving time, if possible. Measure the width of the fish at its widest point, behind the head. Drape fish with cheesecloth to help hold its shape.

Place fish in a vessel of appropriate size so that, ideally, it can be covered by water by 1 inch. If you are using a fish poacher, tie fish loosely to the rack in a few places. Fill pan with water and add 2 tablespoons coarse salt and 1 teaspoon white vinegar per quart of water. If the side of the fish threatens to break the surface of the water, place a foil tent over the exposed area so that it can steam while the rest is poaching. Bring water rapidly almost to a simmer, reduce heat, and cook, uncovered, at the shiver—170°F. to 180°F. Do not let the liquid get any hotter. Test fish for doneness using the skewer test, p. 79. If the fish is to be served hot, remove it to a serving platter, remove cheesecloth, skin the top side, and carefully remove any dark flesh. Drain platter, garnish, and serve immediately with sauce of choice. If fish is to be served cold, undercook it slightly and let it cool in the poaching liquid. Remove from pan, skin, then chill. Decorate with jelly and vegetable cutouts if desired, garnish, and serve cold with sauce of choice.

An alternate poaching method for fish to be served cold is to bring the liquid just to a simmer, then turn off the heat, cover, and let fish rest in the poaching bath until it is tepid. Then proceed with the instructions above. Another possibility is to do the poaching in a 325°F. oven, but moving a large pan of hot water around can be dangerous. Microwave ovens will also poach well, provided the liquid is not overheated.

GALANTINE OF SALMON

8 to 24 servings

For the most festive occasions, particularly when an array of splendid cold buffet dishes is in order, nothing but caviar is more elegant than a whole poached salmon. This version is boned and stuffed and reassembled into its original shape, so it qualifies as one of those grand and glistening French or Italian creations—more often made with poultry—called *galantines.* Though it requires a bit more preparation time than a whole poached fish, it need not be skinned or elaborately decorated, and it is easier to serve. It is also far easier than the finished product would suggest. It must be prepared in advance and is easiest poached a day ahead. This recipe presupposes that you can locate a vessel large enough to poach a whole salmon. If not, you may remove the tail and even the head, too, but the presentation will not be as impressive. Lacking a serving platter of the right dimensions, you may use a board covered with white paper. Though you might expect to find this recipe with the cold dishes or special events, it is included here because the poaching technique is identical to that for whole fish.

> 1 pound skinless fillets of walleye or whitefish
> 2 eggs
> 1 1/4 teaspoons coarse salt
> 1/4 teaspoon freshly ground white pepper
> 1 cup crème fraîche, or 1 cup heavy cream plus 1/2 teaspoon lemon
>   juice
> 3/4 pound medium shrimp, shelled and deveined
> 2 large or 4 small bunches sorrel, or 12 ounces fresh spinach
> 1 whole salmon (about 8 pounds)
> Coarse salt for poaching
> White vinegar for poaching
> Fish jelly and blanched scallion green and carrot slices (p. 244)
> Watercress or parsley for garnish
> Green Mayonnaise (see recipe)

To prepare the mousse: Trim fillets of all bones and cut them into chunks. Put into a food processor bowl with the eggs, salt, and pepper, and process until smooth, scraping down the sides of the bowl as needed. Chill mixture for at least 30 minutes in the processor bowl. Then process in the *crème fraîche* (or heavy cream, adding the lemon juice last thing) just until smooth, using a pulsing action, scraping down the bowl several times. Do not overprocess. Reserve refrigerated.

To prepare the other filling ingredients: Plunge shrimp into a pan of boiling water and immediately skim them out. Shock with cold water, drain, and reserve. Wash sorrel until it is thoroughly free of grit and remove the tough stems. Plunge it into the boiling water, stir, and immediately drain and shock with cold water. Put sorrel into a large bowl of water so that you can easily spread the leaves. Drain them flat on paper towels. Set aside.

Scale salmon and remove gills. Rinse well. Place the salmon on its stomach and proceed to remove the dorsal fins and backbone with a very sharp knife. Starting at the head on the right side, carefully scrape along the bone to release the flesh. Go ahead and cut through the ribs to keep the belly flap intact. When you get to the tail, neatly sever the flesh and skin to free the right side of the salmon from the tail. Repeat on the left side, this time stopping when you reach the tail, leaving the left side attached to the tail. Use kitchen shears to sever the backbone at the base of the head and at the tail and remove it. You now have the two sides of salmon attached at the head, with the tail attached to the left side.

Place the salmon on one side and fold the other side over the head to get it out of your way. Carefully slice off the ribs, doing as little damage as possible to the belly flap. Trim off the base of the fins as you would in neatening a fillet. Remove the pinbones with tweezers. Turn the fish over and repeat the cleaning process on the other side. The only remaining fins will be the pectorals, which are located at the base of the gill cover, close to where the pelvic fins are located in other roundfish. Remove these with shears. The salmon is now ready for stuffing.

Spread on your work surface several layers of rinsed cheesecloth large enough to generously enclose the fish. Place the salmon in the middle on its right side with the head on the left. Fold the top side over the head and proceed to assemble the stuffing: Cover the bottom side evenly with sorrel leaves, letting them extend several inches over the edges, spread half of the chilled mousse evenly over the area where the salmon is, leaving the extended sorrel leaves plain; arrange the shrimp in a row the length of the mousse. Cover with remaining mousse. Wrap the extended leaves around the mousse and add more leaves as needed to envelope the mousse. Fold the top side of the salmon back in place over the stuffing and make sure salmon neatly encloses the stuffing. Wrap salmon rather snugly with the cheesecloth, then wrap it with kitchen twine in a spiral to secure. Chill for 1 or 2 hours.

Poach the *galantine* according to the instructions in the preceding recipe for whole fish. When it has cooled to room temperature, carefully unwrap it, then cover with foil without touching the surface (to prevent sticking) and chill well.

Carefully transfer *galantine* to a serving platter. See page 244 for decoration instructions. Cool 2 or 3 cups of fish jelly over ice until syrupy, and spoon over the *galantine* until it is lightly filmed. There will probably be a few breaks in the skin to be masked, as well as the eye. Use very simple decorations such as a few flower-cut slices of carrot (one to cover the salmon eye, certainly), and a few strips of scallion green to form stem, leaf, and tendril patterns. Glaze decorations with jelly and chill until serving time.

At serving time, garnish platter with watercress or parsley, and pour Green Mayonnaise into a sauceboat. To carve the *galantine,* use a very sharp or serrated knife. Slice off the tail and put it aside. Cut crosswise slices about 1 inch thick at the wide end and thicker at the narrow tail end. For many small buffet portions, cut the slices into cubes. Serve cold, offering sauce from the sauceboat.

FILLETS OF SOLE BOUGIVAL

4 to 6 servings

This delicate dish is from Andrée's Mediterranean Cuisine, which is now Café Crocodile. It can be prepared largely in advance, with just the poaching and the whisking together of the sauce ingredients to be accomplished at serving time.

2 cups Fish Stock (see recipe), or 2 cups water plus 2 pounds bones of white-fleshed fish, cleaned as for stock
2 cups dry white wine
2 leeks, white only, cut into julienne
2 to 3 celery stalks, cut into julienne
2 carrots, peeled and cut into julienne
2 medium turnips, peeled and cut into julienne
1 cup thinly sliced mushrooms
2 large ripe tomatoes, peeled, seeded, and chopped (about 2 cups chopped pulp)
4 whole fillets of gray sole or other flounder (about 2 pounds)
Coarse salt and freshly ground pepper to taste
4 ounces (1 stick) butter
1/2 cup crème fraîche
Juice of 1 lemon
2 tablespoons chopped parsley

Combine stock (or water and cleaned bones) and wine in a nonreactive saucepan and bring to a simmer. Let simmer, partially covered, while you prepare the vegetables, adding the vegetable trimmings to the pan (all but the turnip skin). Let the stock simmer for about 20 minutes, then strain it through a fine sieve. Rinse out the pan and return the stock to it. Add the prepared vegetables and simmer for about 5 minutes. Remove the vegetables with a skimmer and set aside. Keep the stock hot.

Cut the fillets in half lengthwise and remove the strip of tiny bones. Season the fillets lightly with salt and pepper, and fold them into neat packets, skin (shiny) side in. Place fish in a flameproof baking dish just large enough to hold it in a single layer. Arrange the reserved vegetables evenly over the fish, and pour the hot stock over all. Cook over very low heat for about 2 minutes, or until fish is heated through.

While fish is cooking, prepare the sauce. Melt the butter in a small saucepan and whisk in the *crème fraîche,* a spoonful at a time.

Work over very low heat. Season sauce with salt and pepper, and whisk in the lemon juice and chopped parsley. Pour sauce into a sauceboat.

When fish is done, remove it and the vegetables to a platter and moisten with 1 cup of the broth. Serve immediately, offering the sauce.

POACHED FINNAN HADDIE

4 to 6 servings

This old-fashioned British-Yankee specialty is wonderfully satisfying in an elemental way. To enjoy a dish like this in a restaurant, your best bet is a traditional place like Sweet's; we are hoping to see it turn up on more brunch menus, if not lunch and dinner, too. Preparing it at home is a simple affair, and the smoked fish should be easy enough to find at retail. Many markets carry smoked cod from Fulton's Meyer & Thompson Company, as well as other area companies that buy their cod at Fulton. Smoked haddock from New England or Scotland is not widely available in the United States, but high-quality cod is fine enough. Poached finnan haddie may be served with just a pat of butter—plain or Maître d'Hôtel (see recipe)—and a grinding of pepper, but it is particularly soothing in cold weather with a cream-enriched béchamel or velouté, with or without chopped egg. Boiled or mashed potatoes are the perfect accompaniment. Save the poaching broth to use in a soup or chowder where the smoky flavor would be welcome.

2 pounds finnan haddie fillet, cut into serving pieces
2 cups milk
1 medium onion, peeled and stuck with 2 cloves
2 tablespoons butter
2 tablespoons flour
Coarse salt and freshly ground white pepper to taste
Dash cayenne
About 1/2 teaspoon lemon juice
Water and milk, as needed, for poaching
1 or 2 hard-cooked eggs, peeled and mashed with a fork (optional)
About 1/2 cup heavy cream
1 tablespoon chopped parsley

Soak fish in cold water for up to 1 hour, depending on its saltiness, and then drain. Meanwhile, pour the 2 cups milk into a small nonreactive saucepan and add the onion stuck with cloves. Warm over low heat until it just comes to a boil. Cover and put aside to rest for about 15 minutes. Melt the butter in another nonreactive saucepan and whisk in the flour. Whisk and simmer over low heat for 1 to 2 minutes without coloring. Strain the hot milk into the roux (discard onion), and whisk over low heat until sauce is smooth and thickened. Season sauce lightly with salt, pepper, and cayenne, and let simmer very gently for another 15 minutes if you have the time, stirring often. Stir in the lemon juice and heat briefly. Reserve sauce in a warm place while you poach the fish.

Arrange the drained fish pieces in a single layer in a pan just large enough to hold them. Add water and milk in equal proportions to cover well. Bring just to a simmer, reduce heat, and cook, uncovered, at the shiver—170°F. to 180°F. While fish is poaching, finish the sauce. Bring it to a simmer and add optional mashed eggs. Stir over low heat and thin with heavy cream until you are satisfied with the texture. It should be velvety, not pasty. Correct seasoning. When fish is done, drain briefly, plate, spoon over some hot sauce, sprinkle with a little parsley, and serve immediately.

OYSTERS WITH RED BUTTER SAUCE

4 servings

Here is a nouvelle cuisine classic that bears repeating for its delicacy and elegance. The rice mixture was added for drama and substance; it is not essential. Notice there is no salt or pepper added to the oysters, though you may season the sauce if you feel you must. The red wine must be young and fruity with a bright, purply color in order for the sauce to be a pretty pink. Beaujolais is often the best choice.

20 *bluepoint oysters*
1/2 *cup minced shallots*
1 1/2 *cups red wine*
1 *tablespoon red wine vinegar*
1 1/2 *tablespoons dried instant* wakame*

* A Japanese seaweed that is available in specialty stores and some supermarkets.

*3/4 pound (3 sticks) finest butter, cut into 1-tablespoon pieces, kept cool
    but not cold, plus 2 teaspoons*
1/2 teaspoon white wine vinegar
1 teaspoon coarse salt
1 cup long-grain white rice

Shuck the oysters (retain their liquor) and save the large half shells. Clean half shells well and dry them out a bit in a slow oven.

Combine shallots, wine, and red wine vinegar in a medium-small heavy nonreactive saucepan. Simmer until reduced to only 1 or 2 tablespoons of liquid, and set aside.

Soak wakame in 3 cups water; it will expand incredibly. Drain well and set aside.

Bring about 6 cups water to a boil in a saucepan and add the 2 teaspoons butter, white wine vinegar, and salt. When water returns to a boil, add rice and stir. Return to a boil and stir again. Reduce heat and simmer gently, uncovered, for exactly 15 minutes. Stir in drained wakame and drain mixture well. Return to saucepan and cover. It should rest for about 5 minutes, but if you have not completed the other operations at that time, rice can rest longer and be slightly reheated over low heat.

While rice is cooking, prepare the sauce. Warm the reduction, adding a spoonful of water if it seems dry. Whisk in 3/4 pound butter, a piece at a time. Work on and off low heat to keep the mixture warm enough to melt the butter, but do not overheat it or the emulsion will break down. When all the butter is incorporated, strain sauce and hold it briefly over warm water.

Place the oysters and their liquor in a skillet or small saucepan and heat slightly, just until they plump and the mantles become a bit curly. Drain well and place an oyster in each reserved shell. Keep warm.

Arrange small mounds of hot rice in the center of 4 serving plates. You might also pack rice into buttered darioles or custard cups, and unmold. Surround with oysters, 5 to a plate, and nap each with a spoonful of sauce. Serve immediately.

SALADS AND COOL AND CURED SEAFOOD

See p. 78 for ways to determine proper cooking time.

Whether cooked, raw, pickled, smoked, or salted, seafood can be delicious served cold or cool. Many flavors are most accessible to the palate in the room-temperature range. Also, every kind of seafood that is regularly consumed raw, whether natural or cured, has a particularly appealing texture that would be altered by cooking (remember caviar and velvety smoked salmon, as well as sushi and sashimi). And the flavors associated with cool food—herbal, tangy, smoky—are most refreshing. The sushi and sashimi arts are beyond the scope of this book. Those who are interested in learning the techniques will find entire books devoted to them, including *Japanese Cooking: A Simple Art*, by Shizuo Tsuji (Kodansha International/ Harper & Row, 1980).

As you consider the following recipes that feature uncooked seafood, please refer to the section about seafood safety on p. 66. And for all the recipes, be commonsensical, particularly in hot weather, about how long you let things hang around the house, whether on the table or in the refrigerator. Notice that the *Salade de St. Jacques Fleurie* is the only recipe that includes butter, and it must be served tepid. Otherwise, butter is only successful in bread-and-butter canapés, Scandinavian open-faced sandwiches, and such.

SALADE TIÈDE AU POISSON FUMÉ OU AU MAQUEREAU GRILLÉ

WARM SALAD WITH SMOKED FISH OR GRILLED MARINATED MACKEREL

4 to 6 servings

Tepid salads of this sort are nouvelle cuisine notions that have survived; they remain popular first courses at dinner and main courses at lunchtime. Use smoked salmon, sturgeon, tuna, or sable, alone or in combinations of two or three kinds. Smoked poultry and rabbit are also delicious presented this way. The salad itself is so versatile that it also complements many grilled, broiled, or pan-broiled fish, particularly the marinated mackerel below. Feel free to experiment with other vegetables and flavorings following this general game plan.

3 scallions
1 large clove garlic, peeled, thinly sliced, then cut into fine sticks
3-inch length gingerroot, peeled and cut into finest julienne
1/4 cup rice vinegar
1/2 teaspoon coarse salt
1/2 teaspoon sugar
Dash hot chili oil
Dash Asian dark sesame oil
1/3 cup peanut oil
3 medium bell peppers, 1 each of red, green, and yellow, cleaned and
    cut into thin strips
1 small head Chinese cabbage (napa or celery cabbage), shredded
1 pound smoked fish, thinly sliced, or Grilled Marinated Mackerel
    (recipe follows)
2 teaspoons toasted sesame seeds

Separate scallion white parts from green parts; thinly slice the whites and cut the green parts on the diagonal. Combine garlic, ginger, and scallion whites and reserve. Combine vinegar, salt, sugar, chili oil, and sesame oil, and stir to dissolve the solids. Reserve.

Heat a wok or large skillet over high heat and swirl in the peanut oil. When it begins to smoke, add the garlic mixture and stir-fry a few seconds. Add the peppers and stir-fry another few seconds. Add the cabbage and stir-fry, tossing vigorously, just until cabbage is slightly warmed and threatening to wilt. *Do not overcook.* Immediately pour mixture into a bowl and season it with the vinegar mixture, tossing to combine. Correct seasoning.

If using smoked fish, and the slices are large, cut them in half so that they are not larger than 2 by 3 inches. Arrange neat mounds of salad in the center of dinner plates, and sprinkle lightly with sesame seeds. Ring with overlapping slices of smoked fish, and serve. (If you are using more than one kind of fish, alternate the slices for an attractive look.) If using grilled mackerel, place 1 fillet on each plate. Arrange neat mounds of salad next to fish, sprinkle with sesame seeds, and serve warm.

GRILLED MARINATED MACKEREL

> *2 to 3 medium Atlantic mackerel, about 1 pound each, filleted, pin-bones removed*
> *¼ cup soy sauce*
> *¼ cup sake*
> *2 tablespoons rice vinegar*
> *1 tablespoon sugar*
> *Freshly ground black pepper to taste*
> *2 tablespoons peanut oil*

Carefully score the mackerel skin with a very sharp knife or razor blade: on each fillet make 5 or 6 shallow crosscuts on a slight diagonal, angling the knife toward the head end. There should be 1 fillet per serving. Combine the soy sauce, sake, rice vinegar, sugar, pepper, and 1 tablespoon oil in a nonreactive bowl and add the fillets. Let them marinate, turning occasionally, for about 1 hour at room temperature.

Preheat broiler to high.

Drain fillets and pat dry. Film with remaining oil. Broil fillets close to the source of heat, skin side up, until they are lightly blistered and heated through.

JACQUES PÉPIN'S SALMON TARTARE

8 to 10 first course servings, or up to 50 hors d'oeuvre servings

The uniform quality and availability of fine farm-raised salmon from Norway (and now other North Atlantic countries) are responsible for the possibility of preparing interesting cold dishes that exploit the richness of flavor and texture that raw salmon offers. They should be served the day they are made. Please see Seafood Safety, p. 66. This dish is from one of New York's—indeed, America's—favorite teachers, with good reason. You may present it simply, spooned onto thinly sliced and lightly buttered black bread. Or you may prepare one-inch slices of peeled cucumber and hollow them out with a melon baller, leaving a solid base, and spoon a little of the mixture into each. Jacques also does an elegant first course version, which is described below. The presentation is tricky to describe but really very easy to execute once the details are understood.

THE TARTARE MIXTURE

*2 pounds salmon meat, completely cleaned of all bone, sinew, skin, and
    dark flesh*
2 teaspoons coarse salt
1 teaspoon freshly ground black pepper
1/3 cup finest-quality light olive oil
1 teaspoon grated or finely minced lime zest
1/3 cup lime or lemon juice
1 tablespoon red wine vinegar
*1/2 cup finely chopped onion, washed with cold water, drained, and
    dried*
2 teaspoons peeled, crushed, and finely minced garlic
*1 cup chopped fresh herbs: parsley, tarragon, chives, thyme, chervil, or
    basil, or a combination*
Few drops Tabasco or hot chili oil

THE FINISH

Drained tiny (nonpareil) capers
Extra-virgin olive oil
Freshly ground black pepper to taste
*Lightly buttered slices of black bread, or cucumber cups, or garnishes
    for The Fancy Version (see below)*

Use a large, very sharp knife to chop the trimmed salmon flesh into
hash, not a purée. Combine it with the remaining tartare ingredients,
mix well, and refrigerate. Chill mixture for 1 to 2 hours, then correct
the seasoning.

Just before serving time, sprinkle mixture lightly with capers,
extra-virgin oil, and pepper. Present it with the black bread or spoon
into the cucumber cups.

THE FANCY VERSION

1 recipe Salmon Tartare (see above)
*1 to 1 1/2 pounds salmon, sliced very thinly on the horizontal (as for
    smoked salmon)*
A few tablespoons each lime juice and olive oil
3 or 4 cucumbers
Thirty 1/2-inch-long petal-shaped slices of cucumber skin

Prepare the tartare mixture and refrigerate.

If salmon slices are a bit too thick they can be gently flattened between sheets of wax paper with a large knife. Arrange in a single layer on a large platter(s) and sprinkle with the lime juice and olive oil to evenly moisten. Refrigerate for about 1 hour.

Trim the cucumbers to the length of the diameter of the central part of serving plates, peel them lightly and evenly with a swivel-blade peeler, then slice them with the peeler into broad, even slices, preferably with an even amount of light green on one edge. Use only the meaty part of the cucumber; discard the seeds. Prepare number of slices needed to cover completely the serving plates. Using overlapping slices, arrange the pale-green edges like spokes of a wheel. Center a mound of tartare on each, season with capers, olive oil, and pepper, and wrap each one with marinated salmon slices just to cover in a single layer. Arrange 3 cucumber-skin petals flowerlike in the center of each mound. Serve cool. Bow graciously when your guests applaud.

TUNA (OR SALMON) CARPACCIO, ASIAN-STYLE

4 servings

Carpaccio was invented by Giuseppe Cipriani, the founder of the Cipriani dynasty of hoteliers, at Harry's Bar in Venice. It consists of wafer-thin slices of raw beef (with the hue of Carpaccio's vivid reds) enriched with a light herbal mayonnaise. The dish has been much imitated around the world in recent years, even to the extent of substituting tuna—that beefiest of fish flesh—and salmon for the original ingredient. The most celebrated tuna version in New York is that of Gilbert Le Coze at Le Bernardin. The version below includes an interesting sauce that achieves rich flavor and a creamy texture with the use of Asian ingredients and very little fat. Should you decide to use salmon, make sure it is farm-raised Atlantic.

1 pound tuna, very fresh, with a bright, clear red color, cut from a
*   loin of tuna rather than a steak, if possible*
¹⁄₄ cup tofu
Greens of 2 or 3 scallions, thinly sliced

2 tablespoons rice vinegar
1 teaspoon sugar
3 tablespoons water, or as needed
2 teaspoons wasabi powder, or to taste
2 tablespoons soy oil

THE GARNISHES

Pickled ginger
Fresh coriander sprigs
Soy sauce

Slice tuna across the grain as thinly as possible. Placing the tuna in the freezer for a bit to firm it up will help. Do not freeze. If the slices are not evenly thin or not thin enough, place them between sheets of wax paper and pound very gently with a flat object. Do not tear holes in the slices. Reserve the tuna slices in a single layer or between sheets of wax paper in the refrigerator. You might also proceed to arrange the tuna slices on serving plates: Divide the tuna among 4 dinner plates, paving the surface of each plate (all but the rim) with a thin, even layer of tuna slices. Cover and refrigerate.

Prepare the sauce by placing the tofu, scallions, vinegar, sugar, water, and wasabi in the bowl of a food processor. Process until smooth. Put aside to rest for 5 or 10 minutes, then process in the oil. Strain sauce, discarding solids, and correct seasoning. Sauce should have a very light texture. Thin with a little water, if necessary. Set aside. Roll slices of pickled ginger into 4 rosettes, and set aside.

Just before serving time, arrange tuna on plates if you have not already done so. Place the sauce in a squeeze bottle and decorate each plate with random squiggles of sauce. Place a ginger rosette to one side of each and decorate the rosette with coriander sprigs. Serve cool but not frosty, offering soy sauce on the side.

TUNA TEA SANDWICHES

36 to 48 pieces

East meets West in this whimsical creation, which is delicious and not as precious as it sounds. Again, Asian flavors seem just

right with raw tuna. Actually, the sandwiches are more successful with cocktails than at tea time.

1 1/2 cups mayonnaise, preferably homemade with bland vegetable oil
*   (see recipe)*
Soy sauce to taste
1 tablespoon wasabi powder
One 1 1/4-pound chunk of fresh tuna
1 loaf extra-thin-sliced (melba-sliced) white bread

Divide the mayonnaise between two small bowls. Flavor one by stirring in soy sauce to taste. For the other, mix the wasabi powder with
a little water to make a loose paste. Cover and let it cure for 15
minutes. Then, flavor the second bowl of mayonnaise to taste with the
wasabi. Use a fork or a tiny whisk to mash each addition of wasabi into
a little mayonnaise at the side of the bowl to eliminate lumps before
incorporating it into the whole.

Trim the tuna of any skin and black flesh. Slice tuna into
1/4-inch slices. This is easier if it has spent about 30 minutes in the
freezer before you begin. Put tuna slices between sheets of wax paper
and gently pound them with a meat hammer or the bottom of a small
saucepan until they are nearly half the original thickness and twice the
length and width. Chill until needed, wrapped with something opaque
to keep out light.

Working with 8 slices of bread at a time, line them up on your
work surface in two rows of four slices. Spread half of the slices with
soy-flavored mayonnaise and half with wasabi-flavored mayonnaise.
Pave the first row of bread slices with tuna slices, then flip the second
row of bread slices onto the tuna. Use a sharp knife to separate the
sandwiches if you have extended the tuna slices from sandwich to
sandwich. As sandwiches are assembled, transfer them to a baking
sheet lined with plastic wrap and lightly misted with plain water to
create humidity and prevent drying out. Lightly mist the tops of the
sandwiches and wrap them. Repeat procedure twice until you have 12
large sandwiches. The count is approximate, and you might run out
of tuna before you complete all 12, depending on the thickness of
your slices. Wrap tightly and chill for at least 1 hour.

To finish the sandwiches, use a very sharp knife to slice off the
crusts so that sandwiches are neatly squared. Then slice them diagonally into 4 triangles or crosswise into 4 squares or lengthwise into 3
fingers. Wrap and chill until serving time.

GRAVLAX (GRAVADLAX) OR GRAVAD BLUEFISH OR MACKEREL WITH MUSTARD DILL SAUCE

Each pound of fillet serves 4 to 8 people

Celeste Holm, with obvious pride in her Norwegian heritage, explains that *gravlax* is a cognate, that the fish is seasoned and, figuratively speaking, buried in a grave for a while. There are various etymological explanations, but the certainty is that salt-sugar-and-dill-cured salmon has a wide following in the Northeast. It is a delightful method for using the fine quality farm-raised salmon from Scandinavia that are in good supply year round. The technique also works nicely with very fresh bluefish, an idea from teacher Bims Kolding that has consistently surprised and delighted students. Large mackerel—Atlantic, king, or Spanish—are other good choices.

With the closing of Nyborg Nelson's New York retail store, it became difficult to find Scandinavian prepared foods and condiments. For the sauce, the mustard most popular with transplanted Scandinavians who cannot locate Slott's brand Swedish mustard is Gulden's Spicy Brown. The sauce recipe below is based on one used by New Yorker Diana Stammers, who is English-born but was married to a Swede and resident in his country for some years.

Curing time naturally varies with the size of the fillets. Medium bluefish or mackerel can be ready to serve in as little as twenty-four hours, while large salmon is best after two or three days. All *gravad* fish will keep for a week (in classes we lay down a fish one week to sample the next) plus another day or three. Do not count on more life than that. Low temperatures (under 35°F.) certainly increase the keeping time. A splash of cognac makes the fish especially tasty. Some use a bit of akvavit. Purists insist on no spirits at all.

Fillet of very fresh salmon, bluefish, or mackerel, neatly trimmed
Freshly ground black pepper
Coarse salt
Sugar
Fresh dill
Cognac or akvavit (optional)
Good pumpernickel, thinly sliced
Mustard Dill Sauce (recipe follows)

Carefully remove pinbones from trimmed fillets with tweezers for salmon and a V-cut with a sharp knife for others. Sprinkle flesh with a generous amount of pepper. Combine equal parts of salt and sugar, and coat the fillets, allowing ¼ cup of the mixture per pound of fillet. Cover the bottom of a nonreactive dish—glass is best (a Pyrex "lasagne pan" is ideal) but ceramic or enamel in perfect condition or finest stainless steel will do—with 1 or 2 bunches of dill. Bruising the dill with the side of a heavy knife will help to release its flavor. Arrange fish, flesh side down, on the dill. You may also sandwich the fillets, with dill between, if they are large. Splash on a bit of spirits, if you wish. Cover with plastic wrap and seal well with heavy foil. Refrigerate. Turn fish daily, basting with the brine that will develop, for the length of time indicated above. For the last 12 hours, top with a flat surface slightly smaller than the pan and weight with available heavy objects and refrigerate.

At serving time, remove fish from its pan and discard dill; save juices in case you have leftovers. Slice fish very thinly on a slight diagonal with a very sharp, thin-bladed knife, as for smoked salmon. Hold the knife almost flat. Serve with pumpernickel and Mustard Dill Sauce.

MUSTARD DILL SAUCE

> *8-ounce jar Gulden's Spicy Brown mustard*
> *1 tablespoon corn oil*
> *2 teaspoons white wine vinegar*
> *1½ tablespoons sugar*
> *½ cup finely chopped dill leaves*

Combine ingredients and chill. Correct seasoning. Sauce should be balanced—sweet but not cloyingly so. Serve cool.

POACHED WHOLE COD WITH TUNA SAUCE

8 to 10 servings

This festive warm-weather dish is from Joanna Pruess, New Jersey-based author of *The Supermarket Epicure*. It elevates the lowly cod to *haute* status by using the tonnato sauce that is traditionally reserved for veal. The result is elegant, flavorful, and reasonably priced compared to the luxury fish that are usually presented whole. It tastes best when it is prepared a day in advance. Please see Poached Whole Fish for detailed instructions on poaching.

One 8-pound whole cod, head on
Court Bouillon (see recipe) or salted water for poaching

THE TUNA SAUCE

1⅓ cups mayonnaise, preferably homemade with light olive oil or a
*   combination of extra-virgin olive and vegetable oil (see recipe)*
One 7-ounce can imported tuna in olive oil*
One half to one 2-ounce can anchovy fillets, rinsed and patted dry
¼ cup (nonpareil) capers, drained
¼ cup lemon juice
¾ cup finest-quality light olive oil

THE GARNISHES

2 cucumbers, preferably seedless
1 black olive
Julienne of carrot, lightly steamed and dressed with lemon juice, light
*   olive oil, chopped fresh basil or parsley, and salt and pepper*
*   (optional)*
Snow peas, lightly steamed or blanched (optional)

Clean the cod well, removing the gills and rinsing away all blood. Remove pectoral fins with shears. Wrap in cheesecloth, place in a fish poacher or other large vessel, and pour in court bouillon or salted water to cover by 1 inch. Bring liquid rapidly to a simmer, reduce heat, and poach until done. This could take about 8 minutes for each inch of thickness.

Remove fish to a platter and let it cool for a few minutes. Remove the cheesecloth. Skin the top side. If the head has fallen apart or your platter is not large enough to accommodate it, remove it

---

* Of the imported tunas in olive oil, Progresso is the most available; Pastene is equally fine; the expensive ones in glass jars are best of all.

(saving the cheeks for snacks). Leave the tail intact. When the fish has cooled, cover it loosely with foil and refrigerate for several hours until it is cold.

To prepare the tuna sauce: Make the mayonnaise if you have not already done so. In a food processor bowl, combine the tuna, anchovies, capers, lemon juice, and olive oil and process to a smooth paste. This can also be done in a bowl by hand (with the fingers). Fold the tuna mixture into the mayonnaise until well blended and refrigerate until needed.

Remove all liquid from the fish platter. Spoon tuna sauce generously over the fish and smooth it with a spatula, leaving the tail uncovered. Reserve remaining sauce to pass at the table. Score the cucumbers with a fork and slice them thinly. Cut the slices in half. Starting at the tail end of the fish, arrange cucumber slices over the sauce in overlapping rows to simulate scales, with the rounded sides of the slices directed toward the tail. Stop when you get to the head or what will be made to look like the head if it has been removed. Place a slice or half of the olive where the eye should be. Refrigerate for at least 4 to 6 hours, or preferably overnight. At serving time, add the optional garnish(es) and serve cool, passing the remaining sauce.

DECORATION FOR CHILLED FISH

Once they have been poached or steamed and thoroughly chilled, fish may be decorated with a sparkling jelly and vegetable or fruit cutouts. This is most often done with large whole fish, though small trout are also decorated, as are pieces or fillets of larger fish for certain buffet presentations. If the fish is molded in a decorative mold or just a mixing bowl, with various vegetables or shellfish or salads added, then the creation is an aspic. The jelly must be clarified according to the instructions below so that it will be totally clear; do not attempt to clarify a stock that is very cloudy because it has been poorly made. See the recipe for Fish Stock. Vegetables and fruits for decoration are normally blanched slightly to soften them, to remove excess moisture that would bleed into the jelly, and to brighten the color of greens.

THE JELLY

> *4 cups Fish Stock (see recipe) or court bouillon used to poach fish,*
>   *strained*
> *3 to 4 envelopes unflavored gelatine*
> *2 teaspoons tomato paste (optional)*
> *3 lightly beaten egg whites*
> *3 eggshells*
> *Pinch salt*
> *2 tablespoons cognac or Madeira*

VEGETABLES AND FRUITS THAT SHOULD BE BLANCHED

> *Scallion greens*
> *Leek greens*
> *Lemon, lime, or orange zest*
> *Lengthwise slices of carrot, very thin*
> *Cucumber slices*
> *Radish slices*
> *Peas*

DECORATIONS THAT CAN BE USED AS THEY ARE

> *Olives*
> *Pimiento*
> *Mauve skin of white turnips*
> *Truffles*
> *Cooked egg white*
> *Cucumber skin*
> *Lemon or lime slices*
> *Tomato skin*
> *Dill sprigs*
> *Capers*

To prepare the jelly, pour cold liquid into a pot and sprinkle the gelatine over it. If the liquid isn't very jellied when cold, use the larger amount of gelatine; otherwise, use the smaller. Let sit for 5 minutes undisturbed. If liquid is hot, soften gelatine in ½ cup cold water, then add to hot liquid and proceed. Whisk in tomato paste, egg whites, eggshells, and salt, if needed. Bring rapidly to a boil, whisking constantly to keep impurities in suspension. When liquid begins to boil, stop whisking, lower heat, and simmer gently, undisturbed, for about 5 minutes. Turn off heat and let rest for 5 to 10 minutes. Ladle off the clear liquid and strain it through a clean cloth or paper towel into a stainless-steel bowl. Finish with the liquid in the egg-white residue. Do not push or squeeze the residue. When all liquid is strained, add the cognac or Madeira.

Blanch the vegetables that need it for a few seconds, then skim them out of the boiling water and shock with cold water. Drain all decorations well. It is best to plan the decoration, trim the pieces, and arrange them on a cookie sheet. Use a sharp knife and/or little shaped cutters. Floral patterns—bouquets and vases of flowers—are the most common; there are also possibilities for handsome abstract and geometrical patterns.

Chill fish to be decorated very well and put it on a rack (with a platter under it to catch the drips) or a platter. Place bowl of jelly in a larger bowl of ice water and cool it until it is syrupy, swirling it from time to time. If it is cooled until it is set, it will have to be melted and cooled again. Apply a thin layer of jelly to the fish with a pastry brush. Dip decorations in jelly and apply them to the fish, trimming as needed so that they fit neatly. They should set right away. Rechill the fish as needed if your kitchen is hot. Finish by spooning on a layer of jelly to glaze the fish and the decorations. Chill until serving time. Reuse the jelly that drips through the rack or pools on the platter.

It is traditional to chill a thin layer of jelly—up to ½ inch thick—in a sheet pan, then cut it into cubes at serving time to arrange around the decorated fish. Not only will it add a jewel-like sparkle, but it should be tasty enough to offer a little with each serving.

FELIPE ROJAS-LOMBARDI'S ESCABECHE OF FRESH SARDINES

6 to 12 servings

Here is another tasty *tapa* from The Ballroom. It is easy to make, should be made in advance, and keeps well. This is a classic example of "soused" fish dishes that were invented to preserve the catch for lean days and proved to be tasty as well as practical. Fresh sardines—small herring—from U.S. waters are plentiful in spring and fall, and the ones from Spain and Portugal are becoming more widely available. The frozen ones are all right, too.

3 pounds fresh sardines (12 large ones would be ideal, but a larger
*   quantity of smaller ones is fine)*
½ cup flour
1 cup vegetable oil
1 cup light olive oil
6 cloves garlic, peeled
2 bay leaves
1 teaspoon Spanish paprika
6 to 8 sprigs fresh thyme
3 cups red wine vinegar
1 teaspoon coarse salt

Gently scale the fish, doing as little damage as possible. Slit open the cavity of each fish with a small sharp knife or shears, and remove the entrails with your fingers. Use kitchen shears to cut out the gills. Discard all innards. Rinse fish thoroughly but gently in cold water (sardines are fragile) and drain on paper towels. Just before cooking time, dredge fish in flour, shaking off excess.

In a skillet, heat the vegetable oil to hot and fry the sardines in a single layer, in batches, until golden, turning once. This should only take about 1 minute on each side. As you remove the cooked fish, place them in a serving dish with a little depth to it (to hold the pickling bath). There is no need to blot the fish, and you would not want to drain them after the frying is completed; the juices add flavor. Set sardines aside.

Discard the frying oil and wipe out the skillet. Add the olive oil and heat. When very hot, add garlic and bay leaves. When garlic just begins to color—do not brown—immediately add paprika, thyme, and vinegar. Stir, and bring to a boil. Reduce heat to maintain a simmer, add salt, and cook mixture 5 to 10 minutes (the longer cooking time will slightly decrease acidity, so you must decide how tart you wish the dish to be). Cool mixture to lukewarm and pour it over the sardines. Serve soon (slightly warm), or later in the day at room temperature, or refrigerate and serve within the week, bringing to room temperature before serving.

PICKLED CARP, POLISH-STYLE

5 to 10 servings

Here is one version of the Eastern European pickled freshwater fish that are prepared for special occasions. They are tasty additions to festive buffets, as well as fine first courses. Carp and buffalo are the most usual fish, but you might also use whitefish, pike, walleye, or lake trout. This recipe was influenced by both Jewish and Christian traditions, but the sweet-and-sour aspect is more typical of Jewish cookery in that part of the world. Filleting the fish is not entirely usual, but it does make it easier to serve and eat. Pike cannot be filleted into the neat chunks you want, so, should you use it, cut it into the traditional two-inch steaks.

About 5 pounds whole carp, gutted, scaled, gills removed, rinsed of all
*   blood*
Coarse salt
2 1/2 cups white vinegar: wine or distilled
4 cups cold water
1/4 cup sugar
2 bay leaves
15 whole allspice berries
20 black peppercorns
1 small piece cinnamon stick, about 1/4 inch wide
5 whole cloves
2 strips orange zest, about 3 by 2/3 inches
3 large carrots, sliced
5 medium onions, peeled and sliced, rinsed with cold water, and
*   drained*
1/2 lemon, sliced
2 envelopes unflavored gelatine, softened in 1/2 cup cold water

Make sure fish is thoroughly clean and free of any stray scales. Fillet the fish, reserving the skeleton with the head and tail attached. Cut fillets crosswise into 1 1/2- to 2-inch chunks. Sprinkle fish evenly with coarse salt, or dredge it, and place it in a nonreactive bowl. Salt the skeleton and add it. Cover and refrigerate for at least 30 minutes, up to 2 hours.

In a nonreactive pot large enough to hold all the ingredients, combine vinegar, water, sugar, bay leaves, spices, orange zest, carrots, half of the onions, and 1 teaspoon salt. Rinse the salt off the skeleton and add it, too. Bring mixture to a simmer, lower heat, and simmer gently, uncovered, for 20 minutes, skimming, especially at the beginning, to remove any scum. Add lemon and simmer another 5 minutes, then remove and discard lemon.

Rinse the salt off the fish pieces under running cold water and add them to the pot. If there is not enough liquid to cover the fish, add a little cold water. Poach fish at the shiver—170°F. to 180°F.— until done. Remove fish pieces to a nonreactive bowl or crock, layering and topping them with the remaining onions. Add the softened gelatine to the hot liquid and stir to dissolve. Let liquid rest for a few minutes to settle, then strain it through a fine sieve—preferably lined with cheesecloth or paper towels or a coffee filter—onto the fish and onions. Discard solids in the sieve. Make sure fish is covered by liquid; shift it around if necessary. Let mixture cool, then cover and chill it thoroughly, overnight if possible but at least 6 hours. Liquid should set into a soft jelly. Serve fish cold with a few onion slices on top and some jelly spooned around it.

SALADE DE ST. JACQUES FLEURIE

6 to 8 servings

This suave starter, which could hardly be easier to prepare, is by Alain Sailhac, for some years executive chef at Le Cirque, later at the new "21" Club. Notice that this is a perfect cold-weather combination, featuring bay scallops, mâche, and radicchio—all wintry fare—and a dressing so sinfully rich that it is not a vinaigrette but a *beurre rouge* made with red wine vinegar rather than the more usual red wine. The chive garnish lends a perfect hint of yearning for spring, even though chives are always available from the hothouse or the windowsill. It is difficult to imagine a more elegant synthesis, or a worse choice for summer alfresco dining. Some things just are what they are and you don't mess around with them. Yet, in season, if you must, there are a few nonfatal compromises. Should you be unable to secure genuine Long Island bay scallops (or high-quality bay scallops from New England), you will *not* want to try Florida calicoes; there are some scallops from South America that are genuine bays—they have similar plumpness and delicacy of flavor and texture without the telltale fuzzy-looking white ends that signal a heat treatment for shucking purposes. Sea scallops cut into quarters will also do in a pinch. Mâche could be replaced by Bibb lettuce, if necessary. Mr. Sailhac specifies radicchio di Treviso—the one that looks like loose-leafed red Belgian endive—for its beauty and for its delicate flavor. The more familiar round-headed radicchio di Verona (or Chioggia) is fine.

4 ounces mâche, trimmed and carefully washed
6 ounces radicchio di Treviso, trimmed and carefully washed
12 ounces (3 sticks) cool butter, cut into pieces
1 1/2 pounds genuine bay scallops, tough muscle removed
Salt and freshly ground white pepper to taste
1/4 cup minced shallots
1 cup red wine vinegar
1/4 cup snipped chives (about 1/2 inch long)

Refrigerate mâche and radicchio wrapped in paper towels, but remember to remove them from the refrigerator about 30 minutes before serving so that they will not be too cold.

In a medium nonreactive skillet, melt 4 tablespoons butter and add the scallops and a little salt and pepper. Cook over medium heat, tossing or stirring often, until scallops are plumped and just heated through. Pour into a colander or large sieve and drain, reserving liquid. Reserve scallops in a warm place.

Melt another 4 tablespoons butter in the skillet and sauté shallots gently for a few minutes until they are translucent. Add vinegar and scallop juice and boil until reduced by half. Transfer mixture to a medium nonreactive saucepan, straining to remove solids if you wish. Whisk in the remaining 2 sticks butter, a piece at a time, warming the pan over low heat once or twice as necessary to keep mixture warm. Do not overheat. Season very lightly with salt and pepper only if you feel the need.

Arrange mâche and radicchio on warmed—not hot—platter or plates and drizzle a little sauce evenly over them. Place scallops in the center and cover with sauce. Sprinkle with chives, and serve.

SCALLOPS IN CRÈME FRAÎCHE WITH CORIANDER

About 4 servings

When this summery luncheon dish or starter was put together some years ago, fresh coriander was still a novelty in mainstream American cookery, as was *crème fraîche.* Now that they are both more available—at specialty shops or greengrocers— this dish is easy to provision. You may lower the fat and calories by using sour cream or even yogurt, but *crème fraîche* is best. Scallops are delicious raw, but you might blanch them briefly if you feel the need.

1 pound sea scallops
1/2 cup lime juice
1 large or 2 small seedless cucumbers, or several small unwaxed (Kirby) cucumbers, sliced
1 small clove garlic
Coarse salt and freshly ground white pepper to taste
3/4 cup crème fraîche, *sour cream, or plain yogurt*
2 tablespoons olive oil (optional)
1/3 cup thinly sliced scallions, or 1/4 cup minced shallots
2 tablespoons chopped fresh coriander
Large pinch sugar
2 large ripe tomatoes, seeded, juiced, and diced

THE GARNISHES

1 lime, sliced or cut into wedges
Coriander sprigs

Trim and rinse scallops, then pat them dry. Slice uniformly into coin shapes about ⅜ inch thick. Put scallops in a nonreactive bowl and pour on the lime juice. Marinate, refrigerated, stirring a few times, for 1 to 2 hours. Drain, reserving marinade, and return to the refrigerator.

Pour marinade over cucumbers and let them sit for about 30 minutes.

In a nonreactive bowl, use a fork to mash the garlic to a paste with a little salt. Add the *crème fraîche,* and whisk in the oil. Add the scallions, coriander, sugar, and salt and pepper to taste. Fold in the scallops and taste for seasoning. You may wish to add a few teaspoons of the marinade. Season tomatoes lightly with salt and pepper.

Drain cucumbers, season lightly with salt and pepper, and arrange them in a ring on a platter or shallow bowl. Put the scallop mixture in the middle, and ring it with diced tomatoes. Garnish with lime pieces and coriander sprigs. Serve cool.

TROPICAL SHELLFISH SALAD

4 to 8 servings

This salad is based on the flavors of the famous Central and South American raw fish preparation called *seviche* (or *ceviche*), which is traditionally made with mackerel but is more popular in the United States when a white fish such as snapper or flounder is used. You may use your own choice of fish or shellfish, raw or cooked, or the ingredients below.

1 pound squid, cleaned (p. 65)
1/2 pound sea scallops, trimmed and cut into 1/4-inch slices
1/2 pound lump crabmeat, carefully picked over to remove bits of shell
2/3 cup lime juice
1/3 cup olive oil
1 tablespoon white wine vinegar
1 large onion, white if possible, minced
1 tablespoon chopped green chiles, or more to taste
Drops of Tabasco if chiles are mild
3 tablespoons chopped parsley
2 teaspoons chopped fresh oregano, or 1/2 teaspoon dried oregano
*   toasted in a skillet*
1/2 teaspoon coarse salt
1/2 teaspoon freshly ground black pepper
1 large clove garlic, finely minced

THE GARNISHES

1 large avocado, peeled and sliced lengthwise
Slices of ripe summer tomato

Sprigs of fresh coriander
Green olives (optional)

Slice squid bodies into ½-inch rings. Cut tentacles in half if they are large. Bring a pot of salted water to a boil and add the squid. Blanch briefly, about 10 seconds, then drain and shock with cold water. Drain well. Place the squid, scallops, and crabmeat in a nonreactive bowl, add the lime juice, and marinate 1 to 2 hours, refrigerated. Drain, reserving the juice.

Combine half of the juice with the oil, vinegar, onion, chiles, Tabasco, herbs, seasonings, and garlic, and stir to combine. Fold in the seafood. Refrigerate for at least 30 minutes so that the flavors can marry. Correct seasoning. Put salad on a platter and garnish with avocado, tomato, coriander, and optional olives. Serve cool.

CHILLED SOBA WITH SHRIMP AND SQUID

About 4 servings

This refreshing combination of textures and flavors was inspired by visits to East, on East 44th Street, which is part of a chain of rambunctious Japanese restaurants in the metropolitan area. This dish is particularly well suited to summer lunches and suppers. It can be made elaborate, or as simple as you choose, by including any or all of the garnishes below. The Asian products are available at stores that sell Japanese foods, at neighborhood greengrocers, and, increasingly, even in supermarkets. Japanese cold noodles are traditionally eaten with a dipping sauce on the side, but the average Western diner might be happier pouring the sauce over all.

8 ounces Japanese soba (buckwheat) noodles
Coarse salt
8 ounces medium shrimp
8 to 12 ounces squid

THE DIPPING SAUCE

> 2 teaspoons powdered instant dashi
> 2-inch piece dried kombu (kelp) (optional)
> 1 cup water
> 1/4 cup soy sauce (Kikkoman is fine)
> 1 tablespoon rice vinegar
> 1/4 cup mirin
> 1 teaspoon sugar

THE GARNISHES

> 1/4 large seedless cucumber
> 1 tablespoon wasabi, mixed to a thick paste with cold water
> 4 large mushrooms, thinly sliced, or 4 large dried shiitake mushrooms
> 1/2 bunch watercress, tough stems removed, or 1/2 sheet nori (seaweed)
>   for sushi, toasted, then cut into slivers with scissors or a sharp
>   knife
> 1/4 cup grated red radish or daikon
> 1/4 cup thinly sliced scallion
> Asian dark sesame oil (optional)

Cook soba in a large pot of boiling salted water, stirring a few times, especially in the beginning, and adding 1 cup cold water at 1-minute intervals, until noodles are just tender but still firm. Drain and rinse vigorously with cold water, stirring with the hands to wipe off surface starch. Drain. Chill.

Shell and devein the shrimp, leaving the tail end of the shells intact, if you wish. Lightly score the underside of each shrimp with a very sharp knife to straighten it. Clean and flower-cut the squid (p. 65). Blanch seafood separately in boiling water for a few seconds, just until heated through. Squid will cook in a few seconds, the shrimp in 30 seconds or so. Shock with cold water. Reserve.

Combine dashi powder, optional kombu, water, soy sauce, vinegar, mirin, and sugar in a saucepan and bring to a boil. Lower heat and simmer 2 or 3 minutes. Cool rapidly over ice and set aside. Remove and discard kombu before serving.

Slice cucumber in half lengthwise, then cut thin crosswise slices, keeping them together so they can be fanned out on serving plates. Wasabi should be tightly covered and left to cure for at least

15 minutes or so. If you are using dried mushrooms, they should be soaked in warm water for about 30 minutes, then drained and simmered in the dipping sauce while it is cooking, then removed and sliced.

At serving time, divide noodles among serving bowls, a small clump at a time rather than a large mass. If you have any problems with stickiness, rinse the noodles again in cold water and drain. Garnish with seafood and vegetables in an attractive asymmetrical pattern. Divide sauce among small bowls and let diners stir in wasabi to taste. They may also drizzle on a little sesame oil, if they wish. Sauce may be used for dipping or poured over the noodles. Chopsticks are best but forks are fine, too.

SHRIMP AND ASPARAGUS SALAD

4 servings

This recipe was assembled in the early 1980s and has proved very popular. Notes and memory indicate that it was adapted from Michel Guérard, but the antecedent has disappeared. Nothing like it exists in *Cuisine Minceur* or *Cuisine Gourmande*, both of which were in print at the time. Anyway, it is delicious and very pretty. So, with a bow to M. Guérard. . . .

12 medium or medium-large shrimp
16 medium asparagus spears
1 pound string beans, as young and tender as possible (but not tiny French beans)
2 heads Bibb lettuce
2 tablespoons red wine vinegar
1 tablespoon lemon juice
2 teaspoons Dijon mustard
1 teaspoon green peppercorns in brine, drained and mashed
1 tablespoon minced fresh chervil or parsley
Coarse salt to taste
1/3 cup extra-virgin olive oil
1 tablespoon snipped chives (about 1/2 inch long)

Drop shrimp into boiling salted water and poach them for 30 to 45 seconds, depending on size, just until they are firm and heated through. Drain and shock with cold water, then shell and devein. Hold in the refrigerator.

Trim asparagus to a uniform length of 5 to 6 inches, and beans 3½ to 4 inches, depending on the size of the plates you are using to serve the salad. Use a swivel-blade peeler or sharp paring knife to lightly peel the asparagus stems. Blanch each vegetable in well-salted water to the desired tenderness, then drain, shock with cold water, drain, and chill. Separate the lettuce leaves, then wash, drain, and gently dry them with paper towels. Wrap with towels and refrigerate.

Prepare a vinaigrette by whisking together the vinegar, lemon juice, mustard, peppercorns, chervil or parsley, and salt, then whisk in the oil gradually. Correct seasoning. Set aside.

Arrange the salad on dinner plates: For each plate, make a square raft of beans in the center and rim the square with 4 asparagus spears, letting the *tips* extend beyond the square at each corner, keeping the cut ends flush. Place uniform Bibb leaves on each side of the squares. Place 3 shrimp on each plate, arranging them diagonally on the string beans. Whisk up the vinaigrette and spoon it over the salads. Sprinkle shrimp with chives, and serve.

WARM OYSTER SALAD WITH WINTER VEGETABLES

4 to 6 servings

This is a hearty starter or luncheon dish for cold weather. It could be simplified by using fewer vegetables or, simplest of all, the vegetables could be replaced by raw spinach cleaned and torn into pieces.

1½ pounds kale, washed well, tough stems removed, and finely shredded
Small head red cabbage, shredded
1½ pounds daikon or white turnips, peeled and grated into long shreds
4 tablespoons peanut oil
¼ cup minced shallots
6 tablespoons sherry vinegar
⅛ teaspoon ground cloves
Coarse salt and freshly ground pepper to taste

Light olive oil, as needed
2 slices sturdy white bread, trimmed of crusts and cut into ½-inch cubes
White wine vinegar, as needed
24 bluepoint oysters, shucked, in their liquor

Briefly steam the three individual vegetables just until they lose their raw crispness. Or pour boiling water on them, let sit a minute, and drain. Reserve.

Combine the peanut oil and shallots in a small skillet and heat gently until shallots are tender. Add the sherry vinegar and bring it just to a boil. Pour mixture into a bowl, add the ground cloves, and season lightly with salt and pepper. Set aside. Wash and dry the skillet and heat about 1 cup of olive oil in it until very hot and nearly smoking. Fry the bread cubes until they are golden, then immediately skim them out of the oil so they do not overbrown. Set aside. Pour the oil out of the skillet and reserve the skillet.

Dress each of the vegetables separately with just enough olive oil to lightly film, 1 or 2 teaspoons of wine vinegar, and a little salt and pepper. Arrange equal mounds of vegetables on warmed dinner plates, leaving the centers of the plates empty. Pour the oysters into the reserved skillet and heat briefly, just until the oysters plump and their mantles begin to curl. Drain. Arrange the oysters toward the centers of the plates, leaving the very middle free. Spoon the sauce over the oysters, place some croutons in the center, and serve immediately.

LOBSTER WITH AVOCADO AND CHUTNEY

4 servings

This versatile salad is delicious with a number of kinds of shellfish, but lobster is particularly fine. You might also consider shrimp, scallops, or crabmeat, alone or in combinations. Use only Hass avocados from California, the smallish variety with the dull, rough skin that turns black when the fruit is ready to eat. Avocados are not often properly softened when you find them in the market (and if they are, they are probably bruised) so buy them firm but not rock-hard several days in advance and nurse them along at room temperature, in a paper bag with a few holes in it if you are in a hurry. Refrigerate when they yield to gentle pressure.

1/2 cup lime or lemon juice
1 clove garlic, unpeeled and bruised
1 tablespoon honey or to taste
1/4 cup sweet mango chutney (Major Grey–style)
Coarse salt to taste
Tabasco to taste
2 ripened avocados, not too soft
Two 1 1/4-pound lobsters, steamed, cooled, claw and tail meat removed
  from shells (p. 356)
1 small head Boston lettuce, or 2 small heads Bibb, separated into
  leaves, washed, and dried
4 slices bacon, cooked crisp, drained, and crumbled (optional)
1 heaping tablespoon chopped fresh mint
1 small red onion, peeled, thinly sliced, and separated into rings

Make a sauce by combining lime or lemon juice, garlic, honey, chutney, salt, and Tabasco in a nonreactive bowl. If there are any large mango pieces in the chutney, chop them up a bit and return them to the sauce. Let sit for about 30 minutes, then remove and discard garlic.

To prepare the avocados, cut through the flesh lengthwise, all the way around, and then twist the halves in opposite directions to separate them. To remove the pit that remains in one half, plant your knife in it and twist to release the pit. Peel avocado halves; if the skin does not slip off easily, put halves, cut side down, on your board and gently scrape skin with the blunt edge of a knife. Slice peeled halves lengthwise into wedges about 1/2 inch wide. Add slices to the sauce, baste, and marinate until serving time. (Cover and refrigerate if this is done well in advance.)

Devein lobster tails and carefully slice the meat into neat *medaillons* about 1/4 inch thick. At serving time, place some lettuce leaves on dinner plates and add avocado slices in a ring or crescent. Place the lobster in the middle, 1 claw and the meat of half a tail per serving. Spoon the sauce over the lobster and sprinkle with optional bacon, mint, and onion rings. Serve cool.

MUSSEL AND POTATO SALAD

6 to 8 servings

A salad of this sort was "invented" by Alexandre Dumas Fils and christened *Salade Francillon*. It is also known in classic French cookery as *Salade Dumas* or *Salade à la Japonaise,* a mistaken reference to some supposed Chinese influence. In accordance with French tradition and if the budget allows, you may elevate this dish from earthy to heavenly with the addition of lots of sliced black truffles.

3 pounds small new red potatoes
Coarse salt, as needed
1/4 cup dry vermouth
1/4 cup chopped fresh herbs: a combination of parsley and tarragon, basil, marjoram, or savory
1/2 cup sliced scallions, green and white parts
2 cloves garlic, minced
2 cups shelled steamed mussels (p. 353)
About 1 cup well-seasoned Vinaigrette (see recipe), heavy on the mustard
Freshly ground black pepper to taste
Bibb or Boston lettuce leaves, washed and dried

Scrub potatoes but do not peel. Simmer in well-salted water to cover until just tender. Drain. When potatoes are just cool enough to handle, slice them and add them to a bowl, sprinkling with the vermouth as you go. Add the herbs, scallions, and garlic, and toss gently. Fold in the mussels and enough vinaigrette to moisten the mixture. Add pepper to taste and a little salt if it is needed. Serve tepid to cool, on lettuce leaves.

OCTOPUS SALAD, MEDITERRANEAN-STYLE

4 to 8 servings

Mediterraneans and Asians are the world's major consumers of octopus, so there is a fair bit of it moving through Fulton— usually frozen—to accommodate the tastes of those ethnic groups. If you have not seen it at your fish market, ask. They may very well have some in the back. It will be cleaned. A cleaned weight of 1 to 1½ pounds is ideal for presentation and tenderness, but do not shy away from the larger ones. They just need a little more cooking time. As with other cephalopods, octopus is pleasantly chewy when raw and only becomes tough when it is carelessly cooked. The consensus—East and West—leans toward the preliminary blanching technique below, though there are those who insist octopus must be physically tenderized by bashing it repeatedly against coastal boulders (fisherman-style) or against the kitchen sink. That's fine for those who find it therapeutic, but it isn't necessary. This same kind of salad is delicious made with cooked shrimp, scallops, squid, cuttlefish, mussels, or crabmeat, singly or in combinations.

1 to 1½ pounds cleaned octopus
Coarse salt, as needed
3 tablespoons red wine vinegar
1 tablespoon lemon, lime, or orange juice
1 large clove garlic, minced
Freshly ground black pepper to taste
¼ cup chopped parsley, or a combination of parsley and fresh basil, marjoram, or oregano
⅓ cup fruity olive oil
1 tablespoon tiny (nonpareil) capers, drained (optional)
1 cup juiced, seeded, and diced ripe tomatoes
Watercress, arugula, Boston lettuce, or other greens, washed and dried

Bring a medium pot of water to a boil. Put the octopus in a bowl with a handful of salt and knead and scour it for 1 or 2 minutes. Shake off excess salt and add octopus to the pot of water. Immediately remove the octopus and put it aside while the water returns to a boil. Repeat this dunking 2 or 3 times with rest periods between. Then return octopus to the pot and let it simmer very gently until tender. In Japan, less than 10 minutes is considered proper. In the West, an hour is preferred. Remove octopus and put it aside to cool slowly. Do not be tempted to rush the cooling process in any way. When octopus is completely cooled, nip off and discard the tips of the tentacles, then slice the tentacles thinly on a slight diagonal. Set aside.

In a medium nonreactive bowl, whisk together the vinegar, citrus juice, garlic, salt and pepper to taste, and herb(s). Whisk in the oil gradually. Stir in the capers, tomatoes, and reserved sliced octopus. Cover and refrigerate for about 30 minutes to let the flavors marry. Longer marination will flavor and tenderize the octopus, but it is not necessary. Correct the seasoning. Serve cool or at room temperature, garnished with watercress or other green.

MICHEL FITOUSSI'S LE VIOLET AUX PETALES DE ROSE

ARTICHOKES STUFFED WITH LOBSTER AND STEAK TARTARE

6 servings

Michel Fitoussi came to prominence in the New York restaurant scene in the late 1970s as chef of the famous Palace restaurant, which was then the most expensive place in town. After a stint at 24 Fifth Avenue (where this dish was introduced) he became executive chef of Regine's and the Reginette Brasserie. The following is probably the fanciest surf 'n' turf you will ever encounter. It is also rather easily prepared and largely done in advance. Do not be discouraged by the long list of ingredients; there is an easy logic to the proceedings. This dish is planned as a first course, but it could be served in larger portions for a special late supper (New Year's Eve, champagne, et cetera).

THE ARTICHOKE BOTTOMS

6 artichokes, about 8 ounces each
1/2 lemon
Flour
Salt

THE LOBSTER

1 bay leaf
1 teaspoon peppercorns
1 live lobster, 1 1/4 to 1 1/2 pounds, preferably female

THE MASTER SAUCE

>*2 egg yolks*
>*4 teaspoons Dijon mustard*
>*2 teaspoons red wine vinegar*
>*1 cup light olive oil*
>*Freshly ground pepper to taste*

FOR THE GREEN SAUCE

>*2 cups loosely packed spinach leaves*
>*1/3 cup coarsely chopped celery*
>*1/2 cup loosely packed watercress*
>*1/2 cup loosely packed parsley*
>*2 tablespoons lemon juice*

FOR THE TARTARE

>*2 tablespoons minced shallots*
>*2 tablespoons minced cornichons*
>*1 tablespoon minced capers*
>*2 tablespoons minced parsley*
>*6 ounces carefully trimmed, totally lean fillet of beef*

THE GARNISHES

>*6 teaspoons fine-quality caviar*
>*36 very fresh red rose petals*

To prepare artichoke bottoms: Use a stainless-steel knife to slice off stems so that artichokes will sit level. Rub cut surfaces with lemon to prevent discoloration. Starting at the base, pare away the dark green, removing rows of leaves as you go, to expose the pale center flesh. Once you have exposed a base about 1 1/2 inches deep, slice crosswise to remove remaining leaves. You now have pale green "dishes" that are filled with the fuzzy chokes. These will be removed after cooking. Trim neatly to remove any traces of dark green.

The artichoke bottoms will be cooked *à blanc*. Choose a suitable nonreactive pot and decide how much water you will need to cover the artichokes generously. Place a sieve over the pot and add flour, 1/4 cup for each 6 cups of water. Pour cold water over the flour, rubbing to dissolve the flour. Add salt to taste. Add the artichoke bottoms and bring to a boil. Cover pot, reduce heat to low, and simmer for about 25 minutes, or until bottoms are tender. Remove from heat and cool in the liquid. Before using the artichokes, drain, and scrape out the chokes with a spoon.

In a pot large enough to hold the lobster, add enough water to cover and bay leaf, peppercorns, and salt to taste. Bring to a boil and drop in the lobster. Cover and cook 10 minutes. Drain. When cool enough to handle, remove meat from tail and claws and remove and reserve tomalley (liver, or green glands) and coral, if any. Reserve carcass for another purpose or discard. Thinly slice lobster meat, then mince finely with the tomalley and coral. Set aside.

To make master sauce: Combine egg yolks, mustard, and wine vinegar, and whisk well. Incorporate oil bit by bit to make a mayonnaise. Season to taste with pepper. Divide in half and set aside.

To make green sauce: Drop spinach into boiling water to cover, to wilt, for about 30 seconds. Drain, shock with cold water, and squeeze out most of the moisture. Put the spinach, celery, watercress, and parsley into the bowl of a food processor and process until smooth. Line a small bowl with a thick layer of cheesecloth and scrape the mixture into it. Bring up the ends of the cheesecloth and squeeze the juice from the mixture into the bowl. Whisk 2 tablespoons of this juice and the lemon juice into half of the master sauce and set aside. You might reserve the remaining juice and the pulp for another sauce or for soup.

To make tartare: Flavor the other half of the master sauce with the shallots, cornichons, capers, and parsley. Set aside. Just before serving time, cut the beef into chunks and process until fairly fine but not a purée. You could use a meat grinder, but the processor is much easier to clean. Combine ground beef and minced lobster, and moisten with about ½ cup of the tartare–shallot mixture.

To serve, spoon equal portions of the mixture into each artichoke bottom. Smooth the surface. Top each serving with 1 teaspoon of caviar. Spoon equal portions of the green sauce into the center of each of 6 chilled plates and carefully tilt to swirl the sauce neatly over the flat surface of each plate. Arrange an artichoke bottom in the center of each and arrange 6 rose petals symmetrically around each serving. Serve immediately.

SAUCES AND STOCK

The following is a collection of necessities and auxiliaries. Fish stock is certainly among the former. Readers may make their own decisions about the rest.

FISH STOCK (FOND DE POISSON, FUMET DE POISSON)

Approximately 3 quarts

Fish stock is an important ingredient in many recipes, particularly sauces, soups, stews, braises, and jellied dishes. Fortunately, it is easy to prepare and keeps several days refrigerated and several months frozen. You really should make your own stock for delicate sauces and jellies, clear soups, and other dishes where the flavor and clarity of the liquid are nakedly obvious. For best results, remember to simmer mixture gently—do not boil—uncovered, and skim carefully, particularly in the beginning. For the clearest stock, sprinkle the bones generously with coarse salt, refrigerate for one or two hours, then rinse well to remove the salt. To clarify, see Decoration for Chilled Fish.

The traditional handy-dandy substitute for fish stock is bottled clam juice diluted with an equal volume of water. It will do for dishes where there are so many other flavorings that the liquid is only just a footnote. Many fine fish markets now make their own stock, in answer to the demand. If you trust their fish you should be able to trust their stock, again, for uses where the stock is not the star. Another possibility in the also-ran category, for emergencies, is the fish bouillon cube made by Knorr; it is of course long on salt and short on natural gelatine, but it is far more palatable than one could expect such a product to be.

3 to 4 pounds fish heads, bones, and trimmings (mild, lean fish only),
    *gills removed and all blood washed away**
Shrimp, crab, crayfish, or lobster shells (optional)
2 onions, sliced

---

* If your fishmonger has no bones, use whiting instead.

1 leek, white and pale green parts, sliced (optional)
1 stalk celery, sliced
A handful of mushroom stems and trimmings (optional)
A few parsley stems
1 bay leaf
1 teaspoon dried leaf thyme
12 peppercorns
1 teaspoon lemon juice
2 cups dry white wine
Cold water, to cover

Place all ingredients in a stockpot. Bring almost to a boil, then lower the heat. Simmer gently, *uncovered,* for 30 to 35 minutes, 40 minutes maximum. Skim away the grayish foam that forms, particularly during the first half of the cooking time. Strain stock through a fine strainer (discard solids). You may reduce stock by about one-third—by simmering it—to intensify the flavor. Reduction to a concentrate or *glace* is not recommended for fish stock because the freshness and delicacy are lost. But if you are making a stock with shellfish shells alone, you may reduce it to a concentrate.

COURT BOUILLON

Court bouillon is used mainly for poaching and is normally a white-wine court bouillion made with exactly the same ingredients as Fish Stock but without the bones. Combine ingredients, simmer gently 20 to 30 minutes, strain, and add 2 tablespoons coarse salt per quart.

BEURRE BLANC AND BEURRE ROUGE (OR BEURRE ROSE)
WHITE AND RED BUTTER SAUCES

About 2 cups

The darlings of nouvelle and post-nouvelle cuisine chefs, butter sauces are actually old-fashioned, sinfully delicious, and really very easy to make once the mystery is dispelled. Both white and red butter sauces are delicious with seafood, and may be flavored with a wide variety of savory herbs and spices, provided the flavoring is subtle. This basic recipe has no salt or pepper added—it assumes that the delicate white-fleshed seafood it is to accompany has been properly seasoned. If you use red wine, it must be a light, young wine with a bright, purply color. Beaujolais is often the best choice.

¾ cup minced shallots
2 cups dry white or red wine
1 tablespoon white or red wine vinegar
1 pound finest unsalted butter, cut into 1-tablespoon pieces, kept cool

In a heavy nonreactive saucepan, combine shallots, wine, and wine vinegar, and bring to a boil. Lower heat and simmer until reduced to a few tablespoons liquid, being careful not to scorch it. Reduction may be made in advance and rewarmed at serving time. If it seems very dry, add a spoonful of water or cream, *not* wine. Whisk in the pieces of butter one at a time. Whisk steadily but not furiously. Work on and off low heat to keep the mixture warm enough so that the butter will melt but not overheat, let alone simmer, or the emulsion will break down. When all the butter is incorporated, strain if desired, and serve as soon as possible. You may hold it for maybe 1 hour over *warm* water if necessary. Do not reheat.

LEMON BUTTER

1 cup

Just a simple little flavor boost for delicate fish, lemon butter is as easy as any sauce you might prepare. Notice that the zest has more oomph than the juice, which adds more tartness than lemony flavor. Try this with other citrus fruits as well.

8 ounces (2 sticks) butter
Zest of 1 lemon, removed with a swivel-blade peeler
1 teaspoon lemon juice

Warm the butter in a small saucepan and add the zest after twisting each piece over the pan to release the essential oil. Add the juice and bring the butter almost to a simmer. Cover and simmer very gently for up to 5 minutes. Put aside to rest for at least 15 minutes, then strain, discarding solids. Warm for service. Whisk vigorously just before serving to smooth somewhat, but do not expect it to become really creamy.

MUSTARD CREAM

About 1 cup

This is an easy sauce that students have liked very much through the years. It is particularly tasty with bluefish or mackerel broiled with nothing more than a splash of white wine in the pan, a little salt and pepper, and a film of butter on the surface.

2 cups heavy cream
2 tablespoons Dijon mustard, or to taste
Pan juices from broiled fish

Pour cream into a heavy nonreactive saucepan and reduce by half. Broil fish until done, then whisk mustard and pan juices into the cream. Reheat sauce, plate fish, top with a little sauce, and serve.

ROASTED SHALLOT SAUCE

About 1 1/2 cups

Here is an easy preparation to accompany baked or broiled fillets or whole fish. It may be prepared totally fat-free, or it may be velvetized with a butter enrichment.

6 ounces whole shallots
About 1 1/4 cups Fish Stock (see recipe)
Coarse salt and freshly ground white pepper to taste
Pan juices from baked or broiled fish
4 tablespoons butter, at room temperature (optional)

Preheat oven to 300°F.

Place whole shallots in a single layer in a small baking dish and place in oven. Roast until fragrant and very tender to the touch, about

45 minutes or so, depending upon size. Remove from oven. When shallots are cool enough to handle, squeeze flesh from the skins, and discard skins. Trim any discolored parts from the flesh and purée the flesh in a food processor until smooth, adding enough fish stock to make a light sauce. Season to taste with salt and pepper. Scrape into a nonreactive saucepan and set aside.

Bake or broil fish until done and remove to a platter. Deglaze pan with a little fish stock and strain pan juices into the sauce. Reheat sauce, swirl in the optional butter, correct seasoning, and serve hot.

TWO LOW-FAT "SPA" SAUCES

Following are two sheer purée sauces inspired by the national interest in "California cooking," represented in the New York area by avowed practitioners of same and, most famously, by Seppi Renggli and his famous spa menu at The Four Seasons. They are of interest not just because they are healthy but because the lack of palate-coating fat (or small amount used) lets the flavors zing right through. Either sauce may be served with grilled fish or shellfish or with Scallop Mousse.

RED OR YELLOW PEPPER PURÉE

About 1 cup

For a special added smoky flavor, roast and peel the peppers before cleaning them. If they are roasted, the sauce will not need sieving.

> *3 large red or yellow bell peppers*
> *1 clove garlic, peeled and minced*
> *Large pinch coarse salt*
> *Dash cayenne*
> *1 tablespoon red or white wine vinegar (red for red peppers, white for yellow), or to taste*
> *2 tablespoons water*
> *1 tablespoon extra-virgin olive oil (optional)*

Remove caps, seeds, and membranes from the peppers and chop them coarsely. Put peppers in a heavy nonreactive saucepan with the remaining ingredients. Cover and bring to a simmer. Reduce heat and simmer very gently until peppers are very tender, up to 30 minutes (roasted peppers may be tender in half the time). Purée mixture in a food processor until very smooth. Rub mixture through a fine sieve or a food mill. Correct seasoning. Serve hot or at room temperature.

GREEN SAUCE

About 1 cup

> *2 cups tightly packed fresh greens: watercress, spinach, sorrel, parsley,*
> *   and a few celery leaves (at least 3 kinds)*
> *3 scallions, whites and greens separated, trimmed and coarsely chopped*
> *1 large clove garlic, peeled and minced*
> *Large pinch coarse salt*
> *3/8 teaspoon freshly ground black pepper*
> *Dash cayenne*
> *1 to 2 tablespoons extra-virgin olive oil*
> *Fish Stock (see recipe), as needed*
> *1 tablespoon red wine vinegar*

Plunge the greens into a pot of boiling water and blanch for 30 seconds, adding the scallion greens for the last 5 seconds. Drain and shock with cold water. Squeeze greens rather dry and chop them coarsely. Put greens into the bowl of a food processor with the scallion whites, garlic, seasonings, and oil. Process to a smooth purée, adding stock as needed to achieve the texture of a light sauce. For the most elegant smoothness, rub mixture through a fine sieve or food mill. At serving time, whisk in the vinegar and correct seasoning. Serve at room temperature.

RHUBARB SAUCE FOR GRILLED MACKEREL

About 2 cups

> This is a variation on the traditional gooseberry sauce that is served with spring mackerel in Britain and the north of France. Since gooseberries are not normally grown commercially in the United States (they can carry a dreaded pine tree blight), it is possible to substitute rhubarb and achieve a similar acidity, if not the same color and flavor. This sauce is also good with

tuna, herring, and sturgeon. The butter version is particularly delicate, but the lean version is just as tasty in its different way.

1 pound rhubarb
½ cup dry white wine
2 to 3 tablespoons sugar
1 tablespoon finest-quality French crème de cassis
Large pinch coarse salt
4 ounces (1 stick) butter, at room temperature (optional)

Trim the rhubarb and slice it into ½-inch pieces. Put it in a nonreactive saucepan with the wine and 2 tablespoons sugar, and bring to a simmer. Cover and simmer until rhubarb is tender, 10 to 15 minutes. Purée mixture in a food processor or food mill. If you use a processor you may feel the need to pass the sauce through a fine sieve, but this is not essential. Reheat with crème de cassis and salt and more sugar if it is needed to balance the flavor. At serving time, cut the optional butter into pieces and swirl into the hot sauce. Serve right away.

SHEER TOMATO SAUCE WITH PERNOD

About 2½ cups

This sauce has a delicate texture that makes it suitable to accompany Scallop Mousse and several other recipes in this book. Gauge the seasonings to complement the main event so that you will not overpower it. Even people who are not wildly fond of anise flavor find a touch of Pernod delicious in this sauce. You may reduce the butter and/or oil by half and make it even lower in fat than it already is.

1 tablespoon butter
1 tablespoon light olive oil
1 large clove garlic, minced
¼ cup minced shallots
2 cups chopped tomato pulp, fresh or canned
1 tablespoon tomato paste
1 cup Fish Stock (see recipe)

*A cheesecloth sachet containing 1 small bay leaf, ¹/₂ teaspoon dried leaf
thyme, and a few parsley stems*
Coarse salt and freshly ground pepper to taste
Pernod to taste

Warm the butter and oil in a wide saucepan or skillet, and add the
garlic and shallots. Heat gently, just until vegetables are fragrant. Add
the remaining ingredients except for the Pernod. Cover and simmer
gently for 20 minutes. Remove and discard the sachet. Purée the
mixture in a food processor, blender, or food mill. Wipe out the pan
and return the puréed sauce to it. If sauce seems *very* thin, reduce it
over moderate heat. Add Pernod to taste, starting with 1 or 2 teaspoons. Correct seasoning. Serve hot.

RED SAUCE WITH BASIL

About 2 quarts

Here is the simplest all-purpose tomato sauce, the kind you
could enjoy nearly every day and never tire of. It is ideal for
pasta, alone or with fish or shellfish added, as in Pasta with
Tuna and Tomato Sauce (see recipe). It is also tasty spooned
over freshly cooked fish of any sort. It keeps for up to a week
in the refrigerator and may be frozen for six months or better.
Fresh mint is another fine herb choice.

¹/₂ cup light olive oil
3 cups chopped onions
1 rounded tablespoon minced garlic
*Two 35-ounce cans imported plum tomatoes with their liquid, crushed
by hand or whirled in a food processor until coarsely chopped*
Coarse salt and freshly ground black pepper to taste
Pinches of sugar, depending on the acidity of the tomatoes
¹/₃ cup chopped fresh basil leaves

Heat the oil in a large skillet and add the onions, tossing to coat with
oil. Cook over high heat, stirring often, until onions are wilted. Reduce heat to low and cook, stirring occasionally, until onions are very
tender and slightly golden. Stir in garlic and cook briefly, just until

fragrant. Add tomatoes, salt and pepper, and a little sugar (transfer to a pot if skillet is not deep enough to hold everything). Bring to a simmer, lower heat, and cook gently for about 30 minutes, adding the basil for the last 5 minutes. If it seems to be getting too thick, partially cover. Correct seasoning. Serve hot.

PANFRIED ONION TOPPING FOR FISH

1 serving

A relish rather than a sauce, this is a very tasty, homey way to finish plain-cooked fillets or steaks. It is based on a red snapper dish by Chef Hermann Rainer sampled at the dizzying heights of Windows on the World in the World Trade Center. Instead of being cooked *very* slowly to a dense, sweet marmalade—in approved nouvelle cuisine fashion—the onions are cooked a bit faster until nicely caramelized with a hint of fried-onion flavor. If the fish is properly seasoned, the onions do not need any salt or pepper. Spinach or other greens make ideal accompaniments because the onions also go very well with them. You may prepare any quantity you wish if you have skillet(s) large enough. It keeps well.

1 medium to medium-large onion, peeled and thinly sliced
¼ cup light olive oil

Heat the oil in a skillet over high heat and add the onion. (If you are preparing a large quantity, add onions a large handful at a time, letting them cook down a little between additions, so that there is never a layer thick enough to cause the onions to steam rather than fry.) When the onion is wilted, reduce heat to low, and continue cooking, stirring occasionally, until onion is a rich brown color. Drain and serve over freshly cooked fish. If prepared in advance, undercook slightly, then finish cooking and drain at serving time.

TWO COCKTAIL SAUCES FOR OYSTERS ON THE HALF SHELL

Oyster snobs and even some really nice people eschew thick red cocktail sauces in favor of a spritz of lemon juice and a grinding of black pepper, or a sophisticated sauce that complements the briny bivalves without overpowering them. The two sauces below are ideal offerings for occasions when you wish something a little more elegant than just lemon and pepper. The former is a traditional French sauce named for the cracked pepper that is an important ingredient. The latter is from New Jersey–based chef Jack Freedman. They are also tasty served with clams on the half shell.

SAUCE MIGNONETTE

4 to 8 servings

> *¼ cup minced shallots*
> *⅓ cup red wine vinegar*
> *1 teaspoon black peppercorns, coarsely cracked*
> *Large pinch coarse salt*

Combine ingredients and serve.

RICE VINEGAR DIP

4 to 8 servings

> *½ cup rice vinegar*
> *2 tablespoons sugar*
> *1 teaspoon soy sauce*
> *¼ cup minced or finely grated peeled and seeded cucumber*
> *Coarse salt and white pepper to taste*
> *Wasabi (Japanese green horseradish)*
> *Sliced pickled ginger*
> *Cucumber cups or slices*

Combine rice vinegar, sugar, and soy sauce, and mix until sugar dissolves. Add grated cucumber and salt and pepper. Chill mixture. Mix wasabi with cold water to make a paste; cover and let sit for 15 minutes. Serve sauce in tiny ramekins. Garnish plates with pickled ginger and cucumber cups with a dab of wasabi paste in them.

SKARPSÅS

About 2½ cups

Any English-speaking person who has perused a Swedish cook-book will attest to the startling number of cognates that pepper the culinary language. "Sharp sauce" is the idea here, and it is apt. This recipe is from a charming young Swede named Mikael Möller who is with the well-known downtown catering firm Charlotte's. We met at a seafood conference where he was representing a company in Westhampton Beach, Long Island, called New Generation Smokery, which produces a remark-able line of high-quality cured foods. That is why he thought of this sauce, which is traditionally served with hot-smoked salmon. It will also do nicely with other smoked fish (not cold-smoked salmon) or cold poached salmon or trout. When served with fresh fish rather than smoked, the sauce needs a little salt and a bit more mustard.

½ cup distilled white vinegar
½ cup sugar
½ cup water
5 egg yolks
1 cup heavy cream, very cold
1 tablespoon coarse-grain mustard, or to taste
¼ cup minced chives or scallion greens

Combine vinegar, sugar, and water in a heavy nonreactive saucepan, and bring to a boil, swirling to dissolve the sugar. Simmer for a few minutes and put aside. Whisk the egg yolks in a bowl until they begin to lighten. Carefully whisk in a little of the hot syrup to temper the yolks, then carefully whisk the yolk mixture into the saucepan. Whisk-ing or stirring constantly, over low heat or in a double boiler, cook the mixture until it forms a light custard. Once frothy bubbles subside and a hint of steam develops, it will be close to done. Because of its translucence, the mixture is difficult to judge by the coat-the-spoon test. Mikael suggests that you stick a finger into the mixture and blow on it. When it is done, the custard will hold its shape on your finger. Pour the custard into a medium mixing bowl and cool, stirring vigor-ously for the first minute.

Close to serving time, chill a balloon whisk, mixing bowl, and the cream in the freezer for a few minutes, if possible. Fold the mustard into the cooled custard. Beat the cream just until it holds soft peaks. Do *not* beat until stiff. Gently whisk about one-fourth of the cream into the custard to lighten it, then fold in the rest. Fold in the chives, and serve. The custard stabilizes the cream well, so leftovers may be refrigerated and served again within 1 or 2 days with only a slight loss of lightness.

COMPOUND BUTTERS

About 8 servings each

Flavored butters are simple to prepare—often easier to handle than a sauce—and delightful for flavoring a piece of just-cooked fish that has been broiled, grilled, poached, steamed, or otherwise prepared with no more seasoning than a little salt and pepper. They may also be whisked into a sauce to enrich it or added to a baked fish just before it is done. All the variations below are for eight ounces (2 sticks) fine unsalted butter. Proportions for the flavorings should be adjusted according to their piquancy and your taste. Bring the plain butter to a cool room temperature, knead in the flavoring(s), roll the mixture in wax paper or parchment into a log of desired diameter, and chill. At serving time, slice *medaillons* of butter, place on the hot fish, and serve immediately. That's it.

HERB BUTTER

2 tablespoons finely chopped fresh herbs, 1 variety or combinations

MAÎTRE D'HÔTEL BUTTER

2 heaping tablespoons chopped parsley
1 tablespoon lemon juice
Pinches coarse salt and freshly ground pepper

SNAIL BUTTER

This is named for its affinity with snails, as in *Escargots à la Bourguignonne.*

2 large cloves garlic, minced
1/4 cup minced shallots
2 tablespoons chopped parsley
1 tablespoon Pernod (optional)
1/2 teaspoon coarse salt
Large pinch freshly ground pepper

ANCHOVY BUTTER

One or two 2-ounce tins flat anchovy fillets, drained and mashed to a paste

MUSTARD BUTTER

2 tablespoons Dijon or coarse-grain mustard

CITRUS BUTTER

2 teaspoons grated zest of lemon, lime, orange, or grapefruit
1 to 2 teaspoons lemon, lime, orange, or grapefruit juice

FIVE-SPICE (OR STAR ANISE) BUTTER

2 teaspoons ground five-spice powder or star anise

GINGER BUTTER

2 tablespoons grated fresh gingerroot with juice

SAFFRON BUTTER

1/2 cup dry white wine
3 tablespoons minced shallots
2 large pinches thread saffron, crumbled

Combine ingredients in a small nonreactive saucepan and reduce to 1 tablespoon liquid. Strain, discarding solids. Cool the reduction, then knead it into the butter.

MAYONNAISE

Generous 1 ½ cups

One of the most versatile and most-loved cold sauces requires only the few good ingredients below. Add one egg white if you prepare it in a food processor, blender, or mixer. The white stuff in jars cannot be considered a true mayonnaise, containing as it does a good bit of water and sugar and a very bland oil, usually soy. But it has its uses as a sandwich spread and even in cooking a few nostalgia foods such as Deviled Crab (see recipe). In emergencies it can be perked up with the addition of a few tablespoons of extra-virgin olive oil. Occasionally the blandness of vegetable oil is exactly what you want—as in Tartar Sauce with Chile and Coriander—but olive oil is usually the first choice. Whipped *crème fraîche* or whipped heavy cream may be substituted for mayonnaise in flavored sauces, making them a little more delicate.

2 egg yolks
1 egg white (optional)
2 teaspoons Dijon mustard
¼ teaspoon coarse salt
¼ teaspoon white pepper
1 ½ cups light olive oil, or a blend of extra-virgin olive and bland
    vegetable oil
1 teaspoon lemon juice, or to taste
A little hot water

Combine yolks, egg white (if needed), mustard, salt, and pepper, and whisk (or process) until mixture begins to lighten in color. Whisk (or process) in the oil slowly, by drops in the beginning, adding lemon juice once the emulsion begins to thicken. When all the oil has been added, correct seasoning, and thin with a little hot water to desired texture.

GREEN MAYONNAISE

To above recipe for Mayonnaise, add ½ cup finely chopped fresh herbs of choice: parsley, tarragon, chervil, chives, watercress, or shallots. You might want to use parsley and dill or basil and garlic.

SOUTHWESTERN TARTAR SAUCE

To above recipe for Mayonnaise, made with lime juice instead of lemon, add ¼ teaspoon cayenne, 2 teaspoons chili powder, 1 tablespoon minced hot green chile, ¼ cup chopped fresh coriander, ½ teaspoon grated lime zest, and 1 small clove garlic, mashed to a paste with a little salt.

TARTAR SAUCE WITH CHILE AND CORIANDER

To above recipe for Mayonnaise, made with bland vegetable oil (or use bottled mayonnaise), add chopped fresh coriander leaves, minced hot green chile, lime juice, mashed garlic, Asian fish sauce, and sugar to taste.

SAFFRON MAYONNAISE

To above recipe for Mayonnaise, add the wine-shallot-saffron liquid reduction for Saffron Butter (see recipe) to taste.

YOGURT SAUCES

For low-fat purposes, yogurt, preferably homemade, may be used in place of mayonnaise in the preceding recipes. The results will be different but interesting if the mixture is seasoned well. The most successful yogurt sauce for cold fish is a Lime-Chive Yogurt Sauce made with 1 pint plain yogurt, lime juice to taste (about 3 tablespoons), 1 bunch chives, snipped, and coarse salt, freshly ground white pepper, and pinches of sugar to taste.

VINAIGRETTE

Vinaigrettes are not just for salads. Particularly in recent years they have begun to turn up as sauces for all manner of hot and cold seafood. And the sauce itself may also be either hot or cold. The classic proportions of three to four parts oil to one part vinegar—depending on the acidity of the vinegar—still pertain, though the oil is often decreased or replaced in part by reduced stock or egg white. Mustard, garlic, shallots, fresh herbs, and even truffles are welcome additions. With all the oils and vinegars on the market, cooks have a broad range of flavor choices, all the way from the Mediterranean classic of extra-virgin olive oil and red wine vinegar to an Asian sauce made with peanut oil and rice vinegar, flavored with dark sesame oil and soy sauce. One of the tastiest variations was made famous in the late 1970s by Jean and Pierre Troisgros: It is a small amount of olive oil and wine vinegar vinaigrette flavored with tarragon, parsley, and a touch of tomato paste, whisked into a purée of peeled, seeded, and juiced perfectly ripe summer tomatoes. Whatever the flavors, vinaigrettes require the finest ingredients and are generally best when they are freshly made. You may combine everything but the oil in a bowl and gradually whisk in the oil to form a light emulsion, or you may combine all ingredients in a jar, seal, and shake until combined.

APPLE HORSERADISH SAUCE FOR SMOKED FISH

About ³/₄ cup

This is an easy sauce for hot-smoked fish of almost any sort, including sturgeon, whitefish, shark, bluefish, and jack.

¹/₂ cup sour cream
¹/₃ cup finely grated peeled and cored apple
3 tablespoons finely grated horseradish, preferably fresh
Coarse salt to taste

Combine ingredients and chill. Correct seasoning. Serve cool.

SOUTHEAST ASIAN SAUCE WITH COCONUT CREAM

About ³/₄ cup

To add a tropical Asian touch to grilled fish—fillets, steaks, or whole fish—prepare this variation of Southeast Asian Dipping Sauce that includes coconut cream.

1 large trimmed and seeded hot green chile (jalapeño or serrano)
2 large cloves garlic, peeled
¹/₈ teaspoon ground fennel seed or aniseed
3 tablespoons Asian fish sauce
3 tablespoons lime or lemon juice
3 tablespoons water
¹/₂ cup canned coconut cream, stirred well to homogenize it

Chop chile and garlic coarsely, and put them into the bowl of a food processor. Add remaining ingredients and process until mixture is fairly smooth, scraping down the sides of the bowl from time to time. You may strain sauce if you wish. Serve at room temperature.

TARATOOR

MIDDLE EASTERN TAHINI SAUCE

About 1 ¹/₂ cups

Though a flavor combination of this sort is served with nearly all manner of foodstuffs in Middle Eastern kitchens (both native and transplanted), it is particularly tasty with fish that is simply baked, broiled, or grilled. You might serve this sauce with hot, freshly cooked fish, but it seems even better if the fish is prepared in advance and allowed to come to room temperature. The sesame butter called *tahini* is becoming widely available beyond markets that cater to Middle Eastern tastes—all health-food stores stock it, for instance.

1 clove garlic, peeled
¹/₄ teaspoon coarse salt, or to taste
²/₃ cup tahini

About ¹/₄ cup lemon juice
Water, as needed
Heaping ¹/₄ cup chopped parsley

Mash the garlic and salt to a paste with a mortar and pestle or in a bowl
with a fork. Do not use a processor for this one. Mix in the tahini and
add the lemon juice. The addition of liquid causes tahini to stiffen, so
you will now have to work in a little water at a time until the mixture
relaxes into a sauce similar to a light mayonnaise. Stir in the parsley,
and correct seasoning. Serve at room temperature.

SOUPS AND STEWS

See p. 78 for ways to determine proper cooking time.

Be they delicate starters or hearty main courses, savory soups and stews are as soul-warming as any foods in the world. Though they might seem best suited to cold weather, even in climates that are not touched by anything that the rest of us would call winter there are strong traditions for satisfying heat-it-up-and-ladle-it-forth dishes. Some of these tropical and near-tropical favorites are surprisingly rich, in which case they sport a spiciness that stimulates perspiration (if no other bodily excitement), which helps humans survive sweltering conditions. Anyway, wherever and whenever cooks are planning something fluent, available fish and shellfish of every sort are versatile and popular.

A note is in order about one of America's favorite creations, gumbo. The most popular explanation of its origins is an attempt to create a New World *bouillabaisse* using Louisiana ingredients. If so, the evolved dish is quite different, but the roux base does speak of French antecedents. Traditional gumbos are rich soup/stews that might include any available meats and/or seafoods but always (with one exception, a gumbo with lots of greens called Gumbo z'Herbes) start with a brown roux and the aromatic vegetable mixture in Crab and Shrimp Filé Gumbo. The roux is more a flavoring agent than a thickener—the darker the roux, the less thickening power the flour retains—so gumbos have another thickener as well. The word *gumbo* comes from an African name for okra, an African vegetable, so you would expect all gumbos to receive their singular texture from the gooey sap of okra pods. However, the Acadian settlers in the bayou country were introduced by the native Choctaw Indians to powdered dried sassafras leaf, which produces a texture identical to okra even though the two plants have nothing in common botanically. So there are okra gumbos that reflect the Creole tradition of New Orleans proper and the plantation country, and filé gumbos that are more representative of Acadian (Cajun) cooking. Though the two traditions overlap, no purist would think of using both okra and filé. Rice is always served with gumbo but never cooked in it.

BILLI-BI

4 to 6 servings

This is considered by many to be the most elegant soup in the world, with good reason. It is also ridiculously simple to make, assuming that you have the broth from a batch of steamed mussels. It is perfect just as it is, but you may add a few mussels and an herb sprig, if you wish.

1 1/2 cups heavy cream
4 egg yolks
Dash cayenne
4 cups hot, well-flavored mussel broth (p. 353)

THE GARNISHES

A handful of steamed, shucked mussels (optional)
Tiny sprigs of fresh chervil or curly parsley (optional)

Whisk cream, egg yolks, and cayenne together in a heavy nonreactive saucepan and carefully whisk in the hot broth. Heat gently, stirring constantly, until hot and steamy, but do not let it get near a simmer or the yolks will curdle. Correct seasoning, and serve immediately, plain or with optional garnishes.

SOPA AL CUARTO DE HORA

QUARTER-HOUR SOUP

About 6 servings

In various parts of Spain one can find on restaurant menus a seafood soup that is made from available ingredients, the constants being shellfish, aromatic vegetables and tomatoes, raw ham, rice, hard-cooked egg, and pieces of whatever white-fleshed fish happens to be around, often hake. The name comes from the fifteen minutes of finishing time required to cook the rice and fish. The following recipe is relatively authentic, considering that no two cooks make it the same way or necessarily

the same way twice. It is included not because it is famous here
or made well or often by any particular local restaurant or
cook, but because it should be all of the above.

*½ to ¾ pound fillet of white-fleshed fish: cod, hake, ling, monkfish,
blackfish, ocean pout, wolffish*
*6 cups liquid: 1 cup dry white wine or 1 tablespoon lemon juice;
strained juice from canned tomatoes; 1 cup or more Fish Stock (see
recipe) or bottled clam juice; and water to make up the balance*
*12 littleneck clams, scrubbed and soaked in 2 or 3 changes of cold,
salted water*
*½ pound medium shrimp, peeled and cut into 3 to 4 pieces, shells
reserved*
¼ cup olive oil
1 medium onion, peeled and finely chopped
*2 to 3 ounces finely chopped ham, preferably raw-cured (prosciutto is
the best substitute for serrano ham)*
1 large clove garlic, peeled and minced
1 cup imported canned tomatoes, crushed by hand
Coarse salt and freshly ground black pepper to taste
Large pinch dried thyme
Large pinch cayenne
½ teaspoon sweet paprika
*2 tablespoons long-grain white rice, soaked in cold water 30 minutes
and drained*
1 hard-cooked egg, peeled and chopped
1 tablespoon chopped parsley

Trim any skin from fillets and cut them into ¾-inch cubes. Reserve
trimmings. In a large saucepan, bring the 6 cups of liquid to a boil and
add the clams. Cover and simmer until clams open, 5 minutes or so.
Remove clams with a slotted spoon and reserve. You may shell the
clams and chop the meat, or you may reserve the clams whole or on
the half shell. Add to the pot the shrimp shells and any bones or
trimmings from the fish. Cover and simmer gently for up to 20 minutes while you prepare the remaining ingredients.

In a large, heavy saucepan, heat the olive oil and add the onion
and ham. Cook gently until the onion is tender. Add garlic and cook
briefly. Add the tomatoes and strain in the broth, being careful to
avoid any sand from the clams at the bottom of the pot. Add the

seasonings and bring to a boil. Reduce heat and simmer, covered, for about 15 minutes. Correct seasoning. May be prepared in advance up to this point.

About 15 minutes before serving time, bring soup base to a boil and add rice. Cover and simmer 10 minutes, then add fish. Simmer 4 minutes more, and add shrimp. Simmer 1 minute more, then stir in egg, parsley, and chopped or whole clams. Serve hot.

FISH DUMPLING SOUP

6 to 8 servings

On the assumption that everyone who is interested in making gefilte fish already has a trusted recipe, here instead is a variation that produces a warming soup for cold weather. It is inspired by Eastern European liver dumpling soup. You may use whitefish, pike, walleye, carp, or buffalo, or a combination. Save the bones from the fish you choose and get some extra from the fish market.

THE BROTH

3 pounds fish bones, heads, and skin from any mild, white fish, gills removed, all blood rinsed away
Coarse salt, as needed
4 quarts cold water
3 medium onions, chunked
3 carrots, sliced
2 ribs celery, sliced
1 large clove garlic, unpeeled and bruised
4 or 5 parsley stems
1 small bay leaf
2 tablespoons white vinegar: wine or distilled
1 teaspoon sugar
2 whole cloves
10 black peppercorns

THE DUMPLINGS

> *1 pound skinless fillet of freshwater fish*
> *1 medium onion, peeled and chopped*
> *1 egg*
> *1 tablespoon matzo meal or cracker crumbs*
> *1 teaspoon coarse salt*
> *¹/₃ teaspoon freshly ground white pepper*
> *3 tablespoons chopped parsley*
> *Chilled plain seltzer or club soda, as needed*

First sprinkle the bones, heads, and skin—including the trimmings from the fillet for the dumplings—generously with coarse salt and refrigerate for at least 30 minutes, up to 2 hours. Rinse with cold running water to remove the salt and place in a large nonreactive pot. Add remaining broth ingredients and bring to a boil. Lower heat and simmer gently for 30 to 40 minutes, no longer. Skim well in the beginning to keep the broth clear. Strain broth through a clean towel, paper towel, or a coffee filter. Correct seasoning. Reserve.

Slice fillet rather thinly with a sharp knife to break up the connective tissue, and place it in the bowl of a food processor. Process just until mixture is almost smooth, scraping down the bowl often. Add the chopped onion, egg, matzo meal or cracker crumbs, salt, pepper, and 2 tablespoons of the parsley. Pulse a few times just until nearly blended. Scrape mixture out onto a board and begin to chop it with a large, heavy knife, using the knife to scrape the mixture back into a mound when your chopping has flattened it. Continue chopping for 5 minutes or more, until mixture is well blended. The hand chopping produces a lighter result than processing alone. If possible, chill mixture for at least 30 minutes.

Bring the reserved broth to a simmer in a nonreactive pot. With the fingers, work some seltzer into the chilled dumpling mixture to lighten it. Work quickly and lightly, incorporating up to ½ cup seltzer. Mixture should be just barely firm enough to hold its shape. Using 2 teaspoons or a small meat-baller tongs dipped in cold water, form lumps of mixture and poach them in the hot broth; 10 to 15 minutes of poaching time is sufficient. Serve hot with a large pinch of the remaining parsley added to each portion. Leftovers are delicious reheated, or the dumplings can be served as cold nibbles.

RED SNAPPER IN HERBED TOMATO BROTH WITH JULIENNE OF VEGETABLES

6 servings

This dish is very light and fresh-tasting. Of course you may use any lean, white fish you happen to find. Steamed mussels or tiny clams would make a tasty addition; use the broth in place of part of the stock and add the shellfish at the last moment to warm through. The dish is also successful without the julienned vegetables. You might wish to serve this with a little rice or orzo cooked in stock and added to the bottom of the soup tureen or plates before the soup is ladled in.

¼ cup minced shallots, or ½ cup minced onion
2 large cloves garlic, finely minced
1 teaspoon butter
1 teaspoon light olive oil
2 large or 3 medium very ripe summer tomatoes, peeled, seeded, juiced,
    and finely chopped, or 2 cups chopped pulp of imported canned
    tomatoes
1 cup dry white wine
3 cups Fish Stock (see recipe) or water
1 or 2 anchovy fillets, finely chopped (optional)
Pinch sugar
1½ teaspoons coarse salt, or to taste
½ teaspoon freshly ground white pepper
¼ cup finely chopped parsley, or a combination of parsley and fresh
    basil
1 cup fine julienne of carrots
1 cup fine julienne of celery
1 cup fine julienne of leeks
1 pound skinless fillet of red snapper or other lean, white fish, cut into
    ¾-inch cubes

In a heavy kettle, combine the shallots, garlic, butter, and oil, and heat gently, stirring often, until vegetables are fragrant and softened. Do not brown or scorch. Add tomatoes, wine, stock or water, anchovy fillet(s), seasonings, and half of the chopped herb(s). Reserve remaining herb(s). Bring mixture to a boil, lower heat, and simmer, covered, for 15 to 20 minutes. Remove from heat.

Just before serving time, reheat soup and add carrots. Simmer gently for 5 minutes. Add celery, leeks, and fish, and heat gently, below the simmer, until fish is just heated through, about 5 minutes. Correct seasoning. Serve hot, sprinkled with remaining herb(s).

CRAB AND SHRIMP FILÉ GUMBO

6 to 8 servings

This is quite simply the best gumbo there is, in the opinion of everyone who has tried it. And students have often reported their success with this recipe at home. Cleaning the crabs is really very easy and fun, too, when you get the hang of it. Please read about gumbos, p. 286. Charming old Creole recipes say, "First you make your roux." Unless you are making a quantity of roux for several uses, it is best to get the vegetables and, in this case, the seafood ready first, so that when the roux is the perfect color you can dump in the vegetables—thus lowering the temperature so the roux cannot burn—and cook them right in the roux. The vegetables need not be measured with care and you may be generous with everything but celery. The seasonings, however, should be balanced exactly as written, except for salt and cayenne to taste. This gumbo is unusual in that it contains no tomatoes and seems just right without them; you could add some if you felt the need. The luxury crabmeat and oyster addition at the end is not at all necessary, but it is fun for special occasions. Like other gumbos, this is best the day after it is made. Some people like to pick up the gumbo crabs and chew on them, while others do not. Suit yourself. Gumbo filé powder (ground dried sassafras leaves) is available in specialty shops.

THE SHELLFISH

2 quarts water
6 live blue crabs, preferably female (p. 64), rinsed well
1 pound small to medium shrimp

THE VEGETABLES

>*2 cups chopped onions*
>*1 cup diced green peppers*
>*1/2 cup chopped celery*
>*3/4 cup thinly sliced scallions*
>*1 tablespoon minced garlic*
>*2 tablespoons chopped parsley*

THE ROUX

>*1/2 cup flour*
>*1/2 cup corn oil*

THE FLAVORINGS

>*3/4 pound smoked garlic sausage (*andouille, kielbasa*), coarsely chopped*
>*A cheesecloth sachet containing 2 bay leaves, 1 teaspoon dried leaf thyme, 4 whole cloves, and 5 whole allspice berries*
>*2 teaspoons coarse salt*
>*3/4 teaspoon ground black pepper*
>*3/4 teaspoon ground white pepper*
>*1/2 teaspoon cayenne, or to taste*
>*1/2 teaspoon Tabasco*
>*1/4 teaspoon ground mace*
>*1 tablespoon lemon juice*

SHELLFISH FOR EXTRAVAGANT OCCASIONS (OPTIONAL)

>*1/2 pound lump crabmeat*
>*12 oysters, shucked and drained*

>*2 tablespoons gumbo filé powder*
>*4 to 6 cups hot cooked Plain White Rice (Basic Western or Boiled) (see recipes)*

Bring the water to a boil in a pot large enough to hold the crabs and add them. Cover and cook 2 to 3 minutes. Remove the crabs with a skimmer or tongs, reserving the liquid, and put them aside until cool

enough to handle. Meanwhile, peel and devein the shrimp, and reserve shells. Refrigerate the shrimp. Add the shells to the liquid and
keep it hot. Clean each crab (p. 64). Pull off the large claws and put
them into the bowl. Break the crab bodies in half and put them into
the bowl. You now have the hot liquid with the shrimp and crab shells
for flavor; the crab claws, broken bodies, and innards reserved together; and the refrigerated raw shrimp. The only discards are the
crab stomach sacs, gills, and mouth parts. Cover the pot and let it
simmer about 20 minutes while you proceed.

Combine the vegetables in a bowl and set aside.

To make the roux: Choose a 6-quart or larger pot with a heavy
bottom. Using the longest whisk you have, combine the flour and oil
in the pot, and begin whisking evenly and steadily—not rapidly—over
high heat. Be very careful to avoid splashes. When the flour begins
to color, reduce the heat and continue whisking evenly until roux is
dark brown, the color of bittersweet chocolate, lowering the heat even
more to avoid burning. Immediately dump in the vegetables and stir
vigorously with a wooden spoon. Cook over moderate heat, stirring
occasionally, until vegetables are tender, about 10 minutes. Strain in
the broth, avoiding the last bit that might have sand in it. Discard
solids. Add the flavorings and the reserved crabs. Bring to a boil,
reduce heat, and simmer gently, partially covered, stirring occasionally, for about 1 hour. Taste for hotness early on and add cayenne to
taste. It may not be added at the end. Add a little water if the gumbo
seems too thick. Texture should be that of a fairly thin stew. Correct
seasoning and remove and discard sachet.

Remove from heat and stir in the reserved shrimp and the
optional luxury shellfish. Sprinkle on the filé powder gradually and stir
it in. Cover and let rest for at least 5 minutes. At serving time, reheat
mixture thoroughly but do not let it boil. Filé powder must lose its
raw taste but boiling can make it stringy. Serve hot in large soup plates
over a portion of rice.

COUNTRY FRENCH FISH SOUP

6 to 8 servings

Of all the wonderful seafood soup/stews in the world, *bouillabaisse* and *bourride* are probably the most famous, both tradi-

tional creations of the French Mediterranean coast. No two cooks are in complete agreement on the precise ingredients for either dish, and it is of course difficult in the United States to obtain the native fish—rouget, rascasse, grondin, conger eel, et cetera—that give them their special character. The advantage of being thousands of miles away from the Mediterranean is that we can create a tasty dish using the available catch and escape the controversy. One hopes. With its creamy texture and *sauce aïoli,* this one is rather like a *bourride.* Choose four to six kinds of fish, if possible, using lean-fleshed saltwater fish such as monkfish, searobin, cod, pollock, hake, whiting, porgy, halibut, tilefish, grouper, ocean perch, red snapper, black sea bass, and seatrout.

3 to 6 pounds fish, the larger amount for whole fish
2 to 3 pounds fish bones or whole whiting, cleaned
1/2 cup olive oil
1 1/2 cups chopped onions
Chopped white of 1 large leek
2 tablespoons minced garlic
2 cups chopped tomatoes
2 cups dry white wine
6 cups water or Fish Stock (see recipe)
3 tablespoons chopped parsley
1 large bay leaf
1/2 teaspoon dried leaf thyme
3 tablespoons chopped fennel leaves, or 1/4 teaspoon fennel seed
1 vial (.2 gram) thread saffron, crumbled
2-inch piece orange zest, chopped
Pernod or Ricard to taste
Coarse salt and freshly ground black pepper to taste
Sauce Aïoli *(recipe follows)*
3 egg yolks
Thick slices of toasted French or Italian bread
Chopped parsley or fennel leaves for garnish

Clean fish and fish bones to remove guts, gills, scales, and all blood. Fillet whole fish and cut all fillets into serving pieces that are as uniform as possible. Keep the varieties of fish separate so that you can add them in order of size and firmness. Add heads, tails, and bones to the extra bones or whiting. Refrigerate the fillets.

Heat the olive oil in a fairly large nonreactive pot. Add onions and leek, and cook gently until tender and slightly golden. Do not brown. Add garlic and cook briefly. Add tomatoes, wine, water or fish stock, herbs, saffron, orange zest, 1 tablespoon Pernod, and the reserved bones. Bring to a boil, lower heat, and simmer gently, uncovered, for about 1 hour. Strain, pressing on the solids to extract as much juice as possible, then discard solids. Wipe out pot and return strained soup to it. Season fairly well with salt, pepper, and Pernod, knowing that the richness of the liaison will mitigate the flavors somewhat.

Just before serving time, reheat soup just to the simmer, and begin adding the pieces of fish in order of size and firmness, starting with larger and firmer pieces and ending with the delicate flesh. Poach gently just until heated through, keeping in mind that these pieces will require only about 6 or 7 minutes per inch of thickness. Remove fish with a slotted spoon or skimmer to a serving platter as it is done, and keep it warm. Whisk together ½ cup *aïoli* and the egg yolks. Temper with hot soup and then whisk into the soup. Heat gently for a few minutes, stirring constantly, until slightly thickened. Do not overheat or yolks might curdle. Adjust seasoning, and serve immediately in soup plates with a piece of toast with a dab of *aïoli* in each one and more *aïoli* on the side. Garnish fish with chopped parsley or fennel and present it, too. Diners may add fish to the soup or eat it separately from plates.

SAUCE AÏOLI

> *1 large head very fresh garlic, or to taste (at least 8 large cloves), peeled*
> *¾ cup trimmed and cubed bread, moistened with 3 tablespoons of the soup broth, or 1 medium potato, peeled and cooked in the broth*
> *2 egg yolks*
> *1 teaspoon white wine vinegar*
> *Coarse salt and freshly ground white pepper to taste*
> *1½ cups fruity, golden olive oil*

Using a mortar and pestle or a food processor, grind garlic, bread or potato, yolks, vinegar, and salt and pepper to a paste, then add oil slowly, as for mayonnaise.

BOUILLABAISSE LE CIRQUE

About 6 servings

Le Cirque owner Sirio Maccioni supplied this elegant *bouillabaisse* recipe, which dates back to the reign of Alain Sailhac. Note that this version is of the *à la parisienne* stamp, featuring a variety of shellfish. Lobster is the only one that any plurality of Marseillaises will admit, and it is the first to go for economy reasons. Clams and mussels make very tasty additions. Use shellfish or not, as you wish, adding more fish if you subtract shellfish. The unusual assembly technique, which includes a twenty-four-hour marination period, produces superior results, but a highly acceptable dish can be achieved with only a few hours of marinating. You will want to use at least three different kinds of white-fleshed saltwater fish. Le Cirque used striped bass, black sea bass, red snapper, monkfish, and flounder. Other choices include cod, seatrout, tilefish, halibut, grouper, porgy, hake, whiting, and searobin. Buy more than twice as much whole fish as the amount of fillet you will need, and save heads and bones. Some purists claim the bread must never be toasted, but most people do toast it.

THE MARINADE

> *2 large cloves garlic, peeled and minced*
> *¼ cup chopped parsley*
> *¼ teaspoon powdered saffron, or an equivalent amount of crumbled thread saffron (about two-thirds of a .2-gram vial)*
> *2 tablespoons olive oil*
> *½ teaspoon ground aniseed (optional)*
> *1 cup stewed tomatoes, fresh or canned, chopped*
> *Coarse salt and freshly ground black pepper to taste*

THE FISH

> *2½ pounds skinless fillet of white-fleshed saltwater fish, cut into serving pieces, bones reserved*
> *About 3 pounds of additional bones*

THE SHELLFISH

> 6 large shrimp
> 6 littleneck clams
> 18 mussels
> Two 1- to 1½-pound lobsters, preferably female (optional)

THE STOCK

> About ⅓ cup olive oil
> 3 medium onions, peeled and coarsely chopped
> 3 leeks, white only, cleaned and chopped
> 1 rib celery, sliced
> 1 cup dry white wine
> 3 quarts water
> 1 tablespoon whole fennel seed
> ½ teaspoon powdered saffron, or an equivalent amount of crumbled
>   thread saffron (about 1½ .2-gram vials)
> 2 bay leaves
> 1 teaspoon dried leaf thyme
> 2 large strips orange zest
> 4 parsley stems
> 1 head garlic, cloves separated and bruised, unpeeled
> 3 cups chopped tomatoes, fresh or canned
> 3 tablespoons tomato paste
> Coarse salt and freshly ground black pepper to taste
>
> 2 tablespoons chopped parsley
> Pernod or Ricard to taste
> 12 thick chunks French or Italian bread, toasted or not as you wish
> Sauce Rouille (recipe follows)

Combine the marinade ingredients in a nonreactive bowl and add the fish fillets. Cover, refrigerate, and let marinate for 24 hours, if possible, turning fish pieces a few times. Remove the gills from fish heads and rinse all bones well to flush out all blood. Soak bones in cold water overnight (for a clear broth). If you lack the refrigerator space for a large bowl of bones and water, then salt the bones lightly and refrigerate, then later rinse them and soak them in cold water for 1 or more hours.

Shell and devein the shrimp. Add shrimp to the marinating fish. Reserve shells. Scrub clams and mussels well and soak them in several changes of salted cold water. Debeard mussels and test to see that each is alive, p. 62. Refrigerate clams and mussels. Turn lobsters on their backs and pierce the head with a large sharp knife. Then cut lobsters in half lengthwise. Pull off tail halves, devein them, and slice them in half crosswise. Pull off large claws and crack them with the blunt side of your heavy knife. Remove and discard the stomach sacs behind the head. Remove the tomalley (green glands, or liver) and the dark green roe, if any, and mash to a paste in a small bowl with the back of a spoon. Add this to the marinating fish, along with the lobster tail pieces and cracked claws. Reserve the lobster body shells with the shrimp shells.

In a large kettle, heat the ⅓ cup olive oil and add the onions, leeks, and celery. Cook gently, without browning, until vegetables are tender, about 15 minutes, adding a little more oil if mixture seems dry. Add the remaining stock ingredients, plus the fish bones and shrimp and lobster shells, and bring to a boil. Reduce heat and simmer mixture gently, uncovered, for 45 minutes. Strain, pressing on the solids to extract as much flavor as possible. Discard solids. Correct seasoning. This may be accomplished well in advance, but if the stock is going to sit around for more than 2 hours or so, it should be cooled, covered, and refrigerated.

Just before serving time, bring the stock to a boil in a suitable pot that is attractive enough to come to the table: enameled cast iron is often the best choice. Add the marinated fish and shellfish and the clams and mussels. Cover and bring to a boil over high heat. Boil for 3 minutes, then turn off the heat and let rest for about 5 minutes. Uncover and stir in parsley and Pernod to taste, being careful not to break up the fish pieces. Serve immediately, offering bread and *rouille.* The *rouille* is stirred into the broth to taste. You might offer a bowl for empty shells. There will be no need for lobster crackers if you have properly cracked the lobster claws in advance.

SAUCE ROUILLE

> *6 large cloves garlic, peeled and trimmed*
> *3/4 cup bread cubes soaked in 3 tablespoons of the soup broth, or 1 medium potato, peeled and cooked in the broth until tender*
> *1 egg yolk*
> *1 hot chile, preferably red, seeded, or 3/4 teaspoon Tabasco, or to taste*
> *1 bottled pimiento, drained*
> *Coarse salt and freshly ground pepper to taste*
> *1 cup fruity olive oil*
> *2 tablespoons hot broth*

Using a mortar and pestle or a food processor, grind the garlic, bread or potato, egg yolk, chile or Tabasco, pimiento, and salt and pepper to a paste. Add the oil slowly, as for mayonnaise. Thin the sauce with hot broth at serving time.

SEAFOOD CORN CHOWDER

6 to 8 servings

Chowder is an English word that is probably based on *chaudière,* a traditional French cooking vessel. The results are not French at all, but all-American and derived in part from cooking techniques developed by the real native New Englanders, American Indians. There is no need to bog down in the old rivalry between creamy New England clam chowder and tomatoey Manhattan clam chowder—each can be delicious so long as the ingredients are fresh and the seasonings well balanced. The chowder below breaks most of the rules by combining a variety of seafood with the usual ingredients for a creamy chowder, plus corn, which is usually reserved for a creamy chowder that has no seafood at all. The mussels are not essential, but they are tasty.

> *12 medium chowder clams (quahogs)*
> *2 pounds mussels*
> *3 cups water*
> *Flour, if desired*
> *1 pound cod or scrod steak or fillet, skin and bones removed, cut into 1/2-inch cubes*

3 ounces salt pork, finely chopped
2 medium onions, finely chopped
1 rib celery, finely chopped
Corn oil, if needed
2 teaspoons flour
2 large russet potatoes, or 3 eastern (Maine), peeled and diced
Coarse salt and freshly ground white pepper to taste
Large pinch thread saffron, crumbled
1/4 teaspoon dried leaf thyme
1 bay leaf
1 cup milk
1 cup heavy cream
1 generous cup fresh corn, cut from the cob, or one 10-ounce package
*   frozen corn, defrosted*

Scrub clams and mussels well and soak them separately in 2 or 3 changes of cold, salted water. Sprinkle on some flour for the final soak, if you wish. Debeard and test mussels (p. 62). Place clams in a heavy saucepan, add the water, cover, and steam until they open, up to 10 minutes, depending on size. Remove clams and shuck them, discarding shells. Chop clams, leaving the soft belly meat rather coarse, but chopping the hard "foot" finely. Add mussels to the saucepan and steam them until they open, 5 minutes or so. Drain, reserving liquid. When cool enough to handle, remove and discard the shells. Reserve mussels with the fish cubes.

In a large heavy saucepan, heat the salt pork gently until the fat is rendered and the bits are crisp. Add the onions and celery. Cook, stirring often, over medium heat until wilted and slightly golden, adding a little corn oil if the mixture is dry. Sprinkle on the flour, mix it in, and cook another minute. Stir in the reserved shellfish liquid (avoid any sand that has settled at the bottom) and chopped clams, cover, and simmer about 15 minutes. Add the potatoes and seasonings. Simmer gently, covered, until potatoes are just tender, about 15 minutes. Remove and discard bay leaf. Add milk, cream, and corn and bring to a simmer. Correct seasoning. Add fish and mussels and heat through; do not boil. Serve hot.

NEW ENGLAND FISH CHOWDER WITH SCALLOPS AND TOMATOES

About 6 servings

This delicious chowder is from New York–based food writer Richard Sax. Though it begins in the style of a classic Yankee chowder, it is even more iconoclastic than the previous one in its use of tomatoes, which add a lovely touch of color and flavor. Notice that it is thickened with a purée of its vegetables instead of flour, for a clean flavor.

6 ounces bacon (7 or 8 slices), cut into 1-inch squares
Vegetable or corn oil, if needed
3 medium-large onions, coarsely chopped
2 ribs celery, thinly sliced
2 pounds Maine (eastern) potatoes, peeled and cut into 1/2-inch dice
3 cups Fish Stock (see recipe)
Cold water, as needed
2 sprigs fresh thyme, or 1/4 teaspoon dried
3 sprigs parsley
1/2 cup heavy cream
2 cups milk, or as needed
Coarse salt and freshly ground black or white pepper to taste
Few drops Tabasco (optional)
2 pounds cod or scrod fillet, skinned and cut into 1-inch cubes
1/2 pound sea scallops, trimmed and cut into 2 or 3 pieces, depending on size
1 1/4 cups drained canned tomatoes, cut into 3/4-inch pieces
6 thin pats of butter
Sweet paprika

Place bacon in a medium-large heavy pot over medium heat. Cook, stirring frequently, adding a little oil if the bacon is sticking, until golden, 8 to 10 minutes. With a slotted spoon, remove bacon pieces to a plate lined with paper towels. Set aside. Pour off and discard all but about 3 tablespoons of bacon fat from the pot. Add the onions and celery to the pot and toss to film them with fat. Cover and cook over medium heat, stirring occasionally, until softened, about 10 minutes. Add the potatoes and stock. Add a little water, if needed, so that the liquid almost covers the vegetables. Bring mixture to a boil. Tie the thyme and parsley in a cheesecloth sachet and tuck it in. Cover, lower the heat, and simmer until potatoes are just tender, 15 to 20 minutes.

With a slotted spoon, transfer half of the vegetables to a food processor or food mill. Purée until smooth, then return the purée to the soup. Add the cream, 2 cups milk, salt to taste, a generous sprinkling of pepper, and a few drops of optional Tabasco. Return the soup to a boil, stirring until smooth. Thin soup with additional milk, if necessary. Remove and discard cheesecloth sachet. (May be prepared in advance to this point.)

Add the fish cubes to the hot soup, cover, and simmer very gently, about 3 minutes. Add the scallops, tomatoes, and reserved bacon, shaking the pan to combine the ingredients without breaking up the fish. Correct seasoning. Cover and simmer 2 minutes, or until the fish and scallops are just opaque and heated through. Serve hot, topping each serving with a pat of butter and a sprinkling of paprika.

MONKFISH STEW WITH FENNEL

6 to 8 servings

This hearty starter or informal main course would be satisfying any time of year, but is particularly good in cold weather. Conveniently, that's fennel season too. Notice that the basic idea here is a creamy New England chowder with an herbal twist. Any white-fleshed fish will do—especially ocean pout and cod—but monkfish is particularly appealing because its firm texture keeps it from flaking into little pieces.

*2 pounds monkfish tail, trimmed of dark flesh, boned, and cut into
    ¹/₂-inch cubes*
1 quart Fish Stock (see recipe)
3 ounces salt pork, finely chopped*
3 tablespoons butter
2 medium onions, finely chopped
1 medium bulb fennel, with leaves if possible
1 pound (2 large) russet or eastern potatoes, peeled and diced
Salt and freshly ground white pepper to taste
Large pinch thread saffron, crumbled (optional)
¹/₄ teaspoon dried leaf thyme
1 bay leaf
Dash cayenne
1 cup milk
1 cup heavy cream
French bread or any good, crusty loaf

* Storing the salt pork in the freezer for 1 or 2 hours will make chopping easier.

First prepare fish so that you will have the bones and trimmings for the stockpot, if you make your own stock. This is the time to start the stock.

In a heavy saucepan, heat the salt pork gently with the butter until pork fat is rendered. Add onions and cook, stirring often, over medium-low heat until onion is wilted. Thinly slice the fennel, then coarsely chop it. Use an inch or so of the stems and reserve the feathery leaves, if there are any. Stir in chopped fennel and continue cooking until all is tender. Add fish stock, potatoes, and seasonings. Simmer gently, covered, until potatoes are just tender, about 15 minutes. Remove and discard bay leaf. Add milk and cream and bring to a simmer. Correct seasoning. Add fish and heat through; do not boil. Serve immediately, garnished with sprigs of fennel leaf. Offer bread on the side.

OYSTER STEW

About 4 servings

Oyster stews of this sort are great cold-weather favorites from Maine to Maryland, if not beyond. In fact, this is one of the very few traditions of oyster cookery in the Northeast, along with fried oysters and pan roasts. It is wonderfully easy to make, and utterly satisfying in its simple way. Do not be tempted to add onion or potato and start turning it into a chowder. Best keep it uncluttered. Oyster crackers are favored by some and shunned by others. Sturdy homebaked-style bread is a fine accompaniment.

2 cups milk
1 cup heavy cream
4 tablespoons butter
24 oysters, shucked and with liquor reserved
Coarse salt and freshly ground white pepper to taste
Dash cayenne
Dash freshly grated nutmeg
Dash medium sherry for each portion
Oyster crackers or good bread

Pour milk and cream into a heavy 2-quart saucepan and put it over low heat to scald. When it begins to reach the shiver, melt butter in a skillet and slide in the oysters along with a little bit of their liquor. Toss skillet over high heat for 1 minute. Add oyster mixture to the milk and cream, along with the salt, pepper, cayenne, and nutmeg. Heat briefly, just until stew is very hot and oysters are plump with curly mantles. Do not boil. Correct seasoning. Serve immediately with a dash of sherry in each portion and crackers or bread on the side.

SQUID STEW

4 to 6 servings

> This is an old family recipe from Diana DiGreggorio, wife of Fulton Fish Market wholesaler Robert DiGreggorio. It is simple to make and just right for a cold-weather supper. A crusty loaf, a salad, and you are all set.

3 tablespoons light olive oil
1 large onion, chopped
2 large cloves garlic, minced
1 teaspoon dried oregano
1 teaspoon dried red pepper flakes
2 cups tomato purée
1/2 cup water
1/2 cup dry white wine
1 1/4 teaspoons coarse salt, or to taste
Large pinch sugar
2 to 2 1/2 pounds (5 medium) russet potatoes, peeled and cut into
* 1-inch cubes*
2 pounds squid, cleaned, tentacles halved if large, bodies cut into rings
* (p. 65)*

In a pot of about 4-quart capacity, heat the oil and sauté onion gently until tender and slightly golden. Do not brown. Add garlic, oregano, and red pepper flakes, and sauté briefly until fragrant. Add tomato purée, water (use the water to rinse out the tomato can if it is empty), wine, salt, and sugar and bring to a simmer. Cover and simmer gently for about 5 minutes.

Stir in potatoes and return the lid. Simmer gently, stirring once or twice, until potatoes are just tender. Add a little water if it seems dry. Correct seasoning. Stir in squid and heat briefly, just until mixture is very hot and threatens to simmer. Serve right away. In the unlikely event that you should have leftovers, be sure to reheat gently to avoid toughening the squid.

SQUID STEWED IN ITS OWN INK

4 to 6 servings

Rich squid stews of a dark sepia hue are important fare in many parts of the Mediterranean. There must be thousands of Italian, Lebanese, or Spanish grandmothers (to name a few) in the Northeast who prepare a similar stew. This one is of the Spanish variety and is from Josefina Howard of Rosa Mexicano. Mrs. Howard makes it for its sauce, which she folds into cooked white rice to add flavor and drama. To that end, she simmers the stew for 2 to 3 hours; when it is to be enjoyed for itself it will have a better texture after only 1 hour of cooking. Ink sacs are often ruptured in the harvesting, so it is not always possible to get the volume of squid ink that you want for a dish of this sort. It is possible to buy prepared squid ink, but it is very expensive and not readily available. Instead you might have a couple of cans of cuttlefish cooked in their ink (*calamares en su tinta*) handy in case you need to add their liquid to your stew. The liquid is salty, so be careful with seasoning.

2 pounds squid, cleaned, sliced, ink sacs reserved (p. 65)
1 cup dry white wine
¼ cup light olive oil
1½ cups chopped onions, preferably white
2 large cloves garlic, peeled
2 cups seeded and juiced chopped tomatoes, fresh or canned
⅛ teaspoon cayenne, or to taste
Water, as needed
Coarse salt to taste
Juice from canned calamares en su tinta *or prepared squid ink, as needed*
4 to 6 cups cooked Plain White Rice (Basic Western or Boiled) or a batch of Polenta (see recipes)

As you clean the squid, reserve the little silvery ink sacs behind the heads in a small bowl and add about ½ cup of wine. Reserve.

Heat the oil in 4-quart or larger pot. Add onions and sauté gently until tender. Add garlic and sauté briefly. Add tomatoes, cayenne, remaining ½ cup wine, about ½ cup water, and reserved squid. Hold off on salt for now. Bring to a simmer, cover, and let simmer very gently.

After about 30 minutes of cooking, stir in the reserved wine-and-ink-sacs mixture, and stir until they have released their ink and colored the stew. If the stew is not a rich brown-black color, add the juice from canned cuttlefish until you are satisfied with the color. Season with salt to taste. Let the stew continue to simmer gently, covered, stirring from time to time and adding water if it seems dry, until squid is done to your liking. This will take as little as 30 minutes more (or cook for a total cooking time of up to 2 hours if you just want the broth; but then the overcooked squid will only be suitable for snacks). Correct seasoning. Serve hot with freshly cooked white rice or polenta. The stew may also be served at room temperature with polenta also at room temperature.

MARISCOS EN SALSA VERDE

SHELLFISH IN GREEN SAUCE, SPANISH-STYLE

4 to 6 servings

Though New York has a shortage of restaurants that prove Spain has a fine, mainstream-European food tradition, even the little neighborhood spots seem to do a creditable job with dishes of this sort. These dishes are excellent for entertaining at home. Some people consider sopping up the sauce with good bread the best part of the dish. You may easily simplify with just one or two kinds of shellfish, adjusting the procedure accordingly; obviously only shrimp and scallops are floured and cooked in oil. Raw mussels and/or clams may be steamed right in the sauce at serving time, but the method below gives more control over the texture and seasonings and is more do-ahead. Shrimp shells will make a tasty broth, but a good fish stock would be needed with scallops alone. The handful of peas is typically Spanish but not essential. This is also delicious (but very un-Spanish) served over pasta.

THE SHELLFISH AND BROTH

> 1 pound medium shrimp, or ½ pound shrimp and ½ pound sea scallops
> 1 cup dry white wine
> 1 cup water
> 1 small bay leaf
> ¼ teaspoon dried leaf thyme
> 1 thick slice lemon
> 1 large onion, chunked
> ½ rib celery, chunked
> 1 ½ pounds mussels, or ¾ pound mussels and 12 littleneck clams, scrubbed and soaked (p. 62)

THE SAUCE

> ¼ cup olive oil
> Coarse salt and freshly ground black pepper to taste
> Flour, as needed
> ½ cup finely chopped onion
> 2 tablespoons minced garlic
> 1 cup chopped parsley
> ½ cup green peas, fresh or frozen (optional)

THE ACCOMPANIMENTS

> Coarse peasanty loaf or Italian bread
> Hot cooked Plain White Rice (Basic Western or Boiled) (see recipes), or boiled potatoes (optional)

Shell the shrimp and put the shells into a large nonreactive saucepan. Reserve shrimp. There is no need to devein them, but you may do so if you wish. If scallops are used, trim off the white muscle on the side and put trimmings in the pan. Cut scallops in half crosswise and reserve them with the shrimp. Add remaining broth ingredients to the pan and top with the mussels and clams. Cover pan and bring to a boil. Cook until shellfish begin to open, about 5 minutes, then remove shellfish with a slotted spoon as they open. Set aside. Simmer the broth, covered, another 15 to 20 minutes. Strain. Reserve broth and discard solids.

Heat the oil in a medium-size flameproof casserole or enameled cast-iron pot, preferably something that can come to table. Season shrimp and scallops lightly with salt and pepper and dust them lightly with flour, shaking off the excess. Sauté briefly, just until they begin to color slightly, about 1 minute on each side. As they are done, remove them to a bowl and set aside. Add the chopped onion to the pan and sauté a few minutes, until tender. Sprinkle on 2 tablespoons flour and stir it in until blended. Cook about 1 minute. Lower heat, add the garlic and cook it *very* gently for about 1 minute. Whisk in the reserved broth and bring it to a boil. Season with salt and pepper. Lower heat and let sauce simmer, stirring occasionally, for 5 to 10 minutes, even longer if it seems watery. Sauce should be light but slightly creamy. (May be prepared in advance to this point.)

At serving time, reheat the sauce to a simmer, and stir in the parsley and optional peas. Correct seasoning. Add the shellfish and any liquid that has accumulated in the bowls; baste, cover, and cook just until shellfish is heated through. Serve hot with bread, and with hot rice or potatoes, if you wish.

SHRIMP (OR CRAWFISH) ETOUFFÉE

About 6 servings

This traditional Louisiana dish—shrimp smothered in a rich, spicy sauce—has been a great favorite with students for some years. It should be prepared in advance. When it is served the day it is made, the shrimp are plump and distinct; with age the shrimp partake of the sauce and become tender and more a part of the whole. Both ways have their charms. Variations on this theme, often prepared with crawfish, are originally Acadian and now a part of Creole cooking as well. As crawfish become more available in the Northeast, it is possible to use them in this recipe, but yield is low, so you would have to pick at least 10 pounds of whole crawfish—a tedious and pricey venture—to get the necessary volume of tail meat. Better to use a generous 1½ pounds prepicked, frozen tails and ½ to 1 pound whole crawfish, lightly crushed, for the broth. This particular etouffée is long on tomato, while some people prefer a "brown gravy" with much less tomato in it.

THE SHRIMP AND THEIR BROTH

2 pounds shrimp
1 cup dry white wine
2 cups water
1/2 lemon, sliced
2 cloves
2 bay leaves
1/2 teaspoon dried leaf thyme
A few parsley stems

THE VEGETABLES

1 cup chopped onions
1 cup chopped scallions
3/4 cup chopped green pepper
1/2 cup chopped celery
1 tablespoon minced garlic

1 1/2 cups chopped tomato pulp, fresh or canned
1/4 cup chopped parsley

THE ROUX

4 ounces (1 stick) butter
1/4 cup flour

THE SEASONINGS

1 1/2 teaspoons salt
*1 1/2 teaspoons freshly ground pepper, preferably a blend of black and
    white*
3/4 teaspoon cayenne
Tabasco to taste
1 tablespoon Worcestershire sauce

2 tablespoons cognac
Boiling water, as needed
*4 to 6 cups hot cooked Plain White Rice (Basic Western or Boiled)
    (see recipes)*

Shell and devein shrimp. Reserve shrimp, refrigerated. Place shells
and broth ingredients in a pot. Cover, bring to a boil, reduce heat, and

simmer about 30 minutes. Let rest about 15 minutes, then strain. Reserve liquid, and discard solids.

Combine the prepared vegetables in two bowls, onions through garlic in one bowl, and tomato and parsley in the other. Set aside.

In a heavy pot large enough to hold the etouffée, melt butter, whisk in flour, and cook over fairly high heat, whisking constantly, until roux is medium brown. Stir in the onion mixture and cook over high heat, stirring often, until tender, about 15 minutes. Stir in the reserved broth, the tomato mixture, salt, pepper, cayenne, Tabasco, and Worcestershire, and bring to a boil. Partially cover and simmer, stirring occasionally, until all is tender, about 30 minutes. Remove from heat. Add reserved shrimp and stir to blend. Stir in cognac. Cover closely and let rest for 1 or 2 hours. Once it has cooled you may refrigerate the mixture and hold it for 1 to 3 days.

At serving time, reheat mixture very gently without boiling, thinning with a little boiling water, if necessary. Sauce should have the texture of a fairly thick soup. Correct seasoning. Serve with rice.

SHRIMP CREOLE

4 to 6 servings

Genuine Shrimp Creole is rich, spicy, and delicious, nothing like the watery stuff with the odd cornstarch thickener served in bad restaurants all over the country. There is some reason to suspect that it is based on Acadian (Cajun) sauce piquante, but the lavish use of tomatoes is more typical of the Spanish influence in New Orleans proper than the New World French traditions of the bayou country. If you can find whole shrimp— heads on—buy about three pounds of them and add the heads to the broth; the flavor addition is excellent.

2 pounds medium shrimp

THE BROTH

3 cups water
1 cup white wine
2 bay leaves
1 teaspoon dried leaf thyme
1/2 lemon, sliced

THE SAUCE

> 2 cups chopped onions
> 1 tablespoon minced garlic
> 1 cup diced green pepper
> 1 cup sliced scallions
> 1 cup chopped celery
> 2 tablespoons chopped parsley
> 3 tablespoons corn oil
> 3 tablespoons butter
> 6 tablespoons flour
> One 35-ounce can tomatoes, juice and all, broken up by hand
> 2 teaspoons coarse salt, or to taste
> 1 teaspoon ground black pepper
> 1 teaspoon ground white pepper
> 1/2 to 1 teaspoon cayenne
> 1/2 teaspoon Tabasco, or to taste
> 1/2 teaspoon sugar, or to taste
>
> 4 to 6 cups hot cooked Plain White Rice (Basic Western or Boiled)
>   (see recipes)

Shell and devein shrimp and refrigerate them. Put the shrimp shells into a pot with the water, wine, bay leaves, thyme, and lemon. Bring to a boil, reduce heat, and simmer, covered, for up to 30 minutes, while you prepare the other ingredients. Combine the onion, garlic, green pepper, scallions, celery, and parsley, and set aside.

Heat the oil and butter in a medium pot and whisk in the flour. Cook over fairly high heat, whisking constantly, lowering the heat once the flour begins to color, until you have a medium-brown roux, the color of milk chocolate. Immediately add the vegetable mixture and stir it in with a wooden spoon. Cook, stirring occasionally, until vegetables are tender, about 10 minutes. Add remaining sauce ingredients and strain in the shrimp-shell broth. Bring mixture to a boil, lower heat, and simmer gently, partially covered, for about 1 hour. Correct seasoning. Add a little water if it seems too thick.

Just before serving time, fold in the shrimp, cover pot, and put it aside for about 15 minutes. Return it almost to a simmer and serve hot with freshly cooked rice.

ME-OON TANG

FISH IN SPICY BROTH, KOREAN-STYLE

4 servings

Though seafood is an important part of the traditional Korean diet, Korean restaurants in the New York area are long on meats, particularly the tabletop barbecues that create such a heady atmosphere. But there are seafood delights to be had as well. Woo Lae Oak of Seoul serves a bubbling cauldron of mysterious and gutsy broth with fish, clams, tofu, and vegetables. As is common with Asian restaurants, the recipe is a deep, dark secret; the version below is a fine approximation of the real thing.

THE BROTH

> *Whites of 4 scallions, thinly sliced*
> *1 tablespoon minced garlic*
> *1 tablespoon minced fresh gingerroot*
> *2 to 3 teaspoons red pepper flakes or chopped dried red chile*
> *6 cups Fish Stock (see recipe)*
> *2 teaspoons soy sauce*
> *2 teaspoons rice vinegar*
> *1/2 teaspoon sugar*
> *1 tablespoon sweet paprika*
> *1/4 cup tomato paste*
> *Coarse salt to taste*
> *2 tablespoons peanut oil*
>
> *2 squares of soft tofu, cut in half horizontally*
> *Four 6-ounce fillets of cod, scrod, porgy, or seatrout not more than*
> *   1 inch thick, skinned, tail ends folded skin side in to make neat*
> *   squares*
> *4 to 6 littleneck clams, scrubbed and soaked*
> *Greens of 4 scallions*
> *Eight 2-inch chunks of Chinese cabbage*
> *1/2 bunch fresh coriander, tough stems removed*
> *Cooked white rice, Chinese or Boiled (see recipes)*

To make the broth: In a small bowl, combine the scallion whites, garlic, ginger, and red pepper flakes, and set aside. Combine remaining broth ingredients, except for the oil, and reserve them in a large bowl. Heat the 2 tablespoons oil in a large saucepan until nearly smoking. Add the scallion mixture and stir-fry briefly, just until it is fragrant. Add the remaining broth ingredients and bring to a boil. Reduce heat and simmer mixture for about 10 minutes. Correct seasoning. This may be prepared in advance.

Before serving time, bring the remaining ingredients, except rice, to room temperature. Place a slice of tofu on top of each fish piece, and set aside. Pour broth into 4-quart flameproof casserole or enameled cast-iron pot (a Chinese sandy pot is ideal), and bring to a boil. If you are using earthenware, use a Flame-Tamer and start with low heat, increasing it to moderate when the broth is hot. High heat is fine for enamelware.

When broth is boiling, add the clams, cover, and cook until they open, up to 5 minutes. Remove clams as they open and set them aside. Return broth to a boil and add the scallion greens, cabbage, and fish-and-tofu portions, making sure the fish is covered with broth. Cover the pot and return broth to a boil. Uncover, add the clams, and strew on the coriander. Cover pot and immediately bring it to the table, still bubbling. Remove the lid so guests can see and smell what you have wrought. If fish pieces are large, return the lid to hold in heat. Otherwise, leave uncovered. After about 10 minutes, the fish will be cooked through and the broth at eating temperature. Serve in soup plates with rice.

SPECIAL EVENTS

See p. 78 for ways to determine proper cooking time.

This category includes dishes that do not fit elsewhere because there is more than one technique used, or because they involve something more than simple, straightforward fish or shellfish cookery. The latter include a pie, a pizza, a papillote, spring rolls, three dishes based on a purée, and three fish baked in pastry. All can be prepared largely in advance and are festive for entertaining of one style or another. Please refer to the other sections if you have questions about specific techniques.

SWORDFISH AND CLAMS, PORTUGUESE-STYLE

6 servings

Portuguese cooking is finally beginning to generate some interest outside the immigrant communities in the Northeast. The following is an unusual variation on the traditional pork and shellfish dish called *carne de porco à Alentejana* with swordfish scallops standing in for the pork cubes. The success of the dish depends on tender little bivalves; if the available littlenecks are too large, try Manila clams from the Pacific Northwest or substitute mussels. A combination of clams and mussels is excellent. In the nothing-new-under-the-sun department, it is fun to observe that the famous onion marmalade of Michel Guérard is not so very different from the first stages of the everyday *refogado* that is the foundation for many Portuguese sauces.

6 tablespoons light olive oil, or as needed
2 pounds Spanish onions, finely chopped
24 very small littleneck clams, or 2 pounds mussels, or a combination
1/2 cup dry white wine
2 large cloves garlic, mashed almost to a paste
2 cups imported canned tomatoes, most of the seeds removed, and crushed by hand, plus about 1/2 cup of the strained juice
1 bay leaf
2 teaspoons sweet paprika
Dash cayenne
Coarse salt
2 to 2 1/2 pounds swordfish, trimmed and sliced into 18 scallops about 1/4 inch thick
Freshly ground black pepper to taste

Flour for dredging
1 tablespoon finely chopped parsley

Heat 4 tablespoons oil in a heavy skillet and add the onions, tossing to film them lightly with oil. Cover and cook over low heat for about 15 minutes or so. Uncover, raise heat, and cook until the moisture they have sweated is reduced. Continue this process—covering and uncovering, lowering and raising heat, sweating and reducing—until the onions have gone beyond golden to a light caramel color. This will take at least 1 hour. Be careful they do not scorch.

Meanwhile, clean shellfish well (p. 62), and steam them with the wine in a pot with a tight-fitting lid, removing them as they open. Reserve shellfish in the shell. Strain broth, being careful to avoid sand. Reserve broth.

When onions are properly done, stir in garlic and cook briefly. Add tomatoes, bay leaf, paprika, cayenne, about ½ teaspoon salt, and the reserved broth. Cover, and simmer mixture until it is the texture of a rich sauce. If it remains thin, uncover and reduce. Discard bay leaf, and correct seasoning. For a more elegant texture you may purée the sauce in a food processor, but this is not necessary. May be prepared in advance.

At serving time, reheat the sauce and warm the shellfish in it. Heat a large heavy skillet until very hot. Season swordfish with pepper and dust *very* lightly with flour. Add remaining 2 tablespoons oil to hot pan, then a layer of fish scallops. Sauté, turning once, until lightly colored and just heated through. Do not overcook. Repeat with remaining fish, adding more oil as needed. As fish is done, blot cooking oil and place fish on a serving platter or 3 scallops each on dinner plates. Spoon on the warmed sauce and shellfish, sprinkle with just a touch of parsley, and serve immediately.

KIBBEE SAMAK

LENTEN SEAFOOD KIBBEE

12 or more main course servings, more than 24 **mezza** *(assorted hors d'oeuvre) servings*

When Middle Eastern Christians give up their beloved lamb (and dairy products) for Lent, one of the traditional dishes for festive family gatherings is this seafood version of the ubiquitous ground lamb and cracked wheat mixture. Here is the recipe of Gladys and William Sabah of Brooklyn. It is generous because it is always prepared for a group, but you might make only half. The wheat is the special boiled, dried, and cracked product that has no substitute. If possible, buy it in a shop that specializes in Middle Eastern foods—ask for fine (#1) burghul. If you buy it in a health-food store, it will be called bulgur and you will have no choice of gauge; it will be medium and that's okay but not as delicate as #1. This kibbee may be eaten warm or at room temperature. It is served with an assortment of vegetables cooked in olive oil with garlic, such as okra and tomatoes or green beans with onions; and, of course, pita and olives.

THE KIBBEE MIXTURE

> 1 1/2 cups burghul (bulgur), fine or medium, rinsed with cold water and squeezed dry
> 3 pounds skinless fillet of haddock (the Sabah's first choice, but hard to find) or cod, carefully trimmed of all bones, cut into chunks, and chilled
> 1 1/2 pounds shrimp, shelled, deveined, cut into chunks, and chilled
> Grated zest of 1 lemon
> Grated zest of 1 orange
> 1/2 bunch fresh coriander leaves, chopped
> Coarse salt and freshly ground pepper to taste
>
> 1 cup olive oil, plus a little more for the baking pan
> 2 cups chopped onions
> 1/2 cup pine nuts
> 1/2 bunch fresh coriander, chopped

The easiest way to handle the burghul is to put it into a bowl, add cold water to cover generously, then pour the whole thing into a sieve lined with a clean towel. Drain, squeeze, and refrigerate. Put the chilled fish and shrimp into a food processor bowl and pulse, scraping down the bowl as needed, until you have the texture of ground meat. (Or use a meat grinder with the fine blade and grind twice.) Do not liquefy! Scrape into a large bowl and add the remaining kibbee ingredients, including the prepared burghul. Mix with the fingers as quickly and lightly as possible, dipping fingers into ice water often, just until ingredients are blended and the burghul begins to "disappear" into the whole. Refrigerate.

Heat ⅓ cup olive oil in a skillet and add the onions and pine nuts. Cook over medium heat, stirring often, until onions are tender. Stir in the coriander. Pour mixture into a bowl and cool.

Preheat oven to 400°F.

Oil a 12-by-18-inch pan with sides—most people use a flat-bottomed roasting pan. Turn half of the kibbee mixture into the pan and spread it evenly, again dipping fingers into ice water as needed. Spoon on the cooled filling mixture and spread it evenly. Top with the remaining kibbee mixture and smooth. Use a long sharp knife dipped into cold water to deeply score the surface into diamond shapes ¾ to 1 inch wide: Make diagonal cuts from corner to corner, then proceed to add parallel slashes in both directions. Drizzle the remaining ⅔ cup oil evenly over all. Bake until heated through and lightly browned, about 45 minutes. Serve warm or at room temperature, cut into diamond wedges or squares.

PATRANI MACHI

SPICED FISH COOKED IN A LEAF

4 servings

Wonderfully exotic, yet easy to make once you have conquered your coconut, this Indian specialty is from teacher Aruna Madnani. The fish of choice in India is pomfret, very abundant there but only available in New York—and only occasionally—in Chinatown. The best substitute here should be butterfish, but it is difficult to find any of the really large ones that are practical for filleting. Better to choose large porgies, crevalle or another of the smaller jacks (permit, rainbow runner, blue runner), cod, flounder, or halibut steaks. Banana leaves can be purchased in markets that cater to Caribbean and Hispanic clienteles and are really the best choice for flavor, authenticity, and beauty of presentation. Bakers' parchment or foil may be used instead of banana leaves. If you use leaves or parchment, this one is perfect for microwaving.

Four 6- to 8-ounce skinless fillets or steaks of fish of choice
1/4 cup white vinegar
5 tablespoons vegetable oil
1/2 cup water
1/2 of a fresh coconut
2 large cloves garlic, peeled and trimmed
2 green chiles (jalapeño or serrano), seeds and caps removed
1 bunch fresh coriander, leaves only
1 teaspoon ground cumin
1 1/2 teaspoons coarse salt
1/4 to 1/2 teaspoon sugar
2 tablespoons lime juice
4 banana leaves (or parchment or foil)

Arrange the fish in a single layer in a skillet, folding fillets (skin side in) if they are thin so that you have neat, squarish packages. Combine vinegar, oil, and water in a saucepan and bring to a boil. Pour mixture over the fish and lift pieces with a spatula to see that they are moistened underneath. Cover skillet. Bring the mixture almost to a simmer over low heat. Remove from heat and set aside to rest for 15 minutes or so, then uncover and cool. Drain, discarding juices.

Drive a screwdriver or a nail into one "eye" of the coconut and drain out the liquid. Use a hammer to crack the coconut. It will be easier to handle if you first heat it in a 325°F. oven for 10 minutes or so. Pry out the meat, using half for this recipe and reserving the remainder for another use. Pare off and discard the brown skin. Combine coconut, garlic, chiles, coriander, cumin, salt, and sugar in the bowl of a food processor and process to a paste, scraping down the sides of the bowl as needed. Process in the lime juice. Set aside. (This can be done as much as a day ahead and refrigerated.)

Use half of the spice paste to smear a layer about 1/4 inch thick and the shape of the fish pieces toward the stem end of each banana leaf or in the center of 14-inch squares of parchment or foil. Place fish on the paste and mask it with the remaining mixture. Fold in the sides of the banana leaves and begin to fold fish over and over until you have rolled up neat packets. If using parchment or foil, seal packages by bringing 2 sides together and folding them until you reach the fish, then folding the 2 open sides under. Tie the banana leaf packages with twine; parchment and foil will not need tying. Cook the fish either by steaming it or baking it, covered, in a preheated 325°F. oven until heated through, about 15 minutes. Banana leaves will just start to turn a dull color. Untie and serve right away.

PIZZA WITH FRESH SARDINES

4 to 6 servings

Anchovies are not the only little fishes that add interest to pizza. In addition to fresh sardines (small herring), you might consider fillets of smelt or strips of mackerel. Freshly steamed tiny clams or mussels are also delicious added at the very last moment to a pizza with these same ingredients. Diehard cheese enthusiasts will have to have some grated or diced mozzarella sprinkled on, but purists will prefer it without.

THE DOUGH

1 envelope active dry yeast
1 cup tepid water
4 cups unbleached all-purpose flour
1 generous teaspoon salt
3 tablespoons light olive oil, plus extra for the bowl and pan

THE TOPPING

Coarse salt to taste
About ⅓ cup light olive oil
4 to 6 sardines, depending on size, filleted
2 teaspoons minced garlic
1 generous tablespoon chopped parsley
1 generous tablespoon chopped fresh oregano or marjoram, or 1 scant
*   teaspoon dried*
One 28-ounce can imported tomatoes, broken up by hand and drained
*   thoroughly in a sieve*
Freshly ground black pepper to taste

Stir the yeast into the water and pour mixture into a medium-large bowl. Add 2 cups of the flour and mix to a soft dough. Cover and set aside in a warm place to proof (rise) for 30 to 45 minutes. Combine remaining flour and salt and mix into the dough with the hands, adding 3 tablespoons oil after things are combined. Knead until dough is smooth and elastic, adding a little more water or flour if necessary. Knead by hand or in a food processor or heavy-duty mixer. Oil a clean bowl, put in the dough, turn it over to coat with oil, cover, and let rise until doubled in volume for 1 to 2 hours, depending on the temperature. For the finest flavor, proof dough overnight in the refrigerator.

Preheat oven to 450°F.

Salt fillets lightly, film with oil, and put aside.

Punch down dough and turn it out onto a floured sheet pan. Working with floured hands, spread dough into a large round or rectangle. Dough should be thin with slightly thicker edges. Brush edges with oil. Combine garlic, parsley, and oregano and sprinkle mixture over the dough. Strew on the tomatoes. Add pepper to taste. Drizzle with remaining oil lightly but evenly. Put in the oven and bake for about 15 minutes, or until lightly browned. Remove from oven and quickly arrange the sardine fillets attractively, skin side up. A pattern like spokes of a wheel is appropriate for a round pizza. Immediately return pizza to the oven and continue baking until it is done, another 10 minutes or so. Cut with a pizza cutter, and serve as quickly as possible.

EEL IN OLIVE OIL WITH GARLIC AND CHILE

4 to 6 first course servings

Like firm silvery pasta with a hint of delicate seafood flavor, baby eels sizzling in olive oil with garlic and dried red chile is among the world's most extraordinary delicacies. The preparation is Bilbao-style, but it is enjoyed throughout Spain and is capable of lifting even the gloom of a Castillian winter. Unfortunately, Spanish elvers are very expensive and difficult to locate in the United States. Memories of eating baby eels in Spain inspired this adult eel version using the same four ingredients. Those who wish to sample the real thing may do so at Café San Martín in Manhattan. The salad version is also worth trying: Poach and cool fillets, drain and combine with the ingredients below plus 1 tablespoon of red wine vinegar. Marinate for an hour or so and taste for salt. Serve cool.

About 2 pounds live American eels (3 to 4 eels)
Coarse salt
1 bay leaf
½ cup light olive oil
4 large cloves garlic, peeled and sliced into 2 to 3 pieces each
3 dried hot red chiles, sliced crosswise with a sharp knife into 3 to 4
    pieces each, most of the seeds removed
1 tablespoon chopped parsley (optional)
Good bread

Stun, gut, and skin the eels (p. 61). Fillet them as you would any other roundfish. Each eel will yield 4 fillets; the pinbones neatly separate the fillets on each side. Cut fillets into uniform lengths of about 3 inches. Poach fillet pieces in salted water to cover with the bay leaf added. Cool in the poaching liquid and set aside.

At serving time, drain and dry the eel pieces. Heat a skillet to very hot and add the oil. When the oil is hot, add the eel pieces and shake them around until they are slightly golden and heated through. Add garlic and chiles. When garlic is just beginning to color, turn the mixture out onto a platter or into a shallow casserole, sprinkle with optional parsley, and serve immediately with bread.

SPRING ROLLS, SOUTHEAST ASIAN-STYLE

About twelve 4-inch rolls, 4 to 6 first course servings

This recipe was inspired by an evening of good food and even better company shared at Indochine, on Lafayette Street across from the Public Theatre. It is not entirely authentic—most mixtures include some ground pork—but it is delicious and fun to prepare. Most of the ingredients should be readily available; even supermarkets carry rice sticks these days, and neighborhood greengrocers stock fish sauce. Asian food shops have both, of course, but Vietnamese rice paper is harder to find. Spring roll wrappers will do, but they are much thicker. Filo leaves, which are easy enough to find in supermarkets and specialty stores, yield a crispness similar to rice paper and are a better substitute than spring roll wrappers.

THE FILLING

1 tablespoon minced garlic
1 tablespoon minced fresh gingerroot
3 scallions, thinly sliced, white and green separated
2 tablespoons Asian fish sauce
1 teaspoon sugar
1 ounce (dry weight) rice sticks (imported rice noodles) or vermicelli
2 tablespoons peanut oil
1/2 pound shelled shrimp or skinned fillet of white-fleshed fish, diced;
*   or crabmeat, picked over to remove all bits of shell; or a combina-*
*   tion*
Ground black pepper to taste

THE WRAPPERS

12 squares Vietnamese rice paper or filo leaves or spring roll wrappers
1/4 cup hot peanut oil (for filo leaves only)

Peanut or soy oil for deep-frying
Southeast Asian Dipping Sauce (recipe follows)

THE GARNISHES

1 bunch fresh mint
12 Boston lettuce leaves, washed and dried, tough stems removed
Thin slices cucumber and/or carrot, marinated in rice vinegar and
*   sugar (optional)*

Combine the garlic, ginger, and scallion whites. Combine the fish sauce and sugar. Cover rice sticks with boiling water, soak about 10 minutes, drain, and cut into 1-inch lengths. If you use vermicelli, drop into boiling water, cook until tender, drain, and cut. Heat the 2 tablespoons oil in a wok until almost smoking. Add the garlic mixture and stir-fry briefly until fragrant. Add the seafood and stir-fry briefly. Add the fish sauce mixture and the scallion greens, and stir-fry for a few seconds to combine. Pour mixture into a bowl and stir in the noodles and pepper to taste. Cool.

To assemble the rolls: Cut wrappers into 6-inch squares. If you use filo, use 2 layers per square (fold sheets in half and cut square with a sharp knife). One at a time, place a square in front of you with a point facing you. For filo only, brush square with a little hot peanut oil and keep remaining squares covered with a towel to prevent drying out. For rice paper or spring roll wrappers, moisten the far corner with a little water. Spoon some filling just above the near corner and begin to roll it up, rather snugly, pausing in the middle to fold in the sides so that roll will be about 4 inches long. Finish rolling and place roll on a platter, seam side down. Repeat with remaining ingredients.

Heat several cups of oil in a wok or other fryer to 375°F. Once the rolls are assembled, they should be fried soon to keep them from getting soggy. Fry briefly, only 30 seconds or so, a few at a time, and drain. They are now ready to be reheated in hot oil or refrigerated or frozen for later use.

At serving time, reheat the oil and fry the rolls until they are crisp and golden, about 1 minute. Present them immediately with the garnishes and a little bowl of dipping sauce for each person. Diners take a lettuce leaf in hand and add a spring roll and mint leaves to taste, roll up the lettuce leaf, dip, and eat. Delicious! The optional cucumber and carrot provide a little change of taste and texture.

SOUTHEAST ASIAN DIPPING SAUCE

2 large dried hot red chiles, or 2 teaspoons dried red pepper flakes
1/8 teaspoon ground fennel seed or aniseed
2 tablespoons sugar
2 large cloves garlic, peeled
3 tablespoons Asian fish sauce
2 tablespoons lime or lemon juice
3 tablespoons water

Combine chiles, fennel seed or aniseed, and sugar in a mortar, blender, or food processor, and crush until chiles are fairly fine. Add garlic and process to a paste. Add liquids and process to combine. Reserve, refrigerated, in a covered container until serving time.

ANDRÉ SOLTNER'S BASS EN CROÛTE

6 to 8 servings

Here is the first of three fish in pastry, a splendid *haute cuisine* dish worthy of the fine reputation of Lutèce. Puff pastry is traditional; you are in luck if you can purchase a fine all-butter dough like the one made by Saucier, Inc.; it is sold frozen in upscale markets and specialty stores. Fine bakeries are other sources of quality product. Otherwise, make a dough of your own. A fine, flaky *pâte brisée* will do nicely. As genuine pike becomes less available, we have to consider alternate seafood for the *mousseline:* walleye and fresh whitefish are fine, as is a combination of whiting and scallops (for body). Mr. Soltner advises *sauce choron,* which is *sauce béarnaise* flavored and colored with tomato purée (only a fresh purée will be properly delicate). The result is very pretty, very good, and very French, but a *Buerre Rouge* or *Buerre Blanc,* or Lemon Butter (see recipes) would also be appropriate.

MOUSSELINE

1 pound fillet of pike, walleye, or whitefish, or ½ pound whiting fillet
*   and ½ pound sea scallops*
3 eggs
1 ¼ teaspoons coarse salt
⅓ teaspoon freshly ground white pepper
2 cups heavy cream

4 pounds whole hybrid striped bass, black sea bass, grouper, seatrout
*   or other delicate white-fleshed fish (two fish may be necessary)*
1 generous teaspoon chopped fresh tarragon
1 generous teaspoon chopped parsley or chervil
2 pounds puff pastry or Pâte Brisée *(recipe follows)*
Flour for rolling the pastry
1 egg beaten with 1 tablespoon cream

To prepare the mousseline: Carefully trim fish of all bones and skin. Cut into chunks and purée in a food processor, adding the eggs and seasonings, scraping down the sides of the bowl often, until you have a very smooth mixture. Chill well. Process in the cream in pulses just until incorporated, stirring with a rubber spatula between pulses until smooth. Chill until needed.

Poach bass in boiling water for 30 seconds. Remove. Skin and fillet fish, being careful to remove all bones. Lay half of fish on a platter lined with plastic wrap or a clean cloth (if you have 4 fillets, arrange these 2 overlapping so that they are shaped as one fillet) and season with tarragon and parsley. Spread on the chilled *mousseline.* Top with remaining fillets, keeping the whole as even as possible. Wrap snugly with plastic wrap or the cloth and refrigerate.

Roll out pastry into a square just larger than the length of the assembled fish and about ⅛ inch thick; cut pastry in half with a crosscut (or roll pastry into 2 rectangles). Place one half on parchment on a baking sheet. Place the fish on this piece of pastry and paint around it with the egg wash of egg and cream. Place the other pastry half on top and carefully seal, removing excess air as you go. Use a pastry wheel to cut the pastry into a fish shape. Reserve trimmings. Spread the surface with egg wash. Decorate as desired with the trimmings, then apply egg wash to the decorations: Give fish an eye and a mouth and define the gill opening with a strip of pastry. Holding it at a slight angle, press the large end of a pastry tip gently into the pastry, cutting about halfway through it, in a continuous pattern of semi-circles to simulate scales. Do not be alarmed if you happen to cut through the pastry in one or two places—this will create a steam vent without doing particular damage to the appearance of the finished dish. Refrigerate for a few hours, if possible.

Bake in a moderate oven (350°F. to 375°F.) for 40 to 45 minutes, or until puffed and nicely browned. Remove from oven, let rest for 5 or 10 minutes, slice crosswise, and serve with sauce of choice.

PÂTE BRISÉE

> *4 cups unbleached all-purpose flour*
> *1 ½ teaspoons salt*
> *12 ounces (3 sticks) very cold butter*
> *Ice water as needed, about ¾ cup*

Combine flour and salt. Cut in butter until it is the consistency of tiny peas. Mix in about ½ cup ice water, handling lightly, then press firmly but without stretching, sprinkling on more ice water as needed, just until pastry is moist enough to hold together. Shape into a ball, wrap, flatten a bit, and chill until needed, at least 30 minutes.

FEUILLETÉ DE SAUMON AU BEURRE BLANC

SALMON IN PUFF PASTRY WITH WHITE BUTTER SAUCE

6 to 8 servings

Here is another classic French-style dish, this one from Chef Alain Sailhac, formerly of the perennially fashionable Le Cirque, and the new "21" Club. While white-fleshed fish in pastry is traditionally stuffed with a fish mousse, salmon works very nicely with the spinach mixture below, for fine flavor and a lovely presentation. You might also use Swiss chard. This is ideal party food for special occasions, and it can be prepared largely in advance. Notice that the fish is blanched and cooled before assembly, to firm it up and settle the moisture so that there is less likelihood of soggy pastry. The sauce is then made from that blanching liquid, rather than from a reduction of wine and shallots only. Mr. Sailhac recommends blanched cucumber, green beans (optional), and rice as accompaniments.

THE SALMON

1 cup dry white wine
1 cup Fish Stock (see recipe)
1/4 cup minced shallots
1 tablespoon white wine vinegar
1 bay leaf
1/4 teaspoon coarse salt
1/2 teaspoon peppercorns
2 pounds salmon fillet (from about 2 1/2 pounds salmon, center cut or tail)

THE STUFFING

1 pound spinach leaves
8 ounces mushrooms
3 tablespoons butter
2 tablespoons minced shallots
1/4 cup Sercial Madeira
Salt and freshly ground pepper to taste
Dash freshly grated nutmeg

*

2 pounds puff pastry or Pâte Brisée *(preceding recipe)*
Flour for rolling the pastry
1 egg, beaten
12 ounces (3 sticks) butter, cool, cut into 1-tablespoon pieces

Combine the wine, stock, shallots, vinegar, and seasonings in a non-reactive pan just large enough to hold the fish in a single layer. Bring mixture to a boil, reduce heat, and simmer, covered, for about 10 minutes. Add salmon and poach, without returning to the simmer, for 5 minutes. Carefully remove salmon without breaking it and put aside to cool. Reduce the broth over fairly high heat to about ¼ cup liquid. Strain liquid into a medium nonreactive saucepan and reserve. Discard solids. Skin salmon fillets, removing the dark flesh against the skin as neatly as possible. Reserve fillets.

To prepare the stuffing: Plunge spinach into a pot of boiling water and wilt, 30 seconds or so. Drain, shock with cold water, squeeze out excess moisture, and chop medium-fine. Finely chop mushrooms, by hand or in a food processor or meat grinder. Heat the 3 tablespoons butter in a skillet, add shallots, and stir over medium heat for about 30 seconds, until fragrant. Add mushrooms and cook, stirring often, until mushrooms give up their liquid and it reduces. Add Madeira and reduce. Season. Stir in spinach and nutmeg and stir mixture over heat until it is well combined and dry. Correct seasoning and turn out into a bowl to cool. Set aside.

Divide puff pastry in half and roll on a lightly floured surface into 2 rectangles about ⅛ inch thick. Place 1 piece on a baking sheet lined with parchment (chill remaining piece) and begin the assembly: Place half of salmon on the pastry and top with spinach mixture. Cover with remaining salmon, turning fillet in the opposite direction so that the whole is as uniform as possible. Paint pastry with egg wash around the salmon. Cover with the reserved pastry, easing it into place, removing excess air, and then pressing all around to seal, letting the egg wash glue the edges together. Use a pastry wheel to neatly trim pastry, either into a fish shape or a neat oval. Decorate as desired, simulating fish scales with the large end of a pastry tip if desired, p. 327, then glaze with egg wash. If possible, assembly should be chilled for at least 30 minutes, up to several hours.

About 1 hour before serving time, preheat oven to 400°F. and bake assembly for 35 to 40 minutes, or until puffed and nicely browned. While fish is baking, prepare the sauce: Warm the reserved reduction and begin whisking in the pieces of butter, 1 at a time. Work off the heat but return pan to the heat as needed to keep the butter melting. Sauce must only be very warm and will break if it overheats. When sauce is finished, put it aside in a warm place. When pastry is done, remove from oven and let rest for about 5 minutes before serving. Slice with a serrated knife and serve with a bit of sauce, passing the rest of the sauce separately.

SEATROUT IN PASTRY

6 to 8 servings

Here, for good measure, is a third fish in pastry, the simplest because it has no stuffing, only some chopped fresh herbs sandwiched between the fillets. And the fillets are not blanched. Far from being an also-ran, it is just as elegant as the preceding two and faster to make.

2 pounds puff pastry or Pâte Brisée *(see recipe)*
Flour for rolling the pastry
2 large (or 4 small) fillets seatrout (about 3 pounds total), skinned
*   and trimmed, all bones removed*
2 tablespoons minced parsley
2 teaspoons minced fresh chives
1 1/2 teaspoons minced fresh tarragon
1/2 teaspoon coarse salt
1/4 teaspoon freshly ground white pepper
Egg wash of 1 egg and 1 egg yolk
Beurre Blanc *or Lemon Butter (see recipes)*

Divide pastry in half and roll on a lightly floured surface into 2 rectangles about 1/8 inch thick. Place 1 piece on a baking sheet lined with parchment (chill the remaining piece of pastry) and begin the assembly: Place half the fish on the pastry, and sprinkle on parsley, chives, tarragon, and salt and pepper. Cover with the remaining fish (skin side down), turning fillet(s) in the opposite direction so that the whole is as uniform as possible. Paint pastry around the fish with egg wash. Cover with the reserved pastry, easing it into place, removing excess air, and then pressing all around to seal, letting the egg wash glue the edges together. Use a pastry wheel to neatly trim pastry, either into a fish shape or a neat oval. Decorate as desired, simulating fish scales with the large end of a pastry tip if you wish (p. 327), then glaze with egg wash. If possible, assembly should be chilled for at least 30 minutes and up to several hours.

Preheat oven to 400° F. and bake assembly for 35 to 40 minutes, or until puffed and nicely browned. When pastry is done, remove from oven and let rest for about 5 minutes before serving. Slice with a serrated knife and serve with some sauce of your choice, passing the rest separately.

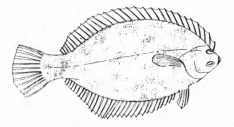

FISHERMAN'S PIE

6 to 8 servings

Delicious as it is, this recipe narrowly made it into the book. At first it seemed a little too old-fashioned to bother with; surely the basic American tomes must have a version for those who are interested. Wrong. And it turns out that no lesser lights than Gilbert Le Coze of Le Bernardin, Anne Rosenzweig of Arcadia, Gérard Pangaud of Aurora, and Steven Mellina of The Manhattan Ocean Club are pleased to feature seafood and potato combos. Granted, they are all using lobster with their spuds; you may certainly use lobster for this recipe if you are feeling flush, but other seafoods complement the earthy simplicity of potatoes as well. You might also prepare a pie with a crust by folding partially cooked vegetables (adding some diced potato) and raw fish into the cooled sauce, pouring the whole into a deep baking dish, topping it with one-half the recipe for *Pâte Brisée* and baking until nicely browned. The version below is easier and less likely to produce overdone fish.

THE FILLING

> 6 cups Fish Stock (see recipe)
> About 20 small white onions, peeled, root ends pierced
> About 20 button mushrooms, very fresh, stems trimmed, or fewer larger
>   ones, halved or quartered
> 6 tablespoons butter
> 6 tablespoons flour
> 3 egg yolks
> 1/2 cup heavy cream
> Coarse salt and freshly ground white pepper to taste
> 1 teaspoon lemon juice, if needed
> Pinch freshly grated nutmeg
>
> 1 1/2 pounds skinned fillet of firm, white-fleshed fish—cod, pollock,
>   blackfish, wolffish, ocean pout, ocean perch—trimmed and cut
>   into 1-inch cubes
> 1 tablespoon chopped fresh tarragon, or 2 tablespoons chopped parsley

THE POTATOES

> 3 pounds russet (Idaho) or eastern (Maine) potatoes, peeled and
>   chunked
> Coarse salt to taste
> 4 tablespoons butter
> About 1/2 cup milk
> Freshly ground white pepper to taste
> 1 egg yolk beaten with 2 tablespoons water
>
> Parsley or tarragon sprigs for garnish

Combine stock, onions, and mushrooms in a large saucepan and bring
to a simmer. Cover partially and simmer just until onions are tender.
Skim out vegetables and reserve. Keep stock hot. In a large, heavy,
nonreactive saucepan, melt the 6 tablespoons butter and whisk in the
flour. Simmer over low heat, stirring constantly, for 1 minute. Whisk
in the stock and bring it to a simmer. Sauce will thicken right away.
Lower heat and let the sauce simmer gently for about 10 minutes,
stirring often. Whisk together the egg yolks and the cream in a bowl,
temper with some of the hot sauce, and whisk the mixture back into

the sauce. Add the reserved onions and mushrooms. Season with salt, pepper, lemon juice (depending on how acidic the stock was), and nutmeg. Cover mixture and set aside. Cut up the fish, mix it with the chopped herbs, and refrigerate.

Preheat oven to 400°F.

Put the cut potatoes into a heavy pot and add water almost to cover and a little salt. Cover pot and bring to a boil. Lower heat and simmer until potatoes are just tender, 20 to 30 minutes. Drain potatoes, saving the liquid. Return pot to the stove, uncover, and shake pot over fairly high heat until potatoes are dry and powdery on the outside. Mash with a potato masher or rice through a food mill. Add butter, milk, and pepper, and stir briskly until smooth, adding milk as needed until the texture is as delicate as mashed potatoes can be (do not make it soupy). Correct seasoning. Spread a thin layer of potato in the bottom of a large, rather shallow heatproof casserole or 2 pie plates. Spoon or pipe a rather high border of potato and brush with the egg yolk mixture. Place in the oven and bake until border is lightly browned, about 10 minutes.

Meanwhile, reheat the filling mixture and add the fish and herbs. Heat, below the simmering point, just until fish is warmed through. Do not overcook. Correct seasoning. If sauce seems too thick, thin with a little of the reserved potato water. Ladle mixture into the hot browned potato shell, garnish with sprigs of parsley or tarragon, and serve immediately.

SCALLOP MOUSSE (AND OTHER MOUSSES)

4 to 8 servings

Velvety *mousselines* of fish and shellfish are French classics that can be prepared in minutes these days with the aid of a food processor. Now that hours of pounding and sieving are no longer required, these mixtures are within the range of any cook's skills and interests, yet no less elegant for the ease of preparation. The name *mousseline* designates the most delicate of foamy mixtures, but in the United States it is normally reserved for *sauce hollandaise* lightened with whipped cream, while preparations of the sort below are called mousses. No matter. This particular mixture is so versatile that it is also the foundation for the two recipes that follow. These proportions are perfect for *sea* scallops, shrimp, and lobster. Scallops will be just right every time unless they have been soaked in water to increase their weight. Always buy scallops that look almost sticky with no standing liquid in the container in which they are displayed.

For most fish, these egg-and-cream proportions will work better with 1 pound trimmed flesh, lest the mousse be too bland. Avoid flounder (not enough flavor to shine through the egg and cream) and any fish other than salmon that does not cook up white. New York chef and teacher Richard Glavin recommends that fish mousses be flavored with a spoonful of a very reduced essence of white wine, shallot, and fish bones. Richard reasons that salt and pepper are insufficient seasonings, that a bland mousse will not be rescued even by a perfect sauce. His results are lovely. Keep everything very cold so that the paste will emulsify the cream properly. There is no way to be certain how albuminous your fish is, and therefore exactly how much cream it will absorb. Do not add all the cream if the mixture seems too loose. And proportions can be varied according to how the mixture will be used. Notice that André Soltner's *mousseline* has extra egg for body because it is a stuffing. Traditionally, only egg whites are used and yolks are really not necessary, but the Michel Guérard formula of 1 whole egg to 1 egg white used below is excellent. For those who *must* reduce fat, the cream may be replaced by very fresh part-skim ricotta or other low-fat fresh white cheese processed until very smooth and thinned with skimmed milk to a texture just thicker than heavy cream. The result is remarkably edible, though of course a completely different experience. Do not try this substitution for stuffings because the mousse will probably weep too much moisture.

3/4 pound sea scallops
1 3/4 teaspoons coarse salt
1/4 teaspoon freshly ground white pepper
1 whole egg and 1 egg white, or 2 egg whites
2 cups crème fraîche, *or 2 cups heavy cream*
1/2 teaspoon lemon juice (if you use heavy cream)
A little butter for the mold(s)

Sauce of choice: Sheer Tomato Sauce with Pernod, Beurre Blanc *or* Beurre Rouge, *Red Pepper Purée, or Green Sauce (see recipes)*
1 teaspoon minced fresh chives, chervil, or parsley

In a food processor, purée the scallops with salt and pepper until very smooth, scraping down the sides of the bowl as needed with a rubber spatula. Process in the whole egg or 1 egg white, and then the remaining egg white. Chill the whole assembly well, for at least 30 minutes, up to several hours.

Replace the processor bowl on the motor and add about one-third of the cream. From this point on, process as little as possible to avoid curdling the cream. Pulse the machine several times, scraping the mixture up from the bottom 1 or 2 times with the spatula to help it receive the cream. When smooth, add another third of the cream and pulse until it is incorporated. Pulse in as much of the remaining cream as the paste will accept and still be just firm enough to hold its shape when a dollop is lifted with the spatula. Scallops normally will take it all. If you use heavy cream, pulse in the lemon juice. Do not overprocess. Chill until needed.

Preheat oven to 350°F.

Bring a pot of water to a boil. Lightly butter four 8-ounce, six 6-ounce, or eight 4-ounce ramekins, or an oval gratin 13 inches from end to end. Add the mixture, smoothing the top(s). Place dish(es) in a roasting pan with sides, place on the extended center rack of the oven, and pour boiling water into the pan to come one-half to one-third of the way up the sides of the dishes. Top with buttered parchment or foil. Carefully slide rack into the oven and bake until a knife inserted into the center comes out clean, 20 to 30 minutes.

To serve, unmold ramekins onto plates, mop up any moisture with a paper towel, and spoon your choice of sauce around. Or sauce plates and spoon a serving of mousse from the gratin onto the sauce. Top with a tiny pinch of chives, chervil, or parsley, and serve immediately.

TERRINE OF SCALLOPS AND SALMON

6 to 8 servings

This one is very pretty and takes only minutes longer to prepare than the basic mousse. It may be served hot or cool.

Scallop Mousse (preceding recipe)
12 ounces fresh spinach
3/4 pound fillet of salmon
A little butter or oil for the pan
Pinch freshly grated nutmeg
Sauce of choice: **Beurre Blanc** *(if served hot) or* **Red Pepper Purée** *(if served cool) (see recipes)*

Prepare scallop mousse mixture and chill it well, still in the processor bowl.

Trim spinach of tough stems and wash it well. Place it in a saucepan with 1 or 2 tablespoons water, cover, and heat until it wilts, 1 or 2 minutes. Drain and shock with cold water. Put spinach in a towel and thoroughly squeeze out moisture. Spinach must be dry. Chop coarsely. Measure ½ cup firmly packed spinach and reserve.

Slice salmon horizontally into sheets about ⅜ inch thick, discarding the skin and trimming the dark flesh from the bottom slice. Pour boiling salted water over the salmon, let it sit for a minute or so, and drain well, cool, then chill.

Preheat oven to 350°F.

Bring a pot of water to a boil. If terrine is to be served hot, lightly butter a 9-by-5-inch loaf pan; use oil if it will be served cool. Choose a pan with sides that the loaf pan will fit into. Return the processor bowl with the mousse mixture to the motor. Remove and reserve two-thirds of the mixture. Add spinach and nutmeg to the remaining mixture and process, scraping as needed, until blended. The spinach will retain some texture.

Make layers in the loaf pan in this order: half the plain scallop mixture, half of the salmon, the spinach mixture, remaining half of the salmon, and remaining half of the scallop mixture.

Cover loaf with a piece of buttered parchment or wax paper. Seal with foil. Nest loaf into the other pan and pour in boiling water to come two-thirds of the way up the sides of the loaf pan. Bake in preheated oven until a knife inserted into the center comes out almost clean, about 30 to 35 minutes. Unmold, mop up any liquid, slice, and serve hot; or cool terrine in its dish, then unmold, and serve. Accompany with sauce of choice.

SEAFOOD SAUSAGES

8 to 10 servings

Seafood sausages make lovely first courses or luncheon dishes and may be flavored and sauced 'most any way you wish. Other seafood might be used for the purée, but the scallop mixture is flavorful and dependable.

Scallop Mousse (see recipe), made with 1 1/2 cups cream
1 pound shelled shrimp, rock shrimp, or salmon fillet (or scallops if you
*   are using a fish mousse), or 12 ounces cooked lobster meat, mus-*
*   sels, or crabmeat, or a combination of any of the above*
2 tablespoons butter
1/4 cup minced shallots
1 tablespoon chopped parsley or other fresh herb
Dash cayenne
Melted butter
Sauce of choice: Sheer Tomato Sauce with Pernod, Green Sauce, or
*   Beurre Blanc (see recipes)*

Prepare the mousse mixture, scrape it into a bowl, and chill it well. Trim whole seafood of choice and cut it into 1/4-inch dice. Reserve. Melt butter in a small skillet and add the shallots. Cook very gently over low heat until shallots are tender. Stir in parsley and cayenne and scrape mixture into a bowl. Cool.

Fold diced seafood and cooled shallot mixture into the mousse mixture. Form mixture into 2 long sausages: Put down a length of foil about 14 to 18 inches on your work surface and cover it with a length of heavy plastic wrap. Brush the central length of plastic wrap with a light film of melted butter. Spoon on half of the mixture in a strip 8 to 12 inches long, depending on how thick you want the sausages to be. Roll up the plastic, twist the ends tightly, and wrap snugly in the foil. Chill. Repeat with remaining mixture.

Place the rolls in a pan long enough to hold them and deep enough for poaching. Add cold water to cover. Weight with a pot lid, roasting rack, or plate to keep them submerged. Bring water to a simmer, reduce heat, and poach at the shiver—170°F. to 180°F.—until firm, about 15 minutes, depending on size. Remove from heat. You may then let sausages rest for up to 15 minutes while you finish your choice of sauce. Remove sausages from the water and, handling them gently, unwrap, drain, and serve in any of the following ways: whole, cut into serving pieces, or sliced and arranged attractively in overlapping slices to display the internal pattern; or they may be prepared in advance, cooled in their wrapping and refrigerated, then reheated at serving time in hot water or in a microwave oven (without the foil, of course).

THE QUILTED GIRAFFE'S LOBSTER AND SCALLOPS WITH SAUTERNES SAUCE

6 servings

This extraordinarily suave dish proves that it is possible to be wickedly extravagant even without champagne, caviar, foie gras, or truffles (though champagne is an ideal beverage choice here). For home cooks who decide to tackle some real power entertaining, here is a winner; the compensation for the pocketbook damage is that the labor is quite simple, as is often the case with precious ingredients. And everything but the final heating can be accomplished well in advance. Do use a genuine Sauternes or Barsac, but certainly not Chateau d'Yquem. The 1.6 ounces of wine left in the bottle is the cook's dividend. If you have beautiful dinner plates bordered with a touch of color—preferably green—and your menu includes adequate vegetables and starch in other courses, you may present this dish naked and unadorned. Otherwise, consider one or more of the suggested garnishes below, using just a few pieces per plate of what you choose.

THE SHELLFISH

Three 1½-pound lobsters
1 pound sea scallops

THE SAUTERNES SAUCE

> *3 cups heavy cream*
> *3 cups Sauternes*
> *1 clove garlic, peeled and bruised*
> *4 shallots, peeled and thinly sliced*
> *4 slices of fresh gingerroot*
> *Pinch ground cumin*
> *Coarse salt and freshly ground white pepper to taste*

SUGGESTED GARNISHES

> *Puff pastry crescents*
> *One or more of the following steamed vegetables: potatoes trimmed into*
> *ovals about 2 inches long; peeled seedless cucumber, cut into*
> *2-inch ovals; baby carrots, peeled, 1 inch of stem left on; baby*
> *turnips, peeled, 1 inch of stem left on; sugar snap peas or snow*
> *peas*

Steam the lobsters, cool, and remove tail and claw meat, reserving the carcass for another stock. Slice tail meat of each into 4 equal *medaillons.* Reserve the tail and claw meat. Trim the scallops of the tough white muscle on the side, and slice them in half crosswise if they are large.

Choose two medium, heavy, nonreactive saucepans. In the first, simmer the cream until it is reduced by one-third to one-half. In the other, combine the Sauternes, garlic, shallots, and ginger, and simmer until reduced to 1 cup. Strain the wine reduction into the cream, and season the mixture lightly with cumin, salt, and pepper. Sauce should be sheer, with just a hint of creamy body.

Add the scallops to the sauce. Let the sauce get just hot enough to poach the scallops but do not let it simmer. When the scallops are nearly done, add the lobster and let it just warm through. Do not overheat. Serve immediately, equally dividing the scallops, tail pieces, claws, and any garnish you want.

LOBSTER, LIGURIAN-STYLE

6 servings

When Franco at Cent'Anni was asked for a seafood recipe, he said, "How about Lobster, Ligurian-Style? It's shellfish with a light tomato sauce with garlic. You take a nice lobster, you take some squid . . ." Without a written recipe there was no hope of duplicating the chef's version, but the recipe below is delicious and perfect for a special occasion. Notice that this dish contains many of the distinctive flavors of the Mediterranean and is Genovese in its free use of herbs—noticeably basil—and its elaborate construction. Spiny lobster is the native crustacean in Liguria, but our Atlantic lobsters do nicely (even better, to some tastes).

THE MUSSEL BROTH

> *1 cup dry white wine*
> *¹/₂ cup water*
> *1 bay leaf*
> *2 sprigs fresh thyme, or ¹/₂ teaspoon dried*
> *Small bunch parsley stems*
> *2 pounds mussels, scrubbed, soaked, tested, and debearded (p. 62)*

> *Three 1¹/₄-pound lobsters, steamed and cooled (p. 356)*
> *1 pound squid*

THE TOMATO SAUCE

> *¹/₄ cup light olive oil*
> *1 cup finely chopped onions*
> *1 tablespoon finely minced garlic*
> *3 cups chopped tomato pulp, fresh or canned*
> *Coarse salt and freshly ground black pepper to taste*

THE GARNISHES

> *6 lemon slices*
> *2 generous tablespoons tiny (nonpareil) capers, drained*
> *2 generous tablespoons chopped black olives*
> *12 anchovy fillets*

*

About ¼ cup light olive oil
2 teaspoons finely minced garlic
¼ cup pine nuts
*½ cup fresh basil, cut into thin shreds (*chiffonade*)*
Italian bread

Combine the wine, water, bay leaf, thyme, and parsley stems in a large, heavy saucepan, cover, and bring to a boil. Reduce heat and simmer for about 10 minutes. Add the cleaned mussels and cover. Steam until mussels open, about 5 minutes. Skim out mussels and put them aside to cool. Strain the broth, being careful to avoid any sand in the bottom of the pot. Discard solids. When mussels are cool enough to handle, shuck them and reserve. Save 6 large double (hinged) mussel shells for garnish.

Split the lobsters (p. 64), and clean, reserving the tomalley and coral. Cover and refrigerate lobsters. Put the reserved tomalley and coral in a blender or processor and purée, adding enough broth to liquefy it. Reserve. Clean the squid as described on p. 65; slice bodies in rings and halve any large tentacles. You now have shucked mussels, broth, mussel shells for garnish, prepared lobster halves, tomalley mixture, and squid.

To prepare the tomato sauce: Heat the ¼ cup olive oil in a wide saucepan, add the onions and cook, stirring, until tender, about 10 minutes. Add the garlic and stir briefly. Add tomato pulp, 1 cup of mussel broth, and salt and pepper to taste. Bring to a boil, reduce heat, and simmer for about 20 minutes, partially covered. Correct seasoning, and reserve.

To prepare the garnishes: Cut halfway through lemon slices and attach one to the hinge of each mussel shell. Spoon some capers into the left shell and some olives into the right shell of each. Crisscross 2 anchovy fillets over each. Reserve.

Just before serving time, preheat oven to 300°F. and reheat the tomato sauce. Place lobster halves, cut side up, in a large baking pan and brush with a little of the olive oil to film. Put lobsters in the oven to warm, about 10 minutes. Heat a large skillet and add the remaining olive oil. When oil is hot, add garlic and pine nuts and heat briefly. Add ½ cup of the tomato sauce, ¼ cup mussel broth, the reserved tomalley mixture, and the squid. Toss over high heat about 30 seconds, then add the basil and the reserved mussels. Toss until all is heated through. Correct seasoning, and serve as quickly as possible.

Film plates with tomato sauce, place a warmed lobster half on each, spoon shellfish mixture into the lobster shells, and garnish each plate with a prepared mussel shell. Serve with bread.

LOBSTER CASSOULET CHEZ JOSEPHINE

4 to 6 servings

This dish proves that perversity can be the mother of invention. Owner Jean Claude Baker's sense of humor led him to ask his chef for a travesty version of the French classic, and this best-seller was born. The seafood sausage is not absolutely essential, but it is fun and it does complete the *cassoulet* theme. You may purchase a high-quality sausage from a specialty store or make your own (p. 337). For this dish, homemade sausages would offer the most variety if they were made with a fish mousse, studded with mussels and/or crabmeat, and well seasoned with cayenne and herbs.

THE BEANS

½ pound (about 1 ⅓ cups) dried black beans, picked over and rinsed
One 12-ounce bottle of beer
1 small onion stuck with 2 cloves
1 bay leaf
Coarse salt and freshly ground pepper to taste

THE SHELLFISH

Two 1 ¼-pound lobsters, steamed, cooled, meat removed from shells (p. 356)
12 sea scallops, trimmed of the whitish muscle on the side, cut in half crosswise if large
12 medium shrimp, shelled and deveined, shells reserved
1 cup dry white wine
8 ounces Seafood Sausage (see recipe) (optional)

2 to 3 tablespoons butter, or as needed
1 cup thinly sliced scallions, green and white parts
1 ½ tablespoons minced garlic

1 cup chopped tomato pulp, fresh or canned
½ teaspoon ground coriander seed
1 teaspoon ground cumin
½ teaspoon cayenne
¼ cup chopped parsley
Coarse salt and freshly ground pepper to taste
About 4 cups hot cooked Plain White Rice (Basic Western or Boiled)
    (see recipes) (optional)

Soak beans overnight in 2 cups of water and the beer. Add 3 cups water, the onion with cloves, and bay leaf, and bring to a simmer. Simmer very gently, covered, until beans are barely tender, at least 1½ hours, adding more water if beans should become dry. Add salt and pepper toward the end of the cooking time. Drain the beans, saving the liquid for another purpose. Discard onion and bay leaf. Reserve beans.

Cut meat from lobster tails into 4 equal *medaillons* each and reserve with the claw meat and the raw scallops and shrimp. Split lobster body shells in half and remove and discard the stomach sacs behind the mouth. Remove and reserve the tomalley and any coral. Put the lobster shells, shrimp shells, and scallop trimmings into a saucepan with the white wine and 3 cups water. Cover, bring to a simmer, and simmer gently for 20 to 30 minutes. Strain broth, discarding solids. Measure 3 cups of broth and reserve remainder for another use. Use a blender or food processor to purée the reserved tomalley and roe, adding enough broth to liquefy it. Add mixture to the broth and reserve. If sausage is homemade, poach it until done, cool, and unwrap. If purchased, leave raw.

Heat a large skillet and add 2 tablespoons of butter. Lightly sauté the shrimp, scallops, lobster meat, and sausages in batches until slightly colored on each side, removing them to a bowl as they are done. Add a little more butter as needed. Cut sausages into serving pieces. Add the scallions to the skillet and cook until wilted. Stir in the garlic and cook briefly. Add the tomato pulp, seasonings, and parsley, and cook briefly. Add the reserved broth and bring to a boil. Reduce heat and simmer gently, uncovered, for about 10 minutes. Pour mixture into a pot of about 4-quart capacity and add the reserved beans. Simmer gently for about 10 minutes more, or until mixture has the texture of a hearty soup. Correct seasoning. May be prepared in advance.

At serving time, reheat the bean mixture and add the shrimp, scallops, and sausages. When they are nearly heated through, add the lobster pieces just to warm them. Do not overcook. Serve hot, with rice if desired.

STEAMING

See p. 78 for ways to determine proper cooking time.

Steaming is an ideal method for cooking fish because it heats the flesh with the least alteration of any technique, subtracting nothing and adding only what the cook has selected in the way of aromatics plus a little moisture. And because it is a moist-heat method, there is less danger of drying out the flesh than there is with some other techniques. But, of course, overcooked is overcooked no matter how it is achieved. Chinese cooks have known for centuries that when they have a perfect fish, one of delicate texture and flavor and just-caught freshness, the only technique to consider is steaming. In Asia this is a matter of respect. There exists no important tradition of steam cookery for fish either in Europe or the New World, a situation that is being remedied as Western cooks learn that steaming need not yield insipidly bland results. Unlike steamed fish, steamed shellfish are standard in Western cooking, as simple as steamed soft-shell clams, or as elaborate as a New England clam bake.

VARIETIES BEST SUITED

Any fish may be steamed, but those with very white, lean flesh and mild flavor seem the most likely candidates because of the simplicity of the preparation and the esthetics of presentation. One would naturally think first of steaming flatfish, sea bass, snapper, grouper, cod, and whiting and hake. However, less lean freshwater fish such as pike, walleye, lake whitefish, perch, and even various trout and char are excellent steamed. And versatile salmon is a natural for this method. Any shellfish might be steamed, but the ones most commonly prepared this way are lobster, mussels, and clams.

TECHNIQUE

Steaming technique is quite simple. All you will need is a heat source, a water source, a platter or plate that can be held above the waterline on which to put the fish, and a lid. Woks work especially well because of their design. Many of them come with steamer racks but, lacking one, simply cross a pair of chopsticks in the bottom of the wok and you have an instant steamer support. Steaming is a good use for woks that will not work for stir-frying, such as a rusted one, or stainless steel, nonstick coated, or electric. It is wise anyway to save a well-seasoned carbon steel wok for oil-based cooking methods.

In addition to steaming directly in the wok, there are bamboo steamer baskets designed to fit into a wok that will work nicely, provided you have a plate that will fit into the basket and be easy to remove safely when it is hot. There are tools like three-pronged pincers that are sold in Asian cookware shops for this purpose. Bamboo steamer baskets have the advantage of stackability, but do not attempt to steam with more than two stacked baskets at a time with a home heat source. It is wise to place a folded dish towel under the plate in the upper basket so that condensation will not drip onto the fish below. There are oversize aluminum layered steamers for professional use that would be nice to have in a home kitchen if you have the budget and the space to store them.

Without a wok or steamer basket, nearly any kitchen should yield the needed equipment: a wide, covered pan; two or three tin cans with both ends removed to place on the bottom of the pan to support a platter (use tuna cans if the pot is shallow); anything that will hold the plate above the waterline, even a folding stainless steel steamer with its center post removed. A little imagination should take care of it. And it is also possible to steam fish in a covered pan in the oven. One important safety measure to learn is that live steam is dangerous, so you must always keep your face well away from the pan when lifting the lid and keep hands and arms protected.

When shellfish are steamed above plain water, as for Steamed Lobster (see recipe), the technique is the same as for fish, except that the platter is replaced by a rack. More often shellfish are steamed in their own juices as in the clam and mussel recipes that follow.

PIERRE BARAN'S RED SNAPPER AUX ECAILLES DE CONCOMBRE

4 servings

Now executive chef at the Knickerbocker Club, Mr. Baran developed this simple and elegant recipe during his years heading the kitchen at Le Cygne, one of Manhattan's loveliest and finest East Side French restaurants. It is surprisingly easy to prepare; the "cucumber scales" look very professional but take only minutes to assemble. Of course all ingredients must be the finest and freshest. Black sea bass is another fine choice, the other fish with the right delicacy and shape. This is a perfect example of the ease with which you may oven steam four portions at once. Notice that you will be creating a white butter sauce using the pan juices with their delicate cucumber and fish flavors. The choice of herbs is individual, and you can substitute parsley for the hard-to-find chervil, but chervil really is best. Potatoes trimmed into neat olive shapes and boiled would be just right if you need a starch.

Two 2 1/2-pound whole red snappers
2 large seedless cucumbers
Coarse salt, as needed
2 large shallots, minced, or a bit more
About 3 ounces melted butter
Freshly ground white pepper to taste
1 cup water
1 cup dry white wine
1/2 pound (2 sticks) finest butter, cool
1 tablespoon minced fresh chervil
1/2 tablespoon minced fresh tarragon
1 tablespoon minced fresh dill

Fillet the fish, trim, and remove all bones. Refrigerate. Wash and score the cucumbers with a fork. Slice them *very* thinly, sprinkle lightly with salt, and set aside for about 10 minutes.

Butter a baking pan just large enough to hold the fish in a single layer—a flat-bottomed stainless-steel roasting pan is best—and sprinkle evenly with the shallots. Place the fish fillets in the pan and brush lightly with a little melted butter. Season lightly with salt and pepper. Drain cucumbers and, starting at the tail end of each fillet, arrange the slices in an overlapping pattern, like the scales of a fish, covering each fish fillet completely. Pour the water around the fillets and seal pan with aluminum foil. Can be prepared in advance to this point.

Preheat oven to 400°F.

Bring the liquid in the baking dish just to a simmer on top of the stove, then place in preheated oven.

Pour the white wine into a medium, heavy, nonreactive saucepan and boil to reduce by more than half. Cut the 1/2 pound butter into pieces of about 1 tablespoon each. Butter should be cool and firm but not icy.

Bake fish for 10 minutes, then test for doneness. When done, remove fish to serving dishes or platter and put in a warm place. Strain the pan juices into the saucepan with the reduced wine. Reduce over high heat to about ¼ cup. Remove from heat and whisk in the cool butter, a piece at a time, returning the pan to low heat from time to time if necessary to keep the mixture warm enough to melt the butter gradually. Do not overheat. Whisk in the herbs. Drain any juices that have accumulated around the fish (save juices to add to fish stock), and blot platter or plates dry with paper towels. Surround fish with the sauce, and serve immediately.

SALMON STEAMED IN CABBAGE LEAVES WITH MUSTARD DILL SAUCE

4 servings

This recipe was developed for a low-fat cookery class, and it proved rich enough to satisfy the *gourmande* in all of us. Lowly cabbage teams well with sophisticated salmon, especially well if the cabbage is savoy, the crinkly green one with the delicate flavor. The sauce has nothing to do with Mustard Dill Sauce for *Gravad* Fish, it just happens to share those two main flavors. Sheer Tomato Sauce with Pernod would also work nicely, as would (horrors!) *Beurre Blanc* (see recipes). Boiled potatoes make a fine accompaniment.

1½ pounds skinned and thoroughly trimmed fillet of salmon (buy a generous piece, a bit more than 1¾ pounds)
Coarse salt and freshly ground white pepper to taste
1 head green cabbage, preferably savoy
1½ cups Fish Stock (see recipe)
2 teaspoons arrowroot or potato starch
3 tablespoons Dijon mustard, or to taste
2 tablespoons snipped fresh dill leaves
Pinch sugar, as needed
Dill sprigs for garnish

If salmon fillet is center cut, fold trimmed belly flaps in to make neat shapes. Cut into eight 3-ounce fingers. Season lightly with salt and pepper, and reserve, refrigerated. Cut out and discard the core of the cabbage and dunk it into a large pot of boiling water just long enough to soften 1 or 2 outer leaves. Remove leaves and return cabbage to the water until you have 8 uniform, attractive leaves. Reserve remaining cabbage for another use.

Cut the hard spine out of each cabbage leaf. Roll each salmon finger in a cabbage leaf as you would roll a grape leaf: Place salmon toward the base of the leaf, fold over the base, tuck in the sides, then roll up. Place packages, seam side down, on a platter or plate(s) that will fit into the steamer setup you have planned.

Heat the water that will provide the steam to cook the salmon. Put the salmon rolls on to steam, and prepare the sauce. Heat 1¼ cups fish stock in a small, heavy, nonreactive saucepan. Combine remaining stock with the arrowroot or potato starch, and whisk mixture into the hot stock. Bring just to a boil. Whisk in mustard and dill and correct seasoning (the pinch of sugar will probably be needed to balance the acidity of the stock and/or mustard). When salmon rolls are done, 6 to 10 minutes per inch of thickness, sauce 4 warmed dinner plates, place 2 salmon rolls on each, garnish with dill sprigs, and serve immediately.

STEAMED BABY COHO SALMON WITH FRESH HERBS

1 serving

This is a simple and versatile little preparation for the tasty trout-sized cohoes that are being farmed in Washington State. The flavors also work nicely with trout or fillets or steaks of adult salmon. Among the herbs you might choose from are parsley, chervil, tarragon, oregano, marjoram, basil, mint, thyme, savory, coriander, and rosemary.

1 baby coho salmon, cleaned
1 or 2 sprigs fresh herb of choice, bruised with a heavy knife
1 small clove garlic, peeled and bruised
1 to 2 teaspoons lemon juice
Coarse salt and freshly ground pepper to taste
1 tablespoon butter, softened
Sprigs of fresh herbs and lemon wedges for garnish

Wash and dry the fish well. Cut about 3 deep slashes, to the bone, on each side of fish. Make the cuts about 1½ inches apart, crosswise, holding the knife at a 45-degree angle toward the head. Rub fish with bruised herb and garlic, lemon juice, and salt and pepper. Let sit at room temperature on serving plate or steaming platter to gain flavor, at least 30 minutes. Just before serving time, rub fish with softened butter and place bruised herb and garlic in the cavity. Steam it just until it is heated through. Serve immediately with herb and lemon garnish.

STEAMED SEA BASS, CANTONESE-STYLE

2 to 4 servings

This is quite simply one of the finest foods in the world, and a snap to prepare at home. In fact, you may actually do a better job of it than a harried cook on a busy night in one of China-town's best restaurants. The technique and ingredients are classically Cantonese. This recipe follows closely the version by chef/teacher Henry Hugh (whose fine cooking does *not* vary under pressure), for many years at Yun Luck, now head of an executive dining room. Though this basic approach is perfect, there are many traditional variations, including one that is equally delicious in its way: Simply add 1 tablespoon fermented (salted) black beans, rinsed and drained, and 1 large clove garlic, mashed, to the raw fish with the vegetables and reduce the soy sauce to 1 tablespoon. Black sea bass is the first choice, but use what is freshest. Dishes of this sort microwave beautifully.

1 whole black sea bass, red snapper, walleye, or gray sole or other
   flounder (about 1½ to 2 pounds)
4 scallions, white part cut into fine julienne and greens into 1-inch
   pieces
2-inch piece fresh gingerroot, peeled and cut into finest julienne
3 tablespoons Chinese light-color soy sauce
2 tablespoons dry sherry
½ teaspoon sugar
2 teaspoons Asian dark sesame oil
Dash hot chili oil
½ bunch coriander sprigs
¼ cup peanut oil

Gut, scale, and remove gills from the fish, leaving it whole and being especially careful to flush out all blood. Dry with towels. Slash the fish crosswise at 2-inch intervals, cutting toward the head with the knife at a 45-degree angle, just to the bone. Repeat on the other side.

Choose a platter just large enough to hold the fish but small enough to fit into the steamer, and strew a few scallion greens and ginger strips on it. Place the fish on the platter and strew remaining scallion greens and ginger. Combine soy sauce, sherry, sugar, sesame oil, and chili oil, and pour about half of the mixture evenly over the fish. Let fish marinate as it comes to room temperature, up to 1 hour but at least 30 minutes.

Place platter in steamer and steam over high heat just until done, remembering that the slashes reduce cooking time to as little as 6 minutes per inch of thickness. Carefully remove fish from steamer and pour off excess juices if the platter seems flooded. Strew scallion whites on the fish and coriander sprigs around it. Pour on remaining marinade mixture. Heat the peanut oil in a small saucepan until very hot. Pour over fish—it should sizzle—and serve immediately.

STEAMED SEA BASS WITH GINGER AND SCALLIONS

1 serving

> Here is Jane Street Seafood Café's version of the Cantonese classic, "oven-steamed" in individual servings. You might also prepare four portions in a roasting pan.

Approximately 8 ounces fillet—1 or 2 pieces—of black sea bass, red snapper, walleye , or gray sole or other flounder
1 tablespoon Asian dark sesame oil
2 tablespoons tamari
¼ cup dry white wine
1 tablespoon grated fresh gingerroot
2 scallions, trimmed and thinly sliced on a steep diagonal

Preheat oven to 375°F.

Trim fish neatly, removing all bones. Place fish in a pie plate, skin side down, and distribute the remaining ingredients over it in the order in which they are listed. Seal with aluminum foil. Bake until done, 15 to 18 minutes. Plate and serve immediately.

OVEN-STEAMED SHRIMP CAFÉ NICHOLSON

1 serving

This is another—but quite different—oven-steamed dish that may be prepared in individual portions in pie plates. Of course you are free to assemble a larger batch if it is more convenient. Café Nicholson is one of New York's more unusual restaurants, in that it is open when chef/owner John Nicholson chooses to open. When patrons speak of the place, the two adjectives that always seem to be used are eccentric, for the proprietor, and romantic, for the tile, marble, and gilt decor.

5 medium shrimp
2 generous tablespoons butter, melted
Coarse salt and freshly ground pepper to taste
1 tablespoon white wine
1 tablespoon lemon juice
2 teaspoons minced shallots
Pinch celery seed
1/2 teaspoon chopped fresh tarragon leaves, or 1/8 teaspoon dried
Paprika

Preheat oven to 400°F.

Use small kitchen shears or sewing scissors to cut along the back of the shrimp shells. Loosen the shrimp from the shells, devein, and tuck them back into their shells. Film a pie plate with a little butter and add the shrimp. Sprinkle on the remaining ingredients, ending with a light dusting of paprika. Seal with aluminum foil. Bake until done, about 15 minutes. Plate and serve immediately.

MOULES À LA MARINIÈRE

STEAMED MUSSELS, MARINER-STYLE (BASIC STEAMED MUSSELS)

Approximately 6 servings

Mussels are among the tastiest, most abundant, and least expensive protein sources around. Luckily, the word has spread beyond the Italian community so that they are now available in most markets in the United States. This steamed mussels dish, some version of which is traditional in all the coastal areas of Europe where the molluscs grow, is delicious served up in large soup plates with some of the broth spooned over. Figure on about 1 quart—1½ pounds—whole mussels per serving. Include good crusty bread, some butter for those who want it, and a bowl for empty shells. This treatment is also the basis for many fine hot and cold dishes, including hors d'oeuvre, salads, and perhaps the most elegant soup in the world. In addition to the suggestions below, please see Mussel and Potato Salad, Billi-bi, and Risotto with Mussels.

10 pounds mussels
2 cups dry white wine
3 leeks, white and pale green only, chopped
3 cloves garlic, minced
½ cup minced shallots
1 bay leaf
¼ teaspoon dried leaf thyme
Small handful parsley stems
4 tablespoons butter
Coarse salt and freshly ground white pepper to taste
2 tablespoons chopped parsley (optional)

Clean mussels thoroughly as described on p. 62. Combine all ingredients but mussels and chopped parsley in a large pot. Bring to a boil, covered, reduce heat, and simmer 5 minutes. Add cleaned mussels and cover tightly. Steam over high heat until shells open, shaking pan occasionally, 5 to 10 minutes. Serve hot, with a tiny sprinkling of the parsley, or cool and reserve for another purpose.

Steamed mussels on the half shell may be made into hors d'oeuvre or first courses. Here are some of the possibilities:

Cold: masked with Green Mayonnaise or Saffron Mayonnaise (see recipes)
Hot: baked with Snail Butter (see recipe)

Steamed mussels may be shucked and marinated in a simple vinaigrette, or combined with other seafood for elaborate salads. They may also be skewered, crumbed, and broiled.

STEAMED SOFT-SHELL CLAMS

Soft-shell, or steamer clams, are normally steamed in just a hint of water and served with melted butter and small cups of broth for rinsing off any remaining sand. The broth is later drunk, with care to avoid any sand at the bottom of the cup. You may find steamers even tastier if you prepare them exactly as the mussels in the preceding recipe. Allow about 1 quart of clams per person. Serve the clams with strained broth, some butter if you wish it, and good bread. The dark skin that covers the "neck" is generally considered too tough to eat and is easily peeled off; however, some people like it and should go ahead and eat it if they wish.

STEAMED LITTLENECKS WITH BLACK BEAN SAUCE

4 first course servings

Here is a Western version of a Cantonese classic that has captured the fancy of many modern chefs because it is so very good. It is also delicious prepared with Manila clams. Fermented black beans are available in specialty stores and Asian shops.

24 littleneck or Manila clams
1 tablespoon minced garlic
2 tablespoons minced fresh gingerroot
2 scallions, thinly sliced, white and green parts separated
1/4 to 1/2 teaspoon dried red pepper flakes to taste
1/4 cup fermented (salted) black beans, well *rinsed and drained*
2 tablespoons dry sherry
1 teaspoon soy sauce
2 teaspoons Asian dark sesame oil
1/3 cup water
2 tablespoons peanut oil

Scrub and soak clams, p. 62. Combine the garlic, ginger, scallion whites, and red pepper flakes and set aside. Combine black beans, sherry, soy sauce, and sesame oil and set aside.

Drain clams and put them in a saucepan with the water. Cover and bring to a boil over high heat. Meanwhile, heat a wok or skillet and add the peanut oil. When it is almost smoking, add the garlic mixture and stir-fry briefly, just until fragrant. Add the black bean mixture, stir it in, and set aside. As the clams open, plate them, then add the broth to the sauce in the wok, being careful to avoid any sand in the bottom of the pan. Bring sauce to a boil, spoon it over the clams, sprinkle on scallion greens, and serve immediately.

STEAMED LOBSTER BEURRE BLANC

4 main course or 8 first course servings

Extravagant? Yes. But for very special occasions there is no more elegant a dish. The plating is based on one pictured in *New York* magazine some years ago from Michel Fitoussi when he was at the Palace. This also serves as a master recipe for lobster steaming—the preferred technique of the majority of fine chefs—and removing the flesh from cooked lobsters.

Four 1 1/4- to 1 1/2-pound lobsters, alive and lively
2 pounds fresh asparagus, as thin as possible
Beurre Blanc (see recipe)

Rig a steamer setup in a large pot or wok as described on p. 346, and put a rack on the support. Add water to come almost up to the rack, cover, and bring to a boil. Place lobsters on the rack—2 at a time if necessary—cover, and steam for 10 to 12 minutes, depending on size. (For other recipes where the lobster will receive no further heating, test for doneness by pulling on one of the small legs: If it breaks off easily, the lobster is done). Remove lobsters from the steamer and cool them in an ice-water bath.

One lobster at a time, break off just the 2 claws and carefully remove the flesh in one piece in this manner: crush just the tip of the small, movable part of the claw and gently wiggle it up and down (not the side-to-side motion it is designed for) to break the cartilage that attaches it. Pull it away from the rest, removing the flat tendon but leaving the meat attached to the large shell. Do not be discouraged if the little piece of meat breaks off with the "thumb"; it can be removed with a pick and plated with the big piece later. Carefully crack the rest of the claw with a lobster cracker and dislodge the flesh. Reserve.

For each lobster, remove the tail from the body by wiggling and pulling it until it breaks free. Reserve the lobster bodies, legs, and arms for another purpose. With heavy shears, cut all the way down the middle of the underside of the tail shell. Carefully remove the meat and trim the body end neatly. Slice in half lengthwise and remove and discard intestine. Reserve. Carefully cut the end of the tail shell—the swimmerets and the last tail shell segment—from the rest of the shell, to use for garnish. For main course servings, cut off as much of the underside as necessary to allow the shell to lie flat. For first course servings, cut the tail shell in half. Reserve.

Cut asparagus spears to a uniform length of about 6 inches. Peel just the outer layer of skin with a swivel-blade peeler.

Steam the asparagus or blanch it in salted water until just tender. Steam the lobster meat just to warm it, being careful not to toughen it. Plate as follows:

For main courses, film warmed (not hot) dinner plates with *Beurre Blanc* and arrange asparagus spears in a fan shape with a whole lobster tail shell at the base. Place tail meat halves in the center, cut side up, and claw meat on either side, and serve immediately. For first course servings, arrange half as much asparagus and the meat of ½ lobster attractively on sauced plates. Add half tail shell to the base of the asparagus spears, and serve.

INDEX